✕ INSIGHT GUIDES

Southern California

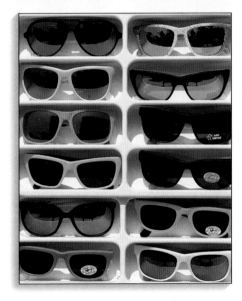

Discovery
CHANNEL

APA PUBLICATIONS

Part of the Langenscheidt Publishing Group

INSIGHT GUIDE

S O U T H E R N
California

Editorial
Update Editor
John Wilcock
Managing Editor
Martha Ellen Zenfell
Editorial Director
Brian Bell

Distribution

UK & Ireland
GeoCenter International Ltd
The Viables Centre, Harrow Way
Basingstoke, Hants RG22 4BJ
Fax: (44) 1256 817988

United States
Langenscheidt Publishers, Inc.
46–35 54th Road, Maspeth, NY 11378
Fax: (1) 718 784 0640

Canada
Thomas Allen & Son Ltd
390 Steelcase Road East
Markham, Ontario L3R 1G2
Fax: (1) 905 475 6747

Australia
Universal Press
1 Waterloo Road
Macquarie Park, NSW 2113
Fax: (61) 2 9888 9074

New Zealand
Hema Maps New Zealand Ltd (HNZ)
Unit D, 24 Ra ORA Drive
East Tamaki, Auckland
Fax: (64) 9 273 6479

Worldwide
Apa Publications GmbH & Co.
Verlag KG (Singapore branch)
38 Joo Koon Road, Singapore 628990
Tel: (65) 865 1600. Fax: (65) 861 6438

Printing

Insight Print Services (Pte) Ltd
38 Joo Koon Road, Singapore 628990
Tel: (65) 865 1600. Fax: (65) 861 6438

©2003 Apa Publications GmbH & Co.
Verlag KG (Singapore branch)
All Rights Reserved
First Edition 1984
Sixth Edition 2001 (Revised 2003)

CONTACTING THE EDITORS
We would appreciate it if readers
would alert us to errors or out-
dated information by writing to:
Insight Guides, P.O. Box 7910,
London SE1 1WE, England.
Fax: (44) 20 7403 0290.
insight@apaguide.demon.co.uk

www.insightguides.com

ABOUT THIS BOOK

This guidebook combines the interests and enthusiasms of two of the world's best-known information providers: Insight Guides, whose titles have set the standard for visual travel guides since 1970, and Discovery Channel, the world's premier source of nonfiction television programming.

The editors of Insight Guides provide practical advice and general understanding about a destination's history, culture, institutions and people. Discovery Channel and its website, www.discovery.com, help millions of viewers explore their world from the comfort of their own home and also encourage them to explore it first-hand.

This fully updated edition of *Insight Guide: Southern California* is carefully structured to convey an understanding of the state as well as to guide readers through its sights and activities:

◆ The **Features** section, indicated by a yellow bar at the top of each page, covers the history, people and culture of the region in a series of informative essays.

◆ The **Places** section, indicated by a blue bar, is a complete guide to all the sights and areas worth visiting. Places of interest are coordinated by number with the maps.

◆ The **Travel Tips** listings section, with an orange bar, provides information on travel, hotels, shops, restaurants and much, much more.

EXPLORE YOUR WORLD
Discovery
CHANNEL

The contributors

This extensively revised edition of *Insight Guide: Southern California* builds on the previous edition, which was supervised, then as now, by London-based, American-born editor **Martha Ellen Zenfell**. As well as looking after the new and updated text, Zenfell also doubled the number of maps and selected more than 100 new images to reflect the glories and contrasts of post-millennium Southern California.

Zenfell and principal writer and updater **John Wilcock** have worked together on many projects, including Insight Guides to the Western States, California and *IG: On the Road* (for which Wilcock took Highway 1 all the way up the coast to Seattle), plus Pocket and Compact Guides to San Diego and Las Vegas. During the course of this book, Wilcock moved from Los Angeles' Topanga Canyon to Ojai near Santa Barbara, famous for its "pink moment" sunsets.

As extensively as Wilcock knows California, no one has better credentials than the Native Americans whose ancestors first settled the land. Despite widespread devastation in past centuries, there are still 300,000 native peoples living there. The chapter detailing their lives and sites was written by **Dolan Eargle**, an authority who has served as an advisory member of the Esselen tribal council, and the author of *The Earth is Our Mother*.

Although revamped many times, this edition still carries influences of the very first Insight Guide to the region and its team of local writers, editors and photographers headed by **Bret Reed Lundberg** and **Ben Kalb**. The book's history section, for example, is a melding of the work by original writer **Joan Talmage Weiss** and John Wilcock, while words by **Sean Wagstaff**, **Karen Klabin** and many, many others too numerous and distant to name help to make this book what it is today. Many thanks for their generous contributions.

The same applies to the photographers – people such as Lundberg himself, whose pictures still grace these pages. His fine work is augmented by the images of **Catherine Karnow**, principal photographer on *Insight Guide: Los Angeles* and other books; **Glyn Genin**, lensman on Insight Compact Guides to *Los Angeles* and *California*, and **Jerry Dennis**, who covered the area for *Insight Pocket Guide: San Diego*. Behind-the-scenes thanks also go to **John Gattuso**, **Sylvia Suddes**, **Lisa Cussans** and **Elizabeth Cook**.

Map Legend

—‒‒	International Boundary
‒ ‒ ‒	State Boundary
⊖	Border Crossing
—•—	National Park/Reserve
‒ ‒ ‒	Ferry Route
Ⓜ	Subway
✈ ✈	Airport: International/Regional
🚌	Bus Station
❶	Tourist Information
✉	Post Office
✝ ✝	Church/Ruins
✝	Monastery
☾	Mosque
✡	Synagogue
🏰	Castle/Ruins
🏛	Mansion/Stately home
∴	Archeological Site
∩	Cave
𝗜	Statue/Monument
★	Place of Interest

The main places of interest in the Places section are coordinated by number with a full-color map (e.g. ❶), and a symbol at the top of every right-hand page tells you where to find the map.

INSIGHT GUIDE
SOUTHERN California

Maps

Inside front cover:
Southern California
Inside back cover:
Los Angeles and the West Side

CONTENTS

Oasis in the desert,
Death Valley

IN SEARCH OF PARADISE

Anglos, Latinos, Asians, African-Americans –
all have succumbed to the California dream

California, the third largest state in the Union, has been actively promoting itself for almost two centuries, and the advertising has never failed to work. The result has been that the state today not only ranks highest in the number of its inhabitants, but no other area of the world can claim such an ethnically diverse population. The students of Los Angeles schools, for instance, speak more than 90 different languages.

The development and growth of California's industries throughout the 19th century brought a tide of immigration. The Chinese initially came as railroad workers on the Central Pacific construction gangs before branching out into agriculture and fishing. African-Americans also came as railroad employees, in smaller numbers at first and then later, during World War II, to fill manufacturing and service jobs. And towards the turn of that century, Japanese immigrants arrived in search of opportunities in the produce industry, a field in which they eventually came to dominate.

Social island

Nothing, however, compared to the tidal wave of Anglos from the Midwest of America during the 1880s (and then again – fleeing the parched "dust bowl" farms of the prairies – in the 1920s and '30s). Already having established major colonies around the San Francisco and Sacramento areas, they saturated Southern California with visions of manifest destiny.

By the mid-20th century, historian Carey McWilliams was already referring to Southern California as an "archipelago of social and ethnic islands, economically interrelated but culturally disparate."

During the 1980s, hundreds of thousands of Mexicans and Central Americans fleeing civil strife and political persecution immigrated, both legally and illegally, to California. Already one in four Californians is a Latino American. It is accepted that Latinos will outnumber Anglos within the next few years, once again becoming the state's majority ethnic group, just as they were when much of the land belonged to Mexico a hundred years earlier. Immigrants from Asia and the Pacific islands are the third largest ethnic community (after Anglos and Latinos), followed by African-Americans. The mix has had significant political implications, a multiculturalism reflected in the offices of both elected and appointed officials.

Reviewing a recent book, *Prismatic Metropolis,* about "inequality in Los Angeles," the *Los Angeles Times* concluded that "the

PRECEDING PAGES: winners of a longboard surfing contest, Huntington Beach; Christmas carriage ride at the Furnace Creek Inn, Death Valley; wall murals on Hollywood Boulevard, Los Angeles.
LEFT: savoring the good life in the San Gabriel Mountains near Los Angeles.

well-educated and skilled usually prosper, but the poorly educated low-skill worker has a harder time making a go of it. Yet the longer immigrants stay, the better off they become. In short, given time, they usually will achieve their California dreams of home ownership and financial security." And so it has been since the state's early days.

Many of the early *Californios* – the Spanish-Mexicans who first followed the missionaries here – were soldiers who stayed when their service was ended, taking advantage of 20-acre (8-hectare) land grants. And before the state even joined the Union, the gold miners were flooding

and suburbs do tend to stay relatively homogeneous, pockets of cultures border one another, stitched by the colorful religions and customs of its people. California is hip-hop and cha-cha wrapped in a gold-flecked sari.

Another country

A wealth of diaries and travelers' tales turned up after the Gold Rush, containing praise for "climate, rapid disappearance of the frontier, agricultural potentialities, cheap living costs, healthfulness, picturesqueness and money-making opportunities," as Glenn S. Dumke summarized it. Dumke wrote in his *The Boom*

in from the Oregon Trail and from as far away as China. Native Americans were becoming strangers in their own land.

In the 1990s, Californians set upon the concept of multiculturalism like a pitbull to the mailman's pantleg, arguing about its meaning in stores, educational institutions, businesses and government. Around the state, celebrations honoring California's multi-ethnicity have cheered their way into the streets in the hopes that unity and goodwill would abound.

What has become more and more evident is that these vastly different people have slowly absorbed each other's habits and styles, epicures and mannerisms. While most California towns

of the Eighties in Southern California that he'd read much of the literature which shared this general tone, despite its content. He quoted Charles Dudley Warner's praise: "This is Paradise. And the climate? Perpetual summer..." Not much later, that early explorer and booster of the Golden State, Charles Nordhoff, was to declare that California was "the cheapest country in the United States to live in," with costs one-third less than in communities back East.

In 1869, the nailing of that final golden spike on the railroad tracks in Utah ushered in the important Iron Horse era. Wealthy Easterners clamored to explore the experience of the West and salesmen with the eternal pitch were meeting the trains and promising to provide it. Henry George had warned earlier in his *Progress and Poverty* what the rail barons with their rights of way would bring about: high prices and inflamed racial prejudice by the railroad's importation of literally thousands of Chinese laborers.

Nevertheless, with the railroads spending thousands of dollars on advertising and promotional offers, the visitors came in floods. Among them was movie supremo Cecil B. De Mille on a search for a place to film a movie. He

THE GREAT OUTDOORS

The outdoors person floats in a sea of possibilities where the sand is fine, the ocean has perfect surfing waves, and wilderness areas of every type are never far away.

tribution for their tales and fables of this new fantasy land where fact and fiction are so convincingly fused. The legend has grown and continues to convince the world that there is indeed this paradise of perpetual sunshine where anybody can become somebody else. A recent show at the Los Angeles County Museum of Art pointed out that after the debut of talking pictures "an entire industry developed around movie stars and their eternally youthful appearance, sumptuous wardrobes and opulent lifestyles."

stopped off in Arizona but got back on the train because he thought California might offer an even better location. The state's first sightseer, you might say.

Fact and fantasy confusion

Next came the birth and explosive growth of Hollywood. By 1930, Hollywood's admired industry was one of America's top ten businesses. The big five studios had worldwide dis-

LEFT: one writer described the state as "hip-hop and cha-cha, wrapped in a gold-flecked sari."
ABOVE: the predominant culture is one colored less by the mind than by the body.

But these, of course, are not the only people who came to see (and sometimes find) paradise. The state has never lacked for its share of eccentrics. Charles Hillinger's recent book, *California Characters, An Array of Amazing People* introduced readers to an old lady living in the Mojave Desert who spent 60 years collecting 80,000 automobile hubcaps; a mountain-top dweller near San Diego who maintains a landing strip for planetary spaceships; and an Escondido soap maker whose labels carry his plans for universal peace. There are numerous others with equally bizarre preoccupations in a state where people expect the unexpected.

It is perhaps the necessity of asserting one's

identity in this Babel-like sea of different ethnic cultures that has made California the state in which more trends and artistic movements take flight and caused East Coast pundits to joke about California's lack of culture.

But this is a short-sighted view, for the predominant culture is something different, one colored less by the mind than by the body. Leaning towards the exotic Far East (or West, depending on one's geographical point of view), the state inevitably adopted the customs of Asian immigrants. Health-conscious Californians submit to strenuous programs of yoga and shiatsu and meditation, in a never-ending

ing volcanoes and bubbling mud pots, bottomless cisterns of pure glacial water, desert wildflowers blooming below sea level.

California has high mountains – the Sierras – that run the length of the state like a spine, north to south, separating forest from desert. It also has the Coast Range to the west that blocks 95 percent of California from a view of the beach; and the San Bernadinos that separate Los Angeles from the Big Valley to the north. The Southern Sierra is an anachronism. Close to the cities of Southern California, it somehow remains more isolated and remote than most of the mountains to the north. Kern Canyon is the

attempt to achieve the physiques of their movie-star gods and the spirtuality of their new immigrant neighbors.

Sun-tanned perfection

The outdoors person in California floats on a sea of possibilities. There really are places where the sand is fine and white, the ocean warm with barreling tubes of perfect surfing waves, and sun-tanned girls in bikinis go twirling down the boardwalk on roller blades. This is a huge and varied state in which there are also hundred-mile wilderness areas of every description, raging whitewater rivers, poppies and lupines springing from canyon walls, fum-

nearest west-slope river to Los Angeles – about six hours away – and it is the entry point to a vast wilderness of high sierra landscape, as well as to the Kern River itself, not to mention the tributaries that comprise some of California's best summer recreation.

The Owens River provides much of the water used by Los Angeles. This once lush valley has been mostly reduced to desert to slake the thirst of the giant city, but along the edge of the eastern slope of the Sierras, there are trickling trout streams and a few sparkling lakes. In the hills and canyons of the region, the lucky few should be able to spot cougar and other big game of the high desert.

The Channel Islands which dot the coast off Santa Barbara and Los Angeles, resemble more than a little the bright-white, dry Greek islands of the Mediterranean. Santa Barbara is a charming town, dominated by a campus of the University of California, where ocean sports take precedence over other forms of outdoors activity. Surfing is easy to learn here, for the waves are pretty small due to a nearby offshore chain of islands. Sailing and windsurfing are also extremely popular.

TRAVELERS' TALES

A wealth of diaries found after the Gold Rush contained praise for "climate, cheap-living costs, healthfulness, picturesqueness and money-making opportunities."

enough to forgo a wetsuit. The underwater hunting, however, is a little picked over until you get close to San Diego.

Then, across the Sierras from the semi-tropical basins of San Diego and Los Angeles is the sharply contrasting landscape of joshua and yucca trees, smooth rolling sandstone, barrel cactus, sagebrush and the abandoned silver mines of the Mojave Desert.

Covering much of the southeast portion of California, the Mojave floats like a mirage out of Arizona, nudging up against the precipice of

Surfing has become a sharply territorial pastime and has gained a somewhat unfriendly reputation. However, if you're willing to settle for less-than-perfect waves, you can paddle out at almost any beach and be assured of a reasonable time. Kids are better off with a "boogey board" and a pair of fins. These missile-fast wave toys have become almost as popular as surfboards, and they're much easier to learn. The diving is interesting here, though not warm

LEFT: although Los Angeles captures most of the limelight, Southern California's towns can be gems, like Julian in San Diego County.
ABOVE: San Diego Wild Animal Park.

the Sierras at their southern extreme. Joshua Tree National Park is a strangely alien place of huge sandstone boulders the color of sunsets and rust, interspersed with oddly shaped joshua and yucca trees.

Desert wildflowers

Death Valley National Park, lying 150 ft (46 meters) below sea level, is the lowest point on the North American continent. Its name is derived from the stupefying heat of summer – when it's not uncommon for a day to break at 130°F (54°C) – and where shade trees are few and far between. In the springtime, however, Death Valley comes to life. Spring rains bring brilliant blooms of cactus and desert wildflowers. Their color is glorious against the spare desert backdrop. Climbing out of the desert toward the eastern ridges of the Sierras will bring adventurous hikers to many trailheads that lead into the vast Sierra wilderness areas.

Final frontier

When California joined the Union in 1850, it was considered to be the final frontier, a land promising spiritual and social riches. Pioneers armed with little more than faith came in search of sunshine, fertile soil, and freedom from oppression. Like the grape vines and citrus trees,

they could bloom under the gentle sun. Boosters furiously sold the fable of the Golden State to the rest of the Union, a dream that more than 150 years later has yet to lose its tenacious hold on the imagination.

The recession that hit California in the early 1990s knocked the smile from its sunny face. As has occurred throughout the history of the state, tensions between ethnic groups amplify when the job market plummets and the window of opportunity slams shut – and illegal immigrants are always the first to feel the blow.

Today, politicians and economists have once again latched onto the issue of immigration, blaming illegal aliens for California's staggering debt. In San Diego, suburban residents have taken action against nearby encampments of immigrants, citing to government officials everything from unsanitary conditions to spouse and child abuse. (Border crossings into San Diego County are so prevalent that there are signs cautioning drivers to be watchful of immigrants running across the highway.)

It has been suggested by the media that California is becoming dangerously Balkanized, that the cities especially are starting to resemble such racially and ethnically driven areas as the former Yugoslavia. What is evident, however, is not that the hope for multiculturalism is withering, but that it is being realized. At the very least from an economic standpoint, many business and political leaders are making a concerted effort to adapt to California's shifting landscape. Neighborhoods that had previously been abandoned after whites fled to the suburbs are now being targeted for revitalization, answering to the new communities they serve.

California epitomizes the best and worst of what being a truly multi-ethnic society can mean. There are some, like San Jose State University professor Shelby Steele, who believe that the obsession with tribalism is a leading factor in causing the sometimes bitter divisiveness throughout the state; viewing others always through the prism of your culture deepens the trenches and hinders society's gains. It's the cult of "other."

Coexistence

Critics of this argument say that recognition of California's many and divergent ethnic groups is the first step towards peaceful coexistence. Promoting minorities to meaningful positions in public policy – whether it be through affirmative action or some nebulous sense of political correctness – will eventually mitigate the issue.

Prior to a recent mayoral election, the *Los Angeles Times* speculated on whether the new mayor would have the foresight to follow Miami's example by welcoming Latino immigrants and offering financial assistance and investment funds for new businesses, or shun them as did San Antonio in Texas. On that decision, the paper said, depended the future civic life of the region. ❑

LEFT: radical recreation, West Coast-style.
RIGHT: one in four Californians is a Latino American.

Decisive Dates

Circa 13000 BC: The first nomads reach what is now known as California.

1542: Portuguese explorer Juan Rodríguez Cabrillo arrives and claims what is now San Diego for Spain.

Pre-1700s: Native Americans inhabit the region, tribes include the Quechan, Chemehuevi, Mohave, Cahuilla, Chumash and Kamia.

1769: Father Junípero Serra builds the first of 21 missions near present-day San Diego.

1771: San Gabriel Mission is founded by Spanish missionaries and *padres*.

1781: Don Felipe de Neve, the Mexican Governor of California, founds Los Angeles.

1833: Santa Barbara's present "Queen of the Missions" is completed, based on a design by the Roman architect Vitruvius.

1840: Sales boom at French immigrant Jean-Louis Vignes' Los Angeles vineyard, at what is now the site of Union Station.

1840s: The first orange groves are planted.

1847: Mexican General Andres Pico surrenders California to American General John Fremont at the Cahuenga Pass.

1848: The Treaty of Guadalupe is signed, fixing present US/Mexico borders. San Diego becomes an American possession.

1849: Gold is discovered at Sutter's Mill in the Sierra foothills – the Gold Rush begins.

1850: California becomes the 31st state in the Union.

1850s: Under successive treaties with the Federal government, native Indian tribes sign away 90 percent of their 7½ million acres (3 million hectares).

1851: A Mormon settlement is established in what has become known as the Inland Empire.

1851–60: Chinese population grows, coming to build railroads and search for gold.

1852: 100,000 miners pass through Los Angeles – it becomes a lawless western town.

1871: The Chinese Massacre – in response to the murder of a white policeman, mass shooting and lynching leaves more than 24 dead.

1872: Raging fires destroy much of San Diego's Old Town.

1873: The plant louse Pylloxera begins to decimate California vineyards.

1882: The first Los Angeles phone book is issued – all three pages of it.

1887: Harvey Wilcox files to form a subdivision on the land of his ranch; Wilcox's wife Daeida names it Hollywood.

1890: Orange County divided from LA County. Population of Los Angeles: 50,000.

1893: Secunda Guasti's enormous San Joaquin Valley Italian Vineyard Company hires hundreds of Italian immigrants.

1905: Abbott Kinney opens his Venetian-style resort near Santa Monica.

1907: Oil derricks proliferate in Los Angeles – Echo Lake is so polluted it catches fire for three days. First house in Beverly Hills is built – individual lots on Sunset Boulevard cost $1,000.

1908: Former Chicago filmmaker William Selig completes *The Count of Monte Cristo*, Southern California's first commercial film.

1910: Los Angeles annexes town of Hollywood.

1911: Hollywood's first movie, *The Law of the Range,* is filmed in a former tavern at Sunset and Gower.

1913: William Mulholland opens his new aqueduct, bringing water from the Owens Valley.

1915: San Diego celebrates the new Panama-California Exposition with the construction of handsome buildings in Balboa Park.

1920: Prohibition hits the US, but proximity to Mexico and offshore bootleggers keep up the spirits of Southern Californians.

1922: Scotty's Castle, a 25-room Spanish-style villa is built in Death Valley by an eccentric millionaire, Albert M. Johnson.

1923: Beverly Hills becomes a movie colony.

1925: An earthquake flattens the town of Santa Barbara, prompting a mandatory code prohibiting the building of unharmonious structures.

1926: Warner Studios adds sound to its feature *Don Juan* and the following year gives Al Jolson dialogue in *The Jazz Singer*.

1927: The first Oscars are presented at LA's Hollywood Roosevelt hotel. Charles Lindbergh completes the first transatlantic flight to Paris, taking off from San Diego in the locally built *Spirit of St Louis*.

1928: A dam in San Fransquito Canyon bursts, sending a wall of water from Santa Clarita to Oxnard; 400 people are killed.

1931: Los Angeles International Airport (known as LAX) is opened.

1932: The Olympic Games are staged in what was then the world's largest stadium, the Coliseum in the downtown area of Los Angeles.

1933: The Long Beach Earthquake (estimated 6.3 on Richter scale) kills 120 in Los Angeles.

1936: Joshua Tree parkland is established.

1939: Union Station, one of the last of the great railroad terminals, opens.

1941: December 7 – Japan's attack on Pearl Harbor brings US into World War II. Night blackouts begin.

1947: The California legislature passes a law against environmental smog.

1950–65: 31,000 acres (12,500 hectares) of orange groves fall to housing development.

1952: Alien Land Act denying land ownership to Orientals is declared unconstitutional.

1955: Disneyland opens in Anaheim.

1957: San Simeon is given to the state following owner William Randolph Hearst's death.

1963: California's population becomes the largest of all US states.

1965: Civil unrest erupts as the Watts Riots, lasting five days, kill 34 people.

1968: Presidential candidate Robert F. Kennedy is assassinated at LA's Ambassador Hotel.

1971: An earthquake measuring 6.6 in the San Fernando Valley claims the lives of 64 people.

1974: The oil tycoon J. Paul Getty donates his Malibu home as a museum.

PRECEDING PAGES: French illustration of early Native Americans outside a California mission.
LEFT: US stamp featuring Juan Rodríguez Cabrillo, credited with the European discovery of California.
RIGHT: the murder trial of football hero O.J. Simpson in the late 1990s had the nation glued to their TVs.

1980: Congress designates more than a million acres of the Mojave Desert as a national scenic area. Former actor and state governor Ronald Reagan becomes the 39th US President.

1990: Water rationing is imposed for the first time in Southern California.

1990s: Early in the decade, the California economy goes into recession, the first in a long time.

1992: The acquittal of LA police officers, charged with beating Rodney King, a black motorist, starts riots which leave 51 people dead.

1994: An earthquake (6.6 on the Richter scale) centered on Northridge in the San Fernando Valley kills 57 people.

1995–97: The Los Angeles trials of football star O.J. Simpson accused (and eventually acquited) of two murders enthrals the nation.

1997: The dramatic suicide of 39 members of the Heaven's Gate alternative religion shines the spotlight on San Diego.

1998: The Getty Center opens to great fanfare, giving Los Angeles the cultural lead over San Francisco.

2001: Disney's California Adventure opens. The state is hit by "rolling blackouts" due to a crisis in the electricity industry.

2002: The long-simmering secession movement erupts into a series of rallies and publicity as residents of Hollywood and the San Fernando Valley demand independence from Los Angeles. ❑

California a prioribus Geographis semper habita fuit quædam pars Continentis, at capta per Hollandos ab Hispanis tabula quædam Geographica compertum est insulam esse et continere ubi latissima est 300 leucas. A Cap. Mendocino uero usq, ad C.S.Lucæ repertum est testibus tabula prædicta et Francisco Gaule extendi in longitudinem 1700 leucarum

A M S

INSULA CALIFORNIÆ

MARE

C. Blanco
C. de S. Sebastian
C. Mendocino
P. Sir Francisco Draco
Punta de los Reyes
P. de monte Rey
P. de Carinda
Punta de la Conception
Canal de S. Barbara
Punta de la Conception
P. de S. Diego
I.S. Cathalina
S. Clement
I. S. Martin
Baia de Todos Santos
B. de S. Quintin
B. de las Virgines
I. de Parnaros
C. d Engano
B. de Francisco
I. S. Marco
B. de S. Simon
I. de Ceintas
Punta de S. Bartolome
I. de la Carre
Sierra Pintada
P. de Roqui
B. de las arenas
R. de S. Cristoual
Punta de S. Apalmat.
I. de S. Martin
P. Malabaja Adena
P. de Ladra Jue
P. de Conou
P. de la Paz

Rey Coromedo
Lago de ora
R. de Aronchi
R. del Tison
R. de Coral
S. Miguel
Las Playas
P. de S. Clara
CALIFORNIA
VER
ZIA. Cilla del Rosario
NIO.
R. de S. Martin
Pueblos de Moqui
Real de Nueua Mexico
G
Astablan
S. Francisco
P. tarlan
Culiacan
P. de Sineloa
R. Guahmaco
S. de Nauito
R. de Potatlan
R. de Pascua
P. I. Mucheres
P. Moruba
S. Miguel
S. A. Puilla
Durango
Sebastian
NUEVA BIS
Endche
Topia
S.
S.
Nombre de Dios
Minas
Ellerens
Zacatecas

Yllao
I. Lanublada
Roca Partida
C. de S. Lucas
Vas d. Bax catha
Las tres Marias
I. de S. Andres
Sierra de Xalisco
C. de Corrientes
Acatlan
Zacotecas
Yeres Ma fronteras
I. Sp. Sancto
Pr. d Singui quipagi
NUES
Xalico
Compostella
N. Sra. de la
Nueva
GALICIA
S. Fateosi
I. del Piloto
Purificatio
Colima
E
Zacatula
Mechoacan

BEGINNINGS

European explorers and Spanish missionaries changed forever the
way of life enjoyed by the first inhabitants of California

The first tenants of the rich land that became California were thought to have been of Hokan ancestry. About 3000 BC, Athabascans migrated onto the land, followed by scores of other Indian tribes. But so many native people died following the late arrival of the white man that anthropologists have had to rely on patchy mission records for their estimates – a reasonable guess being that 230,000 Native Americans originally inhabited the region.

California tribes led a simple life, their igloo-shaped homes of reed providing breezy shelter in summer with deerskin roofs for protection during the rainy season. When it was cool, open fires were built in the homes, holes in the roof allowing the smoke to escape. In warm weather, the men and children were naked except for ornamental jewelry such as necklaces, earrings, bracelets and anklets. They kept warm when needed with robes of bark or crudely tanned pelts. Some groups practiced tattooing. The women wore aprons of deerskins or reeds. Customs, talents and preoccupations varied from tribe to tribe, each with separate identities and languages.

Southern fishermen

In the south, the Chumash tribe, living around what is now Santa Barbara, were adept fishermen who used seashell hooks, traps, nets and vegetable poisons, even catching fish with their bare hands. Shellfish eaten over the centuries have left contemporary historians with mounds of discarded shells, some ranging up to 20 feet (6 meters) deep. Acorn mush was the Chumash tribe's staple food. The women gathered nuts, pounded them to meal in stone mortars, then leached the meal in hot water to remove the poisonous tannic acid. Traces of the Chumash era can still be found as pictographs in isolated caves in the mountainous Los Padres Forest.

LEFT: early European explorers believed California was an island. This map was drawn in 1638.
RIGHT: Father Junípero Serra, the founder of more than 20 missions; the earliest was near San Diego.

Among the crafts left by the Indians, basket-making and canoe-making were the two most outstanding. Baskets were used for cooking, storing and carrying. Twined basketry – crafted from long flexible splints split from spruce roots – was made with great skill. Waterproof, tightly woven baskets were made for cooking,

especially for boiling acorn flour. The Pomo weavers were skilled at making baby carriers, treasure baskets in which to store valuables, various personal effects, snug and cap-like rainhats worn by the women, odd-shaped gambling trays and even asphalt-lined water bottles.

Canoe-making involved easily worked timbers such as red cedar and redwood. The canoes were distinguished by their symmetry, neatness of finish, and frequent decoration. All of this was achieved with limited tools, the principal ones being chisels, curved knives, abrasive stones, wedges and sharkskin. Probably because fishing played such an important part in their lives, the Chumash tribe in particular were expert boat builders. One of their elegant vessels can be admired today at the Santa Barbara County Courthouse.

The California tribes' lifestyle continued and prospered for thousands of years with few major changes and few possessions. The arrival of white people bewildered them but their acquisition of articles such as guns, metal utensils, axes, blankets and cloth inevitably led to a decline of the native arts and crafts. With the coming of the immigrant wagons and the encroachment of white settlements, warfare became a unifying force.

Bands that had been hostile to one another

habitants de Californie

often united against the intruders. But even this did not save them and in the end they were overwhelmed. The culture of all Native Americans was radically changed. They had survived earthquakes and droughts, but the white man was too strong for them.

Fabled island

Hernando Cortés, the Spaniard who went in search of the beautiful Queen Calafia of Baja and ended up conquering Mexico, sailed up the west coast of America. Stumbling upon a "peninsula" which stretched down between the sea and a gulf, he believed he'd found a long-lost fabled island, and he named it "California."

But the European discovery of California is officially credited to Juan Rodríguez Cabrillo, the Portuguese commander of two Spanish caravels, who is thought to have embarked from the Mexican port of Navidad in June 1542. He explored most of the coast of what is now the state of California, entering San Diego Harbor in September 1542 and labeling it "enclosed and very good."

Sixty years later Sebastian Vizcaíno arrived, searching for suitable ports of call for his Manila galleon on its annual return to the Philippines. But the Spanish king, to whom he reported, was also keenly aware of Russian incursions from the north where otter hunting had reached as far south as Bodega Bay near what is now San Francisco.

Vizcaíno gave lasting names to several California sites, such as San Clemente Island, San Diego and Santa Catalina Island. Of more importance was his glowing report on the virtues of the coast, documents that urged Spain to colonize California.

What followed, however, was another century and a half of lassitude until the overland arrival in 1769 of Gaspar de Portola from Baja. Crossing the Santa Ana River and exchanging gifts with friendly tribes, de Portola's band passed the bubbling tar pits of La Brea, through the mountains at Sepulveda Pass to Lake Encino and headed northwards to open up the route to Monterey.

Between 1492 and 1542, Spain had built a fabulously rich empire based on its conquest of the Incas and the Aztecs and by the end of the 16th century had added to it the Philippines. What was needed now was a safe port in which the Spanish galleons heading back to Spain could find haven from Dutch and British pirates. This was Vizcaíno's task.

"The three diarists in the party agree that the practical discovery of most significance was the advantageous site on the Los Angeles River," noted John Caughey in a volume published by the California Historical Society to mark the city's bi-centennial. "Equally important were the numerous able-bodied, alert and amiable Indians because Spanish policy looked towards preserving, Christianizing, Hispanizing and engrossing the natives as an element in the Spanish colony now to be established."

Over the centuries Spain had developed a standard method for settling new territory, using the sword to cut down any opposition from the natives and pacifying the area with the introduction of Christianity. This was the approach used in California where, from 1769 to early in the following century, a chain of 21 Franciscan missions was established between San Diego in the south and Sonoma near San Francisco. These played the major role in enslaving hundreds of coastal Indians into an endless round of work and prayer. Father Junípero Serra, a tireless zealot who stood just 5 feet 2 inches (1.57 meters) in height, was responsible for establishing the first seven missions (San Diego, San Carlos, San Antonio, San

is due to the handful of priests who documented them in their journals. Each mission used Indian converts to set up large-scale "industries" – operations making olive oil, citrus-fruit growing, wine-making, cattle raising, and soap and tallow manufacture.

Complex religious structure

As early as 1775 the members of some tribes rebelled: in an uprising at the San Diego mission, one of the Franciscans was killed. But abolishing age-old tribal customs and introducing a complex religious structure which centered around endless work eventually con-

Gabriel Archangel, San Luis Obispo, San Francisco and San Juan Capistrano), most of which were destroyed in the 1812 earthquake. "Serra's Church" in the San Juan Capistrano mission is the oldest mission building still standing in its original position, and is the only one in which the diminutive padre celebrated mass.

At first the tribes resisted conversion but the might of the church and the zealousness of its priests eventually swept away their old customs. Ironically, our knowledge of those ways

LEFT: early Californians numbered up to 230,000.
ABOVE: the interior of San Gabriel Mission looks much the same as when it was built.

verted the Indians into obedient servants. The object of every mission was to become self-sufficient, to which end its subjects became cooks, blacksmiths, farmers, tanners, vintners or underpaid laborers. Native American men were taught to tend cattle, women to sew.

White diseases such as measles and chicken pox killed thousands. Hundreds more fell ill with venereal diseases and as a result the Indians developed a mortal fear of mission life. But benevolent despotism kept them in the missions and it was their labor that made the system successful. Not until the Mexican government's secularization decrees of 1834 were the native people freed – only to become underpaid peons on the vast ranches. Today, peppering the coast-line and inland areas, are ruins of these once-dominant religious communities, each with its own unique features.

In theory, the Secularization Act of 1834 gave lay administrators and Native Americans the right to ownership of the missions and their property; a potential *ranchero* could ask for as many as 50,000 acres (20,000 hectares). In practice, however, the acts were barely observed: tribes were driven out into a world of treachery and poverty, ill-equipped to deal with white men's laws.

Some returned to the hills, others indentured

themselves as ranch hands or turned to drinking and gambling. Meanwhile the orange groves and the productive gardens were cleared or ploughed up to grow food, and the so-called "string of pearls" (the 21 missions along the coast) were transformed into a patchwork quilt of working ranches.

Many historians believe that for all the good it brought, the mission system promoted out-right slavery under the guise of piety and was at least partly responsible for the ultimate destruction of California's tribal population. Even after the missions had been secularized, pillage of the environment continued for the rest of the century: forests were cut down, hunting lands

confiscated and mining wastes ruined the once-pure salmon streams. Nevertheless, in the fall of 1781, six weeks before the British surren-dered at Yorktown, Felipe de Neve, then gov-ernor of Spanish California, founded the new *pueblo* – or settlement – of Los Angeles. Within three years the founding fathers had started construction on a church to serve as the center-piece of the town's main plaza.

Rural countryside

By 1790, with its population recorded as 139 residents, Los Angeles presented a pleasing sight. Aside from a few fields between the town and the river, the countryside was pretty much as it had looked when de Portola had passed through 30 years previously. The terrain was what geographers call savanna country, grass-land interspersed with groves of California live oak, willow and sycamore trees beside the river, and streams with marshland south of town. The Los Angeles River had been selected as a town site because, unlike the desert washes, it did not dry up in summer. Here, as elsewhere, the early settlers learned the hard way how fickle Californian winters can be: the placid river flooded in 1818, forcing the relocation of the first town square.

Following a 1786 law, the governor became empowered to give land grants, grazing rights and 2,000 head of cattle to the settlers, and thus the early founders were given huge *ranchos* to develop. Many of them went to individuals whose names survive in the modern city. Los Feliz, Las Virgenes, Sepulveda – now better known as freeway off-ramps or "surface" streets – were once haciendas.

It was not until after three centuries of Span-ish rule that Mexico finally broke away. On September 27, 1821, it declared itself a repub-lic from its European motherland.

Coincidentally, secularization of the missions was sought by Spanish-Mexican settlers known as the *Californios*. Eight million acres (3.2 mil-lion hectares) of mission land were fragmented into 800 privately owned ranches with some governors handing out land to their cronies for only a few pennies per acre. ❑

LEFT: Hernando Cortés was prompted to explore the west coast of California in part by reports of the beautiful Queen Calafia of Baja.
RIGHT: missions destroyed many rituals of tribal life.

FROM RANCHOS TO STATEHOOD

Statehood and the Gold Rush changed Southern California from a territory of ramshackle farms into a rich, swaggering retail market

At the onset of the new Mexican republic, soldiers who had finished their time in the army often stayed on in California rather than return to Spain or Mexico. Under Mexican law, a *ranchero* could ask for as many as 50,000 acres (20,000 hectares) and Indian slave labor became part of the plunder.

Orange orchards were cleared for firewood and herds were given to private hands. The predominant lifestyle quickly changed to that of an untamed, frontier-style cattle range, although ranching in this part of the world made few demands upon its owners. With no line fences to patrol and repair on the open range, and no need for vigilance because of branded stock, the *vaquero* had little to do to pass his days but practice feats of horsemanship to improve his masculinity and impress the *señoritas*.

Gold-braided clothes

The *vaquero's* sports were violent, including calf-branding, wild horse roundups, bear hunts, cock and bullfights; his entertainment included dances such as the Spanish fandango and the western waltz, and at fiestas he was bedecked in gold-braided clothes dripping with silver. Crops were plentiful; wildlife included badgers and coyotes; the lordly condor circled overhead while grizzly bear, deer, wolves, mountain lions and wildcats roamed the hills.

Author Richard Henry Dana, who visited in 1835, called the Californians "an idle thriftless people," an observation lent weight by the lifestyle of so many who found it a simple matter to increase their wealth. The sudden influx of prospectors to the northern part of the land created an immense demand for beef which the southerners were ready to supply.

In his novel *Two Years Before the Mast,* Dana described how cattle hides and tallow in 500-lb (227-kg) bags were thrown from the cliffs to the

PRECEDING PAGES: early Americans began to adopt European leisure pursuits.
LEFT: *ranchos* were more Mexican than American.
RIGHT: author Richard Henry Dana.

waiting ships. Accepted as a basic unit of barter, these hides were turned into rugs, blankets, sandals, chaps and saddles. Rawhides were twisted into *reatas* (used for roping cattle) or used to lash timbers together. Meat not eaten immediately was sun-dried as beef jerky or pickled for barter with traders. Fat was rendered into tallow, the basis for candles and soap. Yankee trading ships plied up and down the coast, operating like floating department stores offering mahogany furniture, gleaming copperware, framed mirrors, Irish linen, silk stockings, silver candlesticks, and cashmere shawls. For many of the native-born Americans, these were their first amenities from the civilized world. Sometimes the trading ships, which had survived the precarious Straits of Magellan, would operate up and down the coast for up to an entire year.

A genteel contraband soon developed. To reduce import taxes, ships worked in pairs to transfer cargo from one to the other on the open seas. The partially-emptied ship would then make port and submit to customs inspection. With duties paid, it would rejoin its consort and reverse the transfer. Sometimes the Yankee traders unloaded cargoes in lonely coves and these were eventually smuggled ashore. Both sides fared well: the Yankee traders sailed south with full holds and the *rancheros* displayed their new finery with yet another fiesta.

The weather remained temperate except for the occasional hot, dry, gale-force wind the Indians called "wind of the evil spirits." The Spaniards called them *santanas*, a name which has become corrupted to Santa Ana winds today. An occasional earthquake rumbled down the San

this land of milk and honey on the Pacific Ocean. President Andrew Jackson sent an emissary to Mexico City in the 1830s to purchase California for the sum of $500,000. The plan failed.

War with Mexico

When President James K. Polk took office in 1845 he pledged to acquire California by any means. He felt pressured by English financial interests which plotted to exchange $26 million of defaulted Mexican bonds for the rich land of California. On May 13, 1846, he surprised no one by declaring war on Mexico. A succession of disagreements along the Rio Grande made the

1822 MEXICAN RULE

Andreas Fault. The *rancheros* spent their considerable energy rebuilding damaged haciendas, made from red-tile roofing set on white-painted adobe brick walls, but let the missions fall into ruins. Restoration work began only in the 20th century when the missions were eventually declared historical landmarks.

In 1834 Governor Figueroa issued the first of the Secularization Acts, which in theory gave lay administrators and Indian neophytes the right to ownership of the missions and their property. In practice, however, these acts were widely ignored; secularization drove the Indians out into the world of poverty and helplessness.

Official Washington soon became aware of

STATEHOOD

California was rushed into the Union on September 9, 1850. In November 1849, it had already formed a state government and drafted a constitution which guaranteed the right to "enjoying and defending life and liberty, acquiring, possessing and protecting property, and pursuing and obtaining happiness," a typically Californian mix of the sublime and the practical. By 1850 with LA accorded the status of county seat, the first Protestant church was founded. But the community was still an agricultural hamlet. An 1849 report states: "The town consists of an old adobe church and about a hundred adobe houses scattered about a dusty plaza."

war inevitable, the ultimate prize being possession of Texas. The *Californios* resisted extremely well, considering the forces sent against them.

But this was the high-watermark of their attempt to drive the *Yanquis* (Yankees) from California. The bloodiest battle on Californian soil took place in the Valley of San Pasqual, near Escondido. The Army of the West, commanded by General Stephen W. Kearney, fought a brief battle during which 18 Americans were killed.

Kearney, with his *aide-de-camp,* US naval officer Robert F. Stockton, skirmished with Mexican-Californians at Paso de Bartolo on the San Gabriel River. The *Californios* soon capitulated

flowed on with little change despite becoming a part of the 31st state of the Union. Washington, DC was even further away from California than Mexico City, so communication by land was extremely slow. The *rancheros* had to depend on the Yankee trading ships for supplies. Cattle was still king. But then a new word crept into the news – gold, the first intimation that a major drama was about to unfold.

Tribal lands dwindle

From 1850 onwards the Federal government signed treaties (never ratified by the Senate) under which more than 7 million acres (2.8 mil-

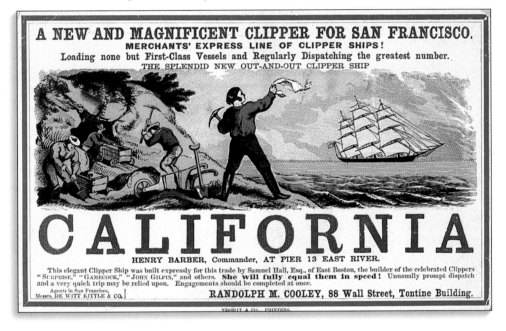

and California's participation in the war ended with the Treaty of Cahuenga.

On July 4 (US Independence Day) 1848, the Treaty of Guadalupe Hidalgo ended the Mexican War. By this treaty, California became a territory of the United States of America; statehood was achieved two years later. Through fierce negotiation, the community of San Diego was saved from being on the south side of the Mexico-California boundary.

In no time at all, Los Angeles became Americanized. But for many, life on the *ranchos*

LEFT: Mexican rule was short-lived.
ABOVE: East Coast poster urging all to "Go West."

lion hectares) of tribal land dwindled to less than 10 percent of that total. Apart from being denied legality and having their labor exploited and their culture destroyed, the Indians themselves had been fatally exposed to disease and alcoholism.

For 30 years after America had acquired Alta California from Mexico, Los Angeles largely remained a Mexican city infused with Latino culture and traditions. But the arrival of the Southern Pacific Railroad triggered a series of land booms with the subsequent influx of Anglo-American, Asian and European immigrants eventually outnumbering Mexicans by 10 to 1.

Soon to suffer from marginalization and racist attitudes were the Chinese, thousands of whom had poured into Northern California from the gold fields and, later, into Los Angeles after their under-unappreciated building of the railroads had been completed.

Gold had been discovered in Placeritas Canyon, north of Mission San Fernando, in 1842 when Francisco Lopez, rounding up stray horses, stopped to rest beneath an oak tree. He opened his knife to uproot some wild onions, and their roots came out attached to a nugget that glittered in the sun. Six years later, gold was discovered in quantity at Sutter's Mill near Sacramento in Northern California.

Word quickly spread East and coincident with

California joining the Union, the stampede began. Soon a torrent of gold-dazzled prospectors were trekking through the Sierras to California. Entire parties in covered wagons made their way west. When they encountered the sheer cliffs of the Sierra Nevada, they winched up the wagons or took them apart and lowered them down the steep precipices.

Good as gold

Although many Angelenos ventured into the gold country, the real wealth lay in selling food to the miners. Their numbers had reached 100,000 by 1852 and food was at a premium, with wildly inflated prices finally creating a mar-

ket for the beef which had once been so much less valuable than the hide. Cattle prices jumped tenfold in a matter of months. Enterprising ranchers employed a single trail boss and four or five *vaqueros* to drive large herds 400 miles (644 km) along the rugged trail north. At one point the animals had to splash through the surf above San Buenaventura.

New money flowed into Los Angeles and, although the Gold Rush produced the city's first population boom, most of the newcomers were the human jetsam of the mining fields. Los Angeles quickly turned into a lawless western town where street killings, shoot-outs and lynchings became commonplace. At one point there was a murder almost every day, Indians not even being counted. In 1855 the mayor quit his position to take part in a lynching, after which he was immediately re-elected.

The boom was soon over, however, and Los Angeles, like the rest of the state, fell into a severe economic depression: banks failed, and merchants went bankrupt. But Los Angeles had grown sixfold in a decade, and racial tension was high between Mexicans and whites as resentment against the Yankee domination grew. By 1860 bullfighting was banned and the first baseball club was formed (at a girls' school), a sure indication of the cultural shift.

Latinos suffered with the onset of the depression of the 1850s. Vigilantes drove 10,000 Mexican miners from the southern mines, aided by a cadre of eager lawyers and greedy Anglo merchants. The merchants, who had advanced credit at exorbitant interest rates, foreclosed on many of the ranchos, ensuring the impoverishment of the Mexican majority in the town. All Spanish land grants were reviewed, and each case had to be heard several times, ensuring that legal fees were suitably exorbitant.

Gold has played a large part in Southern California's history – first, the metal which brought adventurers from all over to the gold fields in the northern part of the state with its obvious spillover effect on the city to the south, and then secondly, the "liquid" gold of oil discoveries. These peppered the region with large oil derricks, in part shaping the automobile-obsessed California culture we know today. ❑

LEFT: Chinese immigrant in traditional dress.
RIGHT: the Gold Rush in the north of California played a significant role in the development of the south.

PUEBLERINA

F.J. Che

AFTER THE GOLD RUSH

The arrival of the railroads, cheap labor and black gold – oil – led

to a boom of tycoons and property in the cities of the south

The Latino population's anger over blatant discrimination soon expressed itself in violence. Many of the overland stagecoaches from the north were preyed upon by roving bands of Mexican outlaws who came to be thought of as folk heroes to the local Latino population; in one 14-year period the Wells Fargo stages were held up 313 times for a total loss of almost half a million dollars.

The most famous of these *banditos*, Tiburcio Vasquez, who hid out in what is now Los Angeles' Laurel Canyon, was captured after a betrayal, but, once in jail, was visited by well-wishers and supporters. A set of famous rocks where he held off the posse that captured him (on the road to Lancaster) now bears his name, and has since been used as the classic Western shoot-out backdrop in scores of movies.

Between 1851 and 1860 the Chinese population increased enormously. Many were laborers imported to help build the transcontinental railroad, and others were drawn by the search for gold. But, after the gold ran out and the railroads had been completed, many moved down to Los Angeles where they became merchants or laborers on the local water-irrigation ditches. On October 23, 1871, touched off by the murder of a white policeman, a mob invaded Chinatown, shooting and lynching at random. More than two dozen Chinese were murdered, – one of the bloodiest incidents in the state.

Polyglot society

But in so many other ways, the fast-growing Asian population had already made an indelible mark on this emerging polyglot society. It is impossible to visualize how the railroads could have been completed or the vast market gardens of Southern California could have evolved without their contribution. Japanese and Chinese market gardens in particular benefited the city; greatly enlarged irrigation systems

---

PRECEDING PAGES: LA streetcar.
LEFT: Spanish influence reflected in tiles.
RIGHT: LA soon became the biggest city in the south.

between 1860 and 1880 not only helped supply the local demand for fresh vegetables, but also produced a surplus of food to ship north up the coast.

Los Angeles and its environs became a major agricultural region. Sheep-raising, which had superseded the cattle culture of the previ-

ous century, was badly hit when thousands of sheep died after the drought of 1877. But sheep and cattle continued to be a mainstay for the area, even as fruits and vegetables grew in trade and importance.

Oranges, in particular, started to become the region's major crop. The fruit had been cultivated as early as 1804 at the San Gabriel Mission and in 1841 William Wolfskill planted a 70-acre (28-hectare) orchard in what is now downtown Los Angeles. But a new seedless variety – the navel orange brought to the area from Bahia in Brazil – established the fruit's popularity. Sometime around 1875, two or three orange trees were sent from the Department of

Agriculture in Washington, DC, to Eliza and Luther Tibbetts in Riverside. which had been budded from a seedless orange. The Tibbetts planted the trees, little knowing that a decade later navel oranges would alter the agricultural, economic and social patterns of the entire region. The Washington navel orange, as the seedless and sweet fruit was officially known, became (in the words of Charles F. Lummis) "not only a fruit but a romance."

Soon, oranges were being shipped statewide but, although in the 1870s experimental shipments were being sent as far afield as St. Louis (they took two months to arrive), it was the

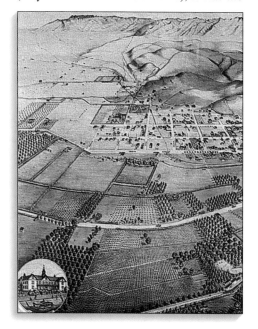

invention of the refrigerated rail car that made oranges a viable crop for shipping far afield. The citrus fruit hit its prime by 1889 when more than 13,000 acres (5,000 hectares) of land in six southern counties were devoted to its cultivation. Growers formed a marketing cooperative, the California Fruit Growers Exchange, famed for its ubiquitous trademark, Sunkist, which today controls 70 percent of the state's entire citrus crop.

Orange groves eventually filled much of the land, not only around Riverside and in the Ojai Valley, but near to the Los Angeles River in downtown LA, where there were still some vineyards (as the name Vignes Street reveals)

and vegetable gardens. The *zanjas*, as the irrigation ditches were called, watered the area and at the same time promptly served the little city as a sewage disposal system.

In 1911, promoters at San Bernardino offered to potential investors 50-acre (20-hectare) groves, already planted, for $5,000.

Orange production peaked in the 1940s. Thereafter, the demand for land for housing development – ironically much of which had been created by people attracted to the state by publicity about the oranges – gradually sent real estate prices too high for many growers to afford. The industry declined for a while, leaving behind some collectable souvenirs. Most of the beautiful orange-crate labels, lithographed with acid-etched granite plates, date from 1885 to the 1950s and were intended for the distributor rather than the consumer. Today some are worth as much as $2,000.

But citrus still manages to be a major crop; current sales top $1 million annually.

Grapes and wine

Within a mere 18 months of him making it, Horace Greeley's "Go West, young man" prediction became a reality. Many boomtowns took root and soon the population of the south equaled that of the north. This vast, semitropical, often desert-like land reached its potential. Thousands of acres of good farmland sold by the railroads at low prices were planted with wheat, oranges, grapes, cotton, tea, tobacco and coffee. Irrigation converted vast tracts of arid waste into fertile land bearing crops.

Agriculture, boosted by rail transportation, became the backbone of Southern California's economy, with grapes and wine becoming primary products. It was the realization that its growth would be limited unless it improved communications with the rest of the continent (and spurred by the example of San Francisco which had earlier become the terminus of the first transcontinental railway) which pressured Los Angeles to connect with the rail system.

Despite competition from San Bernardino, which had easier access, the Southern Pacific Railroad was persuaded to extend a track to Los Angeles where it absorbed Phineas Banning's Los Angeles and San Pedro Railroad. In 1869 the Union Pacific and the Central Pacific had met for a "joining of the rails" at Promontory, Utah, and by 1876 the Southern Pacific line connected San Francisco and Los Angeles. The predicted boom followed.

As the biggest landowners and biggest employers, the immensely rich railroad barons were able to manipulate freight rates, control water supplies, keep thousands of acres for themselves and with their wealth subvert politicians and municipalities. It was many years before state regulation of the railroads became the norm rather than the other way around. When Frank Norris wrote *The Octopus* in 1901, no one had to guess at the reference: the Southern Pacific had its greedy tentacles in every corner of the state.

ization began to take hold. For the next 60 years, California would suffer recurrent bouts of labor strife. The depression was slow to disappear, but California was too rich to suffer permanently. In the next few decades it slowly built up its industrial strength to the point where it could compete with the East Coast.

Boundless orange groves

Southern Pacific had been getting $118 for a first-class ticket, $85 for second-class, Chicago to Los Angeles. By the close of 1876 the highest fare from the Pacific Coast to Missouri was $15. Later it dropped to $10 and, for one day, to

In the winter of 1869–70 a severe drought crippled the state's agriculture. Also, between 1873 and 1875 more than a quarter of a million immigrants came to California. Many were factory workers and few could find work. The "Terrible '70s" had arrived. Those hurt most by the great shrinkage of capital in the 1870s were the state's working people. During the gold and silver rushes California's laborers had enjoyed a rare freedom to move easily from job to job and to dictate working conditions. Now, however, with massive unemployment, union-

a single dollar bill. As a result, waves of passengers and European immigrants flooded Southern California: 100,000 on the Southern Pacific in one year; the Santa Fe, founded in 1859 as the Atchison & Topeka, was bringing in three to four trainloads a day. Land prices jumped tenfold as speculators preyed on the wide-eyed newcomers, drawn by idyllic pictures of boundless orange groves against gloriously clear skies.

Grand hotels were built to form the nexus of still-unformed communities, and new tourism boomed. "We hired the most imaginative liars we could find," said the spokesman for one real estate company. Newcomers were met off the

---

LEFT: Los Angeles depicted in an 1871 lithograph.
ABOVE: workers in a San Gabriel fruit-packing house.

train with music and dancing. In order not to disappoint would-be buyers, speculators were not above sticking oranges on thorny Joshua trees to demonstrate the ubiquity of the fruit.

The arrival in San Diego of the railroad in 1885 caused jealousy in Los Angeles, which did everything it could to discourage its citizens from visiting its southern neighbor. Rail passengers bound for San Diego were intercepted and persuaded that the destination was just a sleepy Mexican town with unpaved streets and no water. Some naive visitors were still clutching the jugs of water they had been sold as they disembarked in the southern city.

Subdividers had barely stepped off the Southern Pacific before they were establishing new towns. One of these entrepreneurs, Harvey Henderson Wilcox, planned a community around his 120-acre (50-hectare) orchard at the edge of the mountains. Chamber of Commerce boosters like to think that Hollywood began with the movies, but the word first appeared in print when Wilcox lettered it on the gate of his farm in 1886. He would have preferred the name "Figwood" himself, figs being the major produce of the orchard spreading around what is now the busy junction of Hollywood and Cahuenga boulevards, but he acceded to the choice of his young second wife Daeida who

had acquired the name from a stranger she met on a train. Topeka-born Wilcox, a paraplegic who got around on crutches, subdivided the property, sold lots, unsuccessfully tried to grow holly, planted pepper trees, and dreamed of a serene, temperance community like that of his native Kansas.

"And then we came," mused Cecil B. De Mille years later, "and Wilcox saw his dream disappear the minute the first camera crews came in. Show people! What a disaster!"

The major attraction for newcomers to the region was climate. Confirming that, as the posters claimed, Southern California was a "Semi-Tropical Paradise," many of those who came on brief visits decided to stay. By the end of the 1880s the wooden sidewalks were crowded with people, night and day; hotel rooms were double-booked and the subsequent building boom brought another wave of bricklayers, carpenters, painters and other craftsmen. Tent cities sprang up on the fringes of town.

Seduction in San Diego

Tent cities of an entirely different kind were going up in San Diego. John D. Spreckels, owner of the new, grand hotel on the Coronado peninsula, was determined that his site would appeal, not only to the rich and famous when it opened in 1888, but also to the snooty locals who, up until that time, had refused to cross the bay. On the strand of beach below the lavish wooden hotel, Spreckels built rows of tent cottages with bare floors, palm thatch roofs and simple furniture, plus a washstand and pitcher. San Diegans, seduced by a weekend on the beach, thronged to the recreation center and restaurant, and danced to live music from the bandshell.

Spreckels was just one of San Diego's visionaries; another was Alonzo Horton, who did for the Downtown area what Spreckels did for the peninsula, ie, extend the boundaries of the city by luring residents away from the town's original mission-era boundaries. Horton was "a plain, typical American western pioneer, with a true vision and optimism infinite," said one orator at Horton's funeral in 1909. Horton's name lives on in San Diego's upscale shopping mall, Horton Plaza.

Just as the northern part of the state had gotten rich from the treasures of the earth so too was Southern California about to undergo its own boom from another kind of gold. In 1892, two decades after earlier strikes had fizzled out, a former gold prospector named Edward Doheny and his partner Charles Canfield struck oil on a vacant lot in downtown Los Angeles. The 160-foot (50-meter) deep gusher at first yielded a modest seven barrels a day but within weeks derricks were shooting up all over the city. They were to become so prolific, in fact, during the next few years that overproduction caused the price of oil to drop to 15¢ a barrel.

Oil, which eventually ushered in the automobile age and turned Wilshire Boulevard – formerly the La Brea Trail – into a major high-

looked like a product in search of a purpose. All of this changed very quickly. Its very abundance inspired experimentation, and in time it not only made the pioneers very rich, it was to trigger massive alterations in lifestyles, and particularly mass transportation.

Big red train cars

Oil-fired engines began hauling Santa Fe trains, and oil-generated electricity drove the Big Red Cars of the Pacific Electric Railroad's 11,000-mile (18,000-km) system which extended like an octopus throughout the region. All this preceded the automobile boom

way, was not taken seriously until the final years of the century. At first, the black stuff that oozed to the surface at the La Brea Tar Pits and in a handful of other spots had found use as water-proofing for boats, huts and sometimes drinking vessels. Experiments demonstrated that it could also be burned in furnaces as a possible replacement for wood. Mixed with sand, it seemed to provide a good paving material.

But when distilled into a flammable spirit, it

LEFT: John D. Spreckels, owner of glamorous Hotel del Coronado, which opened in San Diego in 1888.
ABOVE: coast-to-coast railroads in the north contributed to the economic boom of the south.

which in the next few decades resulted in 450 sq. miles (1,170 sq. km) being blanketed with freeways, airports, factories, oil refineries, subdivisions, movie studios and industry of all kinds. "A completely motorized civilization," was how one chronicler was later to describe Southern California.

Around the time of the train boom, Arthur Freemont Gilmore arrived in Los Angeles from Illinois, and bought 256 acres (104 hectares) of what had once been Rancho La Brea. Finding the land ideal for grazing his cows, he sank a well to find water and instead struck oil. By the time his son Earl graduated from Stanford in 1909, the automobile was well established, and

Earl was to be seen at the corner of Wilshire and La Brea with a red and yellow painted farm wagon holding a large tank full of gasoline. "Fill 'er up, Earl," yelled the drivers of the new-fangled cars as they stopped to wipe their dusty windscreens. They paid 50¢ for five gallons.

A better way to deliver gas was needed, however. On a trip to France another Los Angeleno, Earle C. Anthony, spotted a vendor delivering his product through a hose rather than a funnel. On his return, he set to work with his partner Don Lee and invented the gas pump.

With the coming of the railroad, the discovery of oil, and the acquisition of a reliable flow

Twenty thousand cheering participants ate barbecue and five tons of clams. For 10 years trains continued to bring in the huge quantities of rock needed for the breakwater that protected the city's new deep-water port.

Separate communities to the south and the west of Los Angeles were gradually swallowed up by the city, water being the crucial element that made possible this extraordinarily rapid growth. Rain is, even now, infrequent and unpredictable in Southern California, and the burgeoning population quickly outstripped the capacity of the region's rivers and meager supply of ground water.

of water, Los Angeles tripled in population between 1900 and 1910, from 102,000 to over 320,000, and nearly doubled in area. Neighboring communities such as Hollywood were annexed. The city also grabbed a strip of territory that snaked south to the port of San Pedro. This was a small fishing village that had miraculously won out as the city's harbor despite a heavy-handed campaign by Henry Huntington who had already completed a three-quarter-mile wharf at Santa Monica, serviced exclusively by his own Southern Pacific Railroad.

Despite Huntington's Byzantine politicking in Washington, a party celebrating the new port's location at San Pedro was held in 1899.

Stealing the water

The infamous plot by Los Angeles to steal water from the Owens Valley via a 250-mile (400-km) pipeline over the Tehachapi Mountains made fortunes for a private syndicate. One member was General Moses H. Sherman, whose advance knowledge of what land was about to be enriched came from serving on the city's Board of Water Commissioners. But without the additional water brought by the city's Water Bureau Superintendent William Mulholland, Southern California's growth would have been forever stunted. The farmers of the fertile Owens Valley saw their water rights stolen and the area turned into a wasteland as the water was drained away by the 233-mile (375-km), gravity-fed California aqueduct, a $24.5-million public works spectacular approved by LA voters in 1907.

When the pipeline was completed and the water arrived on November 5, 1913, 30,000 Angelenos gathered near San Fernando to watch the first waters cascading down the open aqueduct at the astonishing rate of 26 million gallons (98 million liters) a day.

The original aqueduct has now been supplemented by a conduit, and today supplies 525 million gallons (over 2 billion liters) of water a day. All firmly believed this supply would take

utes to reach Venice Beach from the city's center. Los Angeles had one of the nation's best public transportation systems when the famous Red Car Line covered the region, spurring further decentralization as communities sprang up along its tracks *(see page 52)*.

No cars needed

At their peak, the trolley companies, with thousands of miles of tracks and overhead power lines, their own power plants and water companies, and hundreds of cars – there were 600 Big Red Cars alone – served 42 towns and carried 225,000 passengers a day. But, gradually,

care of Southern California's thirst forever, but the city has been adding sources ever since. More water from the Parker Dam on the Arizona border arrived in 1941, but it cost the city a staggering $200 million. Electric power now comes mostly from the Hoover Dam on the Colorado River in Nevada about 206 miles (332 km) away.

Despite its size, getting around the Los Angeles region in the early part of the 20th century was not a problem. In 1905 it took just 38 min-

LEFT: workers and pipeline during the aqueduct construction, which brought water to LA from afar.
ABOVE: Santa Monica bath house, 1895.

automobiles strangled the transit system, slowing it down, drawing away passengers. By raising fares to make up for declining revenues, the systems drove away even more passengers. As buses moved in, the trolley tracks were torn up, leaving blighted rights-of-way, many of which remain to this day.

In the 1950s, the designers of Southern California's massive freeway system were forced to follow many of the trolleys' routes to the communities that had sprung up along the lines, and today the region's governments are being forced to spend billions of dollars re-establishing light railway services, in most cases on the original rights-of-way. ❑

I Love You California

Words by
F. B. SILVERWOOD.

Music by
A. F. FRANKENSTEIN.

Will Farrand Wilson.
May 19th 1913.

Copyrighted 1913 by F. B. Silverwood.

Mary Garden stopped Grand Opera to make this California song famous

THE TWENTIETH CENTURY

The rise of Southern California continued with great wealth from agriculture, aviation and another oil boom, but there was smoke on the horizon

During World War I even the formerly dry San Fernando Valley was annexed by Los Angeles which was well on its way to becoming a mega-city. Most of the beach communities resisted incorporation for a time, fearing that LA's "blue laws" – which banned liquor sales on Sunday, – would ruin their best business day of the week. But, finally, they too were absorbed, at least geographically, into the ever-expanding city

Hollywood was one of these towns soon to fall within the grasp of the Los Angeles City Council. In the early 1900s it was a sedate country-club town, the perfect manifestation of Harvey and Daeida Wilcox, the two paragons of propriety who had founded this serene community in the late 1880s. After the town's first formal elections in 1904 drunkenness was prohibited, the sale of liquor was forbidden, and a speed limit of 12 miles an hour (19 km/hour) was rigidly enforced. As late as 1909 the garden town was still the sort of place where Carrie Jacobs Bonds, while staying in her suite at the Hollywood Hotel, could write her famous song "The End of a Perfect Day." A sign at the hotel read "no dogs or actors" before the movie folk transformed the community.

Wilcox himself never actually saw paradise lost. He was dead by the 1890s and his dream was pursued by Daeida and her new husband until her death in 1914, just in time to prevent her from seeing what befell her precious little Hollywood.

Bring on the movies

The Nestor Film Company arrived in 1911 and shot *The Law of the Range* in the Blondeau Tavern – available, as it happened, by virtue of the prohibition ordinances which had been passed at Daeida Wilcox's urging. Two years later Cecil B. De Mille, Jesse Lasky, Samuel

---

PRECEDING PAGES: a new, carefree way of life was beginning to blossom in the sunny south.
LEFT: 1913 song from the Southern California Music Co.
RIGHT: the movie industry makes its mark.

Goldfish (later Goldwyn) and Arthur Friend shot *The Squaw Man*, the first full-length feature made in Hollywood. Within 18 months Lasky's studio occupied a city block.

By 1910, LA had five fiercely competitive newspapers. (*Variety* dates back to the turn of the 20th century but *Daily Variety* did not

appear until 1933; its rival *The Hollywood Reporter* was founded in 1931. Both have an influence far in excess of their 20,000 circulation.) Five years later there were already 15,000 automobiles but still there was no major industry in the area except for real estate. Once here, prospective buyers – many in ill-health, having come for the rejuvenating climate – received bus trips and free lunches to entice them to visit planned subdivisions where they might become customers.

"Nearly everybody in Southern California is more or less in the real estate business," observed one writer in 1948, though it could pertain to any time in the area's history. "That is, nearly everyone figures on what profit he could sell out for and what he could do with the money in some other neighborhood. The homestead handed down from generation to generation is nearly unknown."

Some of the suburban developments began with a bang, some with barely a whimper, but early fanfare was no guarantee of eventual success. Tobacco heir Abbott Kinney reconstituted Venice as a sort of American residential theme park built on what had been marshes and wetlands south of Santa Monica. Gondolas plied the waters of the newly constructed Grand Lagoon in which all the new community's

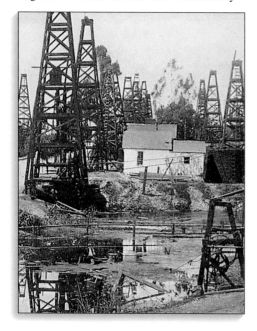

canals terminated. Building lots overlooking the canals were available at $2,700 a piece. Kinney was determined to inject a high level of culture into his ersatz Venice, but after a $16,000 loss on his ambitious first season of opera he lowered his cultural sights.

By 1915, when Barney Oldfield won the first and only Venice Grand Prix, a 300-mile (483-km) automobile chase through local streets, the fledgling movie industry had discovered the town. But Kinney's grand architectural folly eventually went bankrupt and fell on half a century of hard times. In 1958, director Orson Welles used the then-decrepit Venice as the backdrop for his movie *A Touch of Evil.* Most

of Los Angeles agreed: the seedy area had become an enclave of beatniks and artists.

Downtown LA was linked to Pasadena and Santa Monica by an urban railway but, not to be outdone, the Southern Pacific's Collis P. Huntington had, in 1901, devised a vast network of electric trains to cover the entire area called the Red Car Line. "I will join the whole region into one big family," he promised, adding that Los Angeles was "destined to become the most important city in the country, if not in the world. It can extend in any direction, as far as you like." Within a decade his trolley cars on which passengers could ride 20 miles (32 km) for a nickel stretched everywhere from a city whose population had tripled to 300,000.

Transportation revolution

"The whole area within a radius of 70 miles of the city took on a new life," wrote Huntington's biographer Isaac Marcosson in 1914. "Villages became towns; towns blossomed in to miniature cities." When the author Henry James came by on a lecture tour in 1905 he said he'd never seen such an efficient transit system in all his worldwide travels but within five years the *Times* noted that "with thousands of motor cars passing and repassing, the traffic question has become a problem."

A transportation expert brought from back East to anticipate transit needs for the next decade (during which the population was expected to triple again) urged the creation of a planning commission "to replace the present haphazard system of growth." When Los Angeles held its second annual motor show in 1909 it had more cars on its busy streets than any other city in the world.

Other Southern California cities were also in the throes of expansion. When the Panama Canal was completed in 1914, San Diego chose to copy one of San Francisco's ideas and hold a celebratory exposition; as the southernmost US city on the coast, it could be reached by northbound vessels long before its Bay City rival. San Diegans agreed to spare no expense on the Panama-California International Exposition of 1915.

Bertram Goodhue, an expert on Spanish Colonial architecture, was commissioned to design a series of extravagant buildings in Balboa Park, structures which today house most of the city's museums. The exposition spread the southern city's reputation as a place for good living that offered mild, year-round temperatures along with a cost-of-living some three percent less than that of comparable cities.

Santa Barbara, too, undertook an improvement campaign, albeit one that began with a disaster. In 1925, an earthquake destroyed most of the existing buildings. When the time came for reconstruction, the city's leaders imposed a mandatory building code that prohibited anything unharmonious. The result is an entire city built in idealized Spanish Colonial Revival style, one of the prettiest towns in the state.

During the 1920s, Los Angeles experienced

Apart from oil, there was little industry in Southern California but the region had become one of the most productive agricultural regions in the US which it would remain until the eve of World War II. Despite being hampered by a 1913 law that prohibited aliens from owning land, Japanese truck farmers aroused the jealousy of their neighbors with their hard work and skills, although their industriousness was ill rewarded after Pearl Harbor when President Roosevelt's Executive Order 9006 sent 112,000 of them, the majority American-born, to internment camps.

At the end of the war, they saw their property

another oil boom as wells were sunk at Huntington Beach, Signal Hill and Santa Fe Springs. Eventually a forest of derricks stretched from the mountains to the sea. Even Venice, with its canals and gondolas, became an oil city. Confidence men and investors rushed to take advantage of the bonanza by selling shares in non-existent drilling companies. The "Salt Lake Field" in southwestern Los Angeles was developed, followed by fields in Huntington Beach, Santa Fe Springs and Signal Hill.

LEFT: during the 1920s, LA had another oil boom.
ABOVE: in 1927, San Diego served as the take-off point for Charles Lindbergh's transatlantic flight.

sold for taxes and "fees." Italians, Armenians, Slavs, and Anglos, added to the ethnic agricultural mix, but were treated slightly better.

Age of flight

Aviation, which would become a major Southern California industry, had gotten an early start in 1883 when the country's first glider took off near San Diego. Six years after the Wright brothers made their pioneering 59-second flight in North Carolina, Los Angeles hosted America's first international air show partly financed with a $50,000 contribution from Huntington, the railroad magnate.

Among the nearly half a million visitors who

thronged the old Dominguez Ranch to watch Glenn Curtis set a speed record of 55 mph (89 kph) was Glenn Martin, who promptly set up a plant. By the timely arrival of World War I, the plant was turning out at least one plane a day. One of his employees, Donald Douglas, peeled off to begin his own company whose DC3 became the first commercially successful aircraft. Within a couple of years it was carrying 95 percent of all US air traffic.

Cecil B. de Mille had an airport at Fairfax

VENICE VISION

Abbott Kinney's architectural folly of a city by the beach with canals, gondolas and grand opera eventually went bankrupt and fell on half a century of hard times.

struct the airplane on the site of what is now a solar engineering plant south of San Diego airport. Lindbergh had prepared for the ordeal by practicing sleep deprivation in his car in the parking lot. Further aircraft production and defense contracts were to bring considerable prosperity and mass employment to San Diego in the middle years of the 20th century.

The advent of World War II gave a tremendous boost to California's aircraft industry, whose employees increased statewide from

459:—

The box of Fruit I promised you from California

and Wilshire in Hollywood across from one operated by Charlie Chaplin's brother Sydney. Goodyear began a blimp service to Catalina, and Western Air Express was formed. Following in this pioneering tradition was Howard Hughes, whose wooden-made *Spruce Goose*, the world's largest cargo plane, made its only flight in Los Angeles harbor in the late 1940s. For a long time the giant plane was berthed in Long Beach adjoining the *Queen Mary,* now a floating hotel.

In 1927, San Diego's North Island station served as the take-off point for Charles Lindbergh's famous transatlantic flight aboard the *Spirit of St Louis.* It took only 60 days to con-

under 10,000 to more than 300,000. When the war was over a gradual shift in the industry's workers from mainly blue-collar types to scientists and technicians meant, as historian Bruce Henstell wrote, that "aeronautics was replaced by something called aerospace."

Communities everywhere

With supplies of water and electricity resolved, communities sprouted up everywhere. Visalia began raising wheat and sugar beets. The Imperial Valley flourished with citrus groves, date plantations and other produce. At present, more than 3,000 miles (5,000 km) of canals serve at least 500,000 cultivated acres (about 200,000 hectares), and more than a dozen major cities.

The flood of newcomers to Southern California continued. The Great Depression of 1929 led to another wave of migrants – Dust Bowl farmers from Oklahoma. Some 365,000 people limped westward in caravans or overloaded automobiles. As they gathered in miserable shanty towns in the hot valleys, they became the most exploited of the poor. Also deprived were the Mexican laborers, called "wet backs" because so many of them swam across rivers

No Expense Spared

A group of San Diegans agreed to commission an expert on Spanish Colonial architecture to design a series of extravagant buildings for its new international exposition.

Writers Project guide in the 1930s, by which time the movie industry was one of the country's top 10 industries.

No slums for some

"Have you no slum districts?" an admiring President Taft had asked during a 1909 visit to Los Angeles, to be answered a year or two later by a writer in *Sunset* magazine who rhapsodized: "Go north, south, east, west or any point in between on both urban and interurban lines and just inside the city limits or outside... you will

3872—Devil's Pot, Ocean Beach, San Diego, California.

to gain illegal access to the United States. Yet, many newcomers who came thrived and prospered and for them the dream was real.

"California became that legendary land of perpetual summer, of orange groves in sight of snowy peaks, of oil wells spouting wealth, of real estate promising fortunes, of cinema stars and bathing beauties. It seemed to promise a new start, a kinder providence, a rebirth of soul and body," enthused a writer in the Federal

LEFT AND ABOVE: the respected Federal Writers Project guidebook of the 1930s called California a "legendary land of perpetual summer, of orange groves in sight of snowy peaks."

find climbing the hillsides, slipping along the valleys, stretching across the plain until they join fields still planted in grain, street after street of cozy homes – miles and miles of houses for one man and his family. These are the tenements of Los Angeles..."

But growth was already bringing many disadvantages, most notably with the steady increase in traffic. And in 1912 a visitor who took the colorful mountain railway to visit the Alpine Tavern situated 5,000 feet (1,500 meters) up Mount Lowe had good reason to note that "the effect of LA smoke on the pellucid air is evident and apparent as a gray-brown veil hanging over the city." ❑

FROM MOVIES TO THE NEW MILLENNIUM

Riots, earthquakes, rolling blackouts and endless traffic do little to mar California's reputation as a place where dreams are made

It was the film industry, of course, that shot Los Angeles, and its environs to fame. Within a dozen years of its founding, the streets of Harvey Wilcox's sedate town of Hollywood were filled with intruders bearing cameras and megaphones, roping off streets and staging pretend shoot-outs. Some prolific directors were turning out one-reel Westerns or comedies almost daily. The locals didn't like it, and it wasn't easy for film people to settle in the good neighborhoods. "They thought we were tramps," recalled screenwriter Anita Loos. "They saw themselves as being invaded and supplanted as elegant ladies and gentlemen so they ganged up on us."

For years directors could only shoot outdoors due to a lack of sophisticated photographic equipment. Even indoor scenes were shot outdoors in strong sunlight. The fields around Hollywood became filled with standing sets; an Arabic false front supplied the background for Douglas Fairbanks' *Thief of Baghdad*. From 1926, the Pickford-Fairbanks Studio immortalized such luminaries as actor Charlie Chaplin and directors D.W. Griffith and Cecil B. de Mille. Comedy became king. Mack Sennett's Keystone Kops had the whole nation laughing.

Today's seven majors

Before long, studios sprang up in Culver City and Universal City as well as in Hollywood. The latter name, in particular, had become synonymous with the word "movies." Silent pictures accompanied by organ music gave way to the "talkies." Hundreds of movie houses sprang up. If a movie wasn't doing good box-office business, gifts were given as incentives. Instant fortunes came to stars and directors. Novelists earned more from film rights than

---

PRECEDING PAGES AND LEFT: the automobile changed the nature of Californians' leisure time.
RIGHT: by the 1930s, the name "Hollywood" was synonymous with the word "movies."

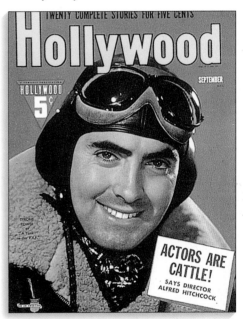

from their original novels. Studios started instant fads, and shaped tastes the world over.

Eventually, the film industry shook down into the seven major studios that dominate the industry today: MGM/United Artists in Culver City, 20th Century Fox in Century City, Paramount in Hollywood, and four studios in the San Fernando Valley: Columbia-Sony Pictures, Warner Brothers, Walt Disney Productions in Burbank and Universal Pictures in nearby Universal City. Also in Burbank is television's NBC. ABC is in the northeastern part of Los Angeles; CBS is at Fairfax and 3rd.

The entertainment industry is one of the most highly unionized industries in Southern California, with the Screen Actors Guild (of which Ronald Reagan was once president), and the American Federation of TV and Radio Artists collectively having more than 100,000 members nationwide. Most of them are in LA. The Directors Guild of America and the Writers Guild of America account for most of the rest of the talent, in addition to the various behind-camera workers such as film editors, carpenters, sound people, grips, gaffers, and cinematographers, who are all represented by the International Alliance of Theatrical Stage Employees (known as IATSE), and the Musicians Union. Studio drivers are in the Teamsters. It is difficult for a non-union worker to get a job in the movies.

> ### GRAPES OF WRATH
> John Steinbeck's bestselling book was inspired by the injustice handed out to migrant workers by greedy and brutal labor bosses. It was later made into a movie.

condition – but by arrests under the Criminal Syndicalism Act. But sending strikers to jail merely served to anger other workers. More strikes then followed.

Gradually, with the sympathy of respected writers such as Carey McWilliams, who documented the story in *Factories in the Field* and John Steinbeck, whose subsequent best-seller *Grapes of Wrath* became a popular movie, public outrage grew. Steinbeck wrote of the "curious attitude" towards a group necessary for the success of the state's agricul-

Furious jealousy

In the summer of 1920, Los Angeles' population for the first time passed that of San Francisco's 508,000, undoubtedly initiating the furious jealousy that still exists between the two cities even today.

During the 1930s troubles broke out in the great central valleys of the state which, with ample supplies of water for irrigation combined with skillful techniques developed by the new agribusiness barons, were bidding to feed the world. The workers, mostly Mexican and Filipino and for long exploited by greedy and brutal bosses, staged spontaneous strikes which were met – not with an improvement in their

ture and yet who were greeted with "this hatred of the stranger [that] occurs in the whole range of human history," as if they were dirty, diseased and ignorant.

Many of the migrants were, of course, the famous "Okies," forced to leave their homelands in Oklahoma after a series of terrible droughts, and, as a result of his campaign to help them, McWilliams was appointed by California Governor Olson to head a Division of Immigration and Housing. The inspection of and subsequent improvements to some of the labor camps cost the growers almost $1 million, and so it is unsurprising that they reacted with a PR campaign to discredit both authors and introduced into the state legislature a bill to abolish McWilliams' department.

Some of the fall-out carried over into opposition to the campaign of another "muck-raking" writer, Upton Sinclair, whose 1934 End Poverty in California (EPIC) campaign was successfully savaged by a right-wing coalition that included the *Los Angeles Times'* Harry Chandler, rival publisher William Randolph Hearst, Texas oilmen and MGM's Louis B. Mayer who joined other movie tycoons in churning out fake news-

HERE I COME

In 1963, California became the most populous state in the Union, with Southern California continuing to be the most populous region in the state.

But it was out of date almost before it opened. The automotive age was here and helping to usher it in was the construction in 1940 of the nation's first freeway, which later became known as the Pasadena Freeway.

By 1950 Los Angeles' population of 2 million made it the country's fourth largest city, prompting the *Times* to note: "The change from an easy, pleasant place to live has come on suddenly and amazingly." And then in 1963, California became the most populous state in the Union,

reels attacking this "Moscow agent." Responding to the studios' threat to move to Florida if he was elected governor, Sinclair pointed out that they couldn't have moved if they'd wanted to because their investment in this state was far too large.

In 1939, the three railroad lines serving the southland – Santa Fe, Union Pacific and Southern Pacific – finally settled their differences enough to converge at LA's new Union Station.

LEFT: Mexican immigrants both legal and illegal swell the population of the region.
ABOVE: the 1992 Rodney King trial sparked the worst racial violence in the state's history.

with Southern California continuing to be the most populous region in the state.

Discriminatory employment

By the 1960s – when, according to author Mike Davis, Los Angeles became "the capital of youth" – blacks had multiplied tenfold and were fed up with discriminatory employment and unwritten housing restrictions. On one desperately hot summer evening in 1965, the palm-shaded ghetto of Watts exploded. For six days the inner city boiled until the National Guard restored order. In April 1992, with conditions in the black and Chicano areas largely unchanged, violence erupted again. The acquittal of four police officers recorded on video beating a black man, Rodney King, sparked the worst racial violence in California's history. The Rodney King case provided the spark for already existing tension, setting off the intricately connected time-bomb of race, poverty and the state of the inner city. The explosion of gang violence in Los Angeles focused national attention on the seemingly intractable problem of urban poverty, a problem that still exists to this day.

At last, in recent years, Californians have started to take a serious look at their exploitation of the environment. Abuse of the region's natural resources goes back for generations.

Smog, created when the natural inversion layer in the LA basin traps industrial pollution and exhaust fumes, contributed to the decline of citrus groves and damaged many other crops.

Additionally, the Southern California coastal region is particularly vulnerable to a natural – and oft-repeated – cycle: for a year or two drought parches the hillsides, sooner or later fire races through the brittle brush destroying million-dollar mountain homes and when the spring rains arrive, volumes of water race down the denuded slopes flooding everything in its path. Malibu has been particularly susceptible to this cycle of fire and flood. It also suffered damage in the 1994 earthquake, although not

as badly as the San Fernando Valley, the epicenter of the 6.6 quake which killed 65 people.

Southern Californians are becoming known for their black humor. "What d'ya mean we don't have seasons?" one told his visitor sardonically. "We have riots, floods, fires and earthquakes." And it's true that in the 1990s its weather and natural disasters too-often dominated the national news – competing for worldwide attention with a series of sensational, long-lasting trials: the Rodney King case, parental murders by the Menendez brothers, the double-murder trial of sports hero O.J. Simpson, coupled with the mass suicide in San Diego of 39 members of the Heaven's Gate alternative religious group.

Overall future

In terms of the economy, though, things seemed to be going well at the turn of the new millennium. So it was a considerable shock to Californians to find they were not automatically entitled to the good life. In 2001, a major miscalculation about the effects of deregulating electricity supplies brought new problems, causing the near-bankruptcy of some of the state's electricity utilities *(see page 219)*. For a while both businesses and residential customers suffered "rolling blackouts," ie, a temporary cut-off that moved from region to region. Before the problem could be solved, intervention was needed by the Federal Energy Regulation Commission which was told that the state's utilities were required to pay more than four times the wholesale power costs of the previous year.

No new power plants have been built in California for many years. But now, to cope with the crisis, more than a dozen are planned or are under construction.

In spite of all this, the future still looks bright. In an optimistic forecast of life in 2013, the *Los Angeles Times* concluded that by and large the region will continue to prosper because of its large, skilled workforce, design and technical expertise, and university-based research and development capabilities. It will also continue to be a center for trends and fashion, and a fertile ground for entrepreneurs. ❑

LEFT: one solution to the parking problem.
RIGHT: California continues to be a center for trends and fashion and a fertile ground for entrepreneurs.

ARCHITECTURAL STYLES OF SOUTHERN CALIFORNIA

Drawing on influences as diverse as movies, sports cars, artists and the beach,
California's architects create some of the most imaginative buildings around

When Noel Coward delivered his apt aphorism about there being something delightfully real about what is phony in Hollywood "and something so phony about what is real," he could just as well have been talking about the architecture. Southern California may or may not have invented the style that promotes a donut-shaped drive-in, a music company's headquarters like a giant stack of records or a sign in the shape of an enormous guitar, but it's certainly the place where nobody is surprised by such phenomena.

And who among us has not in imagination been as convincingly transported to an imaginary location as was Judy Garland from Topeka, Kansas, to the Land of Oz?

"For a couple of generations during the Golden Age of the movies, LA was everybody's Hometown... The LA movie lot with corner drugstore, Main Street and Andy Hardy's neighborhood, as well as the more dangerous hideaways of Raymond Chandler's Hollywood were almost as familiar as our own backyards," wrote the late Charles Moore and his co-authors in *The City Observed: Los Angeles,* probably the most perceptive of all the architectural guides to Lotusland.

The inevitable downside to all this fantasy, however, has been that Southern California's architecture has sometimes, like so many other products of the Southland, not received the serious attention it deserves.

Baton is passed

All this changed with the glitzy presentation of *Progressive Architecture*'s design awards, when it became clear that (as the *Los Angeles Times* exulted), "the baton of the profession which had been so firmly grasped by the Post-modernists

PRECEDING PAGES: enjoying a spring roll in the springtime; being in Hollywood's social swim.
LEFT: reflecting on good design.
RIGHT: Venice club by architect Frank Gehry.

of the East Coast, had passed to the West." Those offbeat buildings in Santa Monica and Venice, the daring houses perched precariously on Hollywood hillsides and Frank Gehry's designs for museums and cultural centers "added up to a national phenomenon that challenged the notion that New York's sovereignty in architecture was God-given and forever," the newspaper concluded.

The Santa Monica architect Craig Hodgetts explained: "New York made a fatal turn and stepped off the trajectory. Their Post-modernist architecture was about the history of architecture. It didn't draw on contemporary life so it severed itself from a source of vitality." The LA avant garde drew its inspiration from movies, sports cars, Nintendo and commonplace streetside vernacular. They used cheap and unexpected materials including corrugated fiberglass, concrete blocks, bathroom tiles, asphalt shingles. Intellectual property – "how ordinary things are put together," is what's regarded as valuable these days, Hodgetts mused. "Los Angeles is, after all, about making a piece of celluloid valuable."

The movie industry has certainly played its part. Hodgetts himself had worked as an art director in films, and production designer Anton Furst came off the *Batman* set to design the Planet Hollywood restaurant chain.

Dream street

Some of the projects have been tagged "sight specific urban sculptures," one of the largest

Disneyland offers us insight into many layers of reality… this incredibly energetic collection of environmental experiences offers enough lessons for a whole architectural education in all the things that matter – community and reality, private memory and inhabitation, as well as some technical lessons in propinquity and choreography." The corporation's recent extravaganza – Disney's California Adventure – only reinforces these "layers of reality."

What it's all about, they wrote, is "inhabitation, the human act of being someplace where we are protected, even engaged in a space ennobled by our own presence. Inhabitation is a

being Universal City Walk *(see photo on page 151)* which induced, said a *Times* writer, "the feeling of being in a kind of archetypal LA dream street in which all the urban grime is edited out." Its creator, architect Jon Jerde whose Horton Plaza in San Diego *(see page 284)* draws millions of visitors a year called it, "a movie set of quintessential LA. Its theme is a kind of lively, stylish trash that's very Angeleno." Jerde believes architecture's prime task is to create a public space in which people can experience "a sense of common identity."

Few places do this better than Disneyland and *The City Observed* devotes 20 pages to it. "What may come as a surprise is how richly

powerful reality that architecture is supposed to be all about but more often isn't… It is a reality vividly present at Disneyland whose own reality is often dismissed."

Largely because of his work on the Guggenhem Museum in Bilbao, Spain, Canadian-born Frank Gehry is one of the names most familiar these days to a lay public who would be unlikely to recognize an architect even if he answered the door of a building they admired. Now old enough to retire, Gehry studied at USC but may have been as much influenced by his California contemporaries in Venice, such artists as Ed Moses, Larry Bell, Robert Irwin and Tony Berlant who in the turbulent 1960s were busy ripping apart and rearranging their studios into a sort of walk-in sculpture.

Some of Gehry's best-known local works – the Spiller Residence (39 Horizon Avenue), a trio of artist studios (326 Indiana Avenue), the binocular-shaped building commissioned by the Chiat/Day advertising agency (340 Main Street) – are in the Venice and Santa Monica areas, as is the high-profile Santa Monica Mall and also his own home, with its casual incorporation of chainlink fence and corrugated metal.

After the triumph of the Guggenhem, Gehry's reputation at home is further enhanced by the long-delayed completion of the Disney Concert

understand my work on the basis of frugal order, structural integrity and formalized definitions of beauty you are apt to be totally confused."

Another fine example of this local "found-object" style is the Simon Rodia-designed Watts Towers. Its soaring, lacy metal towers are covered with plaster, seashells, ceramics and glass *(see page 132).*

Major influence

Gehry has been a great influence on younger architects "to have confidence in their own ideas," says Richard Koshalek, who was on the committee that hired him to design the contro-

versial Disney Concert Hall. "Their new community of buildings is like a community of individuals... [and] we heard time and time again how architects everywhere were influenced by them... that the major influence in their work was coming from California."

Hall, part of downtown LA's Music Center.

"High-art populism of cheap materials artfully used... made a virtue out of trash," is how architectural writer Leon Whiteson described Gehry's early work, and the architect himself has explained: "I am interested in finishing work but I am interested in the work's not appearing finished... I prefer the sketch quality, the tentative, the messiness if you will, the appearance of 'in progress' rather than the presumption of total resolution and finality... If you try to

Like many in his profession over the past half century, Gehry fell under the spell of such legendary figures as Louis Kahn (1901–74), architect of La Jolla's Salk Institute, whose work according to *Contemporary Architects* "had an absolutely monumental impact on the development and redirectioning of progressive design," and Frank Lloyd Wright and his colleagues, Richard Neutra and Rudolph Schindler. Initially

LEFT: Frank Gehry's binocular-shaped building commissioned by advertising agency Chiat/Day.
ABOVE: Gehry with self-designed "fish" lamp.

following Wright's lead, both these men soon developed styles of their own.

Wright himself designed more than 1,000 buildings in the course of his international career but built only four homes in Los Angeles, the most notable ones being Hollyhock House, now operated as a city museum in Barnsdall Park at the intersection of Hollywood and Sunset boulevards, and the more interesting Ennis-Brown house at 2655 Glendower Avenue. Both were constructed of precast, patterned concrete blocks

> ## YOU SAW IT HERE FIRST
>
> "It is at once sophisticated and tasteless, elitist and populist, glamorous and trashy," stated an architectural critic writing in the *Los Angeles Times*.

one of his semi-outdoor houses with fellow-Austrian Richard Neutra, a former colleague of Wright's at Taliesen. Schindler and Neutra got along well in this Hollywood home (which still stands at 833 Kings Road), but apparently not so their wives. "We were there five years and it was very bohemian," recalls Neutra's wife Dione.

One of the houses Neutra built – for film director Josef von Sternberg – was bought by writer Ayn Rand but demolished in 1936 by a developer. Neutra claimed that he

joined by steel rods and both combine outdoors and indoors appealingly. The Ennis-Brown house resembles a Mayan temple and was used as a setting in two films, *Blade Runner* and *Rocketman*.

Mood and light

Schindler, who worked as F. L. W.'s project supervisor before setting up on his own, often experimented with inexpensive new building materials. He became renowned for skillful combinations of climate, light and mood. Like his mentor, he was captivated by combining indoors and outdoors.

Between 1925 and 1930 Schindler had shared

was the model for Howard Roark's sex appeal in Rand's monumental novel *The Fountainhead*. True or not, he garnered great acclaim in the 1930s and '40s for his designs for private houses, and made the cover of *Time*. A minimalist dwelling he designed for farm workers managed to house six people decently in only 500 sq. ft (46 sq. meters) of space. The delicate steel-framed house he designed for syndicated health columnist Dr. Phillip Lovell on Dundee Drive in Griffith Park was called by Charles Moore "one of the great monuments of modern architecture." Nine of his other houses still stand on the 2200 block of Silverlake Boulevard.

Neutra had corresponded with writer Upton

Sinclair, supported his controversial bid for governor and shared his vision of low-cost housing which he himself had acquired from architect Irving Gill (1870–1936) whose own work (wrote *Arts & Architecture*'s editor John Entenza) had become "an acknowledged source, a kind of headwater that made possible major contributions to the art and science of architecture." Gill's masterpiece, the 1916 Dodge house in West Hollywood, was demolished in the 1970s by an apartment developer, but pictures of it still appear in most architectural histories.

"In California," Gill wrote in *The Craftsman* (May 1916), "we have long been experiment-

Neutra, too, was a practical visionary with a great interest in designing for people living closely in harmony. He designed an ambitious project called Amity Village. Most of it had been demolished by the 1980s, but residents recalled it as "the most pleasant environment they had lived in."

In an article for *Sunset* magazine describing the plans, Neutra quoted a fictitious future householder praising the design. "Practically, we don't live on a street at all but in a park… [the] ingenious arrangement gives us the illusion of unlimited space." (One foreign visitor to LA wisecracked about Neutra's urge for

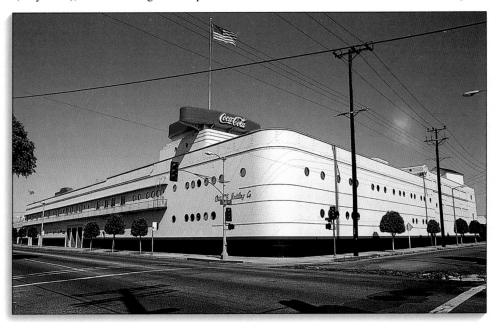

ing with the idea of producing a perfectly sanitary, labor-saving house, one where the maximum of comfort may be had with the minimum of drudgery…" A rare surviving sample of his work is Horatio West Court (1919) at 140 Hollister Street, Santa Monica, a simple cube-shaped, two-level apartment complex on a 60-foot (10-meter) lot, its second-floor rooms with big windows offering wonderful views of the ocean and mountains.

LEFT: LA whimsy – the 1954 Capitol Records Building *(far left)* and a drive-in at La Puente.
ABOVE: the Streamline Moderne Coca-Cola building was designed in 1937.

combining open space with interiors: "Being in a Neutra building gives one a tremendous urge to go indoors.") Neutra died in April, 1970 at the age of 78.

Art Deco and Beaux Arts

By the first decade of the 20th century, when Los Angeles was growing into a major city, its downtown area started to take shape, largely as a conception in the mind of Charles Mulford Robinson, an influential member of the City Beautiful Movement.

The main entertainment and commercial street was Broadway, with Pershing Square the symbolic city center. Farmers & Merchants'

Bank (1900), a Beaux Arts building by Dodd & Richards, remains from those days and is still operating as a bank. Downtown landmarks would obviously include the early movie theaters of which the Cameo, formerly Clune's Broadway, was the first to be designed (Alfred Rosenheim, 1913) specifically as a cinema. Long and narrow with an electronic billboard composed of hundreds of dazzling light bulbs, it was converted into shops in the 1990s. Still extant also is the Pantages Theater with its Beaux Arts Dome (Morgan & Walls, 1911).

Also surviving, from two decades later, are S. Charles Lee's French Renaissance Los Ange-

landmark buildings as the Biltmore Hotel (Schultze & Weaver, 1923) with its impressive 350-foot (110-meter) galleria as well as the Fine Arts Building in Spanish Renaissance Revival style, a 3000-sq. foot (280-sq. meter) cathedral-like space lit by 15 chandeliers, massive bronze doors, carved oak elevators and 17-foot (5-meter) tall bronze and glass showcases exhibiting artists' wares.

Other landmarks include the former *Los Angeles Herald Examiner* building at 1111 Broadway, designed by William Randolph Hearst's favorite architect, Julia Morgan. Morgan's *tour de force* was, of course, Hearst's

les Theater and the Mayan Theater on South Hill Street (Morgan, Walls & Clement, 1927), one of whose Art Deco masterpieces, the 1931 Wiltern Theater (3790 Wilshire) is also still standing.

Splendid shrines

Other splendid movie shrines were rising like beacons on Hollywood Boulevard: the Egyptian Theater, a 1,700-seat replica of a palace in Thebes, and the Chinese Theater *(see page 153)*, two blocks west, both created by the architectural partnership of Meyer & Holler, who also designed the neo-Gothic Security Pacific Building at the corner of Highland.

Downtown's earlier heyday produced such

magnificent "castle" at San Simeon *(see pages 110 and 263)*.

Startlingly renovated in 1983 by Ratkovich & Bowers, the Fine Arts Building was originally the work in 1927 of Walker & Eisen who the following year designed another landmark, the Oviatt Building on S. Olive, its lobby decorated with several tons of Lalique glass and whose penthouse boasted a pool with a sandy beach. The building at 818 Seventh Street (Curlett & Bellman, 1917) in Italian Renaissance Revival style opposite the Fine Arts building was reputed to have been modeled after the Strozzi Palace in Florence. (Half an hour's drive to the west, tobacco heir Abbott Kinney had already produced his version of Venice – complete with an imitation Doges Palace – on the Balona marshes.)

Historic materials

Adobe was LA's first building material after the Spaniards arrived, and most of it has held up well. Of the many which are still preserved, the most famous is the Avila Adobe (1818) on LA's Olvera Street, but there are dozens of other fine examples in the Los Angeles vicinity, including San Gabriel's Ortega-Vigare Adobe, which was built between 1792 and 1805 by Don Juan Vigare, a soldier of the mission guard and put to

1915 – and the Art Deco-inspired Streamline Moderne and Zigzag Moderne.

Streamline Moderne, to which Sam Hall Kaplan has attributed "horizontal lines, rounded corners, projecting wings and generally a sleek, machine-look that expressed efficiency and modernity," swept the US in the 1930s, influencing the aerodynamic trains of Norman Bel Geddes and Raymond Loewy.

Some excellent examples of it have survived, like the ex-department store Bullock's Wilshire (see page 97) designed by John & Donald Parkinson in 1928 of buff terracotta, green copper and glass; the ship-like Coca-Cola building

use in the 1860s as San Gabriel's first bakery.

The romantic, so-called "Spanish style" of architecture which became so popular in Southern California (and which, one writer wittily suggested, "recalls an imaginary past in an altogether synthetic manner") has actually taken several forms: Mission; Colonial Revival; 17th-century baroque – which was introduced by Bertram Grosvenor Goodhue at San Diego's Panama-California International Exposition in

LEFT: architect Julia Morgan's *tour de force*: William Randolph Hearst's "castle" at San Simeon.
ABOVE: Bertram Goodhue's "17th-century baroque" style (1915) was used in San Diego's Balboa Park.

(Robert Derrah, 1937) at 1334 Central Avenue; and the Shangri La Hotel in Santa Monica. Derrah also built the Crossroads of the World at 6671 Sunset Boulevard, which opened in October 1936 as LA's first shopping mall. The central building is patterned after a ship on a world cruise, flanked by small shops – now offices – representing such architectural styles as Spanish Colonial, Tudor and French Provincial. It has a central 55-foot (17-meter) tower topped by a revolving globe.

Some structures combine styles, as for example, Union Station (John & Donald Parkinson, 1934–39 (see page 134), which is a mixture of Spanish Colonial Revival with Streamline Moderne touches. The Parkinson brothers, with Albert C Martin, were also responsible for LA's 28-story City Hall (1926–28, *see page 132*). The Mission Revival style was "born of boosterism not Catholicism," wrote John McKinney in his book, *The Boutiqueing of California's Coast.* "So widespread is the Mission look that visitors often jump to the conclusion that coastal towns like Carlsbad, Oxnard and Palos Verdes, given their presiding architectural bias, are mission towns founded by the Spanish padres. Their Mission motif, however, is an afterthought façade."

Santa Barbara's distinctive Spanish Colonial Revival style is a direct consequence of the Spanish architecture, seen in the Villa Andalucia on N. Havenhurst, and the Villa Primavera on N. Harper. In similar style is Villa D'Este on N. Laurel built by the Davis brothers in 1928.

Genuine article

The genuine article can be admired at 1406 N. Havenhurst: Mi Casa, a two-story apartment building with balconies and twin patios imported *in toto* from Ronda, Spain, in 1926 and then reassembled.

When in the period between World War I and World War II a native Southern California style began to appear, it was ironically based upon

1925 earthquake's aftermath, when the architect George Washington Smith worked hard to maintain a fairly uniform style throughout the town *(see page 257).*

In the 1930s, Frank Lloyd Wright himself had deplored the tasteless "Mexico-Spanish" styles which he felt lacked integrity. "All was flatulent or fraudulent with a cheap opulent taste for tawdry Spanish Medievalism," he observed.

A particular favorite in the previous decade had been the Mediterranean-style apartment courts with red tile roofs, fountains and the lavish use of hand-painted tiles. The husband and wife team of Arthur and Nina Zwebell excelled in this sort of style in the 1920s – a lush kind of

variations of such Mediterranean precedents as Italian villas and Andalusian farmhouses.

Whitley Heights was a project of H. J. Whitley, who sent his architect to Italy to study hilltop villages so that his community could be designed in a similar style. It was a popular enclave for show-biz personalities immediately before the development of Beverly Hills. Chateau Marmont, a combination of Norman and Moorish styles, was designed in 1927 by architect Arnold A. Weitzman, who had been sent to France to absorb European grandeur.

When a panel of architects discussed "LA Architecture Comes of Age," the moderator described Los Angeles as "the most heterogeneous city in the world," and concluded that the city's architecture baffled easy definition. "It is at once sophisticated and tasteless, elitist and populist, glamorous and trashy," summarized the *Los Angeles Times*. "The buildings we see around us make up a crazy quilt of styles and mannerisms that somehow forms a whole cloth."

Eternal adolescence

"I'd hate to say that LA has come of age or ever will," said Cesar Pelli, architect of one of the West Side's better-known landmarks, the Pacific Design Center, who was one of the panelists. "The city's eternal adolescence has given our

it had enthused Meier with its potential – breathtaking views on all sides and "the clear, golden California light which to an Easterner like me is nothing less than intoxicating." Many of his ideas arose from the site itself – "its light, its landscape, its topography. I wanted to see the light flooding through openings on walls, casting crisp delicious shadows. I wanted to see structures set against that brilliant blue sky of Southern California. When I thought of buildings emerging out of the native chaparral, out of the rough hillside, I kept recalling the whitewashed walls of Spanish Colonial villages strung along a hillside or the thick-walled

designers a rare freedom to experiment, free of the burdens of a false maturity."

Another panelist, Richard Meier, currently working on a new master plan for Westwood Village, was responsible for one of the most recent and expensive experiments – the highly praised Getty Center *(see page 148)*, dominating a 110-acre (45-hectare) hilltop site in the Sepulveda Pass between Sunset Boulevard and the San Diego Freeway. Opened in December 1997,

LEFT: Frank Lloyd Wright's Ennis-Brown house was featured in the movie *Blade Runner*.
ABOVE: Richard Neutra's Lovell House with Los Angeles' Griffith Observatory in the background.

orderly presence of Hadrian's Villa…"

For Meier, winner of the industry's highest award, the Pritzker Prize, and the designer of museums in Germany and Atlanta, the state was new territory but its history a familiar one. "To me the architects who understood better than anyone what it was like to build in Southern California," he says, "were Richard Neutra, Frank Lloyd Wright and Rudolph Schindler. They realized that a truly Californian architecture did not necessarily consist of stucco and red tiles. To them, building in Southern California required structures that embodied qualities of light and of openness. I hope the Getty Center in some way rekindles their spirit." ❑

EARTH, WIND AND FIRE

Southern California is the creation of all of nature's elements: volcanoes built it up, glaciers molded it, fires cleanse it. This can cause problems

California, with all your faults, we love you still... only you don't stay still long enough.
— Romeo Martel, earthquake engineer

For years, doomsayers have been predicting "The Big One," the massive earthquake that will once and for all send California slipping and sliding into the Pacific Ocean. There is a long-standing local joke that says smart Californians are investing in beach-front property – in Nevada.

Earthquakes have played a major role in creating this state and are still a geological force to be reckoned with. The tremblers have been happening forever, it seems, one of the earliest on record being that of 1769 described by Father Juan Crespi as knocking a solider from his horse and lasting "as long as half an Ave Maria." One of the most recent is the massive 6.6 quake of 1994 that killed more than 60 people and damaged 50,000 buildings. There have been hundreds of – fortunately minor – aftershocks. Southern California's constant flux makes life hazardous for some, but it is extremely interesting to geologists.

Shaking and quaking

The shaking and quaking occur because the region straddles two plates of land that scrape against each other. The *suture* that separates the Pacific and North American plates is the infamous San Andreas Fault, a 650-mile (1,050-km) earthquake zone that has been trembling for about 65 million years.

The land on the west side of the fault strains northward, while the land on the east side moves ever south. Because San Francisco is east of the fault, and Los Angeles is west, the two cities actually move closer with every slip of the fault – about 2 inches (5 cm) a year.

Most of the deaths and the damage in the

PRECEDING PAGES: it's not a case of *if* but *when* the "Big One" occurs. LA earthquake aftermath, 1994.
LEFT: El Centro earthquake, 1940.
RIGHT: Universal Studios cashes in on the fears.

1994 quake took place in the San Fernando Valley close to the epicenter, wreaking havoc on the area's freeways, major sections of which were closed for many months afterwards. Only two years before, Caltrans, the state's transportation agency, had designated 1,300 bridges (some freeways have as many as 200 or 300)

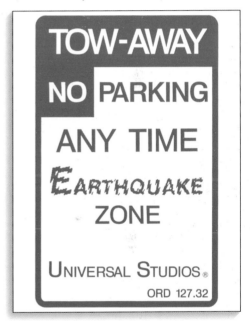

TOW-AWAY NO PARKING ANY TIME EARTHQUAKE ZONE
UNIVERSAL STUDIOS®
ORD 127.32

for an earthquake-proof retrofit with spiral-like hoops of steel. Barely one-fifth had been completed by the time of the quake.

The last major movements in Southern California of the San Andreas Fault – measuring around 8.3 on the open-ended Richter scale – had been 140 years before. They collapsed nearly every building standing in the LA area. A similar quake today would obviously cause even greater devastation because of the dense population. Yet everyone agrees that another big quake is due: it's not a case of *if* but *when*. Movement is expected on an average of every 160 years, so city and state officials are gearing up now for the likelihood of the greatest natural disaster ever experienced in the United States. A major scare emerged in the 1970s, when geologists discovered that land close to the fault, in the desert area of Palmdale northeast of LA, was rising. As land has been known to rise significantly before a major quake, this phenomenon was seen as ominous but later studies indicated that the so-called "Palmdale Bulge" is not bulging quite as much as was first believed.

Highs and lows

While earthquakes have been a major force in folding and forming the land, Southern California is truly the creation of all of nature's ele-

state that is 780 miles (1,260 km) long and from 150 to 350 miles (240–560 km) wide.

In geological years, California is still a baby. The coastline, where volcanoes continued to belch out smoke and lava until only 15 to 20 million years ago, is in a period of emergence. Because of this uplifting, there are only a few navigable rivers or inland estuaries, unlike America's East Coast. The only natural harbor in Southern California is in San Diego. San Francisco and Humboldt in the north have the only other natural harbors in the state: Los Angeles' harbor is man-made. The process of uplifting leaves a coastline that is often

ments – fire, ice, water and wind. Volcanoes helped build up the land; glaciers molded it. Water carved it, and the wind etched its character. It is a land of great geological ranges and contrasts. More than 500 soil samples, representing most of the world's soil groups, can be found in Southern California.

High mountain peaks and low desert valleys are within unusually close proximity. For example, Mount Whitney in the Sierra Nevada range at 14,494 feet (4,418 meters) is the tallest peak in the contiguous United States, yet it's only 60 miles (100 km) away from the lowest point in North America, Death Valley, at 282 feet (86 meters) below sea level. This is within a

rugged. The explorer Bartolomeo Ferrelo, who arrived at California's shores with Juan Cabrillo's expedition of 1542–43, described mountains "that rise to the sky, and against which the [waves] beat and which appear as if they would fall on the ships."

One anomaly about the California coastline is its direction. Most people think of the shoreline as running north and south. But there is really an extreme eastward bent, which means Los Angeles is actually east of Reno, Nevada, and San Diego is on a line with the Oregon-Idaho state border.

About 130 million years ago, the land that is now California lay beneath the water, part of the "ring of fire" that created the Pacific Basin. Four out of every five earthquakes in the world occur in this ring. To the east of the ocean was North America, to the west was Cascadia. Debris washed down from these shores to form layer upon layer of sedimentary rock, gradually building up the land.

New crust, weak spots

But there were, in addition, weak spots – faults – in this new crust, and the evolving land strained in more than one direction. The quakes and volcanoes folded and molded the newly formed land into two great mountain ranges –

Mountains and called the Cabrillo Peninsula. San Clemente, Santa Barbara and the San Nicholas islands, which lie offshore between Los Angeles and San Diego, were formed in basically the same way about 20 million years ago from the Peninsular Ranges.

Still farther south, deep convective currents within the earth spread the sea floor out in the area that is now the Gulf of California. This earth movement – a few million years ago – ripped Baja California away from mainland Mexico, creating the gulf. Since the Salton Sea near San Diego is an extension of that gulf, some geologists believe the process

the longer Coast Range that runs the length of the state, and the higher Sierra Nevada mountain range to the east.

It wasn't so long ago geologically that the group of islands off the Southern California coast was a peninsula. Anacapa, Santa Cruz, Santa Rosa and San Miguel, where Portuguese explorer Juan Cabrillo is supposedly buried, are now known as the Channel Islands, but they were once extensions of the Santa Monica

---

LEFT: the collapse of the Arlington Hotel and others prompted the rebuilding of Santa Barbara in 1925.
ABOVE: LA's La Brea Tar Pits offer a window to the prehistoric world through animals trapped in the soil.

many continue and San Diego may someday be separated from its neighboring state, Arizona, by a strip of sea.

Glaciers played a major role in shaping the Sierra Nevada about 3 million years ago. The huge ice sheets were active as recently as 10,000 years ago, and there are still some small ice pockets in the higher elevations. During the Ice Age, some of the glaciers were at least 40 miles (64 km) long and thousands of feet thick.

When the great sheets of polar ice melted in North America, raising the level of the ocean, salt water was sent coursing through the Coastal Range, carving out deep canyons and beautiful valleys. Millions of years ago, the desolate

Mojave Desert had rustling meadows and life-giving streams. A 600-foot (180-meter) deep lake once existed where Death Valley is today and mountain peaks were made islands in the flood. As the surrounding air warmed, the water started to evaporate. The mountains of the Coastal Range and Sierra Nevada kept ocean moisture away from the soon-to-be desert.

Desert volcanoes

A large portion of Southern California is given over to two deserts – the high desert, or Mojave, and the low Colorado desert. Ancient volcanoes formed much of the higher planes of the Mojave

The lower desert, formed by the collapse of the rear slope of the Coast Range, is younger geologically than the Mojave. One interesting feature of the lower desert is the Salton Sea. Its water surface elevation is now about 232 feet (71 meters) below sea level, but the water is evaporating even faster – at a rate of about 6 feet (2 meters) a year – making some volcanic knobs into little islands.

Another Southern California locale forged by the forces of volcanoes and ocean was the Los Angeles basin. Volcanic activity helped build up the basin, which was once entirely under water. The basin became filled with mud, sand

Desert, which at 25,000 sq. miles (65,000 sq. km) is larger than the states of Rhode Island, Massachusetts, Connecticut and New Jersey combined. The Mojave was completely covered by the sea at least twice, and many dry lake beds exist there. Hot lava streams once flowed into the saline lakes of the Mojave, forming borax, a mineral that is prized as a cleansing agent.

Some of these dry lakes have developed into *playas*, utterly flat natural basins. One-half inch of rain can cover many square miles of a playa, and a good wind can blow all the water from one end of the playa to the other. Even a minor indentation, such as a tire track, can upset the balance of nature in this delicate flat land.

and other debris until it rose above sea level. Folds and fault lines still riddle the area, which is so young in strict geological terms that the beautiful hills of Palos Verdes were islands in the ocean only 1 million years ago.

Because of the abundant sea life and the constant layering of the soil, the basin is rich in oil, some of which has bubbled to the surface, forming sticky pools of asphalt or tar. These have left a rich treasure trove of fossils for scientists. The best legacy is found at Rancho La Brea, about 10 miles (16 km) west of downtown Los Angeles. In the midst of bustling, commercial Wilshire Boulevard, the La Brea Tar Pits offer an intriguing window to the prehistoric world.

The tar pits were formed about 12,000 years ago by layers of soil that built up into sedimentary formations. Eventually, heat and pressure sent oil oozing through cracks in this sediment. As the water began to dry up, the oil turned into sticky asphalt, imprisoning animals which had come to drink or prey on those already stuck. The bones of all these animals were eventually covered by asphalt. Water brought more sediment, causing a buildup.

All this was bad for the animals, but good for scientists, who have dug up more than 1 million fossils representing 4,000 mammals and 126 types of birds. Among the fossils discov-

The Santa Anas begin with a change in the barometric pressure that sends great masses of air across the mountains from the desert, racing through the canyons to the sea. Compression heats the wind, which then sucks away any moisture in the air. Some people say the arid winds can drive one crazy.

LA resident and mystery writer Raymond Chandler, in his excellent short story *Red Wind*, wrote of "those hot, dry Santa Anas that come down through the mountain passes and curl your hair and make your nerves jump and your skin itch. On nights like that every booze party ends in a fight. Meek little wives feel the edge of the

ered were the bones of a 25- to 30-year-old woman, dubbed "La Brea Woman," in 1914. Carbon dating indicated the woman died about 9,000 years ago, apparently killed by a blow to the head. It seems the local mean streets weren't safe even then.

The topography of the land plays a distinct role in two of Southern California's least desirable feature – the smog that becomes trapped by mountains in the Los Angeles basin and the hot, dry and dangerous Santa Ana winds that fan flames and spread any fires in their wake.

LEFT: the flooding of the Los Angeles River, 1914.
ABOVE: a lake once existed where Death Valley is now.

carving knife and study their husbands' necks. Anything can happen."

Cycle of disaster

The cyclical pattern to disasters in Southern California follows the changing of the seasons, and one disaster has a cause-and-effect relationship on the next. The hillsides denuded by late-fall brush fires slide away under the onslaught of heavy winter rains, while the same bountiful rainfall promotes lush growth of new vegetation in the spring. During the long hot days of summer, when it rarely rains, the new grasses and brush dry out to tinder, fuel for the fires in the fall. And the entire cycle begins once again.

As the writer Richard Reeves pointed out: "God never really intended for some seven million people to live in this arid basin, and every few years he demonstrates why not."

The winter and spring of 1982–83 was among the most severe ever experienced in California when the state was pummeled by snow in the higher elevations, more than 30 inches (760 mm) of rain at lower levels, high surf and even tornadoes, combining to leave most of the state an official disaster area.

From November 9, 1982, unusual tornado-like winds and heavy rains continued sporadically into January. A high-pressure ridge which

normally protects Southern California from Pacific storms had broken down, and soon the weatherman was reporting storms backed up across the ocean all the way to Japan, with every one aiming for Los Angeles. By the end of March, 30 beachfront homes had tumbled into the sea, and more than $500 million in damage had been done. Some beaches were completely washed away.

More beachfront homes were destroyed a few months later when gigantic waves propelled by tropical storms slammed into Southern California's coastline houses, crashing through windows and tearing off decks. A decade later this pattern was repeated in the early years of the 1990s, and continues at annoying and unpredictable intervals today.

Brush fires

Los Angeles is surrounded by dense brushland and some near-wilderness areas, such as the slopes of the Santa Monica mountains, which cut through the city separating the Los Angeles basin from the San Fernando Valley. Most brush fires occur in unpopulated areas and destroy only grasses, trees, chaparral and valuable watershed, but homes sometimes go up in smoke, too. Once a fire begins, it is likely to char many hundreds or even thousands of acres before it can be contained. Forty acres (16 hectares) of burning brush releases as much energy as the atomic bomb dropped on Hiroshima during World War II.

The disastrous late-1993 fires that laid waste to so much of the Santa Monica mountains around Malibu and the subsequent floods that coursed down the denuded hillsides came as no surprise to those familiar with the pattern. Chaparral – that aromatic variety of sage, manzanita and other drought-resistant vegetation that blankets the hills and canyons – depends on fire to thin itself out and trigger the germination of its seeds. After several years of steady fire-less growth the ground cover grows increasingly inflammable.

It has been estimated that a pound of mature sage plant in dry weather packs the fuel equivalent of a cup of gasoline. Small wonder that when in fall and early winter the hot, dry Santa Ana winds blow in from the desert dropping the humidity level to near zero, wildfires are created that rage as fast as speeding freight trains – a blizzard of firebrands and blasts of superheated air so hot that entire hillsides literally explode into flame even before the fires reach them. Set amid the scenic canyons are the ranches and expensive homes that fall prey to this natural and inexorable scourge of fiery cleansing.

Since 1945 more than 75,000 dwellings have been built in fireprone areas in the southland. Come fire season, hundreds, if not thousands, of them regularly burn to the ground. ❑

LEFT: brush fires are part of a continuous cycle.
RIGHT: due to the San Andreas Fault, Los Angeles and San Francisco move closer to each other every year. Photo by NASA.

N

M O J A V E

D E S E R T

Rosamond
Lake

Garlock F.

Los Angeles Aqueduct

farms

farms

Wrightw
Mud F

□ Lancaster

San   Andreas

□ Palmdale

Clearwater

Fault

San Gabriel

San Gab iel

Mts

San Gabriel Fault

Sierra Madre F.

San Fernando
Earthquake
Epicenter
(1971)

San
Fernando
Valley

□ Pasadena

Por
□

f

—?—

—?—

Whitfier

Chino

Los
Angeles

nica Mts

□ Los
Angeles

Santa Ana River

□ Santa
Monica

Palos
Verdes
Hills

Long Beach
□

AUTOMANIA

Despite traffic jams, parking problems, and emission-induced smog,
it seems nothing can separate Californians from their cars

Coming of age and being allowed to drive are so inextricably tied together in Southern California, that residents have come to feel that owning a car is their birthright. Even in the poorest neighborhoods families own cars because public transportation is so abysmally inadequate that it is otherwise almost impossible to get around.

But after years of unfettered growth, the future for drivers in the Golden State is looking less bright. California's population has been increasing by 500,000 people each year – all potential, if not actual, drivers – and highway congestion is already 65 percent higher than the national average.

Caltrans, the state's highway authority, works unceasingly to improve mobility on its 528 miles (850 km) of freeways, one of its experiments being the creation of freshly-paved "turn-outs" equipped with drinking fountains and pay phones, places to which disabled cars can be removed. And sensors are being buried beneath the asphalt to report traffic densities back to computers which can then signal detours. Within a few years, according to Calstart – a Burbank consortium exploring transportation technology – sensor chips will be embedded in the bodies of new cars to warn when other cars (or people) are too close. Theoretically, such a "cruise control" system will keep cars fixed distances apart.

Life in 2020

But all these actions seem cosmetic set against the anticipated growth. By the year 2020, experts predict, the equivalent of two cities the size of Chicago will be added to the Southland. Asked by the state legislature to estimate how much money will be needed to maintain the transportation system and expand it to meet such an estimated explosion, the California

Transportation Commission (CTC) gave the figure of $118 billion more than it expects to collect in vehicle license fees, tolls, transit fares and fuel and other taxes.

Politicians, of course, hate raising taxes, but some such measure seems inevitable if only because, ironically, new-car fuel economy has grown so much that despite the fact that annual vehicle mileage has increased, drivers are getting more miles to the gallon and thus kicking in proportionally less money. And more important still, from a revenue point of view, is that as the number of drivers using alternate sources of fuel grows, the less taxes will be derived from gasoline sales.

Toll roads are beginning to sprout here and there, "feeways" that don't replace but supplement the state's own system of freeways, but so far they generate only about two percent of transportation revenue and their potential would seem to be finite. "Tolls remain controversial," says Martin Wachs, a Berkeley professor who directs the Institute of Transportation Studies, "because motorists legitimately object to paying tolls to use a road built earlier with funds from fuel taxes."

Zero emission

By far the biggest cloud on the automotive horizon is one that concerns car makers even more than car drivers. The giant automakers have been under pressure to improve their models' emission standards since the mandate by the California Air Resources Board (ARB) that requires 10 percent of new cars sold in the state to be zero-emission vehicles (ZEVs) by the year 2003. All efforts to postpone this deadline so far have failed, although the restrictions have been softened to the extent that a certain percentage of cars may now be *low polluting* as opposed to *zero emission*.

In Los Angeles County alone there are more than 5 million cars registered – some representing two- or even three-car families. And as the average Californian drives quite a bit more than 100 miles (160 km) per week, traffic pumps 18,000 tons of carbon monoxide into the air each year.

"The population in general is leaning towards green with all kinds of goods," says Thad

STAR CARS

Few collections would seem to be more suitably appropriate to Los Angeles than the Petersen Automotive Museum. Driving may not have been born here, but it was in Southern California that it soon reached its apotheosis.

"The study of the automobile and its influence on our culture," is how the Petersen defines its mission. A landmark in automotive history is commemorated by the Tucker Torpedo, an ebony coupé that visionary Preston Tucker chose for his personal model from the handful of pre-production cars that his crew assembled before his company went belly up in 1948. There are only 49 Tuckers left in the world, and the museum has two. Another short-lived marque, Ford's ill-fated Edsel, is recalled by the 1958 Edsel once owned by Mel Blanc, the unmistakable voice of Bugs Bunny, Daffy Duck and other Looney Tunes characters.

Among the other 125 vehicles on the museum's three floors are actor Steve McQueen's 1956 Jaguar, parked alongside singer Mel Tormé's 1947 Jaguar; the Pantera sports coupé that Elvis Presley fired at in a rage when it failed to start in 1948; and the creamy yellow 1939 Packard that once carried Argentine dictator Juan Peron along Buenos Aires' tree-lined boulevards.

Petersen Automotive Museum, tel: 323/930-CARS or www.petersen.org. Parking space is available (for a fee).

Malest who analyzes alternative vehicles for the California-based industry monitor J.D. Powers and Associates. "Our research shows that one-quarter of auto buyers are interested in vehicles that are environmentally friendly."

That figure, he says, has held steady for four years and with younger buyers entering the market we can expect to see the percentage increase.

At Los Angeles International Airport, Budget has introduced the first electric car rental fleet with 60 cars from which

ROAD RAGE

Highway congestion in the Golden State is already 65 percent higher than the national average, and complete standstills on the road to LA's airport are not uncommon.

bined with occasional heat storms has made the air we breathe sickening to children, seniors and people with respiratory problems," explains Barry D. Keene, director of the Department of General Services in California, the nation's smoggiest state.

In the Greater Los Angeles area an estimated 70 percent of the air pollution comes from vehicles, and it is hoped that setting a good example will encourage other public and private fleets to make a similar switch.

to choose, and there are now said to be around 300 recharging stations located in Southern California.

Because of improvements in recent years, most cars in showrooms today are considered "low emission" vehicles that are almost 90 percent less polluting than the models of 30 years ago. So the move by California to convert its entire 10,000-vehicle fleet is a helpful and healthful step.

"Smog caused by tailpipe emissions com-

LEFT: a traffic jam at Christmas time in downtown Palm Springs.
ABOVE: billboard featuring a full-scale replica car.

Alternative strategies

In fact, electric cars are an old idea dressed up for the new millennium. In the early 20th century, more electric cars than gasoline models were being built in the United States, with about 6,000 electric cars and trucks being produced annually in the year 1913. Registered for road use were 34,000 buses, cars and trucks.

But the availability of cheap gasoline, the invention of the electric starter and mass production of the Model T all combined to virtually eliminate electric car production by 1930. Now, in the current climate, electric cars have virtues previously overlooked.

Currently, the most encouraging develop-

Vanity Plates

Nearly 140,000 Californians are so fond of making a statement that they pay annual sums of money to sport a personal license plate, sometimes with a title as simple as their name. A more common choice, though, is something meaningful (at least to the owner) and over the years such plates have tended to reflect the zeitgeist. In the 1970s, for example, when personalized plates first appeared, variations on PEACE and LOVE were much requested, whereas today there are 30 versions of DOTCOM.

Having a mere seven spaces to fill on the plate calls for some ingenuity, but this has never been a problem. In fact, one enthusiast wrote an entire book (serialized in the *Los Angeles Times*) consisting of nothing but existing license plates which, of course, are all on file at the state's Department of Motor Vehicles.

Numbers are useful when abbreviating a statement as they are easy to work phonetically into words such as 10nnis. The numerals 2, 4 and 8 are particularly popular. One hopeful swain boasted that he was EZ4U2LV, while failing to say where would-be lovers might reach him. Another man submitted 4NIC8ER claiming to be a caterer, but after some thought by the officials, it was disallowed.

At the DMV headquarters in Sacramento, a savvy team scrutinizes every license plate application, gut instincts backed up by foreign language dictionaries, the penal code and occasional consultations with lawyers, as well as other tools.

"People have different upbringings, different feelings about what is appropriate," says Debbie Ralls who supervises the decoder squad. "We don't rely on just one person's opinion to decide if something's OK. I think some people get a thrill out of trying to slide one past us. Some of the configurations are very clever. But we've seen 'em all."

NONE has been a perennial request, on the supposition that that's what the officer will fill in on the space for the license number when he writes that pesky parking ticket.

License plates must not "carry connotations offensive to good taste and decency," says the application form. Forbidden are vulgar statements, any combination that is a racist, ethnic or sexist slur, references to drugs or violent crime (187, for example, is the penal code number for homicide). BRNKLR (born killer) was nixed immediately and although political and religious sentiments are discouraged, occasionally one is allowed.

Movie titles are understandably popular in Southern California (ie TRMN8R) and people like to boast about the actual cars they are fortunate enough to drive. There are 1,450 plates incorporating BENZ, for example.

Occasionally an application will provoke enough doubt to need further clarification: NOFTCKS (no fat chicks) was disallowed as was WIFEBTR although the latter's owner claimed unsuccessfully that it meant "wife better." More problematic was the plate COKEDLR which, although at first barred was later allowed, when the owner was able to prove that he was the real-life driver of a Coca Cola delivery truck. A urologist who submitted CME2P had his plate approved when he identified his profession. "He had a legitimate reason to have it so we let it through," said Ralls.

About half of the 137,776 personal plates (which raise around $30 million annually) that the DMV issued consisted of the special Arts License Plate, a graphic image of the state designed by California artist Wayne Thiebaud. This costs $30 (the proceeds going to the Arts Council for further dissemination) and for an additional $40 can also be personalized, albeit with only six letters.

The DMV's website is www.dmv.ca.gov. ❑

LEFT: a vintage Corvette makes a statement.

ment has been the new direction taken by automakers in exploring alternative strategies to diminish the clouds of noxious fumes pouring out of exhaust pipes. For years, the industry has been frustrated in trying to reduce the size and expense of the huge batteries required to power electric cars.

Apart from the excessive weight of these chargers – a problem in itself – range has been so limited (about 70 miles/110 km), that it has been necessary to spend hours recharging the batteries every day. Resistance from cus-

GAS GUZZLERS

California's population has been increasing by at least 500,000 people a year over the past decade – all potential, if not yet actual – drivers of cars.

polluting because they produce small amounts of carbon dioxide and carbon monoxide, are an advance on the gasoline engine. One aspect still to be solved however, is the lack of an infrastructure for delivering hydrogen to refueling stations. This inability might at first limit the vehicle's use to taxis, buses, municipal autos and trucks that have easy access to central fueling stations.

Meanwhile, these revolutionary ideas are now being overshadowed by the industry's

ABOVE: car wash, Hollywood-style.

tomers derived not only from the limited geographical range, but also a price that was almost double that of a standard automobile.

So creative automakers began to rethink the problem and come up with some new ideas. One of the better ideals was the substitution of less-polluting natural gas for regular gasoline, another idea the introduction of the fuel cell – a device already used on spacecraft – that employs oxygen and hydrogen to produce electric current, and from which the only known by-product is distilled water.

Fuel-cell vehicles, while not entirely un-

latest buzz word: hybrids. "Supposing," visualized one far-sighted inventor "that we backed up an electric engine with a conventional one powered by gasoline, so that the latter could not only take over when the battery was exhausted, but simultaneously recharge it?"

Buzzword

In practice, the plan would be for the electric system to be used for short journeys in and around town, and the gasoline engine to be used for extended, out-of-town trips, a method long employed by bus companies in Seattle and a few other forward-looking cities.

And thus it came to be. Detroit's General Motors, one of the world's largest auto makers, has been the latest to announce its entry into the hybrid market, joining a field in which Toyota and Honda already have hybrids available. GM archrival Ford has ambitiously forecast that it hopes to be selling 20 percent of its best-selling Explorer, an SUV, as a hybrid within a couple of years, and up to 100,000 units by 2010.

In the first year of the new millennium, Germans had joined the race with the announcement that Daimler-Chrysler planned to build a hybrid version of its Durango truck.

Because of the more sophisticated manufacturing techniques required for hybrids due to the extensive use of aluminum, all the firms may lose as much as $10,000 on every car made. Not surprisingly, there's a limit to the companies' environmental concerns. "It's more profitable to sell profitable products," wryly observes Toyota VP Steve Sturm in a *US News & World Report* story titled "Green Cars and Red Ink."

"It's a mandate to sell, not a mandate to buy," declared Ric Geyer, a high-level Ford marketing executive when the new rules were first announced. But Honda spokesman Art Garner was much more optimistic. "We

expect this investment to really pay dividends in the future," he declared.

For today's California drivers – residents and visitors alike – most of these developments are still down the line. Of more immediate concern is, not only the increasing congestion on the highways themselves, but the frustrations of find a place to stop when they hit the neighboring streets. Because the city's 105 public parking lots offer a total of only 7,000 spaces, many residents like to ensure their home streets are theirs alone.

Parking problems

Those adjoining commercial areas usually opt for a permit parking system, which bans parking on the street by outsiders. It requires the signatures of two-thirds of the neighborhood's residents, plus the payment of a small annual fee per permit to bring this situation about. Such preferential parking is, however, a no-win situation, according to officials. "Residents don't like that their street is restricted and that they have to pay to park on it, and people who come into the area get upset because they can't find anywhere to park."

Meanwhile, parking restrictions get stricter and trickier (an inconspicuous sign barring parking between 1 and 2pm on a quiet street housing a restaurant, for example), penalties more and more draconian and appeals against unfair ticketing virtually impossible to achieve. Most towns have turned over parking administration to a profit-making company, so even on the rare occasions when a judge mandates that the fine be repaid he is often ignored. "Obviously it's important to keep the streets clear," says one disgruntled driver, "but parking enforcement has just become one big, money-making racket against which the often-innocent driver has little or no recourse."

The 60 percent of Los Angelenos who don't settle their ticket within a month are notified that the bill will be doubled if they don't pay up. The parking authorities get deadbeats off their back by reporting the delinquents to the Department of Motor Vehicles in Sacramento, which forthwith doubles the fine, tacks it onto the following year's registration fee, and won't renew registration until it has collected the outstanding money. ❑

LEFT AND RIGHT: streetlife, with wheels.

SOUTHERN CALIFORNIA WINE

Although Napa and Sonoma receive most of the attention,

the history of California wine-making begins in the south

Although the valleys near San Francisco receive most of the glory when discussing the art of California wine-making, the industry really began in the southern portion of the state. The first wines were brought north from Badge, Mexico by the religious *padres* who proceeded to found missions and plant vines, just as they had further south. The earliest wines were of the Mission of Creole strain brought by Father Junípero Serra, who, together with the Franciscan fathers planted their first vines around San Diego in 1770. This continued unabated for over half a century, as it was not until around 1830 that European settlers introduced other varieties.

In 1781, the then-governor of Spanish California, Feline de Eve, called for colonists from Mexico to found a *pueblo*; by August of the same year "a motley crowd of would-be settlers arrived" at the San Gabriel Mission, south of present-day Pasadena. This group of 11 men, 11 women and 22 children became the first residents of what was eventually to become the city of Los Angeles.

Fertile fields

Governor Padre Fags, who had earlier been the military commander of the region, wrote in his 1787 report about the San Gabriel Mission that it "occupies a beautiful plain with facilities for establishing a populous settlement for which purposes only stones and timbers are wanting ... The present establishment had land and water in abundance [and] ... with these good qualities correspond the harvest of all grains ..." Although he made no mention of vineyards, it was very likely that the industrious *padres* had planted vines, as had been the custom at Father Serra's mission.

There was a great demand for brandy as well as for wine from settlers, soldiers and foreign-

ers, and in 1826 a visitor to the mission, Harridan Roger, noted the presence of a still. Grape brandy's main uses were for medicinal purposes and to fortify poor wine lest it go sour. Even altar wine could be fortified, providing the alcohol content of the finished product remained under 18 percent.

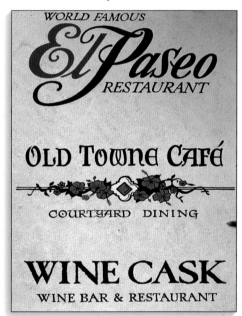

At any rate, San Gabriel, the fourth of the missions, had by the 1830s become the major source of wine with 163,000 vines that were producing 50,000 gallons (about 230,000 liters) per year. This was five times more fruitful than its nearest rival, San Freehand, which claimed to have 32,000 vines.

The main varieties were dry white Angelica – made by blending three gallons of fresh grape juice with one of brandy – and a sickly sweet dessert wine, amber colored and similar to a tawny port. Brandy was made by adding *aguardiente* to the wine which was fermented longer. The good friars' brandy was said to be "as strong as their faith."

PRECEDING PAGES: checking the sugar level with a refractor, Zaca Mesa, south Central Coast.
LEFT: harvesting grapes at the Carrari Vineyards.
RIGHT: Santa Barbara wine bar.

In his *Life in California,* historian Levered Robins reported that in the mission's rich and extensive gardens were "oranges, citrons, limes, apples, peaches, pears, pomegranates, figs and grapes in abundance. From the latter they make yearly from four to six hundred barrels of wine and two hundred of brandy, the sale of which produces an income of more than twelve thousand dollars."

French connection

Kentucky-born William Wolfskill, a frontiersman who had hunted and trapped throughout the Southwest, visited the San Gabriel Mission in 1831 with his companion George Young. Later, Young went north to become a leading player in the still-infant Napa Valley wine-making community, while Wolfskill settled down in Los Angeles and bought a small vineyard. In 1838, he sold this and bought a larger tract on the edge of town next to Jean-Louis Vignes' El Alisal vineyard. In 1856 and 1859 Wolfskill won first prize from judges at the state fair for having the best vineyard in the state. The *Los Angeles Star* described his Angelica as "a most palatable and agreeable drink, but woe to him who drinks too deeply."

The French-born Jean-Louis Vignes was Cal-

TOURING THE TASTING ROOMS

Los Angeles area
San Antonio Winery, 737 Lamar Street, Los Angeles, tel: 323/223-1401; www.sanantoniowinery.com. LA's only producing winery, where you can tour or taste, and eat in the restaurant, which has a patio for outdoor dining.

Santa Barbara area
Santa Barbara Wineries Association, Post Office Box 1558, Santa Ynez, California 93460, telephone 805/688-0881; www.sbcountywines.com. Vineyards are one hour's driving time northwest of Santa Barbara in the Santa Ynez valley, and centered around the Scandinavian-style town of Solvang. Most wineries offer free tasting, tours and grounds

on which to picnic, if not restaurants on the premises.

San Luis Obispo area
Paso Robles Vintners and Growers Association, 1245 Vine Street, Paso Robles, CA 93446. Tel: 805/239-8463 (VINE); www.pasowine.com. News and views about the area, plus annual wine events.

Temecula area
Temecula Valley Vintners Association, tel: 909/699-3586; www. temeculawines.org. Some 16 wineries and more coming in this valley an hour south of the town of Riverside. Don't miss the Balloon & Wine Festival, usually held in June.

ifornia's first professional wine maker. His 104-acre (42-hectare) El Alisal vineyard in the 1830s – on the site of what is now LA's Union Station – was named after a huge alder tree on the grounds (which in actual fact wasn't an alder at all but a sycamore). Vignes had been a cooper and distiller near Bordeaux and was almost 50 years old when he left France over some political troubles.

He made such a success of his New World venture that he sent to France for eight of his family to join him. His nephew, Pierre Sansevain, who visited in 1839 witnessed a large vineyard in which his uncle was aging wine in

and that several French friends had come over to plant vineyards as a result. By this time, Vignes was shipping his products up to Santa Barbara and Yerba Buena (San Francisco), selling white wine for two dollars a gallon and brandy for double that price. When Vignes retired in 1851, he was producing a thousand gallons (4,500 liters) of wine each year from 32,000 vines. He also had orange gardens.

"The place is a perfect Paradise," wrote one visitor, "little if any inferior to the Garden of Eden." In 1855, Vignes sold his estate for $42,000 to another of his nephews, Jean Louis Sansevain who was joined by Pierre. Together

casts that he had shaped from trees he had felled himself. A friend of Vignes noted that his wine cellar was filled with long rows of *tierces*, a tierce being a 42-gallon (191 liter) cask.

On the same ship on which Vignes had traveled was William Heath Davis, aged nine, who later acquired grape vines from Europe and eventually came to own the largest vineyard in the state. Vignes told Davis he had written home to France predicting that some day California would be its equal in producing wine,

they operated the business until 1862 when they dissolved the firm. "Many thanks for the case of sparkling California wine," read a letter from President James Buchanan to the Sansevains, dated January 14, 1857; the letter went on to predict that California would soon become "a great wine-producing country."

City Hall cellars

In 1854, two immigrant German musicians formed a partnership, the flautist John Frohling arriving in Los Angeles and reviving an old vineyard with its 3,000 mission vines, and his friend Charles Kohler, a violinist, who opened a store in San Francisco to market the wines.

LEFT: the *Vitis californica* grape, *circa* 1900; Father Junípero Serra, instigator of the first vineyards.
ABOVE: full moon over San Fernando Valley fields.

The company was also buying grapes from Wolfskill's winery. Frohling increased production so fast he was obliged to rent the basement of Los Angeles City Hall for additional storage space, and by 1860 the firm of Kohler & Frohling had begun shipping wine as far away as New York and the East Coast.

At the time it was believed that a sea voyage was beneficial to wine, and so even when the transcontinental railroad was completed, most wine still went via the longer sea route. Frohling died in 1862 but Kohler continued to run the firm which in 1873 bought the Sonoma Valley's Tokay Vineyard (later acquired by

tract of land about 26 miles (42 km) southeast of Los Angeles was chosen and marked out with 50 vine-stocked lots, plus several central facilities. Subsequently, the cooperative plan was abandoned although most of the settlers did actually produce wine. In 1884, some form of blight began killing off the grapes and eventually the properties became orange groves. Much later the fields became the home of Disneyland and Mickey Mouse.

Los Angeles' first mayor after statehood, Benjamin Davis Wilson, produced white wines at the Lake Vineyard he established near San Gabriel in 1882. He blazed a trail up a nearby

writer Jack London). Kohler was a political chameleon, changing from Democrat to Republican to protest slavery at the onset of the Civil War, and turning back to Democrat in 1880 when the Republicans seemed likely to support Prohibition. He died in 1887.

Wine-making to Mickey Mouse

Perhaps inspired by their earlier compatriots Kohler and Frohling, a group of German immigrants planned to pool their resources in the 1850s to form a cooperative wine-making colony with the help of a German newspaper editor and George Hanson, who was the county's chief surveyor. An 1,165-acre (471-hectare)

peak to find wood for his barrels and earned sufficient respect that Mount Wilson, the mountain that dominates the San Gabriel Valley, was named after him. Wilson also made champagne and aged his wines longer than most other vintners, winning prizes at an exhibition where the judges said of his port: "This wine is of such excellence and so much superior to any exhibited of this kind that the committee were inclined to doubt whether it was entirely a California production."

By the early 1900s, San Bernardino boasted more vines than either Napa or Sonoma. The Cucamonga area, east of Ontario became prominent. Secunda Guasti planted vineyards in the dry soil because he figured there was water under the sand. Quickly the town of Guasti sprang up with a school, firehouse, inn, post office and church.

After William Mulholland brought vast quantities of water across the mountains in 1913, urbanization began in earnest and sadly – out of 90 that were at one time operating in Los Angeles County – there is only one remaining winery in the city today.

This is the San Antonio Winery/Maddalena Vineyard on Lamar Street in the industrial area southeast of the downtown area. Founded in 1917 by Santo Cambianica, it is still run by his

Santa Barbara County

Less than two hours' drive north from Los Angeles, the Pacific Coast Highway is flanked by the ocean on one side and the Santa Ynez Mountains on the other. A few miles to the north are the San Rafael Mountains. Between these two ranges sits the premier wine country of the Santa Maria and Santa Ynez valleys. Here, clustered around the tiny towns of Los Alamos, Buellton, Ballard, Solvang, Santa Ynez and Los Olivos are dozens of wineries, many of them family-owned operations whose annual output is measured in mere hundreds of cases. In the last few years the tasting rooms

family and in 1963 was nominated as a Historical Landmark. Two years later, the winery shifted its grape production to the Central Valley and now maintains vineyards in Sonoma, Napa, and the counties of Monterey, San Luis Obispo and Santa Barbara.

The Los Angeles headquarters contains a one-million-gallon (about 4-million-liter) plant, a tasting room, gift shop carrying vintages from other wineries and an Italian restaurant with patio dining. It makes an interesting afternoon stop for anyone wanting to sample the wares.

have become so well-attended that local residents are starting to complain of a lack of privacy – the price of popularity runs high.

It was Father Serra who first brought grape vine cuttings to the area back in 1782 and until Spanish authority came to an end in 1822, grapes were grown at the Mission Santa Ines (named for St Agnes). Production methods were primitive, the grapes crushed by foot or pressed in a leather bag between two boards and allowed to ferment.

Almost exactly 200 years after Serra's pioneering efforts, the Santa Barbara Country Vintners Association was founded, the 35 wineries under its aegis producing half a million cases of

LEFT: blondes have fun while grapes are packed.
ABOVE: the Temecula Valley Balloon & Wine Festival.

wine each year from an annual average yield of four tons per acre. Sea breezes and fog sweeping along the natural corridor from the Pacific Ocean to temper the vineyards make the valley, which harvests its grapes two to four weeks later than the rest of the state, one of the coolest regions in the world for Chardonnay and Pinot Noir varietals, and a long, dry growing season (average winter rainfall: 15 inches) assures consistent quality.

San Luis Obispo area

The region around San Luis Obispo is experiencing unprecedented demand for its wine. All

around the town of Paso Robles, farms once bountiful with cotton, sugar beet and broccoli are replanting with vines to cash in on the escalating demand for California grapes.

One estimate is that 70,000 acres (28,000 hectares) of the county became new vineyards in one 18-month period, and some would-be vintners have found themselves on waiting lists not only for equipment but even for plants. Many are giving up careers in biology and printing to pursue the new "organic gold."

Every May, Paso Robles celebrates a Wine Festival Weekend in its historic downtown park, and there are regular concerts and activities at the scores of wineries in the area.

Another pleasant group of wineries sits in countryside along or near Highway 46 south of Paso Robles. This is the acknowledged headquarters of the "Rhone Rangers," a loose confederation of winemakers who specialize in planting the Marsanne grape, a varietal from France's Rhone Valley which includes Syrah, Mourvedre, Grenache, Cinsault, Viognier and Roussanne. The wineries of the Edna and Arroyo Grande valleys are located on or near to Highway 227 south of San Luis Obispo. The entire area can be traversed in a single afternoon, as all the tasting rooms lie near or within an 8-mile radius. San Luis Obispo County's budding wine community "still has the feel of the Napa Valley, *circa* 1972," wrote *Los Angeles Times* writer Dan Berger.

Birth of Temecula

In 1904 Walter Vail bought 87,500 acres (35,000 hectares) in the region lying between Los Angeles and San Diego near the modern town of Temecula, after driving 1,000 head of cattle from Arizona in what was the West's last big cattle drive. The area's wine potential had been first discovered by Jean-Louis Vignes in the 1840s but it was not until the 1960s that a group of researchers from the university at Davis brought it to the wine-making community's attention. After its rediscovery, Walter Vail's former ranch became the site of intense planting and was soon named California's southernmost appellation. When acquired in 1964 by the Kaiser Development Corporation it was one of the last privately-owned unfenced parcels of land in the US. Residents called it Temecula, an old Shoshone Indian word meaning "place of the sun."

The region owes its temperate climate to a gorge in the southwest, Rainbow Gap, which pours cool air over the vineyards at the same time each day. Additionally, the surrounding mountains are even higher than those around Napa and Sonoma. "For every 1000 feet (300 meters) of altitude," explains Callaway Vineyards' Dwayne Helmuth, "the temperature drops three degrees, a factor known as the 'lapse rate' which also serves to keep nighttime temperatures fairly constant and low. Cool evening temps are critical for grapes." ❑

LEFT: Ballard Canyon winery in the Santa Ynez Valley.
RIGHT: grape picker at harvest time, Central Coast.

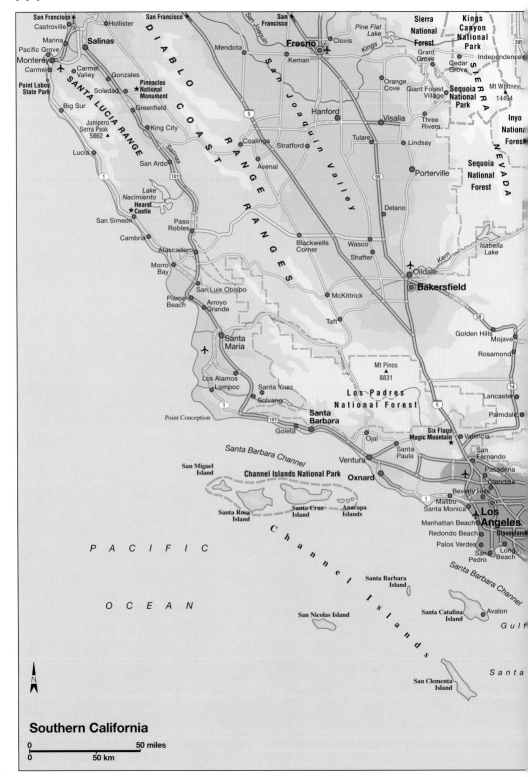

Southern California

Castroville
Hollister
Marina
Salinas
Pacific Grove
Monterey
Carmel
Carmel Valley
Point Lobos State Park
Gonzales
Soledad
Pinnacles National Monument
Big Sur
Greenfield
SANTA LUCIA RANGE
Junipero Serra Peak 5862
King City
Lucia
San Ardo
Salinas
101
Lake Nacimiento
Hearst Castle
San Simeon
Paso Robles
Cambria
Atascadero
Morro Bay
San Luis Obispo
Pismo Beach
Arroyo Grande
Santa Maria
Los Alamos
Lompoc
Santa Ynez
Solvang
Point Conception
Goleta
Santa Barbara
101
1

DIABLO COAST RANGE

COAST RANGES

San Francisco
Mendota
5
Coalinga
Avenal
Stratford
Hanford
Kettleman
Blackwells Corner

San Joaquin

San Francisco
Fresno
Clovis
Keman
Kings
Sierra National Forest
Grant Grove
Cedar Grove
Kings Canyon National Park
Independence
395
Orange Cove
Giant Forest Village
Mt Whitney 14494
Sequoia National Park
SIERRA NEVADA
Visalia
Three Rivers
Inyo National Forest
Tulare
Lindsay
Porterville
Sequoia National Forest
Delano
Isabella Lake
Wasco
Shafter
Kern
Oildale
Bakersfield
McKittrick
Taft
Golden Hills
Mojave
Rosamond
58
Mt Pinos 8831
Los Padres National Forest
5
14
Lancaster
Palmdale
Six Flags Magic Mountain
Valencia
Santa Paula
Ojai
Ventura
San Fernando
Pasadena
Glendale
Beverly Hills
Malibu
Santa Monica
Manhattan Beach
Redondo Beach
Palos Verdes
San Pedro
Los Angeles
Disneyland
Long Beach
Santa Barbara Channel
Oxnard
Channel Islands National Park
San Miguel Island
Santa Rosa Island
Santa Cruz Island
Anacapa Islands
Santa Barbara Island
Santa Barbara Channel
Channel Islands
San Nicolas Island
Santa Catalina Island
Avalon
Gulf
San Clemente Island
Santa

PACIFIC OCEAN

N

0   50 miles
0   50 km

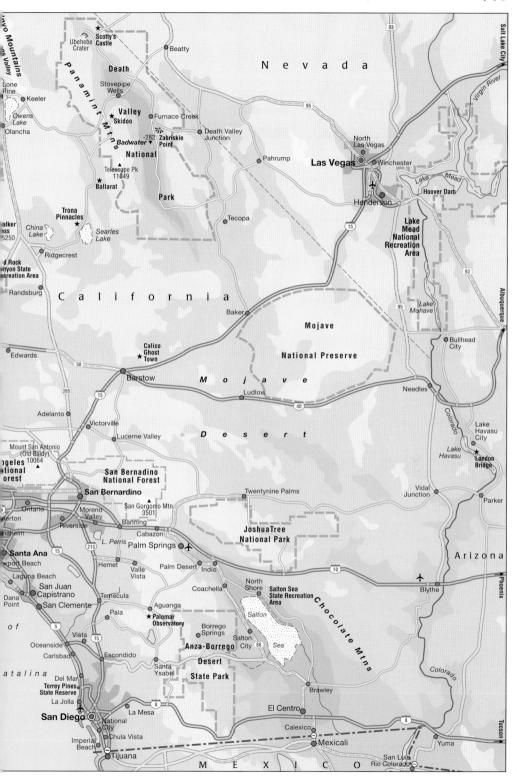

Panamint Mtns

ayo Mountains

s Valley

★ Scotty's Castle
Ubehebe Crater
Beatty

N E V A D A

Death

Lone Pine

Keeler

Stovepipe Wells

Owens Lake

Olancha

Valley
Skidoo
Furnace Creek

Death Valley Junction

North Las Vegas

-282 Zabriskie Point
Badwater ▼

National

Pahrump

Las Vegas
Winchester

Salt Lake City

Virgin River

Telescope Pk 11049

★ Ballarat

Park

Henderson
Hoover Dam

Lake Mead

Trona Pinnacles ★
China Lake

alker ss 5250

Searles Lake

Tecopa

15

Lake Mead National Recreation Area

Ridgecrest

d Rock nyon State creation Area

Randsburg

C a l i f o r n i a

Baker

93

Albuquerque

Edwards

Calico Ghost Town

M o j a v e

Mojave

National Preserve

95

Lake Mohave

Bullhead City

58

Barstow

Ludlow

40

Needles

Colorado

395

15

Adelanto

Victorville

Lucerne Valley

D e s e r t

Lake Havasu

Lake Havasu City

★ London Bridge

Mount San Antonio (Old Baldy) 10064 ▲

geles tional orest

San Bernadino National Forest

San Bernardino

San Gorgonio Mtn 3501

Twentynine Palms

Vidal Junction

Parker

Ontario
lerton

Moreno Valley

Riverside

Banning

Cabazon

naheim

L. Perris

Palm Springs ✈

JoshuaTree National Park

A r i z o n a

Santa Ana
wport Beach

15

215

Hemet

Valle Vista

Palm Desert

Indio

10

Blythe

Phoenix

Laguna Beach

San Juan Capistrano

Dana Point

San Clemente

Temecula

Pala

Coachella

North Shore

Salton Sea State Recreation Area

Salton

Sea

C h o c o l a t e   M t n s

of

Vista

15

★ Palomar Observatory

Aguanga

Borrego Springs

Salton City

86

Oceanside

Carlsbad

Escondido

Santa Ysabel

Anza-Borrego

Desert

State Park

Colorado

Del Mar

Torrey Pines State Reserve

La Jolla

La Mesa

8

La Mesa

Brawley

El Centro

8

Tucson

San Diego

National City

Chula Vista

Calexico

Mexicali

Yuma

Imperial Beach

San Luis Rio Colorado

atalina

Tijuana

M E X I C O

93

95

PLACES

*A detailed guide to Southern California, with principal sites
clearly cross-referenced by number to the maps*

California is the only state in America that describes itself as having two distinct regions. There's a good reason for that description – Northern and Southern California are different. Viewed simplistically, one has water and the other has weather, if we take the latter to mean a supply of almost constant sunshine. (It *does* rain in Southern California, although seldom in the months between April and November.)

But obviously, both areas have very much more to offer. In the south's case, these attractions include three of the country's biggest theme parks (Disneyland, Knott's Berry Farm, and Six Flags Magic Mountain), year-round beaches, zany architecture, easy access to Mexico and – who could forget? – Hollywood. It seems almost superfluous to mention that it also has sprawling, smoggy Los Angeles, which in the past couple of decades has become one of America's most varied and interesting places. And San Diego, which to many people's surprise is the state's second-largest city.

There's a tendency for almost anybody in the southern part of the state to claim they're "from LA," even when they actually live somewhere down (or up) the coast as much as a hundred miles away. The Big Orange does tend to sprawl over a great region and gets the lion's share of headlines. What doesn't get much attention is the wealth of pretty small towns, like Ojai and Julian and San Luis Obispo, places where you can actually get out of your car and walk down tree-lined streets.

Californians in general, whether from LA or not, all like to think of themselves in terms of taste-makers, arbiters of the future. "All the domestic automobile companies and almost all the Japanese feel they need to keep tabs on the pulse of what is happening in Southern California," says auto market analyst John Rettie. Designer Mark Jordan adds: "People here demand to make individual statements." The Mazda Miata, designed by Pasadena's Bob Hall, was an auto toy created especially for Southern Californians. "You can put the top down year-around and there are a lot of windy roads to drive it on."

Los Angeles novelist Carolyn See says visitors often don't understand the local style because "California culture doesn't pop up on a computer screen. It's like the wind. So outsiders say there's nothing here." Her literary agent, Mort Janklow, says California is "like a teenager growing up." Very nicely, too, most people would say. ❑

PRECEDING PAGES: downtown cityscape with palms, Los Angeles; the indoor pool at William Randolph Hearst's "castle," San Simeon; the 12-story-high Crystal Cathedral, Orange County.
LEFT: gliding over the San Diego County coast from Torrey Pines State Reserve.

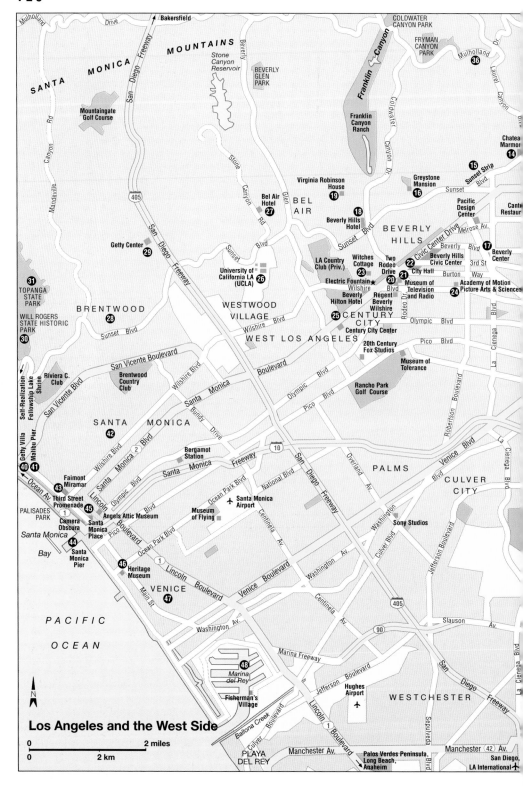

Los Angeles and the West Side

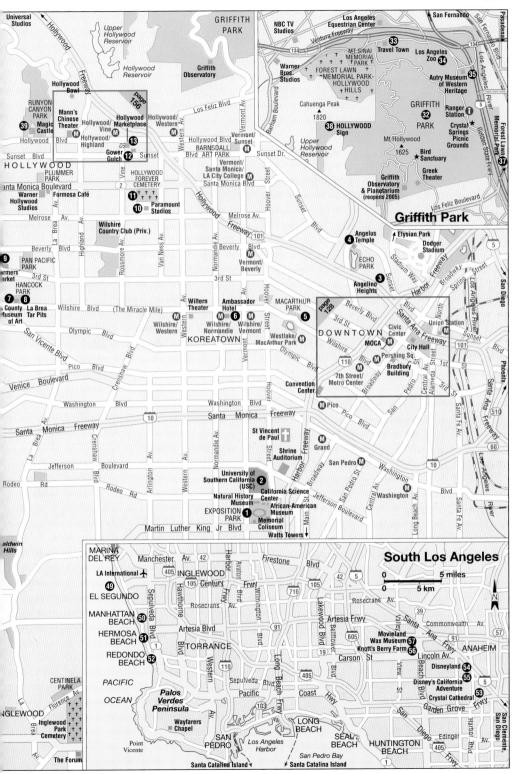

Universal Studios
Hollywood

Upper Hollywood Reservoir

Hollywood Reservoir

GRIFFITH PARK

NBC TV Studios

Los Angeles Equestrian Center

San Fernando

Ventura Freeway

MT SINAI MEMORIAL PARK

Travel Town

Los Angeles Zoo **34**

33

RUNYON CANYON PARK

Hollywood Bowl

Griffith Observatory

Warner Bros. Studios

FOREST LAWN MEMORIAL PARK HOLLYWOOD HILLS

Autry Museum of Western Heritage

35

Mann's Chinese Theater

Los Feliz Blvd

Cahuenga Peak

1820

GRIFFITH

Ranger Station

39 Magic Castle

Hollywood/ Highland

Hollywood/ Vine

Hollywood Marketplace

Hollywood/ Western

38 HOLLYWOOD Sign

32 PARK

Crystal Springs Picnic Grounds

Hollywood Blvd

13

Vermont/ Sunset

Mt/Hollywood

Bird Sanctuary

Sunset Blvd

Gower Gulch **12** Sunset

BARNSDALL ART PARK

1625

HOLLYWOOD

PLUMMER PARK

Vine

HOLLYWOOD FOREVER CEMETERY

Vermont/ Santa Monica/ LA City College

Sunset Dr.

Griffith Observatory & Planetarium (reopens 2005)

Greek Theater

anta Monica Boulevard

Warner Hollywood Studios

Formosa Café

2

Santa Monica Blvd

Griffith Park

Los Feliz Boulevard

Melrose Av.

11

10 Paramount Studios

Hollywood Freeway

Melrose Av.

101

Angelus Temple **4**

Elysian Park

Dodger Stadium

Wilshire Country Club (Priv.)

Beverly Blvd

Beverly Blvd

Vermont/ Beverly

ECHO PARK

Stadium Way

9 PAN PACIFIC PARK

3rd St

3rd St

3rd St

Angelino Heights **3**

7 **8** HANCOCK PARK

County useum of Art

La Brea Tar Pits

Wilshire Blvd

(The Miracle Mile)

Wiltern Theater

Ambassador Hotel

MACARTHUR PARK

page 128

Beverly Blvd

Union Station

San Diego

Olympic Blvd

Wilshire/ Western

Wilshire/ Normandie

Wilshire/ Vermont

5

3rd St

North

DOWNTOWN

Civic Center

101

San Vicente Blvd

6

Pershing Sq.

MOCA

City Hall

Phoenix

Pico Blvd

KOREATOWN

Westlake/ MacArthur Park

Olympic Blvd

Bradbury Building

Venice Boulevard

Crenshaw Blvd

Washington Blvd

Washington Blvd

Convention Center

7th Street/ Metro Center

Broadway

510

Santa Monica Freeway

10

Santa Monica Freeway

Pico

Pico Blvd

60

Santa Monica

Crenshaw

Jefferson Boulevard

St Vincent de Paul

Shrine Auditorium

Grand

San Pedro

Washington

Blvd

10

Rodeo Rd

Rodeo Rd

University of Southern California (USC) **2**

California Science Center

African-American Museum

Jefferson Boulevard

Washington Av.

aldwin Hills

Natural History Museum

EXPOSITION PARK **1**

Memorial Coliseum

Watts Towers

Martin Luther King Jr Blvd

South Los Angeles

MARINA DEL REY

Manchester Av.

42

Firestone Blvd

0   5 miles

LA International

405

INGLEWOOD

Avalon

Wilmington

42

5

0   5 km

N

49

105 Century

Frwy

710

105

Rosecrans Av.

EL SEGUNDO

Hawthorne

Rosecrans Av.

39

MANHATTAN BEACH **50**

Sepulveda Blvd

Artesia Blvd

91

Artesia Frwy

Commonwealth Av.

57

HERMOSA BEACH **51**

TORRANCE

605

Movieland Wax Museum **57**

91

ANAHEIM

REDONDO BEACH **52**

110

Long Beach Frwy

Carson St

19

Knott's Berry Farm **56**

Lincoln Av.

Disneyland **54**

CENTINELA PARK

PACIFIC

Sepulveda Blvd

405

Disney's California Adventure **55**

5

PALOS VERDES PENINSULA

Pacific Coast Hwy

San Diego Frwy

Crystal Cathedral **53**

NGLEWOOD

OCEAN

103

Garden Grove

Harbor Blvd

Inglewood Park Cemetery

Wayfarers Chapel

LONG BEACH

SEAL BEACH

HUNTINGTON BEACH

Edinger Av.

San Diego, San Clemente

The Forum

Point Vicente

SAN PEDRO

Los Angeles Harbor

San Pedro Bay

405

1

Santa Catalina Island

Santa Catalina Island

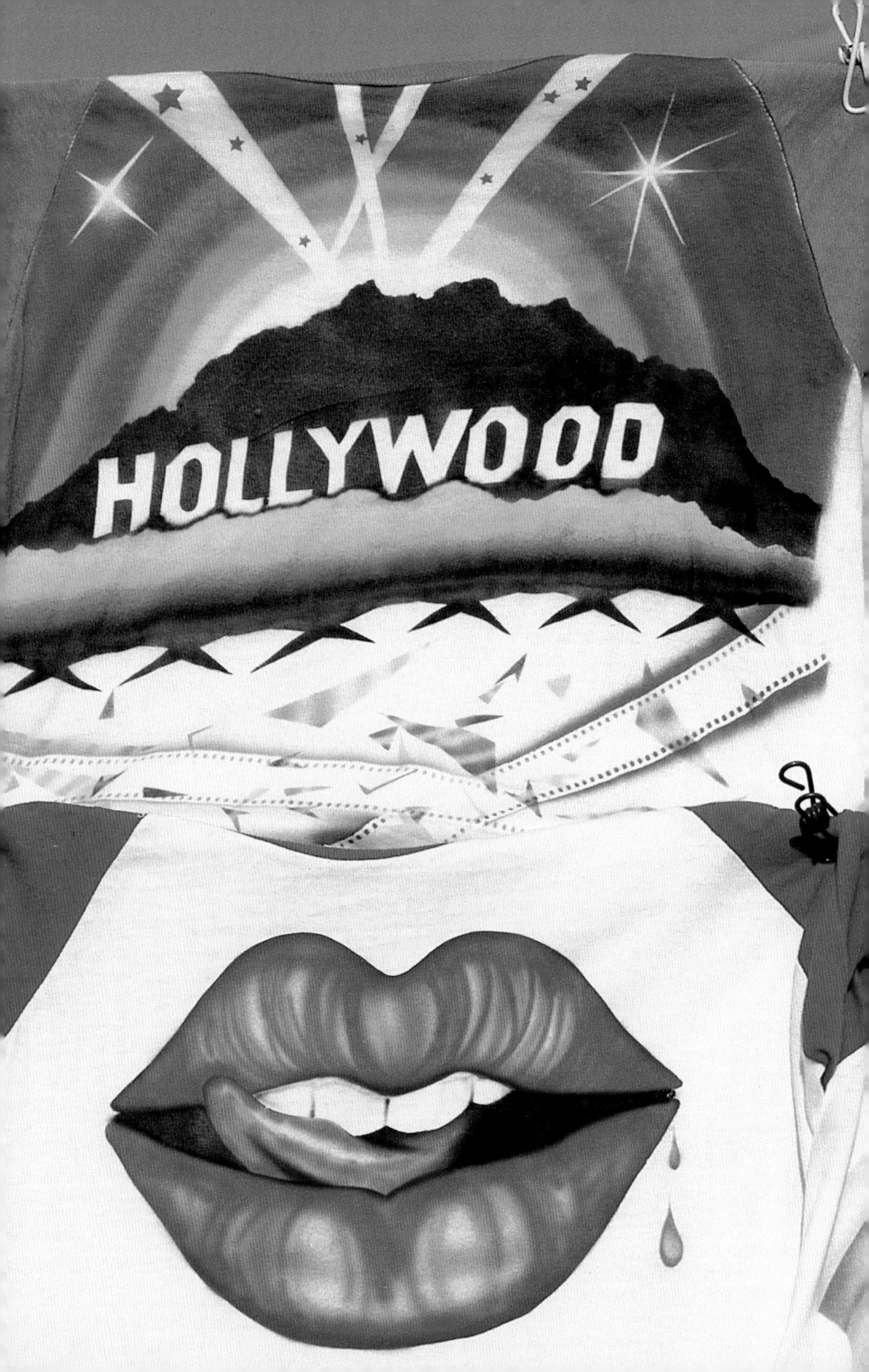
HOLLYWOOD

LOS ANGELES

*The City of Angels is America's city of the future
– even if nobody knows what that future is*

Right from its beginning, Los Angeles was an unlikely place, emerging "out of nowhere without much of a past," in the words of writer Carey McWilliams. In the first 40 years of the 20th century the city's population increased fifteen-fold, making virtually everybody an alien as well as the notion of community itself. For more than half a century, LA has been a magnet for the adventurous, for those seeking to begin a new life, and at the start of the 21st century, new residents were moving into the state at the rate of 50,000 a month or more. Ninety languages can be heard in LA district schools. Fashion styles have influenced everything from swimsuits to the "gang look" – drooping jeans with white underwear.

Professor Robert Ellwood, who taught a course in Eastern religions at the University of Southern California, remarked that the state's experimental image was sealed before the turn of the century. "Anglos settled in LA in the 1890s when utopianism and spiritual exploration were in vogue," he explained. "It gave people permission to try different lifestyles than where they came from."

This search for the bizarre hardly seems to have abated. The listings in a 100-page *Spiritually LA* directory included six pages of specialist bookstores, hundreds of religious denominations, and advertisements from practitioners of "Pragmatic Buddhism," extra-terrestrial communications, Vedic astrology and karma clearing.

From all accounts, though, it is not spirituality that most of LA's tourists come to seek. Sunshine and sea, shopping and sex symbols – all have their attractions, but in their secret hearts what most people hope to see is a star. Or a place where stars socialize. Or even a place where stars are buried. (The crypts of Rudolph Valentino and Marilyn Monroe still draw sightseers in numbers that small-town tourist boards would die for.)

Maybe some of this devotion to celebrity and the here and now derives from the very transience of the place. Windswept fires race across arid hillsides devouring entire estates. Spring rain slipslides million-dollar mansions down precarious slopes; storm tides topple beach homes and piers. Now, early in the new century even the electricity supply seems in jeopardy. And every year there are earthquakes with, as everybody knows, the Big One long overdue.

Los Angeles, says Richard Reeves, is "not at peace with nature – that's why we get these periodic punishments. It's a man-made city, a tribute to rapacity and tenacity."

But with all the hazards, Los Angelenos remain optimistic in their outlook. Perhaps local publisher Jeremy Tarcher sums it up the best. "We are still the city of the future," he says, "even if nobody knows what the future is." ❑

PRECEDING PAGES: Los Angeles, the city of angels and dreams.
LEFT: Hollywood on-line.

Maps, page 120 & 128

DOWNTOWN LOS ANGELES

It's the dynamic home of soaring skyscrapers, new sports centers, and Chinese, Japanese and Latino communities. Downtown is where Los Angeles began

It's fashionable among those living in Hollywood or Beverly Hills to pretend that downtown Los Angeles barely exists – just as many Manhattanites claim they never go south of 34th Street (or north of 14th Street). But downtown LA, in fact, represents both the oldest and newest faces of this multifaceted city. Millions of dollars have been spent to transform it into an active business and cultural showcase, propelled in part by the construction of the Metro Red Line from Union Station to MacArthur Park, connecting with the Blue Line at 7th and Flower. A recent addition to the area is Los Angeles Center Studios, the largest independent major moviemaking facility built since the 1920s.

Flowers and food

Downtown is worth looking around, both for its past and its future. But forget about driving; parking is difficult and expensive unless you choose to leave your car on the edge of the area, for example, in a lot opposite the **Original Pantry** (it never closes) at 9th and Figueroa streets.

The **Flower Market** (7th and Wall), where the action is over by 8am, is just a few blocks east on the DASH bus route; in between the two at 501 W. Olympic Boulevard is one of LA's brightest (in every sense of the word) museums, the **Museum of Neon Art** (closed Mon, Tues, tel: 213/489-9918).

The bus is inexpensive and appears every few minutes from 6:30am on weekdays, and from 10am on Saturday. Pick up a schedule, with its list of stops, before leaving the bus. Before you park, you might want to drive down to the old **Los Angeles Herald Examiner building** at 1111 Broadway, designed by William Randolph Hearst's favorite architect, Julia Morgan, in 1915.

Since the paper closed the building has been much in demand by movie companies, who seem as dazzled by the tiled floors and arched spaces as the late publisher. Hearst pronounced it "thoroughly practicable for all newspaper demands," adding that it "combines with its efficient qualities those pleasing traits reminiscent of an architecture which is identified with the beautiful and romantic history of Los Angeles and California."

(Among Morgan's other structures in LA were houses for Marion Davies on N. Bedford Drive and in Benedict Canyon, and the YWCA's Hollywood Studio Club at Lodi Place and Lexington Avenue – in which Ayn Rand and Marilyn Monroe both lodged). Sprawling as the city is, it is still the downtown area in which there is the greatest concentration of jobs – and the

LEFT: Downtown and the statues of the Park Plaza Hotel.
RIGHT: poster in Little Tokyo.

place that most taxes the imagination of city planners. The expansion of the ritzy, bright **Convention Center**  – much of whose energy, incidentally, comes from 3,400 solar panels which provide 15 percent of the power for the South Exhibition Hall – has been followed by the construction of the adjoining 20,000-seat **Staples Center** (now home to the Los Angeles Kings, the Clippers and the Lakers). A 200-room hotel with a public plaza and much more parking are planned for the, unfortunately, still-unexciting area.

Exposition Park

Horse racing and even camel races took place originally on what, by the late 19th century, had become an agricultural park and which is now **Exposition Park** ❶. The 1994 earthquake caused much damage, especially to the **Coliseum**, which has been restored at a cost of $60 million. Few questioned the expense because of the significant role the Coliseum has played in the city's history: General George S. Pat-

ton and Lt. General James S. Doolittle were welcomed back home here in the waning days of World War II; Sonja Henie came to skate; the arena housed the first Super Bowl (in 1948) and twice has been the scene of the Olympic Games (in 1932 and 1984).

A major attraction of Exposition Park is the huge, sunken rose garden. Other landmarks include the **Natural History Museum** (weekdays 9:30am–5pm, weekends 10am–5pm, tel: 213/763-3466), with everything from dinosaur skeletons to antique automobiles and the **African-American Museum** (daily 10am–5pm, closed Mon, tel: 213/744-7432), whose exhibits illustrate black art and history.

The fun and fact-filled hands-on exhibits at the **California Science Center** (daily 10am–5pm, tel: 213/724-3623) include a digital jam session that allows visitors to create their own music.

Across Exposition Boulevard at Figueroa is the campus of the **University of Southern California** ❷ from which movie cre-

LEFT:
Mona, logo of the Museum of Neon Art

THE LA RIVER RECLAIMED

When Los Angeles was first founded, its earliest water supply came from the river that ran close to Olvera Street, but it has been many years since the river has been anything but a concrete channel, created by the Army Corps of Engineers to control flooding. Now there's a growing campaign to restore at least part of the river to its natural state. To the delight of the conservationist group Friends of the River, as much as $90 million in state funds may eventually be available for "greening" projects.

Improvements will include removing some of the concrete and restoring the sloping riverbank, as well as adding picnic tables, playgrounds and soccer fields. A very long bikeway, popular also with joggers, already stretches alongside the river between Burbank and Atwater Village, with an entryway where Zoo Drive meets Riverside Drive.

The most ambitious proposal is for a 62-acre (25-hectare) park – the first created in almost 20 years – at the abandoned Southern Pacific Railroad yard on San Fernando Road. Another likely site is at the confluence of the river and the Arroyo Seco beside the Pasadena Freeway. Los Angeles fares poorly for parkland. Only 10 percent of land within the city limits is designated as open space, compared with 27 percent of New York and 25 percent of San Francisco.

Maps, page 120 & 128

ators George Lucas and Steven Spielberg once graduated and in whose grounds many films have been shot, among them *The Graduate* and *The Hunchback of Notre Dame*. Walking tours of the huge and attractive campus can be arranged by appointment (weekdays 10am–3pm, tel: 213/740-6605).

At USC's northeast corner, where Figueroa and Jefferson meet, is the striking **Shrine Auditorium** in which Darryl F. Zanuck restaged the 1912 Democratic convention for his cinematic flop *Wilson*. It was also the site of the humiliating confrontation between Judy Garland and James Mason in the 1954 weepie *A Star Is Born,* and the place where Michael Jackson caught fire while making a Pepsi commercial. Such is the substance of legend in LaLaland.

The big Victorian mansions along Washington and Jefferson boulevards have been mostly either abandoned or converted into apartment houses but along West Adams, a few blocks to the north, the private enclave of Chester Place remains much as it was. Oil tycoon Edward Doheny's distinctive residence (which he is said to have paid for in gold coins) now houses the faculty from Mount St Mary's college which owns many of the surrounding buildings. It was Doheny who paid for the construction of **St Vincent de Paul Church**, with its landmark 90-foot (27-meter) dome, at the end of the block on which the Tudoresque house at **649 West Adams** was the home (at different times) of movie stars Fatty Arbuckle and Theda Bara.

Walking tour

Returning to Downtown proper, you might want to begin your walking tour by heading up Figueroa past the **Seventh Market Plaza ❺**, a stylish mall whose sunken plaza with its open-air restaurant sits among three-story palm trees shading smart department stores. Among the interesting art work scattered around the plaza is a stooping bronze businessman on the north side of the Citicorp Center. Cross the

BELOW: the Staples Center, Downtown's sports arena.

street and walk half a block to the **Fine Arts Building** at 811 West 7th, where its artists' studios were long ago converted to offices. Built in 1936, it was lovingly restored in the 1980s. A medieval-style lobby with 15 chandeliers and a tiled fountain hosts drawings of some of the ambitious artwork planned for 30 stations of the city's Metro system.

Strong silhouettes

Admire the gaudy, gilded facade of the **Home Savings Building** as you head back to Figueroa. The stepped, white tower of the **777 Building** ("subtle profiles and strong silhouettes," says one critic) was created by Argentine-born Cesar Pelli, also responsible for the distinctive Pacific Design Center (known locally as "the Blue Whale") in West Hollywood. A low-key fountain by Eric Orr sits outside the **Sanwa Bank** building in the 80-foot (24-meter) high Art Deco lobby in which, among acres of brown marble, sit two of the largest plants ever seen in captivity.

The **First Interstate World Center** ● is one of the tallest buildings in the West.

From Arco Plaza across the street an escalator leads into the glitzy **Westin Bonaventure Hotel** ● with its multi-level lounges and engaging perspectives, and from which a bridge heads from the second floor into the other **Arco Plaza** dotted with enormous sculptures by the likes of Rauschenberg, Stella and Mark DiSuvero. Not far away at 333 S. Grand Street is the **Wells Fargo History Museum** (weekdays 9am–4pm, tel: 213/253-7166), whose delightful exhibits include an old stagecoach and a gold nugget worth at least $2 million.

Downtown street life is at its most active on **Broadway**, where silent screen comic Harold Lloyd once swung from a long-gone clockface in the film *Safety Last*. The fabled 1893 **Bradbury Building** ● (weekdays 9am–6pm, weekends 9–5, tel: 213/626-1893) in all its wrought-iron and oak-paneled glory was the site of the office of hard-boiled private eye Philip Marlowe

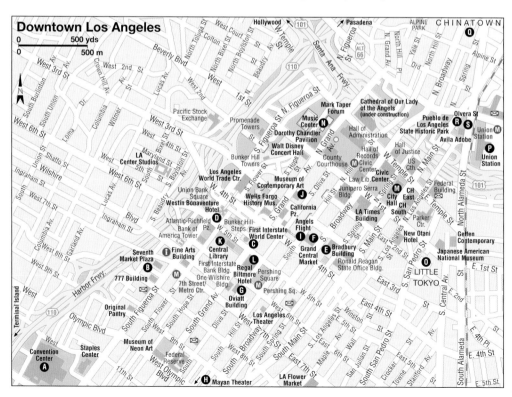

Downtown Los Angeles

Map on page 128

in the 1969 movie of Raymond Chandler's *The Little Sister*.

Chandler, the revered documenter of the Los Angeles of the 1940s, felt it was a city "rich and vigorous and full of pride… a city lost and beaten and full of emptiness." More than half a century later it seems appropriate to warn visitors that there have been some incidents of violence at Downtown nightspots.

The last of the grand movie palaces, Charles Lee's fine **Los Angeles Theater** opened on Broadway with the premiere of Charlie Chaplin's *City Lights* in 1931. It had an art gallery, mahogany-paneled ballroom, baroque ceiling, fountain and kiddies playroom, and is still operating down the street.

Million-dollar movie

Broadway's other attractions include the lively **Grand Central Market ❻** with its fascinating mix of food and knickknacks, and juice bars where you can sit and watch all the action. The market adjoins one of the city's earliest movie palaces, the gala **Million Dollar Movie Theater**. Founded by showman Sid Grauman, it had a grand opening on February 1, 1918, with Charlie Chaplin, Mary Pickford and Lillian Gish in attendance to applaud Mack Sennett's comedy *The Silent Man*.

Top Mexican stars played the theater in the 1950s but the decline of Mexican cinema in the 1970s, coupled with the predominance of other ethnic groups in the area, forced the theater to rent its premises to an evangelist preacher.

Other distinctive downtown buildings include the **Oviatt Building ❼** (South Olive and 6th streets), whose lobby is still decorated with more than a ton of rare Lalique glass, and the fanciful **Mayan Theater ❽** at Hill and Olympic Boulevard (10th Street), where Norma Jean Baker is said to have appeared as a stripper long before she became Marilyn Monroe and which has been described as "somewhere between a pre-Columbian Temple and a wedding cake iced by a madman."

BELOW: Asian resident; Grand Central Market.

Its architects were also responsible for the eye-catching former Uniroyal Tire Factory beside US 405 in the city of Commerce, which is now a discount shopping center. Built in 1929 to resemble the palace of Sargon II in the old Assyrian city of Khorsabad, the theater's 1,700-foot (500-meter) long facade is embellished with winged bulls with human faces, bass reliefs of kings, and lotus flowers.

In 1928 the designers of Downtown's Oviatt Building firm were also responsible for the greatly-admired Richfield Tower (since demolished and replaced by Arco Towers) but another of their Art Deco masterpieces survives. This is the 1931 **Wiltern Theater** (west of town at 3790 Wilshire), although it too was threatened with destruction a decade ago. Happily the Wiltern survived intact, its candy-colored lobby awash in stylized Egyptian columns, dazzling tiled fountains, exotic bas reliefs, hand-painted ceiling murals of the solar system, frosty chandeliers and a green marble bar. In the 2,300-seat auditorium is the world's second largest organ, as well as a huge gold and silver sunburst exploding from an ornate and fiery orange ceiling.

Contemporary art

Behind Grand Central market is the legendary funicular railway **Angel's Flight ❶**, lovingly restored after years of neglect and disuse. Its 25¢ rides were proving enormously popular until the railway was closed after the millennium when a man was accidentally killed on it, and its reopening has not yet been announced. When operating, it ascends the hill to **California Plaza**, where plumes of water and waterfalls frame the outdoor stages and where tables and chairs are set around food stalls. Angel's Flight is on the 15-site walking tour that includes Bunker Hill Steps and the Bradbury Building, marked with bronze tableaux.

Also on California Plaza is the excellent **Museum of Contemporary Art ❷** (daily 11am–5pm, closed Mon, tel: 213/626-6222) known locally as MOCA, in a build-

BELOW: the Hyatt Regency's Broadway Plaza.

Map on page 128

ing designed by Arata Isozaki. Outside is an eye-catching fountain which is a favorite spot to meet friends.

Central Downtown

What might be termed the center of Downtown is around the attractive **Central Library** ❸ (guided tours, tel: 213/228-7000), which houses two million books and is twice the size of the previous one which was the victim of arson. The Central is the creation of visionary Ira Yellin, the lively Grand Central Market entrepreneur who also owns the Bradbury Building. "This part of town has a human dimension and Broadway can eventually become a *real* city walk," he declared, the "city walk" being a reference to Universal Studio's popular attraction.

The **Regal Biltmore Hotel** ❹ on Olive Street has an elaborate vaulted ceiling of hand-painted friezes and roundelles by Italian artist Giovanni Smareldi, who also created works for several Vatican palaces and the White House. It was here where

MGM's art director Cedric Gibbons is said to have used a napkin to sketch a design for the still unnamed Oscar statue.

The Biltmore, with its awe-inspiring lobby and enormous photograph of attendees at the 1937 Academy Awards, was the largest hotel in the west when it opened in 1923, its lobby festooned with frescoes, murals, and a cherub and cloud ceiling. "Sumptuous churrigueresque splendor," said one observer, cognizant of the grand two-story Rendezvous Court with its elaborate Spanish ceiling painted in soft tones of gold, green and black. German chandeliers dangle above a bubbling marble fountain surrounded by potted palms, and the double stairway leads to an elaborate Spanish Renaissance balcony.

One block east of the Biltmore is the redesigned **Pershing Square**. It may be less seedy than the earlier version, but it is also more sterile. In line with these times it also lacks any public toilets. The northeast corner of the square was in 1887 the site of Hazard's Pavilion – demolished in

BELOW:
NASA captures the California coastline.

1985 – where at different times George Gershwin, John Philip Sousa and Igor Stravinsky demonstrated their musical talents before it became the headquarters of the Los Angeles Philharmonic. Known earlier as Clune's Auditorium, the scene of lectures by Booker T. Washington and Mark Twain, it has a celebrated place in early movie history as the venue for D.W. Griffith's *Birth of a Nation,* which packed in audiences for two straight years.

At nearby Flower and 7th streets is **the terminus of the Blue Line Metro**, which runs down to Long Beach through Watts and the internationally admired, 100-foot (30-meter) high **Watts Towers** (tel: 213/847-4646), which is now open every weekend. Lovingly constructed over 33 years as a tribute to his adopted land by the penniless Italian tilesetter Simon Rodia, the towers can be spotted from the train as it approaches 103rd Street. Composed of broken bottles, pottery shards, tile, pebbles and steel rods all stuccoed together and covered with 70,000 seashells, the towers are a set of sculptures so ahead of their time that they were unappreciated for years: vandals tried to destroy them and, more than once, the city planned to pull them down.

Movie icon

The around-town DASH bus passes **City Hall Ⓜ**, which is also a movie icon, having starred in many TV shows and movies. Perhaps its best known "role" was as the *Daily Planet* building in the *Superman* TV series. Until 1957 when steel structures became commonplace City Hall was the only Downtown building allowed higher than 13 stories because it was believed to be earthquake proof. In keeping with its function, the mortar with which it was built contained sand from every California county, water from every mission and cement from every cement mill.

Now City Hall has been strengthened to withstand an 8.1 earthquake which everybody hopes will never arrive. A 4-foot (1-meter) wide dry underground moat with

BELOW: City Hall presides over the LA Street Festival; famous Watts Towers.

Map
on page
128

steel sliders will allow room for motion. Reinforced concrete walls replace hollow clay block walls. At its base, high-tech shock absorbers can move up to a foot in any direction. And the building is now once again topped by the beacon first installed to celebrate Lindbergh's flight across the Atlantic.

Near City Hall on Spring Street is the *Los Angeles Times* **Building** where interesting stories and a short video history of the state's biggest newspaper are displayed in the lobby. Tours are available (tel: 213/237-5000) if reservations are made one week ahead.

Music city

After long delays, the Frank Gehry-designed **Disney Concert Hall** is at last scheduled to open. The concert hall is the offbeat jewel of the four-theater **Music Center ⓝ** (tel: 213/972-7483), whose other classy components are the **Dorothy Chandler Pavilion**, the **Mark Taper Forum** and the **Ahmanson Theater**. The

surrounding garden contains a restaurant, café and bookstore.

Soon another Downtown landmark will be completed, the $163-million cathedral, **Our Lady of the Angels** (one day to be known as OLA) by Spanish architect Jose Rafael Moneo, around whose huge plaza will be mission-style colonnades, gardens and a conference center.

The ultimate plan, to be completed by 2005, is for an enormous urban park through which will run a reconfigured Grand Avenue along which pedestrians can walk between the grand buildings.

East of City Hall is the **New Otani Hotel** with its lovely Japanese garden off the fourth floor created by famous landscape artist Sentaru Iwaki. The hotel sits at the edge of **Little Tokyo ⓞ**, whose interesting stores include a fully stocked branch of the worldwide Japanese department store chain, Yaohan Plaza. At 369 First Street, adjoining the Geffen Contemporary, is the **Japanese American National Museum** (daily 10am–5pm, till

BELOW:
LA has one of the fastest-growing Asian populations in the nation.

8pm on Thurs, tel: 213/625-0414). Designed by architect Gyo Obata, the spectacular museum overlooks a lovely, ancient Buddhist Temple and attracts almost one quarter of a million visitors each year. A public art project in the sidewalk commemorates six decades of Japanese-American life.

Stratospheric ceilings

In the northeast corner of town is majestic **Union Station P**, which opened in 1939 complete with leather seats and stratospheric ceiling. This was where movie stars often disembarked after their cross-country tours, and has been seen in scores of old black-and-white newsreels.

Nicely maintained by Amtrak, which operates about 20 trains a day up the coast, down to the Mexican border and into the desert, it has become a money-making star itself with lucrative rentals to production crews for such movies as *Bugsy* and *Grand Canyon*. LA's subway system, the **Metro Red Line**, intersects with the Blue Line (south to Long Beach) at 7th Street. The Red Line runs to Hollywood and North Hollywood. Behind the station sits the glass-roofed **Gateway Transit Center**, the mural- and fountain-filled transportation hub of the region.

The DASH bus stops at the station enroute to and from "touristy" Olvera Street and then heads to the far edge of **Chinatown Q** at Bernard. Just around the corner on Broadway, the gaudy Oriental stereotypes of **Gin Ling Way** surround a stage-sized plaza. Chinatown's main street is scruffily interesting, an exotic supermarket of everything from live fish to caged chickens, with scarcely a word of English to be heard.

Today's Chinatown replaces a gaudier earlier version (burned down in 1948) that was partly the inspiration of a Paramount set designer after most of the original Chinese area had been razed to build Union Station. During excavations for the Metro Line, various artifacts from the original Chinatown (like opium pipes, ivory dice,

BELOW: Union Station opened in 1939 and has featured in many movies.

Map on page 128

coins) were dug up near Union Station and are on exhibit at 425 South Main Street. Today's Chinatown population is estimated at around 15,000, and steadily rising each year.

Strolling *mariachi*

Three long blocks south (easily achieved on the bus) is **Olvera Street ®** with its working craftsmen, Mexican stalls and strolling *mariachi* who serenade diners as they sip frozen margaritas and eat lunch under the sidewalk awning of pretty **La Golondrina**, the city's first brick building (1850). This was home to the Pellenconi family whose piano, a neighborly gift, sits across the street in the older (restored) **Avila Adobe ⑤** (daily 9am–4pm, till 5pm in summer, tel: 213/628-1274).

Here on what began as Wine Street is where the town of El Pueblo de Nuestra Señora a la Reina de Los Angeles began in 1780, when Felipe de Neve, California's first governor, laid out what was eventualy to become California's biggest city. Apart

from being reinforced after a 1922 earthquake, the Avila Adobe, home of a prosperous rancher who died in 1832, has remained pretty much as it was left by his widow when she died 23 years later.

After her death, the neighborhood steadily deteriorated and by 1890 was best known for "Nigger Alley," a rowdy block of saloons, gambling houses and cockfighting whose badly exploited ethnic minority community had been vastly increased by an influx of Chinese laborers discharged on the completion of the transcontinental railroads. Lynchings and racial attacks punctuated the latter half of the century. Walking tours of the area (free) are conducted most mornings, tel: 213/628-1274).

A massive mural painted in 1932 by the celebrated Mexican artist David Alfaro Siqueiros and covered over by city officials who were offended by its radical theme, has been restored in Olvera Street's **Italian Hall**. Other notable landmarks include the **Pico House**, the city's first

BELOW: today's Chinatown replaces an earlier one on the same site.

three-story building and once its finest hotel; the **Garnier House** (1890) and the adjoining **Helman Quon building**, originally a Chinese store but now a Parks Department office that offers tours of the neighborhood. Take a look in the firehouse for the picture of Blackie, the city's last working firehorse.

Between the **Plaza Church** (1818), scene of an annual Easter ceremony when children bring their pets to be blessed, and Union Station, is a statue of Father Junípero Serra (1713–84), founder of the chain of missions that still stretches for hundreds of miles up the coast.

First suburb

Heading west along Sunset Boulevard for a mile or two brings you to what was the city's first suburb, **Angelino Heights ❸**, once connected to Downtown via a 15-minute trolley ride that ran along Temple Street. In the early 1900s, prosperous businessmen thought the views and the convenience were worth paying $10,000 or so

for homes which are today worth many times that. In the silent-movie days Mack Sennett filmed on these residential streets where Gloria Swanson and Mary Pickford had already taken up residence. In 1929, western lawman Wyatt Earp died, aged 80, in a cottage at 4000 West 17th Street, near Crenshaw and Washington boulevards. A school now stands there.

Carroll Avenue's fame today derives from a group of Queen Anne-style houses, all of which have been lovingly preserved, and supplemented by others transported from elsewhere. Together they constitute a collection of more than 50 classic homes, the largest group in Southern California. The fine **1300 block**, for example, has been listed in the National Register of Historic Places.

Below Angelino Heights beside **Echo Park Lake** is the **Angelus Temple ❹** from which broadcasts by the charismatic evangelist Aimee Semple McPherson attracted nationwide attention back in 1920. Radio's first preacher had no difficulty filling the 5,000 seats in her Four Square Gospel Tabernacle four times every Sunday, using such dramatic tricks as chasing the devil across stage with a pitchfork and "arresting" him from the seat of a highway patrol motorcycle. Audiotapes of Aimee's sermons are still on sale in the adjoining shop.

Three miles (5 km) northeast of Downtown, the area between **Hollenbeck** and **Lincoln Parks** is the mainspring of a lively Chicano community; the intersection of Boyle Avenue and 1st Street in **Boyle Heights** where *mariachi* musicians meet in the evening (and which has in the past become gang territory, so be alert) is somewhat optimistically scheduled for redevelopment.

You'll need your car to reach the preserved Victorian homes of **Heritage Square** (weekends 11:30am–4:30pm, tel: 626/449-0193) at Avenue 43, near the Pasadena Freeway and the fascinating **Southwest Museum** (daily 10am–5pm, closed Mon, tel: 323/221-2164) on Museum Drive, with its Native American artifacts and relics of Los Angeles's short but compelling history. ❑

Maps, page 120 & 128

LEFT: the First Interstate World Center, one of the tallest buildings in the West. **RIGHT:** beauty on Cinco de Mayo parade route.

Map on page 120

HOLLYWOOD AND THE WEST SIDE

Beverly Hills, Rodeo Drive, the hilltop Getty Center: when people talk of Hollywood opulence and grandeur, this is where they mean

When Sunset Boulevard was still a dusty track heading westwards from Downtown, it was Wilshire Boulevard to the south – running almost parallel and at times 3 miles (5 km) away – that became the major road out to the coast. And the automobile made it so. Wilshire was developed by H. Gaylord Wilshire, who made millions from peddling a questionable metal collar which – like the copper bands which are in vogue today – was supposed to be a cure-all for numerous ailments and maladies. Gaylord died in 1927 when Wilshire was well on its way to becoming the longest, widest boulevard in the country, intersected by 200 streets.

Nowadays though, Wilshire is showing its age with sleazy **MacArthur Park** ❺ – once a garbage dump – being the most visible sign of its decline. The recent $8 million restoration and the Metro station have partially succeeded in breathing new life into the area, but be aware this is no place for the unwary pedestrian.

Moviemaker's favorite

On the park's northwest corner, the **Park Plaza Hotel**'s sensational lobby is a favorite of moviemakers. Opened in 1927 as the Elks Club, it is built of reinforced concrete etched to look like stone. Still doing business as lodgings are actor Fred McMurray's **Bryson Apartment Hotel**; the "white stucco palace" at 2701 Wilshire of Raymond Chandler's *Lady in the Lake* fame; and the nearby **Talmadge** in whose lobby hangs a portrait of Norma Talmadge, the original co-owner along with her husband, Fox studio boss Joseph Schenck. Just past the park are the **Los Altos** apartments (1925), whose early tenants included Clara Bow, Bette Davis and June Allyson.

The beautiful and venerable Art Deco building that opened to great fanfare as

Bullock's Wilshire, the city's first suburban department store whose early salesgirls included Angela Lansbury and the future First Lady Pat Nixon, is now a law library *(see photograph on page 97)*.

At the corner of Crenshaw, the site now occupied by an insurance company, was the rambling mansion depicted as Norma Desmond's residence in the movie *Sunset Boulevard*. Built in 1924, it was owned by a former wife of billionaire J. Paul Getty when Billy Wilder spotted it and rented it for his 1950 film. Wilder installed a swimming pool, stained glass windows and a pipe organ, rented an Isotta Fraschini car to park in the driveway and signed up Glo-

LEFT: scents-sational Rodeo Drive. **RIGHT:** Hollywood: famous 7 days a week.

ria Swanson, to make what is surely the most famous of Hollywood movies. The mansion was used once again – for a swimming pool scene in the James Dean classic *Rebel Without a Cause* – before being demolished in the 1950s.

Another has-been is the **Ambassador Hotel ❻**, once fabled for the showbiz types who attended (and performed in) its ultra-chic nightclub, the Coconut Grove, and later infamous as the site of Robert Kennedy's assassination. The hotel is currently closed and used mostly for local film shoots until its future is decided.

At **Hancock Park**, on Wilshire near Fairfax, is the **LA County Museum of Art ❼** which is about to close and be reconstructed to the design of the trendy Dutch architect Rem Koolhaas. The fascinating **La Brea Tar Pits ❽**, at the George C. Page Museum (closed Mon, tel: 323/934-7243) are a major tourist attraction. In the 1860s, Rancho La Brea had been bought for $2.50 an acre by Major Henry Hancock, who quarried asphalt and shipped tar to San Francisco to pave streets. In 1899 the oil company geologists moved in and fossils were discovered. They identified some of the bones as belonging to extinct sabre-toothed tigers, dire wolves and giant sloths.

9,000 years ago

After a decade of oil drilling, Henry's son George allowed LA County to examine the site, deeding the 23-acre (9-hectare) ranch to the county in 1913. The skeleton of an Indian woman from 9,000 years ago was found, but no other humans among what was literally millions of bones. Local industrialist George C. Page paid for a museum in 1972 and excavations for this uncovered skeletons of complete animals which had been trapped in the tar as they came to drink.

There is terrific al fresco eating and lots of free parking at the nearby **Farmers' Market ❾** (open daily until early evening, tel: 323/923-9211) where from 1934 farmers could park their trucks and

BELOW: Gloria Swanson's swansong in *Sunset Boulevard.*

Map
on page
120

sell produce from the back. A huge shopping mall, **the Grove**, opened next door in 2002; the mall and the market are connected with a free trolley.

Just north of here, until burned down by an arsonist in 1989, was the **Pan Pacific Auditorium** – site of Elvis Presley concerts, Harlem Globetrotters performances and other spectacles such as the Ice Capades, for 54 years.

Sunset Boulevard gate

For Noo Yawk vibes check out the legendary **Canter's Restaurant** on Fairfax Avenue, a 24-hour delicatessen where brusqueness is the approved style. But some visitors find glamour in just the idea of that. Most of the well-known movie studios which earned Hollywood its reputation have long moved out – although MGM in Culver City and Fox in Century City are not too far away – but the imposing gate seen in *Sunset Boulevard* still guards the entrance to **Paramount Studios ⑩** on Melrose at Van Ness Avenue. More

recently, TV shows such as *Cheers* and *Frasier* have been made here.

Tours are sometimes available, so you, too, can glide through those famous gilded gates like a movie diva. Speaking of divas, Mae West ("It's not the men in my life, it's the life in my men") lived for nearly 50 years within walking distance of the studio (not that she walked) amid gilded Louis XV furniture in a sixth-floor apartment in Ravenswood on Rossmore Avenue, until her death aged 94 in 1987.

And fans who were not even born when silent star Rudolph Valentino died in 1926 seek out his grave (and those of Douglas Fairbanks, Cecil B. de Mille, Eleanor Powell and Marion Davies) in the adjoining **Hollywood Forever Cemetery ⑪** which, under new management, has instituted such innovations as "video biographies" and a name change; undoubtedly everyone will, however, refer to the cemetery by its original name forever.

The **Formosa Cafe** at 7156 Santa Monica Boulevard, which once served as an

BELOW:
the cast roars
out loud over
a 1920s
comedy script.

unofficial commissary for film studios like United Artists, has been designated a historic landmark due to its priceless collection of autographed photos of former customers – Frank Sinatra, Marilyn Monroe, Elvis Presley, and Howard Hughes (who once borrowed $20 off the late owner, Lem Quon).

Visiting this low-key establishment is a good way to spot the stars, as meetings and after-work cocktails still happen here regularly due to the proximity of so many movie and TV studios. The Formosa played a featured role in the 1997 film noir *LA Confidential*, and it was here that Kevin Spacey and Kim Basinger were offered their roles by director Curtis Hanson. Rumor has it that Robert Redford and a cinema company plan to open a movie and retail complex at the corner of La Brea and Santa Monica that will essentially be built around the Formosa

Memories of moviedom's low-budget Westerns are evoked by **Gower Gulch** ⓬, a frontier-style shopping center opposite

CBS on the corner at Sunset and Gower where Hollywood's first film studio, the Nestor Film Company, paid $40 to rent a defunct tavern in 1911.

The television station across the street replaced the old Warner Brothers studio where in 1927 Al Jolson emoted in *The Jazz Singer*. Just north of Sunset on Vine Street, Cecil B. De Mille and Jesse Lasky filmed *The Squaw Man* in 1913, Hollywood's first full-length feature. Paying homage to its location, the McDonald's here on Vine Street is decked out in the style of *Casablanca*.

A bust of Rudolph Valentino stands in the minuscule **De Longpre Park** on Cherokee, named after the flower painter whose gorgeous house and gardens near Wilcox Street and Hollywood Boulevard were Hollywood's first tourist attraction. (Kansas-born Harvey Wilcox and his wife Daieda were the founders of a temperance community they called Hollywood which encircled their extensive orchards.)

Hollywood Marketplace

On Hollywood Boulevard near Vine Street, a renovated **Cinerama Dome Theater** will be the centerpiece of the glitzy **Hollywood Marketplace** ⓭, a huge entertainment and retail center designed in matching late-'50s architectural style with a health club, 15-screen movie theater plus shops, offices, eating places and 2,000 parking places.

A favorite with such macho stars as Errol Flynn, Clark Gable and John Wayne was the **Hollywood Athletic Club**, 6525 Sunset, where Cornel Wilde was once a fencing instructor and in whose pool Buster Crabbe trained before winning a gold medal at the 1932 Olympics and becoming the star of the movie *Tarzan*. Valentino maintained a penthouse apartment here from whose balcony Wayne once threw billiard balls at passing cars. The swimming pool has long gone but today's stars such as Madonna and Kevin Costner can occasionally be seen having dinner in the restaurant or playing pool in the billiard room.

On the opposite side of the road at 6530 Sunset is the West Side's nicest pub, the **Cat & Fiddle**, built around an attractive

LEFT: ironing out the problems of the day in time for a night out.

Map on page 120

Mediterranean-style patio where patrons can sip British beers and enjoy such typical pub grub as bangers and mash when not busy inside playing darts.

The castle-like **Chateau Marmont** ⓮, on Sunset near Laurel Canyon, where Paul Newman met Joanne Woodward, is famous not only because of guests such as Arturo Toscanini, Greta Garbo and Howard Hughes, but also as the place where John Belushi died.

Interesting architecture is prolific in this area, with many delightful examples of a lush Spanish style to be found in the blocks between Sunset Boulevard and Fountain Avenue, west of Crescent Heights. Some of these – including the **Villa Primavera** (1300 N. Harper); the **Patio del Moro** (8229 Fountain); and the **Villa Andalucia** (1473 N. Havenhurst) were the work of the husband-and-wife architectural team of Arthur and Nina Zwebell. Others, like **Villa D'Este** (1355 N. Laurel), were done by the Davis brothers, Pierpont and Walter.

All date to the 1920s, as does the apartment house at 1305 N. Harper where Marlene Dietrich is said to have stayed when she first arrived in 1930. **Mi Casa** (1406 N. Havenhurst) is the genuine article: an irresistible row of balconied apartments around twin patios brought bodily from Ronda, Spain, in 1926, and since designated as a national historic place.

The city's denizens have always had an ambivalent attitude about the local architecture and what survives seems to be largely a matter of chance. Most of the steamy 1930s nightclubs on Sunset Strip – Ciro's at 8433 Sunset, the Mocambo (at 8588) and the Trocadero – are gone, although some weed-covered steps at 8610 Sunset mark the site where the Trocadero (the house pianist was Nat King Cole) once stood, and the **Comedy Store** adapted the Ciro's building.

Sunset Strip

Commercial buildings first went up on Hollywood's famous **Sunset Strip** ⓯ in 1924 but it remained a two-lane dirt road

BELOW: Sunset Strip is now best-known for its rock clubs.

until 1935 when it was widened, paved and (the following year) strewn with flowers by a low-flying plane to mark the dedication ceremony. Secret gambling clubs were one of the street's earliest features, followed by the famous nightclubs around which swirl many of the legends of early moviedom.

The Trocadero, for example, founded by *The Hollywood Reporter*'s publisher Billy Wilkerson, was a favorite haunt of Ronald Reagan, Judy Garland and Lana Turner as well as powerful columnists Hedda Hopper and Louella Parsons. It was Wilkerson who discovered 15-year-old Lana Turner (then Julia Turner) in the Top Hat Café and introduced her to the agent Zeppo Marx.

Other discoveries were made at the Mocambo where one night, an attractive dancer named Margaret Cansino was spotted by director Howard Hawks and studio boss Harry Cohn who signed her up to co-star – under the new name of Rita Hayworth – with Cary Grant in *Only Angels Have Wings*. When the club first opened it got some valuable publicity after the ASPCA nearby demanded that the club close during the day so its collection of cockatoos, parakeets and macaws could get some sleep.

Dominating the hill above Sunset at 501 North Doheny is the **Greystone Mansion** ⓰, its 18-acre (7-hectare) garden popular with visitors, the house itself being rented out to movie companies. It was seen in *The Loved One* and *Ghostbusters II*. Built at a cost of $6 million in 1926 by the city's first oil millionaire, Charles Doheny, it is now owned by the community of Beverly Hills.

Down La Cienega at Beverly Boulevard is the **Beverly Center** ⓱. For 30 years, until 1974, an amusement park and oil wells stood on the site of what is now an eight-level mall. Stars including Geena Davis, Phil Collins and Bernardette Peters have been spotted in one or another of its plethora of shops, restaurants and movie theaters. Its parking levels can be so confusing that one customer hailed a taxi to drive him around until he remembered where he had left his car.

Beverly Hills

Drilling for oil on what was once the Rancho Rodeo de las Aguas is what led to the birth of Beverly Hills: the unsuccessful oil prospectors subsequently decided to develop the land. One-acre (half-hectare) lots were offered for under $1,000 along Sunset where in 1912 Burton Green built the **Beverly Hills Hotel** ⓲ to be the focal point of the new community. A legendary watering hole for everyone from Spencer Tracy to Marilyn Monroe, it was bought in 1987 by the Sultan of Brunei, who spent $100 million (on top of the $185 million purchase price) renovating it.

One of Beverly Hills' earliest homes – and the only one open to the public – is the **Virginia Robinson House** ⓳, built in 1911 for the son and daughter-in-law of the Robinson department store chain founder. The lushly landscaped gardens include a mini forest of palm trees and flower-filled terraces.

Filmdom's elite built ever-bigger homes in this elegant area, first of all not far from Sunset: George Burns and Gracie Allen at

LEFT: everyone from Spencer Tracy to Marilyn Monroe spent time here.

Map on page 120

720 N. Maple Drive; Groucho Marx at 710 Hillcrest and Edward G. Robinson with his vast art collection in an English-type brick residence at 910 N. Rexford Drive. After Ginger Rogers chose to live at the highest point of Beverly Hills, building a gleaming soda fountain into her one-story house at 1605 Gilcrest Drive, more and more stars fanned out into the hills and canyons, especially around **Mulholland Drive**, the spectacular highway running along the crest of the Santa Monica Mountains.

In 1918 Mary Pickford and Douglas Fairbanks, soon followed by others, targeted Benedict Canyon, converting an old hunting lodge on Summit Drive into Pickfair (demolished by controversial financier Meshulam Riklis and his then-wife starlet Pia Zadora); Chaplin lived, apparently with rented furniture, at 1085 Summit Drive, with Fred Astaire at number 1121; Rudolph Valentino luxuriated in Falcon's Lair at 1436 Bella Drive; and the home of Roman Polanski and Sharon Tate at 10050 Cicelo Drive was the scene of the murders in 1969 by members of the Charles Manson family.

Cher lived for many years in an Egyptian-style house in the canyon. But perhaps the most spectacular home was the enormous mansion on a 16-acre (6.5-hectare) estate created in 1927 by silent movie comic Harold Lloyd, who died there in 1971. The estate, which included a golf course and canoe waterway, has now been reduced in size but the 25-room house, Green Acres, can still be glimpsed behind an iron gate at 1225 Benedict Canyon.

At the canyon's lower end, along immaculate North Roxbury Drive, lived Marlene Dietrich (822), Jimmy Stewart (918) and Lucille Ball (1000). Greta Garbo's home was nearby at 1027 Chevy Chase Drive.

Rodeo Drive

A self-guided tour of Beverly Hills, taking in most of the interesting sights should begin at the **Visitors Bureau** (daily 9am–5pm, tel: 800/345-2210) where you can pick up a map before heading up the street to the Moorish-style **Israel Discount**

BELOW: everyone from Brad Pitt to Julia Roberts shops until they drop here.

Bank, with its onion dome, which began as a theater in 1925. Go along Wilshire past the famous department stores and the Beaux Arts-style **Regent Beverly Wilshire Hotel** to fabled **Rodeo Drive** and its companion **Two Rodeo Drive** ⓴. The latter – a little cobbled street with fountains that featured in the movie *Pretty Woman* – is a replica of what only Hollywood could believe to be an authentic olde-worlde European backwater.

Rich and famous

Between them, the Rodeos are the height of retail royalty. The most famous names in fashion are here: Dior, Chanel, Armani and Gucci, along with jewelers like Tiffany and Cartier. It is here that the rich and famous do their shopping, and where the tourists window-shop while hoping to spot a star.

Futher down at 322 N. Rodeo there's a little-known (rather ordinary) Frank Lloyd Wright building. More interesting are Richard Meier's **Museum of Television and Radio** ⓴ (tel: 310/785-1000) and the Artists and Writers Building, a Spanish Colonial office block which has housed many of the film colony's famous writers at one time or another since it went up in 1924. Both are around the corner on Santa Monica Boulevard.

Continuing east, you'll pass the distinctive post office and, at the corner of Rexford Drive and the main boulevard, handsome **City Hall** ⓴ with its tiled dome. City Hall is opposite **Beverly Gardens**, which stretches for 14 blocks and includes an interesting cactus garden. The Gaudi-esque **O'Neill House** at 507 N. Rodeo, and – a few blocks away – the bizarre **Witches Cottage** ⓴ at 516 Walden Drive, are uniquely interesting, the latter beginning life as a 1921 movie set designed to look like the home of the fairy-tale witch in Hansel and Gretel before being moved to this site lock, stock and barrel.

Santa Monica and Wilshire boulevards intersect at the far side of Beverly Hills beside the **Electric Fountain**, a structure that caused traffic jams when it was first

BELOW: Rodeo Drive: "the most staggering display of luxury in the Western world."

Map on page 120

erected in 1930. Almost opposite is the distinctive marble and glass building by architect I.M. Pei for the **Creative Artists Agency**, its lobby dominated by a gigantic Roy Lichtenstein painting.

Golden Globe awards

The annual Golden Globe Awards are staged at Merv Griffin's **Beverly Hilton Hotel** across the busy intersection, while the home base of the Oscars is several blocks back east at 8949 Wilshire, where the **Academy of Motion Picture Arts and Sciences** ❷ (tel: 310/247-3000) maintains a movie-themed exhibit in the lobby.

Santa Monica Boulevard heads west past the skyscrapers of **Century City** ❷, centered around the luxurious Century Park Hotel and another upscale shopping center. The Century City site was once part of the studio back lot of 20th Century Fox, which now occupies only the adjoining southern portion.

Wilshire Boulevard swerves slightly northwest out of Beverly Hills along the southern flank of **Westwood** village, once the headquarters of William Fox' newsreel operations but now better known as a college town because it adjoins the pleasant, tree-shaded **University of California** in Los Angeles (**UCLA**) ❷, whose 130 buildings include Schoenberg Hall (named after the renowned composer who taught here), Bunche Hall Library and the Frederick S. Wight Art Gallery, all of which are open to the public. UCLA's main entrance is on Hilgard Avenue, just south of Sunset, and the first stop should be at the **Visitor Center** (tel: 310/8252278) in Murphy Hall, which dispenses maps and information about tours, free movies and concerts.

The gated community of ultra-chic Bel Air is north of Sunset, the road up through Stone Canyon passing what some people think of as LA's nicest hideaway hotel, the **Bel Air Hotel** ❷, its peaceful grounds intersected by a stream along which glide graceful swans. Grace Kelly lived here for much of her movie career.

Back on Sunset, the boulevard begins a

series of dizzying loops and curves passing through **Brentwood** , where the half-mile stretch of San Vicente Boulevard between Wilshire and Bundy attracts shoppers and café-sitters. Brentwood has been home to many stars: Raymond Chandler had a home at 12216 Shetland Place; Joan Crawford lived at 426 Bristol Avenue; Shirley Temple at 227 Rockingham Road; and Marilyn Monroe died in a bungalow at 12305 Fifth Helena Drive.

Dwarfing all these in recent interest and attention was the 1996 double murder on Rockingham Drive outside of the house of the football star O.J. Simpson of his wife Nicole and her friend Ron Goldman. The trial ended in O.J.'s acquittal, but the house was sold to pay his legal bills.

Getty Center

Sunset heads through the attractive area of **Pacific Palisades** before sweeping down to the Pacific Coast Highway. High on a hilltop overlooking the intersection of San Diego (I-405) and Santa Monica (I-10) freeways is the **Getty Center** (closed Mon and most holidays, tel: 310/440-7300; www.getty.edu, possibly America's richest and most spectacular museum. The center was designed by architect Richard Meier and took 13 years to complete. Anyone visiting the (free) Getty Center during the week before 4pm must pay for a space in the parking lot from which they are transported to the hilltop; on weekends and after 4pm parking is free. (The MTA 561 bus also stops at the parking lot). Five buildings, connected by balconies set around an open courtyard, house the permanent collection.

This includes masterpieces by Rembrandt, van Gogh, Monet, Renoir and Cézanne, as well as drawings by Michelangelo, Leonardo and Raphael, sculptures by Cellini, Bernini and Canova, Renaissance ceramics and glass plus medieval illuminated manuscripts. There are 14 galleries devoted to French furniture and decorative art, and one of the world's largest collection of photographs from 1839 to David Hockney's contemporary assem-

BELOW: the Getty Center stole the cultural limelight from San Francisco.

Map
on page
120

blages. Photography curator Weston Naef says that if all 60,000 photographs could be exhibited at once it would require 30 miles (48km) of wall space. Gallery interiors were designed by Thierry Despont, the architect of Bill Gates' extravagant mansion in Seattle.

The 742-acre (300-hectare) Getty Center site, which cost a relatively minor $20 million, houses 11 separate structures including the Circular Research Institute with its library and archives; a 450-seat auditorium; and a restaurant/café whose terrace offers what are probably the best views of the entire city. Part of the site is occupied by a garden designed by artist Robert Irwin, with a maze, trees, stone and thousands of plants. A brook runs through it downhill to a reflecting pool.

Buddhist grottoes

On his death in 1976, oil tycoon J. Paul Getty left stock worth $700 million to the museum he founded in his Malibu home *(see page 163)*. Today his endowment is worth several billion dollars, a percentage of which under US tax law has to be spent each year. In 1996, the foundation had to spend $110 million on art and archival material alone. The activities of the Getty's Conservation Institute include preserving Buddhist grottoes in China and prehistoric footprints in Tanzania.

Just before the coast, on the left, is a sharp turnoff from Sunset to the pretty lakeside shrine of the **Self Realization Fellowship** (free parking). A mile or two before that it's worth making a right, going uphill to the **Will Rogers State Historic Park ㉚** (daily 10:30am–4:30pm, tel: 310/454-8212). The state has maintained the ranch pretty much as it was when the cowboy star lived in it, and polo matches are played on the grounds most weekends. A trail leads from the ranch up into **Topanga State Park ㉛**, which ends at Entrada Road in Topanga Canyon. If you park your car at either end, arrange to be picked up at the Sunset end because you won't want to hike all the way back. ❑

BELOW:
Pacific
Palisades
of long ago.

Map on page 120

HOLLYWOOD BOULEVARD

Stars, stars everywhere: in front of Mann's Chinese Theater, along Hollywood's Walk of Fame, picking up an Oscar, or stepping onto that final stage in the sky

Hollywood Boulevard begins at Barnsdall Park where Sunset veers left to run parallel until the former peters off into the hills around Laurel Canyon about 4 miles (6 km) to the west. Being the northernmost of the east/west boulevards – the others are Wilshire and Santa Monica – it offers easy access to Griffith Park, the Hollywood Reservoir and the Hollywood Freeway, which runs through Cahuenga Pass to Universal Studios and the San Fernando Valley.

One of the largest city parks in America, **Griffith Park** ㉜ has something to offer almost everybody, and on an average weekend more than 50,000 visitors come in search of it *(see page 186)*. Most of these people arrive by car – which is what you'll need to explore the park. Caution should be exercised: sections of the park are both lonely and dangerous and have sometimes been a dumping ground for bodies, often killed elsewhere. During daylight there are usually enough people around to discourage troublemakers, but don't take any chances.

No buses run into Griffith Park, but an MTA from Downtown runs along Los Feliz Boulevard on its southern border. Bicycles can be rented on Los Feliz, and horses can also be hired for a few hours to ride along some of the 53 miles (85 km) of semi-rural bridle trails. One trail that originates from near the zoo runs alongside the Los Angeles River.

The park was a gift to the city by Griffith J. Griffith, a Welsh immigrant who, after making his fortune, took up residence here. Because of its size, the park is best described by areas: the entrance from Vermont Avenue leads to the **Greek Theater** (open-air concerts in summer); the **Bird Sanctuary** (walking tours on Sundays); and – a long uphill drive – the **Griffith Observatory**, which will be familiar to visitors who have seen its distinctive facade in *Rebel Without A Cause* or *Battlestar Galactica*. The Observatory is closed to the public for major renovations until January 2005.

Free map

The eastern entrance from the Golden State freeway leads into the Crystal Springs picnic grounds and also to the **Ranger Station** (tel: 323/913-4688), where you can pick up a free map. The northern entrance, near the freeways' intersection, leads onto Zoo Drive at the western end of which both children and adults play trains on Sundays, riding on model railway cars pulled by powerful steam or diesel-powered engines. **Travel Town** ㉝, a free transportation museum, is an ele-

LEFT: a rarely seen view of a famous sign. **RIGHT:** Universal City Walk.

phants' graveyard of old trains, plus cable and trolley cars and antique fire engines.

At the park's eastern side, adjoining the golf course, is the 113-acre (46-hectare) **Los Angeles Zoo** N (daily 10am–5pm, tel: 323/644-4200), with many endangered species. The different sections are far enough apart to make it worthwhile riding the little train.

A recreation of a Western town, together with clips from vintage movies, are part of the fare for visitors to the **Autry Museum of Western Heritage** N (Tues–Sun 10am–5pm, tel: 323/667-2000) along Zoo Drive, which is really quite absorbing and continually stages a dramatic re-enactment of the shoot-out at the OK Corral. On display are guns, clothing and holsters from the likes of Wyatt Earp, Teddy Roosevelt and Annie Oakley, and clips from classic old Western movies are screened on a regular basis.

Next to Griffith Park's entrance at Riverside and Memorial Drive is a fountain dedicated to William Mulholland, the man who brought Los Angeles its first reliable water supply from the Owens Valley in 1913. Although Mulholland was accused of the "rape of the Owens Valley" by some, he is nonetheless memorialized today by one of LA's most famous streets, **Mulholland Drive** N, the stunning 50-mile (80-km) scenic route across the Santa Monica Mountains from the Hollywood Hills to the Pacific Coast Highway north of Malibu.

Mulholland is one of the glories of the region and although it is bisected by most of the canyons that run through these mountains, access is probably easiest from where it begins at the Cahuenga Pass. Dozens of lavish homes are cantilevered off the steep hillsides and, from the spine of the range, a 360°-view offers sensational panoramas across the mountains of both the Valley and the West Side, the string of lights after dusk resembling the view coming into Los Angeles by plane. One section – between the San Diego Freeway and Topanga Canyon – has been left unpaved, restricting driving to about 20 mph (32 kph).

While this lends a wonderfully unspoiled aura by day, this stretch is best avoided after dark when it becomes attractive to outlaws of one kind or another. At noon on most Sundays, the **Rock Store** at 30325 Mulholland Highway has become an informal meeting place for scores of the area's motorcyclists, including (occasionally) a movie star or two.

Famous cemetery

One of LA's crowning glories is **Forest Lawn Memorial Park** N (daily 8am–5pm, tel: 800/204-3131), with two locations flanking Griffith Park. The branch in **Glendale** *(see page 186; photograph on page 191)* was the inspiration for Evelyn Waugh's 1948 novel *The Loved One*. Among the celebrities buried here are the entire Walt Disney family, including brother, mother and father, as well as Humphrey Bogart, Clark Gable and Carole Lombard. There are reproductions of famous churches from around the world, a stained-glass interpretation of da Vinci's *The Last Supper* and the world's largest

LEFT: stars at your feet: the Walk of Fame.

Map
on page
120

religious painting, *The Crucifixion* by Jan Stykam, measuring 195 feet (59 meters) by 45 feet (14 meters). This branch is dedicated to early American history, featuring bronze and marble statuary including a replica of the Liberty Bell.

A recent addition is a large, three-dimensional mandala by Tibetan sculptor Pema Namdol Thaye, dedicated to world peace. Another branch of Forest Lawn, in the Hollywood Hills, was the final resting place of Buster Keaton, director Fritz Lang and Liberace, among others. All of the park's literature carefully avoids the word "cemetery," preferring to quote founder Huber Eaton's vision of "the greenest, most enchanting park that you ever saw."

Sign of the city

BELOW:
Mann's
Chinese
Theater.

The famous 450-foot (137-meter) long **HOLLYWOOD sign** 🅴 has obviously always been a magnet for curious visitors, but access has been kept as inconvenient as possible via a shrub and cactus-covered hill off Beachwood Drive. Now infra-red detection devices and radar-activated cameras have been installed around it to keep intruders at least 1,500 feet (457 meters) away. An easier alternative for curious explorers is to view it from the relatively unvisited **Hollywood Reservoir**, a favorite jogging spot for locals. It's easy to get lost in the tangled streets but if you head up Ivar north of Franklin, turn left on Dix Street and then right on Holly Drive and again on Deep Dell Place you'll be on Weidlake Drive, which dead-ends at the reservoir itself.

Continuing along Hollywood Boulevard, the building at Hollywood and Cahuenga opened as a bank in 1921 with Charlie Chaplin and Cecil B. de Mille among its customers. Upstairs was the fictitious offices of Raymond Chandler's wise-cracking detective, Philip Marlowe. At 2919 Lankershim Boulevard in the Cahuenga Pass which joins Hollywood to the Valley is the **Campo de Cahuenga**. This little-known spot is where the 1847 peace treaty was signed which ended the

powerful and extremely influential (for California) Mexican–American War. Visitors should alight at the Universal City stop of the Metro line, the same stop as for **Universal Studios** and **Universal City Walk** *(see page187).*

From seedy to starry

Hollywood Boulevard first came to life in 1923 when the fledgling Chamber of Commerce persuaded its shopkeepers to leave their lights on after 9pm, and achieved worldwide fame the following year with the Christmas Parade, its success assured by the willingness of big-name stars to take part.

Millions of dollars'-worth of improvements, renovations and rebuilding are taking place in a no-holds-barred attempt to bring glamor back to a street that had gained a reputation for seediness. Hollywood Chamber of Commerce executive director Leron Gubler says it is more than a renovation. "We are creating an entirely new destination, " he promises, which is a

good thing as about one-third of Los Angeles's annual visitors are said to spend time in Hollywood.

The Hollywood that most visitors come to see begins back in the city at Vine Street, where Judy Garland and James Dean are the first stars along the sidewalk **Walk of Fame Ⓐ**. The Walk of Fame was part of a major restoration of the street back in 1956 when the first batch of stars were cemented into the sidewalk: Burt Lancaster, Ronald Colman, Joanne Woodward and Preston Foster are just some of the stars that were immortalized.

New plaques are installed roughly every month – the star or her/his agent or manager pays several thousand dollars for the privilege – and dates of future ceremonies can be obtained by writing to the Hollywood Historic Trust, 6255 Sunset, Suite 911, LA 90028, which is the same address to which can be sent nominations for future honorees.

Along this part of the walk is beautiful **Pantages Ⓑ**, America's first Art Deco

BELOW: prints from the forecourt of Mann's Chinese Theater; El Capitan theater.

Map on page 156

theater, which opened in 1930 with *Floradora* starring Marion Davies and from 1949 to 1959 hosted the Oscar ceremonies. The lessee of the Pantages promises to present at least 132 weeks per year of Broadway shows in his 3,585-seat theater. There's a DASH bus stop opposite, and others right along Hollywood Boulevard.

Hooray for Hollywood

One side effect of the long-overdue renovation work has been to uncover forgotten artifacts from an earlier era. The gothic, terra cotta face of the 12-story **Equitable Building**, next to the Pantages, has already been uncovered and peeling back layers of plaster and paint from another building has revealed a sign for the old Pig 'n' Whistle café to which Rudolf Valentino, Shirley Temple and other luminaries would adjourn for late-night snacks after attending a movie at the Egyptian Theater next door.

Across from **Frederick's of Hollywood ⓒ** with its museum of famous bras, is the

Information Center (Mon–Sat 9am–5pm, tel: 213/689-8822) located in the Queen Anne style **Janes House**, bought by Herman and Mary Janes in 1903, and the only remaining example of the graceful houses that once lined the boulevard. For 15 years, until 1926, it served as a school and was attended by the children of Cecil B. de Mille, Douglas Fairbanks and Charlie Chaplin, among others.

Take steep Whitley Terrace here up to **Whitley Heights ⓓ**, a community of elegant mansions much favored by movie stars of the Gloria Swanson-era preceding the rise of Beverly Hills. A request by current residents to fence off the community with a gate was rejected. Pedestrian access is easier off **Highland Avenue** just before the big yellow barn (moved here long ago) which served as the original de Mille and Lasky movie studio. After being damaged by a fire in 1997, it has been transformed into the **Hollywood Studio Museum ⓔ** (open weekends), housing movieland's historical artifacts.

BELOW: contemporary café society.

Back down on the ground, and next to Frederick's of Hollywood is the well-known **Larry Edmund's Bookstore ⑤** (Mon–Sat 10am–6pm, tel: 323/463-3273), a peerless source of Hollywoodiana. Two blocks further west is the wonderful 1922 **Egyptian Theater ⑥**, a 1,700-seat replica of a palace in Thebes which in its heyday had a man on the roof dressed as an Egyptian sentry in white robes announcing screening times to the passersby below.

Completely rebuilt internally, the Egyptian houses the **American Cinematheque** which has four-times-daily showings of *Forever Hollywood* with commentary by contemporary stars. The legendary **Musso & Frank Grill ⑪**, across the street, was the favorite hangout of noted writers Nathanael West, William Faulkner and Raymond Chandler

Near Highland Avenue are the veteran **Hollywood Wax Museum ①** (Sun–Thurs 10am–midnight, till 1 am Fri, Sat, tel: 323/462-5991) on the site of the old Monmartre Café where Joan Crawford flirted

and danced. Elvis Presley's star on the Walk of Fame is also here and, across the street, fronting **Ripley's Believe It or Not ①** (daily 10am–10pm, tel: 323/466-6335), those of Marilyn Monroe and Tom Cruise.

Famous footprints

Like its companion the Egyptian two blocks east, incredible **Mann's Chinese Theater ⑯** (just west of Hollywood and Highland) is a famous landmark mostly notable for its forecourt of well-known footprints etched in cement, from Mary Pickford's delicate imprints to the hoofs of Roy Rogers' horse.

Rising above the subway station at Hollywood and Highland is an enormous complex which includes, among other facilities, the **Kodak Theater ⑫**, home to the Academy Awards. The Kodak was purpose-built for the Oscar ceremonies, with a dramatic entrance for equally dramatic arrivals, and a red terrazzo floor underneath the red carpet so that tourists can hold reenactments year-round. The Gov-

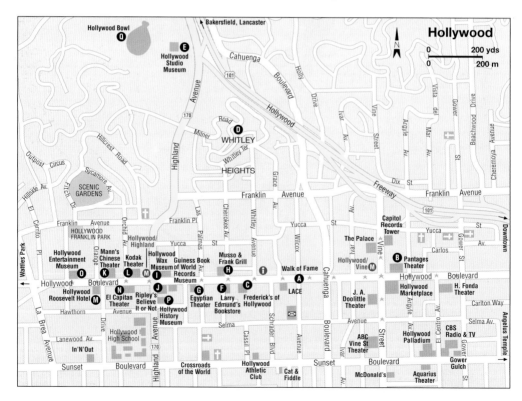

Map on page 156

ernor's Ball is held upstairs in a newly built ballroom designed to evoke the Art Deco look of an ocean liner. When the Kodak is not involved in high-profile Oscar affairs, concerts and theater productions are held on the site.

First Oscars

Across the boulevard is the fabulous Spanish Colonial-meets-Art Deco **Hollywood Roosevelt Hotel** Ⓜ where the first Oscars were held in 1929, and whose mezzanine floor displays a treasure trove of wonderful memorabilia, including the first Technicolor camera used in Disney's *Silly Symphonies* cartoons. Almost adjoining is another theater, the **El Capitan** Ⓝ, which has been restored to its original Art Deco glory by the Walt Disney company.

One block west of the development, the **Hollywood Entertainment Museum** Ⓞ (daily 11am–6pm;. from 10am in summer, closed Wed, tel: 323/465-7900) contains some of the cosmetic and clothing items formerly on show in the Max Factor

BELOW:
Hollywood
Boulevard at
Christmas.

Building. Its "back lot" is filled with artifacts from old movies and exhibits include the bar from the long-running television show *Cheers* and the control room of the *Enterprise* in *Star Trek*.

In the Foley Room, visitors are given props and invited to accompany a short film that is then played back with their own sound effects. A host of interactive attractions include short commentaries from stars like Tina Turner, Orson Wells and Walt Disney, and there are stars' cast-off clothing for sale, a scale model of Hollywood, and a dizzying six-minute film montage shown every half hour. The wonderful old Max Factor building itself is set to open as the **Hollywood History Museum** Ⓟ, offering "exhibits from the film capital's most memorable eras."

Going north along Highland Avenue leads to the **Hollywood Bowl** Ⓠ, an amphitheater with 17,000 seats which stages nightly "Symphonies Under the Stars" concerts all summer. A little-known secret is that some of the Tues-

day, Thursday and Friday morning rehearsals are open to the public (call 323/850-2000 for information). The free **Hollywood Bowl Museum** (closed Monday) specializes in shows featuring film music performed in the Bowl and exhibits range from the music for Disney's *Fantasia* to Mancini's original score for *The Pink Panther*.

Legendary counter

A movieplex and shopping mall stands on the site of the former Schwabs Drugstore at 8024 Sunset, a prime hangout for unemployed stars, directors and other movie types until it eventually closed in 1983. Charlie Chaplin, legend has it, liked to take a place behind the counter and make his own milkshakes.

F. Scott Fitzgerald once suffered a heart attack in Schwabs while buying cigarettes, and composer Harold Arlen said the light coming from the windows as he walked past one day inspired him to write the song that would immortalize Judy Garland: "Somewhere Over the Rainbow."

Guitar Heaven, the Guitar Center and several similar shops are located at Sunset and Gardener. In the cluster is the Sunset Grill, made famous in an Eagles song; nearby is the Garden Street School where Michael Jackson studied. Beyond La Brea the boulevard segues into Laurel Canyon, but it's worth going half a dozen blocks along Franklin to N. Sycamore to take a look at the **Yamashiro** restaurant, a recreated Japanese palace, and its Victorian neighbor, the **Magic Castle 39**.

For 30 years the castle has been a private club where some of the country's top magicians have performed for each other. The biggest magician of all, Harry Houdini, had a terraced estate about a mile up **Laurel Canyon** near Lookout Mountain Road, the spooky, untouched ruins of which are said to be haunted. In the early part of the 20th century a trackless tram ran up the canyon, but today visitors must walk or drive. ❑

Map on page 120

BELOW: seeking out the stars.

The Oscars

The first Oscar ceremony, an intimate affair, took place at the Hotel Roosevelt on May 16, 1929, and shortly after the new millennium moved into the Kodak Theater right across the street in the Hollywood and Highland complex. Despite their worldwide popularity, the awards – voted by 5,722 members of the Academy of Motion Picture Arts and Sciences (roughly one-quarter of them actors) – have never lacked for critics.

In the opinion of Peter H. Brown, who covered Hollywood for both the *Los Angeles Times* and the *Washington Post*, the Oscars were awards made by the establishment to the establishment. It was the way you played the game, he said, that won you an Oscar, not how well you played it. In the early days (according to Brown's book *The Real Oscar*), Louis B. Mayer was a person whose whims could come true; if he didn't want an MGM player nominated, no force could override his veto.

It was Mayer who hosted the Oscars' first dinner meeting and his personal lawyer who drew up the by-laws. Eleven of the founder members were from MGM, the company which took 155 nominations and 33 Oscars in the first decade, twice as many as Warners, three times as many as RKO and four times as many as Columbia. According to Joan Crawford, the committee merely formalized decisions already made by a few key producers. "You'd have to be some ninny to vote against the studio that has your contract or that produces your pictures; your future depends on theirs."

King Vidor, whose movie *The Crowd* should have been nominated when the 300 Academy members first met to vote, and who never won an Oscar despite a successful life-long career in the industry, said: "I'm a great admirer of the Academy. It was nearly ruined by the big studio men who founded it."

In any event, the Academy's members were not known for their guts: in 1936 when the 3,000-member Screen Actors' Guild, the 500-member Writers Guild and the fledgling Directors Guild of America asked their members to boycott that year's ceremony to protest the studios' antagonism to the unions, screenwriter Dudley Nichols and director John Ford were the only nominees who refused to show up for their crack at an award. Seeking favorable publicity, the Academy granted an honorary award to D.W. Griffith, who had been jobless and ignored by the industry for a decade. Many stars didn't come but 1,200 of the movies' middle ranks did show up. The next day, director Frank Capra demanded the Academy end their eight-year battle to stall unionism in what was by now the US's fourth largest industry.

A study in 1947 showed that an Oscar for Best Picture added $2 million to the box office take. Humphrey Bogart once suggested that all five Oscar nominees should recite Hamlet's "To be or not to be" soliloquy before an audience of voters, presumably as a test of actorly skills which, of course, the existing selection process lacks.

The New York film critics are sometimes felt to judge the stars' acting ability more fairly than the Academy. The New York group, as well as the Los Angeles critics, the Foreign Press Association (with their Golden Globes) and the National Board of Review all give their awards before the Oscars, for which their choices often become predictions. ❑

RIGHT: Michael Douglas and Cher share the acting awards for 1988.

Map
on page
120

THE LA SEASHORE

*Malibu, Santa Monica, Venice Beach
and Muscle Beach – this is where Hollywood
meets the sand and the sea*

Where Sunset Boulevard meets the Pacific Coast Highway is only around a mile from the fabulous **Getty Villa** ⓴. The villa, modeled on a 1st-century Italian country house, is the former home of many of the treasures collected by J.Paul Getty which have since moved to the Getty Center *(see page 148)*. When the villa reopens after extensive interior renovations, it will, fittingly enough, house more than 50,000 objects, ranged thematically, which have been extracted from the Antiquities Collection.

A couple of miles north of Sunset, rugged **Topanga Canyon Boulevard** leads off the Pacific Coast HIghway (often abbreviated as PCH) into the Santa Monica Mountains and down the other side into the **San Fernando Valley**, 10 miles (16 km) in all. Apart from the post office and some small shops at about the midway point, there is no place to pass on this two-lane highway. Various side roads – mostly dead-ends – trickle off the boulevard but most of the canyon is undeveloped, thickly forested oak and chaparral sweeping down the rocky hillsides from the vast and lovely **Topanga State Park** (entrance from Entrada), with its extensive network of hiking and riding trails.

Dramatic drive

About half a mile before the boulevard reaches the Valley, a left turn can be made along Mulholland Highway which offers a sinuously dramatic two-hour drive back towards the coast. Off US 101 is Las Virgenes Road which passes through Malibu Canyon. This area has been the scene of such movies as *Planet of the Apes* (1968) the supposedly Welsh *How Green Was My Valley* (1941), lots of Tarzan films, and the setting for the *M*A*S*H* television series.

Back on Mulholland is the **Paramount Ranch** where the series *Dr. Quinn, Medicine Woman* was shot and where on summer nights there are occasional screenings of silent movies. Farther along are the Peter Strauss Ranch with a multitude of shady picnic spots and a famous biker hangout, the Rock Store, serving burgers and chicken. The Kanan Dune Road, a main highway, is subject to landslides and flooding and thus occasionally closed.

The beach-dotted Malibu coastline stretches for miles, beginning past Topanga Canyon and ending roughly where Mulholland Highway meets PCH. Just north of the little **Malibu Pier** ⓴ is the historic **Adamson House**, built in 1927 as a wedding gift by her new husband for Rhoda May, the former Michigan schoolteacher whose first husband Frederick Rindge had founded Malibu 40 years before.

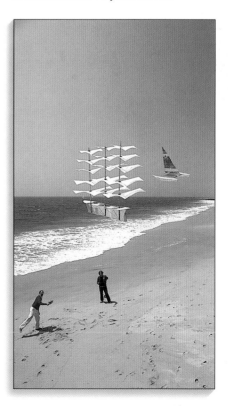

PRECEDING PAGES: leaving the city and heading for Santa Monica. **LEFT:** life's a ball if you live near the beach. **RIGHT:** Venice.

One year after Rindge's death in 1905, May built a 20-mile (32-km) railroad on the property and thus for 20 years thwarted plans by the Southern Pacific to penetrate the estate. Finally after a succession of legal battles, the coastal highway was built and the property opened up to the outside world. The Adamson House, covered with tiles from the Rindges' Malibu Pottery (it burned down in 1902) is as attractive outside as inside. This is fortunate because the interior, with its little museum packed with photographs of the early Malibu community, is open only two days of the week. There's a small fee, and a movie is shown depicting Malibu's history.

Malibu gold

Even when the house is closed you can drive or walk up the lane (or even off the beach) and admire the tiled terrace, the lovely fountains, bottle-glass windows and well-kept gardens. The adjacent lagoon is a preserved wetland and home to ducks, herons and pelicans.

Frederick Rindge paid only $10 per acre for the vast area he bought back in 1887 (oceanfront lots now cost at least $50,000 per foot) and a display in the museum reveals that the true Malibu gold is real estate: crooner Bing Crosby's house cost him just $8,700 in 1931 and was bought for almost $2 million by Robert Redford half a century later.

Visible from the highway is the castle-like **Serra Retreat** in the mountains, a 50-room mansion that May was still building when she died in 1942. It now belongs to the Franciscan Order.

Dozens of stars live hidden away in Malibu, some of them along the well-guarded **Malibu Beach Colony** at the junction of PCH and Webb Way, but the only place they're likely to be seen in public is the **Colony Mall** shopping center about a mile to the north of the pier. More interesting is the **Malibu Country Mart**, a collection of little shops, cafés and a movie theater centered around a kids' playground about halfway between the pier and the mall.

BELOW: the Getty Villa is based on a 1st-century Italian country house.

Map on page 120

Broad Beach, like so much of the Malibu coastline, is private but only down to the mean high-tide line. Which means that as long as you stay on wet sand you have every right to be there. Maybe you'll spot a superstar jogging. Easily-missed access to the beach is in the 3100 and 3200 block of Broad Beach Road. **Zuma beach**, **Will Rogers beach** and **Pt Dume state beach** are public but understandably get pretty crowded. Riptides sometimes make the beaches unsafe for swimming, but you can check conditions by calling the lifeguards: tel: 310/457-9701.

Beaches and more beaches

Beaches north of Malibu include **Leo Carrillo** (where Mulholland Highway meets PCH), which being a state rather than a county beach, allows both camping and alcohol. The water is clean (but chilly). Three delightful, but easily missed "pocket beaches" are **El Pescador**, **La Piedra** and **El Matador**, the last of which is the most exciting. All are awkward to reach down winding paths from miniature parking lots, but each is isolated, rugged and romantic.

The stretch of PCH between Malibu and Topanga Canyon to the south has been closed scores of times in recent winters due to fires, flooding, high seas and/or mudslides but most of the time it is an attractive drive. The highway continues south past several public beaches, flanked (mainly at the northern end) by enormous mansions alongside the shore which were mostly built by moviedom's former elite.

The grandest estate, at 415 Pacific Coast Highway, was the 118-room compound designed by William Randolph Hearst's favorite architect Julia Morgan for the newspaper tycoon and his paramour Marion Davies. In 1945 the house was sold for $600,000 to Joseph Drown, owner of the Bel Air Hotel, who turned it into a beach hotel and club. Only the lavish servants' quarters survive today as a private club, the adjoining paddle tennis court sitting on the site of the former Hollywood Swimming Club where the seminal surfer Duke

BELOW: the exclusive Malibu Beach Colony.

Kahanamoka worked out alongside world champion swimmer Johnny Weissmuller.

In those days, before the breakwater extended the beach, the sea came to within 50 feet (15 meters) of most of the homes. It was another famous architect, Richard Neutra, who created Mae West's home at number 514.

Twentieth Century Fox boss Darryl Zanuck lived at 546 PCH; Harry Warner of Warner Brothers lived at 607, later to be occupied by Paramount Pictures' founder Jesse Lasky; and the lavish villa at 625, designed by MGM art director Cedric Gibbons for Louis B. Mayer, became a trysting place for Marilyn Monroe and President John F. Kennedy when it was the home of actor Peter Lawford. During the 1960 Democratic convention held in Los Angeles, it served JFK as the western White House.

Santa Monica

The "Bay City," setting of many of Raymond Chandler's detective novels, is where Wilshire and Sunset boulevards meet the ocean, albeit a couple of miles apart. Busy **Santa Monica** ㊷ is the largest coastal town in the 100-mile (160-km) stretch between Oxnard and Long Beach. Once it took a full day's stagecoach ride to get here from downtown LA, but when the freeway opened in 1966 the trip was cut to half an hour (depending on traffic). Recently, Santa Monica has undergone something of a renaissance, having been "discovered" as the perfect site by Hollywood types who have a preference for conducting their business beside the seaside.

The California Incline ascends from the Pacific Coast Highway up the cliffs to eucalyptus-lined **Palisades Park** just north of Wilshire Boulevard where the **Fairmont Miramar Hotel** ㊸ now sits in spacious grounds, the enormous fig tree outside the lobby having been planted by a member of the family more than a century ago. After arriving in the US in 1924, Greta Garbo spent the next three years living at the Miramar. The hotel was once the home of silver tycoon John P. Jones, a Nevada

BELOW: Santa Monica was the "Bay City" of many of Raymond Chandler's mysteries.

Map on page 120

senator who, with his partner Col. Robert Baker founded Santa Monica in 1892, dedicating Palisades Park to the city "forever." Santa Monica is one of those all-too-rare walker's towns, offering the opportunity to admire the surroundings at a leisurely pace. Note the two stylish Art Deco hotels: the Georgian and the Shangri La across from the park. Clark Gable was a regular at the Georgian's basement speakeasy.

Adjoining an office and apartment complex called **Champagne Towers** – once owned by bandleader Lawrence Welk, whose national TV program was broadcast for years from the now-defunct Aragon ballroom in nearby Venice – the General Telephone Building was the site of a long-running television series, *Marcus Welby M.D.* The nearby **Wilshire Palisades Building** won an award for its architects in 1960, and the distinctive **Queen Anne house** at 1333 Ocean Avenue was once owned by Gussie Moran, a tennis star who was also well known for her frilly undergarments. (A similar house, on Colorado Avenue, houses **Angels Attic Museum**, Thurs–Sun, 12:30–4:30pm, tel: 310/394-8331, filled with antique toys and dolls.)

Solar-powered

Farther south is the delightful century-old **Santa Monica Pier** ㊹ with restaurants, an amusement park containing the world's only solar-powered ferris wheel, and a famous carousel (closed Mon) that appeared in *The Sting*. There are concerts on the pier every Sunday in spring, and dancing once a week in summer. But your first stop might well be to pick up maps and guides from the **Visitor Center** (tel: 310/393-7593) where Ocean Avenue meets Santa Monica Boulevard. There's a rare **Camera Obscura** (tel: 310/458-8644) with free admission via the Senior Recreational Center.

Santa Monica authorities have a predilection for art on the beach. In recent years this has taken the form of a giant roller that marked out a mini cityscape in the sand, and several examples of unconventional sculpture. South of the pier are two huge *Singing Chairs* by sculptor Douglas Hollis, powered by aluminum tubes which turn the breeze into music (of a particular sort).

Three blocks inland from the information kiosk is the town's busiest center, the spacious **Third Street Promenade** ㊺, an always-crowded pedestrian street with strolling musicians and entertainers giving impromptu performances. It leads on to sparkling **Santa Monica Place**, an attractive, upscale mall designed by the internationally acclaimed architect Frank Gehry with major department stores, and scores of eating places and shops. The adjoining five-story parking lot permits three hours of free parking before 5pm. On Wednesday and Saturday mornings, the street is taken over by a **farmers' market**

Undiscovered by many visitors is trendy **Montana Avenue**, a few blocks above Wilshire, which has become a popular hang-out for local actors with its variety of little stores, sidewalk cafés, a movie theater and a library.

Separated from the rest of town by the freeway, Santa Monica's **Main Street** is several blocks to the south and is fre-

quented more by locals than visitors. Here, the **Heritage Museum** ⓐ in an 1894 house at 2612 Main Street is filled with period items, and stages such long-lasting shows as the one devoted to the Harvey Girls (the waitresses who served in the chain of restaurants along the route of the Santa Fe Railway). And maybe you'll never see your star along Hollywood's Walk of Fame, but for a fee, the Heritage Museum will sand-blast your name onto a brick.

Approximately 30 of the town's art galleries, along with its **Museum of Art** (closed Mon and Tues, tel: 310/586-6488) have moved about a mile inland to attractive **Bergamot Station** (closed Mon, tel: 310/829-5854), a large warehouse complex and railroad junction. The name *bergamot* comes from flowering plants that flourished here long ago.

Venice

South of Santa Monica Pier, a walkway and bicycle path adjoins the beach all the way down to Venice, and buses run up and down Ocean Avenue. The closer you get to **Venice** ⓐ, the odder the ambiance. An early favorite with Charlie Chaplin, the boardwalk is today jammed almost around the clock with assorted characters who appear to be auditioning for some unexplained contemporary epic: rainbow-haired punks, a guitar-bearing roller blader in robe and turban, lunatic dreamers, outrageous conmen, barely dressed cyclists, psychics, chain-saw jugglers and the bicep-bound boasters of legendary **Muscle Beach** (tel: 310/458-8301).

There are sidewalk cafés at which it's a relief to rest and watch all this activity, which includes chess games with giant-sized pieces on a huge board. One of the beach's oldest traditions is the weekend gatherings of the Drum Circle, a shifting group of percussionists from all over the region who present a non-stop wall of sound that is not always fully appreciated by the neighbors.

There is another, less-explored Venice a few blocks to the east. After you have

BELOW: Venice street scene.

Map on page 120

noted **St Mark's**, the bar/restaurant/dance-hall on **Windward Avenue**, whose colonnaded arches are meant to evoke visions of St Mark's Square in Venice's Italian namesake, walk east to the post office which earlier in the 20th century was where most of the canals met. Many of these canals are now paved over, but a few blocks to the south is what remains of the watery network, a charmingly tranquil area of deep canals lined with houses in a myriad of styles, mostly with gardens full of flowers that only grow in the hot sunshine.

Ducks and geese line the walkways which, twice a year, most of the 1,200 residents gather to clean up, at the same time as painting the bridges.

Grand schemes

When tobacco magnate Abbott Kinney invested millions in creating his Venice from what was 160 acres (65 hectares) of worthless marshland at the turn of the 20th century, he lined the canals with Japanese lanterns, imported gondolas from Italy, encircled the project with a miniature railroad and sold 592 housing lots. Visitors who paid 25¢ to take the new railroad from downtown Los Angeles ended a busy day on the (now-abandoned) pier watching an armored trumpeter serenade the sunset from a replica of Juan Cabrillo's medieval flagship before retiring for the night in St Mark's Hotel, modeled after the Doge's Palace. Venice became Southern California's major playground, often luring as many as 30,000 visitors – one-tenth of the city's then population – on weekends.

Despite Kinney's ambitious plans, which included hiring Sarah Bernhardt and the Chicago Symphony Orchestra for his 3,500-seat auditorium, and staging beauty contests and a Grand Prix motor race, he was obliged to scale down the attractions towards more plebeian audiences; from then on the project gradually deteriorated.

The collapse of Kinney's dream was speeded first by the discovery of oil (which resulted in 163 wells probing the area by 1931) and secondly by the shortage of

BELOW: near Muscle Beach.

fresh water. Like so many neighboring communities, Venice was obliged to come under the aegis of Los Angeles if it wanted to be sure of a regular water supply. With incorporation came a preference for paved roads over canals.

In any case, Kinney's circulation system for what was originally 16 miles (26 km) of canals with seawater pulsing through 30-inch (76-cm) pipes from every fresh tide, proved unworkable, and the canals themselves became sand-clogged and stagnant. The dream was gone.

A couple of decades ago, an overhaul of the area was completed, with the canals dredged and refilled, the adjoining paths repaired and some of the bridges rebuilt. Kinney's name and dream was memorialized in **Abbott Kinney Boulevard** – connecting Main Street with Marina del Rey – a street which has enticing little cafés, restaurants and shops.

Some of the city's most interesting murals can be seen in the streets around here – Christina Schlesinger's *Marc Cha-gall Comes to Venice Beach* at 801 Ocean Front Walk, and farther down, Emily Winters' *Endangered Species* outside the headquarters of SPARC, an organization which sponsors such public art. SPARC's big triumph is *The Great Wall of Los Angeles* covering half a mile beside the Los Angeles River in Van Nuys, on which 400 people worked between 1976 and 1983.

Phony but charming

South of Venice, before Los Angeles airport, is a sea-filled complex which on the map is shaped like the stern of a gondola. This is **Marina del Rey ㊽**, a marina and condo complex whose chief attraction for visitors is **Fisherman's Village** (the "lighthouse" is a fast food stand) with a multitude of restaurants for lunch. Although entirely phony, Fisherman's Village has considerable charm.

These range from the reasonably-priced Mexican fare to Shanghai Red's, which has all the appealing ambiance of a century-old inn but has actually been there for only

BELOW: landing at LAX, LA's international airport.

Map
on page
120

a few decades, or since the marina began. Growing in popularity here is "moonlight kayaking," group expeditions into the bay with illuminated paddles, followed by dinner at a nearby café. At the end of Basin D is a shallow-water family beach known, appropriately, as **"Mother's Beach."**

The concrete-lined **Ballona Creek** that separates the marina from **Playa del Rey** was badly polluted until recently; on another note, preservationists seem to finally be winning the battle of the Ballona Wetlands to save wild birds from the ravages of the developers.

MGM's backlots once overlooked the 9½-mile (15 km) creek, along which "Indians" paddled in canoes, and where spectators watched the skyhigh flames from "the burning of Atlanta" during the filming of *Gone With the Wind.*

Los Angeles airport

BELOW:
sunset on the
SoCal coast.

Hundreds of tons of sandbags have been dumped in the sea off broad, sandy **Dockweiler State Beach** to provide what's claimed to be North America's first artificial surfing reef. Dockwell is just south of thundering **Los Angeles International Airport (LAX)**, one of the busiest airports in the United States. (It also has traffic-filled freeways, so leave plenty of time if catching a plane.) Behind the south end of Dockweiler is **El Segundo ㊾**; nearby is **Inglewood**, home of Hollywood Park and the Forum, LA's most prestigious sports-entertainment complex. On the El Segundo Dunes, buckwheat has been planted to preserve the endangered blue butterfly native to the area.

Beyond El Segundo are three successive beach towns: **Manhattan ㊿**, **Hermosa ㊾** and **Redondo ㊾**. There's not a great deal to choose between them apart from their rivalry about which offers the best surfing. (Hermosa is the most vociferous claimant). All the beaches have piers, and it's well worth strolling to the end of any one of them. Surrounded by water and caressed by sea-breezes, it's easy to understand why so many people want to live near the ocean while remaining close to the city.   ❑

Map
on page
120

ANAHEIM

*With its wealth of restaurants, hotels and theme parks,
including the recent Disney's California Adventure,
Anaheim pulls in the crowds*

Anaheim's biggest attraction is its collection of amusement parks and similar attractions of which Disneyland is by far the best known. MTA bus 460 runs down to Disneyland but if you have a car (and limited time) you could just squeeze Disneyland and a visit to the Crystal Cathedral at Garden Grove into the same day and still manage to have dinner while watching the jousting at Medieval Times.

It would need another excursion to explore Knott's Berry Farm (almost as big as Disneyland), but you could combine that with a visit to the Movieland Wax Museum or one of the fun attractions at nearby Irvine such as **Lion Country Safari** or **Irvine Meadows**, an amphitheater that stages big-name entertainment.

Anaheim overnight

Another alternative, obviously, is to stay in the Anaheim area overnight. Disneyland itself has some fairly pricey if amusing hotels (with thousands of rooms) conveniently located on the grounds, but there are cheaper motels on West and Ball roads and the branches of most major hotel chains operate free shuttle buses to the park. The tourist board claims that there are 18,000 hotel rooms within walking distance of Disneyland but even with a car you'll probably do a lot of walking, so come prepared.

In fact, so gung-ho is Anaheim in making the most of itself − employing high-level marketing firms to make sure the world knows of its attractions; offering transporation links from Anaheim to Universal Studios − that the City of Los Angeles is starting to run scared.

Downtown LA, whose staple income is the lucrative convention trade, is not sure it can compete with the "new-look" and in many ways more convenient Anaheim, and is itself looking for ways to lure trade fairs and conventions away from the suburbs and back to the city. It will be interesting to see how the tug-of-war develops.

The most "grown-up" of Anaheim's attractions is the architecturally fascinating **Crystal Cathedral** ❸ (12141 Lewis Street, Garden Grove, visitors welcome Mon–Sat at 9:30 and 11am, tel: 714/544-5679). The headquarters of evangelist and preacher Robert Schuller, the cathedral is constructed from a labyrinth of steel trusses covered with more than 10,000 panes of shimmering glass *(see photograph on page 112)*.

Designed in 1980 by Philip Johnson, the body of the building is in the shape of a star. The cathedral's interior is as awesome as its facade, containing one of the

**PRECEDING
PAGES:**
dressed
to thrill.
LEFT:
Mr Michael
Mouse.
RIGHT:
kidding around.

largest pipe organs in the world. During some of the balmier Sunday morning services, the huge glass doors are opened so that the drive-in congregation in their cars outside can have an unobstructed view.

Disneyland ❺ (daily till late, tel: 714/220-5200; www.disneyland.com) was first opened in 1955 inspired, Walt Disney once said, by his realization that he didn't know a safe and friendly park where he could take his family to have fun together. Disneyland and TV grew up together after loans from ABC-TV got the amusement park off the ground:

Disney repaid the favor by producing a weekly show that was not only an ongoing commercial for the fledgling park, but one that also brought the television network vast audiences. In keeping with the folksy theme, **Tom Sawyer Island** – the only section of the park designed by Walt himself – evokes memories of Hannibal, Missouri, which was near his birthplace, as well as being the small-town home of author Mark Twain.

Mickey's world

One of Disney's early designers, John Hench, referred to Walt's knack for putting "little touches of humanity" into everything he did. Hench said that Mickey Mouse's appeal has something to do with his body shape – all circles, all-round, harmless and non-threatening. In fact, because of a height restriction – you can't have Mickey towering too much over his fans – most of the besuited mouse persons in Disneyland are girls.

What tourists never get to see is the immensely intricate backstage operation that keeps the park operating so smoothly. If visitors were somehow to sneak in just before opening time, they might spot divers emerging from one of the delightful **Magic Kingdom**'s ponds, pools and rivers, having made their nightly inspection of the lifelike underwater creatures that add so much authenticity to the various boat and submarine rides. The divers find lost or abandoned objects, too: cameras, keys, shoes and even crutches.

BELOW: Disney's California Adventure – Hollywood section.

Map
on page
120

Originally, visitors paid for each ride. Then the park tried issuing ticket books with different-value rides, but that resulted in the lesser attractions getting disproportionate attention. Eventually the single, all-in admission price was introduced that still prevails. Walt, living for long periods at a time in a private apartment above the Fire Station on Main Street, was always wandering around trying to devise better ways of crowd control, a policy that's still followed. Each Disneyland day now closes with a piece of fiber optic wizardry called **High Magic**, a spectacular journey which replaced the aeons-old Main Street Electrical Parade.

Early arrival advised

There's no successful way to avoid the crowds and the lengthy line-ups at Disneyland, especially in summertime. Obviously, it helps to get there as soon as the place opens (Disneyland's **Main Street** opens at 8:30am, half an hour before the rest of the park) and head straight for the most popular rides. To avoid backtracking, it's probably wise to cover the park logically, one "land" at a time. As at least two of the most popular rides – Star Tours and Space Mountain, neither for the faint-hearted – are both in **Tomorrowland** (now refreshed and improved, utilizing all the best new technology money can buy), it might be an idea to position yourself at the top of Main Street.

Main Street's premature opening (to encourage you to take your time browsing in the souvenir shops) is also helpful if you want to get information and maps (found in **City Hall**), exchange foreign currency or get credit card advances, rent a camera or camcorder, hire wheels for the baby or for grandma (just inside the main entrance), stash your surplus items in a locker (adjoining Disney Clothiers), and attend to your infant (Baby Center, near the **Magic Castle**).

Fantasyland might well be the kids' favorite "land," but some of its rides such as Peter Pan's Flight and Snow White's

Scary Adventure seem to be aimed as much at adults as at children. How much time you have available will pretty much decide the shape of your itinerary.

Whatever happens, try not to miss **New Orleans Square** with its nearby Pirates of the Caribbean and **Haunted Mansion,** also recently upgraded. **Adventureland** is fun, with its eclectic mixture of architectural styles from Mexican to what one writer described as "Beverly Hills French." The hokey but still really amusing **Big Thunder Mountain Railroad**, the **Enchanted Tiki Room** (talking birds and flowers) and **Mark Twain Steamboat** are all good fun, and the night-time spectacular **Fantasmic** is such a sensation that crowds start jostling for good viewpoints two hours' before the show starts. Also good for visitors of all ages is the **Indiana Jones Adventure**: riders board decrepit jeeps after the Jungle Cruise and head through doors into a creepy world of fake bats, spiders, rats and snakes.

There's no sign stating "the original," but Disneyland – as opposed to Disney World in Florida or Disneyland, Paris – is the official home of his characters. Over the years, the influence of these characters has spread around the globe, and while the world has changed dramatically, they have continued to bring pleasure and familiarity. But that doesn't mean Walt's first-born has stagnated – Disney's team has been careful not only to maintain its pristine operation, but also to introduce new major attractions every five years. Now, they have expanded with the most ambitious program since the original began in 1955.

A California adventure

The culmination of a $1.4 billion program is the creation of the **Disneyland Resort,** which includes not only the improvements to the Magic Kingdom and the existing hotels but also **Disney's California Adventure** ⑤⑤, a 55-acre (22-hectare) theme park with a 750-room luxury hotel and a huge shopping, dining

BELOW: finishing the day with a bang.

Map on page 120

and entertainment center. Although its attractions are undeniable, Californians themselves have been underwhelmed by this venture, probably because they have the real thing on their doorstep. Still, most visitors are from out of state, and it seems hard for Disney to put a foot wrong.

Entering under a replica of the Golden Gate Bridge, California Adventure (which charges a separate admission fee) is comprised of three themed "lands" focusing on the beach, Hollywood movie-making and the state's natural wonders.

The **Hollywood Pictures Backlot** section explains how certain special effects are achieved and is celebrated with the **Muppet Vision 3D**, which has been a hit at Disney/MGM Studios in Florida; also featured is the ride **Superstar Limo**, plus a fun interactive animation studio and the **Hyperion Theater** hosting live shows.

Paradise Pier, representing California beach culture, has a Disney twist. A huge orange peels away to reveal a thrill ride,

while the giant rollercoaster (the fastest in either park) races around a silhouette of Mickey Mouse's head. **The Golden State** celebrates the early jet-test pilot days with **Condor Flats,** and includes a simulation thrill ride that takes you gliding over California landmarks as if riding a hang glider.

Pacific Wharf is where to find the shops and restaurants. Straddling Disneyland and Disney's California Adventure is **Downtown Disney** (no charge) which features plenty of dining, shopping, and entertainment options, including a House of Blues, Rainforest Cafe, Wolfgang Puck's and a huge 16-screen cinema. The **Grand Californian Hotel** has been touted as a rival to the most luxurious of Orange County hotels, and has its own entrance to the California Adventure.

Beyond Disneyland

Another attraction in Anaheim, situated on Beach Boulevard, is **Adventure City** (daily in summer, weekends off-season, tel:

BELOW: Laurel, Hardy, and the Movieland Wax Museum.

714/236-9300, whose attractions include 17 rides and a petting farm. In nearby Buena Park is **Knott's Berry Farm** ⑳ (daily 10am–6pm, later in summer, tel: 714/220-5220), a recreated 19th-century gold town. The theme park grew out of a roadside snack bar operated by farmer Walter Knotts and his wife Cordelia. The Knotts' reputation for tasty chicken dinners and thick slabs of boysenberry pie (served on the couple's wedding china) spread far and wide.

Individual attention

Knott's Berry Farm actually predates its Disney rival by a few years, but is in many ways just as interesting and a little funkier. The characters are more primitive than high-tech and the staff charm tourists with individual attention.

At the town hall, for example, a "horse thief" will chat with strangers, and visitors to the jail are always amazed to have an unseen jailer call them by their first name and make remarks about what

they look like or are wearing. Or at one of the arcades, a costumed gunslinger will challenge some passer-by to confront him in what usually turns out to be a humiliating showdown.

Old West Ghost Town offers the opportunity to pan for gold, a stagecoach ride, a watery log ride and stunt and vaudeville shows in a section of the park where the lines are often pretty short. In the contemporary side of the park, various other theme areas include the Roaring '20s and a colorful tribute to Southern California beach culture, with its surf-inspired dual roller coaster called the Windjammer. Kids love the cartoon-themed Camp Snoopy with its miniature train and other rides, and the Kingdom of the Dinosaurs, an indoor trip through Earth's prehistoric era.

One of Knotts' most intriguing attractions is **Mystery Lodge**, what it terms "a multi-sensory journey deep into the Native North American West." In a cave set among totem poles and waterfalls, visitors' imaginations are challenged by the venerable Old Storyteller.

Knotts, too, has been expanding and to celebrate its 80th birthday added a huge water adventure park, **Soak City USA**, immediately adjoining the main park.

California corny

And speaking of corny, what could be sillier than paying to eat a meal with your bare hands in a fake castle, bowing to a fake king and queen and egging on some pretend-knights in a battle whose outcome is already fixed? Well, hundreds of enthusiastic customers do it every night and enjoy themselves at **Medieval Times** (tel: 714/523-1100) on Beach Boulevard. What the heck, you have to eat dinner somewhere.

In the same block is another family-style dinner attraction, **Wild Bill's Extravaganza** (tel: 714/522-4611) and on Katella Avenue is **The Sun Theatre** (tel: 714/712-2700) which features Country and Western performers. ❑

● *Other attractions in Orange County are listed in the chapter starting on page 275.*

Map on page 120

LEFT: Pluto and friend. **RIGHT:** the slippery slope at Knott's Berry Farm.

Map on page 186

SAN FERNANDO AND SAN GABRIEL VALLEYS

The valleys of Los Angeles County
contain historic homes, secluded gardens,
superior shopping malls, and a world-class movie studio

All of the vague and amorphous references to the valleys and canyons of the area around Los Angeles merit some clarification. Of the three main valleys, the smallest is **Santa Clarita Valley**, known for its abundance of produce stands and the looming presence of the Six Flags Magic Mountain amusement park; next is **San Gabriel Valley**, which stretches through Pasadena and Monterey Park toward Riverside and San Bernardino. But the star of the three is the dry, vast and sprawling San Fernando Valley, and it is this one to which people are referring when they simply say "The Valley."

Various passes and canyons are byways to and from the Valley: **Sepulveda Pass** connects it to West Los Angeles via the San Diego Freeway; the **Cahuenga Pass** cuts through to Hollywood. **Laurel Canyon** connects Studio City and West Hollywood, and **Coldwater Canyon** connects Sherman Oaks to Beverly Hills. The last of the large canyons, **Topanga** and **Malibu**, provide rustic, dramatic routes from the Valley to the ocean.

San Fernando Valley

Far from being a typical glitzy tourist attraction, the **San Fernando Valley ❶** possesses a low profile – or did until it was devastated by the 1994 Northridge earthquake whose 6.6 magnitude inflicted $2 billion of damage and destroyed 50,000 homes. Before that, many of LA's long-time residents knew almost nothing of the Valley – save that it's the area northwest of LA which floods after heavy rain and bakes in a dry, desert heat layered in smog in the summer. It was always that place they drove through on their way north to ski. In contrast to neighboring areas, the Valley is a staggeringly flat expanse of land about 24 miles (39 km) wide and 12 miles

(19 km) north to south, covering an acreage as large as Chicago. It is bounded by the Ventura county line on the west, the San Gabriel Mountains on the north, the Verdugo Mountains on the east and the Santa Monica Mountains and Hollywood Hills on the south. Beginning in the 1990s, a well-funded campaign began for the Valley to secede from the city of Los Angeles, although it is expected that the battle will continue for years.

The west and south sides are the more affluent, with communities like Encino and Tarzana boasting average incomes almost double the LA average. Tarzana was named after the jungle character in the novels of

PRECEDING PAGES: Huntington Gardens in Pasadena, San Gabriel Valley. **LEFT:** welcome to LA County. **RIGHT:** Galleria shopping in Sherman Oaks, San Fernando Valley.

Edgar Rice Burroughs, whose estate covered much of the area in 1919, and Encino is the home of the Michael Jackson family and a handful of sports stars. Heavy industry is mostly concentrated in the northern area, around Pacoima and Sylmar. The neighborhood of San Fernando, its population now predominantly Latino, has retained much of its low-key atmosphere.

Perfect grid

Were it a city unto itself, the Valley would be the fifth largest in the country, topped only by New York, Chicago, Houston and, of course, Los Angeles. The Valley is not a city in itself, but two of its communities – **Burbank ❷** and Glendale – are. All the other areas are neighborhoods within the City of Los Angeles, and between them compose nearly one-third of LA's population. By annexing the Valley in 1915, Los Angeles added a staggering 177 sq. miles (458 sq. km) to its existing 108, and all of that has systematically filled up with a perfect grid of uniform single-family homes, bungalows and shopping centers.

The valley more or less begins with **Griffith Park** *(see page 151)*, the immense and attraction-filled preserve that begins at Los Feliz Boulevard and extends all the way to the Ventura Freeway.

Glendale ❸ has earned some recent fame for its astonishingly eclectic mix of cuisines – over a dozen – to be found in the cafés and restaurants in two blocks along Brand Avenue between Lexington Drive and Wilson Avenue. Glendale's 100-acre (40-hectare) **Grand Central Business Center** sits on the site of the former airport, where celebrities held all-night farewell parties for their friends undertaking the 16-hour flight to New York.

The glorious **Brand Library and Art Center** (closed Mon, Wed, Sun, tel: 818/548-2051) houses the art and music section of the city's public library in a Moorish-style mansion. Inspired by the East Indian Pavilion at the Chicago World's Fair, it was built in 1904 by Leslie C. Brand; the landscaped grounds are a perfect spot for picnics. Used as the locale for TV shows and movies, the mansion with its Tiffany glass windows and silken wall coverings has been described by one writer as "a *nouveau* Taj Mahal."

Before leaving Glendale, you might want to check out an interesting home called **The Doctor's House** (it was occupied by four of them in succession), with its Victorian parlor and such quaint artifacts as an Edison Home Phonograph. Preserved by the local historical society, it had to be

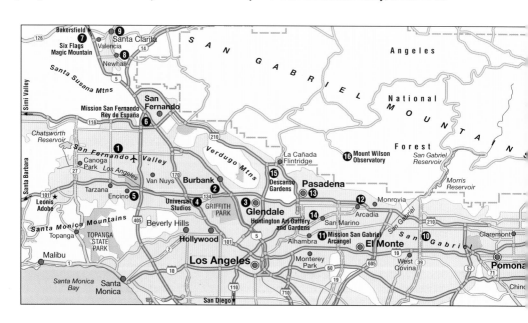

Map
on page
186

chopped in half to be moved from its original location to Mountain Street in Brand Park, where it was reassembled.

The San Fernando Valley is home to most of Los Angeles' working TV and movie studios. In just a short space you can come across the **Walt Disney Studios** and **CBS Studio Center**, but neither are open to the public. **Warners Bros. Studios**, where *ER* and *Friends* are made, offers a 2-hour tour for grown-ups (no kids allowed), while the NBC **Studio Tour** is a fairly serious 90-minute look at the rigors involved in putting together a television show. The grandaddy of all tours, though, is the one hosted by **Universal Studios** ❹.

Craziest things in the world

"Just think of what this would mean to see the inside workings of the biggest moving picture plant in the whole, wide world," wrote founder Carl Laemmle in a 1915 ad when Universal first opened. "A whole city where everybody is engaged in the making of motion pictures; a fairyland where the craziest things in the world happen!"

Universal (open daily 8am–7pm, in winter 9am–7pm, tel: 818/622-3801) offers conducted tours past working film sets while touring what is in effect an amusement park. Many of its young guides

regard the job as the first phase in what they hope will be a successful acting career. An entertaining, 2-hour tram ride visits a gargantuan King Kong, the giant mechanical shark from *Jaws* and – through the perils of a collapsing bridge – avalanches, a flash flood, earthquakes and the parting of the Red Sea.

A recent addition is the mind-blowing Terminator 2: 3D based on the movie by James Cameron, who also directed *Titanic*. Other highlights include Jurassic Park, assembled with the aid of Steven Spielberg's notes and models for the movie; the fiery "Backdraft" and a chance to beam aboard the *Starship Enterprise*.

You can also catch a glimpse of numerous outdoor sets, including the creepy Bates mansion from *Psycho* and the facades from *Back to the Future*, a movie which has now spawned an amusement ride of its own. Shooting Star Ranch, a sprawling restaurant beside the main gate, offers entertainment for the family while they eat.

Universal CityWalk, a glittery shopping-restaurant mall with one-of-a-kind shops, a neon art museum, street performers and a multi-screen cinema, opened here in 1993 (*see photo on page 151*) and has recently been enlarged. City Walk has been

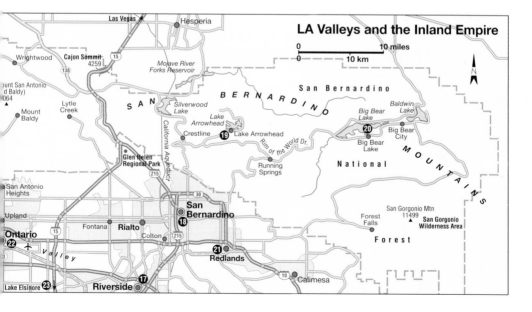

described by some observers as a proto-type of the kind of street that could revitalize dying city centers, as it is, in the common parlance, a "controlled environment." Othe people, while deploring its artificiality, concede that its safety compensates for its lack of soul. Either way, it's worth making the trip, open between 11am and 11pm every day. Admission is free but there is a fee for parking; budget-conscious visitors can take a bus or the Metro Rail to Universal City and take a studio tram from there. There is also a bus from Anaheim to Universal City, tel: 800/UNIVERSAL, free with the purchase of a full-priced admission ticket to the studios.

Mall country

Some of LA's major restaurants have branched out into the Valley, bringing what's been called "310 food" to the 818 area code. More than anything, this is mall country. "You eat, you shop. It's the Valley," as one Sherman Oaks resident defines it. Shopping the Valley is easy, if only

because parking is abundant compared with the rest of Los Angeles, although the burgeoning population, combined with meager public transportation, has slowed traffic. There are super mega-malls like the **Sherman Oaks Galleria**, whose recent renovation added a 16-movie theater complex and a pedestrian plaza. This is in mid-Valley about halfway between **Topanga Plaza** to the west and **Glendale Galleria** nearer to LA; at the western end, too, are **Woodland Hills Promenade**, **Town and Country Shopping Center** and **Plaza de Oro** in Encino.

Ventura Boulevard runs right through the Valley offering an immense range of shops and restaurants. Just north of the boulevard is the astonishing **Encino Oak** (located within the Town and Country Shopping Center on Ventura Boulevard), claimed somewhat dubiously to be over 1,000 years old. The branches spread 150 feet (46 meters) and the trunk is over 25 feet (8 meters) around.

Before the 1994 earthquake damage, 21-

BELOW: monkeying around at Universal Studios.

UNIVERSAL PROPS DEPARTMENT

Although MGM sold its collection of movie props in 1970 and 20th Century Fox unloaded such items as gorilla mannequins from the *Planet of the Apes* and Paul Newman's bicycle from *Butch Cassidy and the Sundance Kid* soon after, Universal Studios still maintains its prop museum as it has done since its early days. In a three-story building on the backlot of Universal Studios are 400,000 props of every kind, ranging from items used in Boris Karloff's 1932 *The Mummy* to the 1914-era folding wood and cane deck chair used by actress Meryl Streep in *Out of Africa.* Unfortunately, it is rarely open to the public.

Suits of armor, life-sized tigers and an entire corridor of Greek, Roman, Medieval, and Colonial statues share space with barber-shop chairs and reproductions of Meiji-style bronze samurai, not to overlook paintings "in the style of" Renoir, Monet, Picasso and Rothko. Universal's prop department was started in 1915 and by the time of Hollywood's Golden Age it was such an essential part of the studio that for any determined director the right prop had become as important as the script. Erich von Stroheim is said to have halted production on *The Wedding March* in 1927 to await the arrival of an authentic, early-9th century Russian bed for ZaSu Pitts to sleep on during a crucial scene.

Map on page 186

mile (34 km) Ventura was beginning to resemble a mini-Wilshire Corridor, with a strip near Van Nuys Boulevard taking on the aura of trendy Melrose Avenue. This is the home of **Antique Row**, comprising shops on Sherman Way in Canoga Park specializing in Americana, from memorabilia and collectibles to bric-a-brac.

Pumpkin king

At the Valley's western end, on Calabasas Road near Mulholland Drive is the **Leonis Adobe** (Wed–Sun 1–4pm, tel: 818/223-6511), a one-story 1844 farmhouse which was transformed by "King of Calabasas" (*pumpkin* in Spanish) Miguel Leonis into this charming gingerbread home, fully restored and furnished.

The **Plummer House** (on the same property), which now serves as the park visitor center, is a Victorian cottage transported from Hollywood in 1875.

Orcutt Ranch Horticulture Center (daily 8am–5pm, tel: 818/346-7449) in **Canoga Park** perfectly recalls a vanished moment in California history – citrus groves bounded by majestic and stately oaks, ancient on their native soil. When the Orcutts purchased the 200-acre (80-hectare) estate in 1917 they named it *Rancho Sombra del Roble*, ranch in the shadow of the oak, which is quite literally the case. One magnificent oak tree is estimated to be 700 years old. The gardens, lavish with statuary and sundials, have proved to be popular for picnics and weddings. The orange groves are open to the public on a weekend announced in June or July, with the proceeds augmenting the garden's city-allotted budget.

On Vanowen Street in Canoga Park, is **Shadow Ranch**, a restored 1870 ranch house built by LA pioneer Albert Workman and located on the remaining few acres of what was a 60,000-acre (24,000-hectare) wheat ranch. The stands of eucalyptus are said to have sired most of the towering trees that now blanket the state, and the ranch is used as a community center.

The Japanese Garden (9:30am–4pm,

BELOW: Universal Studios is San Fernando's most visited attraction.

tel: 818/756-8166) in **Van Nuys**, a 6-acre (2-hectare) botanical delight, was created in the 1980s by the Donald C. Tillman Water Reclamation Plant. Three morning tours visit a trio of gardens in distinctly different styles. On some summer weekdays there are "sunset" tours; advance reservations are essential.

Encino ❺ has its **Rancho de los Encinos State Historic Park** (closed Mon, Tues, tel: 818/784-4849), originally the site of a Native American village and later a stagecoach stop. The property later became a ranch which belonged to the de la Osa family, who planted vineyards and orchards and raised cattle. Amid the acres of manicured lawns, duck ponds and eucalyptus and citrus groves is the **de la Osa adobe**, built in 1849 and full of period furnishings. A blacksmith shop and a French Provincial home have recently reopened following repairs for eathquake damage.

West of the Ventura Freeway, Las Virgenes Road, winding up through the Santa Monica Mountains to Malibu, makes for a pleasant drive. Just off the road near Mulholland Highway – a wonderful drive in itself all the way to the Pacific Coast Highway – the exotic, looming spires of the **Venkateswara Hindu Temple** entice many a passer-by.

World's longest mural

The **Tujunga Wash Mural** (west wall of the concrete flood control channel at Coldwater Canyon Boulevard between Burbank Boulevard and Oxnard Street in North Hollywood) stretches for a full half-mile and purports to be the world's longest mural. It recounts the history of California from dinosaurs to the present, warts and all, so it's an interesting learning experience for participants (it's a collaborative effort) and visitors alike.

Near the junction of US Highway 5 and US Highway 405 in **Mission Hills** is the **Mission San Fernando Rey de España ❻** (daily 9am–4:30pm, tel: 818/361-0186), California's 17th mission, founded in 1797. Its long and tumultuous history has been

BELOW: good cakes to feed the crowds.

Map on page 186

marked by complete destruction in two major earthquakes (in 1806 and 1971) and subsequent reconstruction. The tour of the working, sleeping and recreation areas and an extensive collection of artifacts vividly recreate a sense of day-to-day mission life.

The nearby **Andres Pico Adobe**, the oldest home in San Fernando and second oldest in the Los Angeles area, was built by tribes from the mission in 1834 and restored in 1930 after many decades of disuse. To the northeast, the very different **San Sylmar Tower of Beauty Museum** on Bledso Road in Sylmar, a private museum owned and operated by the Merle Norman Cosmetic Co., offers a world-class collection of antiques, vintage automobiles, rare musical instruments and music boxes. Tours require reservations, so call ahead; children under 12 not allowed.

Santa Clarita Valley

US Highway 5 continues northwest into the **Santa Clarita Valley** to Valencia, site of **Six Flags Magic Mountain** – now

BELOW RIGHT: Glendale's Forest Lawn Memorial Park, final resting place for the great and the dead.

called **Xtreme Park** ❼ (daily from 10am, tel: 818/367-5965) – an amusement park that has over 2,000 rides and attractions. A recent acquisition, the 85-mph (137-kph) rollercoaster Goliath, plunges hair-raisingly down a heart-stoppingly steep drop that kids love.

Up in **Newhall** ❽, on San Fernando Road, is the **William S. Hart Museum** (guided tours Wed–Sun, tel: 805/254-4584) a Spanish Colonial-type mansion on a 265-acre (107-hectare) park which has been designated as a wilderness area and is open daily. It was deeded to Los Angeles County by the famous silent-screen cowboy who mandated that admission be free. This area was very familiar to western stars, many of whom – Hopalong Cassidy, Gene Autry, Roy Rogers, Dale Evans – used to hang out in the old Newhall Pharmacy.

Gene Autry's Melody Ranch in adjoining **Santa Clarita** ❾ was the scene of movies as far back as 1911. There are still three other movie studios in town, plus one in nearby Valencia. The Santa Clarita

VALLEY HISTORY

The San Fernando Valley remained rural for more than 100 years after Father Juan Crespi's discovery of this "very pleasant and spacious valley" in 1769. He named the area "Valle de Santa Catalina de Bononia de los Encinos," which has been whittled down to Encino, the Spanish word for oak and now the name of a well-known Valley neighborhood. Later, along came magnates such as Isaac Lankershim and I.N. Van Nuys (after whom boulevards are named) to divide up the land in anticipation of the inevitable boom, due to its proximity to ever-growing Los Angeles.

By 1907, the still-expanding Valley population stagnated for the first time over the very probem that has plagued Southern California ever since its inception: the need for more water. City water chief William Mulholland's ambitious project to bring water hundreds of miles south from Owens Valley eventually came to fruition in 1913 after which farming boomed – especially the 15,000 acres (6,070 hectares) of orange groves that became synonymous with Southern California. Bing Crosby's hit recording "I'm Going to Never More Roam and Make the San Fernando Valley My Home" remained on the hit parade for 22 weeks in 1944. Almost 40 years later, Frank and Moon Zappa's "Valley Girl" again drew attention to LA's most extensive suburbs.

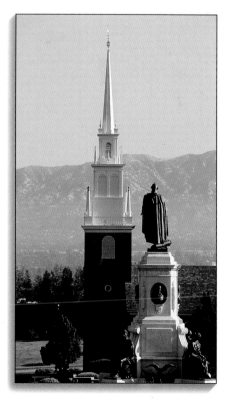

school board was once involved in a dispute over naming a local high school after Tiburcio Vasquez, a local horse thief who still stirs controversy even today, with some regarding him as a kind of Latino Robin Hood and others a publicity-conscious bandit who gained support by writing glamorous "confessions" of his life before being hanged in 1875. The school is a stone's throw from the 745-acre (300-hectare) **Vasquez Rocks Park** – also the scene of many movies.

San Gabriel Valley

Ten years before Los Angeles was even a gleam in anybody's eye, the major settlement in the **San Gabriel Valley** ⑩ was the **Mission San Gabriel Arcangel** ⑪ (daily 9am–5pm, tel: 626/457-3035) whose friars eventually presided over a million acres (400,000 hectares) of land rich with vineyards, olive groves, and extensive cattle ranches. By the middle of the 19th century, however, with the secularization of the missions, the valley had been divided among numerous ranches, some of which in turn gave way to independent communities such as **Arcadia** ⑫, San Marino and Pasadena. The much-renovated mission, damaged by several earthquakes since its founding in 1771, was where California's oranges were first grown early in the 20th century. Its winery on Mission Drive in San Gabriel now serves as a **museum** which can be visited. Surviving from a similar time are the nearby remains of the **Ortega-Vigare Adobe** which adjoins the mission-style **Playhouse**, built in the 1920s.

One of the original ranchos was bought by the silver tycoon "Lucky" Baldwin in 1875, whose fretwork Queen Anne- style guest cottage still sits in Arcadia on what is now the **State and County Arboretum** (open daily, tel: 626/821-3222). Peacocks wander among the palm trees and historic buildings, which include the former Santa Anita railroad depot.

Open every day of the year, it offers a guided tram tour around its 30,000 plants spread around a natural lagoon. Access is

BELOW: lounging in the park.

Map on page 186

via Interstate 10, from the Baldwin Avenue exit. The estate has appeared in numerous movies, the most famous being the "jungle" through which Humphrey Bogart pulled the *African Queen* in 1951. Garden paths wind around statuesque palm trees, a waterfall and tropical greenhouse. Visitors doggedly in pursuit of the past can visit the **El Monte Historical Museum** (closed Mon, early Aug, tel: 626/580-2232), whose historical exhibits include an early 1900s schoolroom and a Victorian parlor. Arcadia is best known today for its **Santa Anita Park** (tel: 626/574-7223), 5 miles (8 km) southeast of Pasadena. At this historic racetrack, thoroughbred horses compete between October and April.

The Rose Bowl

Pasadena ⑬ is a fairly commonplace town which comes fully alive once a year during the Rose Bowl football game and the famous **Tournament of Roses Parade**. These New Year's Day extravaganzas attract hordes of onlookers, some of whom arrive as early as 72 hours before parade time to be assured of the best viewing spot. After the parade, the mobile flower garden of floats is routed to a nearby park, where entries remain on display for two days.

The parade is followed soon after by the longest-running collegiate football championship in the nation: the **Rose Bowl**. Since 1923, two outstanding gridiron teams have lined up against each other in Pasadena's Rose Bowl stadium inside **Brookside Park**, cheered on by over 100,000 dedicated, screaming fans. It's an American phenomenon.

In 1911, the chewing-gum magnate William Wrigley built the fabulous **Wrigley Mansion**, which conducts free afternoon tours (usually Thurs) for the first half of each year. The mansion is now the headquarters for the Tournament of Roses which, 80 years ago, replaced a pagan celebration, the Battle of the Flowers, when citizens welcomed spring as the rest of the country was still deep in winter. Those were the days when investing in Califor-

BELOW: the Rose Bowl, Pasadena.

nia real estate became a national preoccupation and the hucksters and promoters were out in force greeting arriving prospectors with bands at the railway station.

Old Pasadena

Adjoining the Civic Auditorium in the center of town, the spiffy **Paseo Colorado** is a stylish replacement for an aging plaza mall, abutting on a pedestrian walkway and containing an ingenious mix of shops, restaurants and housing. Three blocks west, the quaint 20-block **Old Pasadena** area remains the major magnet for visitors in search of night life.

Several interesting Pasadena houses from the early 1900s are well worth inspecting, but most of them close mid-afternoon. Near the freeway at Walnut and Orange Grove is the 18-room art and antique-filled **Fenyes Mansion** (guided tours Thurs–Sun, tel: 626/577-1660), home of the Pasadena Historical Society, and where D.W. Griffith shot one of his first films. Half a block away, the impressive

California-style "bungalow" known as the **Gamble House** (Thurs–Sun noon–3pm, tel: 626/793-3334) was built for David Gamble (of Procter & Gamble, America's biggest soap company) in 1908 at a cost of $50,000 when an average three-bedroom house cost less than $1,500. The house is terraced and tiled with wood, incorporating teak, cedar, maple and mahogany. It is a much-admired product of the Arts and Crafts Movement, of which the Ohio-born Greene brothers, Charles Sumner (born 1876) and Henry Mather (1870) were noted members. Impressive from the outside (and so worth admiring even when closed), the interior is a knockout, but to see it you must reserve a place on one of the small tours.

Pasadena contains seven other **Greene and Greene bungalows** (Arroyo Terrace), as well as the house that Alice Millard challenged Frank Lloyd Wright to build for $5,000 on Prospect Crescent. The Arts and Crafts Movement, begun by William Morris and John Ruskin in reaction to the blight

BELOW: two views of the 1908 Gamble House, a fine example from the Arts and Crafts Movement.

Map
on page
186

of industrialization in England, eschewed meaningless ornamentation and emphasized harmony with nature and natural sources. Two other stylish buildings from the era when Pasadena was a popular resort are the **Hotel Green** and adjoining apartment building, and the **Ritz-Carlton Hotel**, on Oak Knoll Avenue.

Timeless opulence

With a vine-covered Moorish facade, the hotel's interior is decorated with Oriental carpets and marbled hallways presenting a style which has been termed "timeless opulence." The Grand Ballroom contains two Viennese chandeliers from 1836. The redwood Picture Bridge, on the grounds, displays triangular oil paintings depicting Californian scenes, distinguishing this as the only covered picture bridge in the United States.

Just before the freeway is the **Norton Simon Museum** (Thurs–Sun noon–4pm, tel: 626/449-6840) with its world-class collection of Asian and Western art spanning 2,000 years and including works by Goya, Degas, Picasso, Rembrandt and Cézanne. **The Pacific Asia Museum** (Wed–Sun 10am–5pm, tel: 626/449-2742), in a delightful building on N. Los Robles, is also worthwhile. Children will enjoy the hands-on attractions of **Kidspace** (Fri, Sat 10am–5pm, afternoons Sun–Thurs, tel: 626/449-9143) with hands-on exhibits.

Pasadena's major attraction (which, strictly speaking, is in **San Marino**) is the **Huntington Art Gallery and Gardens** ⓮ (daily 10:30am–4:30pm, tel: 626/405-2141). Just past the California Institute of Technology on California Street near Allen Street, walk down to Orlando to enter the gardens and **fabulous library** of Henry Edwards Huntington, a railroad magnate, who, with his wife Arabella, assembled one of the most important collections of art and rare books in the US.

Past the orange grove is an immense lawn lined with 17th-century statues and flanked by a garden of camellias (in winter, azaleas). Through the colorful Shakespeare

BELOW:
the library of
Pasadena's
Huntington
estate; books
include a 1410
edition of the
*Canterbury
Tales.*

garden, with its bust of the bard and almost all of the flowers mentioned in his works, is the library which boasts an astonishing four million items, among those on show being a 1410 edition of Chaucer's *Canterbury Tales*, a Gutenberg Bible, Audubon prints and an early Shakespeare folio. Huntington was a world-class collector in the Hearstian mode.

Sound of birds

Because the gardens occupy more than 100 acres (40 hectares), it's not difficult to find yourself in some tranquil spot with nothing but the sound of birds for company. After crossing the little red bridge over the carp-filled lake and climbing the steps you'll find yourself in the Rose Garden and just in time for tea (reservations required) at the charming **Rose Garden Room**.

The most treasures are to be found in the **Huntington Gallery** (the family home from 1850 to 1927), with the main gallery offering several world-famous paintings: Thomas Gainsborough's *Blue Boy* (*circa*

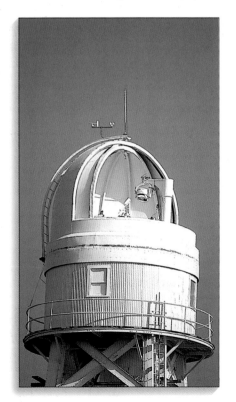

1770); Thomas Lawrence's *Pinkie* (1794); Sir Joshua Reynolds' *Mrs Siddons* (1784); and a famous landscape by John Constable, *View on the Stour* (1822) and Gilbert Stuart's 1797 painting of George Washington.

On Old Mill Road, also in San Marino, is **El Molino Viejo** (Tues–Sun 1pm–4pm, tel: 626/449-5458), an adobe structure dating back to 1816 which is now the southern headquarters of the California Historical Society, but originally housed the first water-powered grist mill in the region. It was built by Native Americans from the Mission San Gabriel Arcangel.

North of Pasadena, off Interstate Highway 210, the **Descanso Gardens** ⓯ (daily 9am–4:30pm, tel: 626/821-3222) in La Cañada Flintridge cover what remains of a 30,000-acre (12,000-hectare) ranch. The 165-acre (67-hectare) gardens take a good couple of hours to explore. The oak and camellia woodlands – more than 600 varieties, constituting one of the largest camellia collections in the world – began as landscaping along the private drive to a 22-room house built in 1938 by *Daily News* publisher E. Manchester Boddy.

The beautiful, rampant camellias are augmented by winding, shady trails, a lilac garden, the Descanso Rose History Garden (a timeline of roses from Cleopatra's day to ours) and **the Japanese Garden** and **Teahouse**, which serves tea and cookies. The gardens are organized so that something is blooming whatever time of year you arrive.

Head up State Route 2 north of La Canada Flintridge and then east onto the Angeles Crest Highway to journey into the soaring **San Gabriel Mountains**. The San Gabriel's highest peak, towering **Mount San Antonio** (also known as "Old Baldy") is almost 5,000 feet (1,524 meters) higher than the **Mount Wilson Observatory** ⓰, itself a lofty 5,700 feet (1,500 meters) above sea level.

Apart from the twisting and winding of the Angeles Crest Highway, things have not changed much since the 1890s, when the explorer and naturalist John Muir called the San Gabriel range "more rigidly inaccessible than any other I ever attempted to penetrate." ❑

Map on page 186

LEFT: the Mount Wilson Observatory is many thousands of feet above sea level. **RIGHT:** winter on Mount San Antonio, also known as "Old Baldy."

Map
on page
186

THE INLAND EMPIRE

The Inland Empire is the area between San Diego County and three
sets of mountains – the San Gabriels to the west, Mount San Jacinto
to the east and the San Bernardinos to the north

The name "Inland Empire," used in all of California's commercial promotion, is thought to have been derived from a local radio station's advertising campaign of the 1940s. This somewhat isolated area between three mountain ranges escapes the attention of many tourists, leaving it a pleasantly secluded place for hiking and relaxing. The climate might at first seem confusing to newcomers, as the native plants and shrubs covering the hillsides bloom from February through May; by summer they have taken on a stark, naked winter look. The hills become green again in winter, and then the cycle begins again.

Popular retreat

Because of its physical beauty – lakes, mountains and streams – and secluded position, the area has long been a popular retreat. Father Francisco Dumetz founded an extension of the San Gabriel Mission here in the early 1800s, followed a few decades later by wagonloads of Mormons. The Mormons were quick to put their plans into practice: astute farmers, businessmen and city planners, the spiritual pioneers set to work planting wheat, harvesting lumber, and founding the town of San Bernardino.

To protect their political interests and assure their "theocracy in the wilderness," the Mormons lobbied for the creation in 1853 of San Bernardino County, which became one of the largest counties in the continental United States and remains so today.

Eventually disputes over land between the Mormon and non-Mormon inhabitants soured the experiment and when in 1857 Mormon leader Brigham Young called for the return of all the "faithful" to Salt Lake City, a host of bargain hunters arrived to bid on the well-built homes and businesses.

Down by the Riverside

Before being given the name the "Inland Empire," this region was known as the Citrus Belt. Around Riverside, Redlands and Ontario, groves of oranges, lemons and other citrus fruits sprang up in the 1890s, financed by well-educated and ambitious urbanites. **Riverside ⑰** is the home of the California orange, which dates from the mid-1870s when Eliza and Luther Tibbetts planted three orange saplings nurtured from the bud of a Brazilian seedless orange. (One of these parent trees is still in Riverside today, blossoming and producing oranges more than 130 years later.)

Riverside's famous **Mission Inn** (daily guided tours, tel: 909/781-8241), built in

PRECEDING PAGES: hot air over the Perris Valley.
LEFT: Riverside's Mission Inn is a monument to Spanish Revival architecture.
RIGHT: Big Bear Lake.

the 1880s and a monument to Spanish Revival architecture, is a US Historic Landmark. Beginning as a 12-room adobe and continually expanded from 1902 onwards, the block-long hotel is complete with gargoyles, flying buttresses and spiral staircases, Tiffany stained glass windows, and the goldleaf altar from a 17th-century Mexican church.

Many of the rooms have been refurbished, often with a Spanish Catholic theme: there are 900 bells, crosses and international dolls inside and outside the premises. President Theodore Roosevelt once stayed here; other celebrated visitors have been Richard and Pat Nixon, who held their wedding party in the hotel, and Ronald and Nancy Reagan, who chose it for their honeymoon.

Dating from about the same time is the **Bettner House**, constructed in 1891 in Queen Anne style. Built on Magnolia Avenue by a wealthy widow, the house is operated as the **Riverside Municipal Museum** (Tues–Fri 9am–5pm, closed Mon afternoon, weekends 11am–5pm, tel: 909/782-5273), with exhibits on local history and Indian culture. On State Route 215, southeast of town, there is an aircraft museum at **March Air Force Base** (tel: 909/697-6600). The University of California's **Riverside campus** includes a 37-acre (15-hectare) botanical garden specializing in plants of Latin America, Australia and South Africa.

San Bernardino

San Bernardino ⓑ is not much of a tourist attraction apart from the **County Museum** (closed Mon, tel: 909/307-2669), with a unique collection of birds' eggs. A plaque marks the site of the Mormon Stockade at 3rd Street and Arrowhead Avenue, and there are a few Native American reservations outside town.

San Bernardino's big agricultrual event is the National Orange Show, a 10-day celebration of the winter citrus harvest at the county fairgrounds in mid-March. Held annually since 1915, it includes sports and

BELOW LEFT: Riverside fruit pickers, *circa* 1900. The region was known for its citrus fruit.

INLAND EMPIRE HISTORY

In 1810, Father Francisco Dumetz from the San Gabriel Mission stopped in this beautiful valley near the mountain foothills. Noting that it was the feast day of an Italian saint, San Bernardino of Siena, he gave the mountains and the valley this name. In what came to be an *asistencia* (extension) of the San Gabriel Mission, sporadic services were held in the small building until 1834. (Now part of the San Bernardino County Museum system, the *asistencia* underwent major restoration in the 1930s.) By the 1840s, families such as the Lugos were carving up the acreage of the San Bernardino Valley for cattle and horse ranches and seeking protection from rustlers. The Lugos employed the Native American Cahuilla chief Juan Antonio and his band of warriors to protect their interests. Juan Antonio became the "watchdog" of the valley – in effect the commander of a pioneer police force.

In 1851, three years after California became an American state thanks to the impetus of the Gold Rush, 150 wagonloads of Mormons arrived at the Cajon Pass after a difficult trip from Utah. Here, between the San Bernardino and San Gabriel mountains, they bought 36,000 acres (14,500 hectares) of land from Antonio Lugo for $77,000. This 500-strong settlement became a model for future Mormon development of the Inland Empire.

Map on page 186

entertainment events along with exhibits and festivities. The restored **Asistencia Mission de San Gabriel** (Wed–Sat 10am–5pm, Sun 1pm–5pm, tel: 909/793-5402) has a wedding chapel which recalls valley life as it was in the 1830s and 1840s. In San Bernardino's western suburb of **Rialto**, the **Historical Society Museum** is located in an attractive craftsman-style wooden structure and in **Colton**, just to the south, is the **Pioneer Memorial Park**, burial site of many early-day settlers from a community destroyed by floods in 1862.

Three miles (5 km) to the north, a huge arrowhead cut into the mountain is a local landmark. **Glen Helen Regional Park**, 10 miles (16 km) northwest of the city center, has some 500 acres (200 hectares) perfect for camping, boating and fishing.

Rim of the World Drive

State Route 18 leads to Lake Arrowhead and Big Bear Lake along a spectacular, winding 101-mile (163-km) route into the San Bernardino National Forest known as the **Rim of the World Drive**. First opened in 1915, it features beautiful vistas and awesome landscapes, although when the forest was first established in 1893 by President Benjamin Harrison, naturalist Francis Saunders was heard to observe: "They seem austere, barren and uninviting." At first impression this might seem true, yet they are now popular year-round outdoor recreation areas. The road begins at **Crestline**, once a logging area for the 1850s Mormon colony at San Bernardino. It is located at about 5,000 feet (1,500 meters) near Lake Gregory.

The mountains divide the deserts of the north from the verdant valleys to the south and are dominated by one of the tallest peaks in Southern California, **Mount San Gorgonio**, which stands 11,499 feet (3,505 meters) from the desert floor. The foothills of the San Bernardino Mountains are covered with chaparral, a green-gray shrub, with forests on the higher elevations. Because this range runs east-to-west,

BELOW: cruising along Lake Arrowhead – an upscale retreat for Los Angelenos.

the light and shadow patterns created by the sun provide an unusual beauty.

Mile-high **Lake Arrowhead**  (tel: 909/337-3705), now an upscale colony of fine homes built by Hollywood personalities and wealthy businessmen, was created in 1891 with the damming of Little Bear Creek, and flourished as a popular resort in the 1920s. Tourists are attracted by its shops, restaurants and hotel, as well as a lake cruise on the *Arrowhead Queen* (operates daily, tel: 909/336-6992).

Near Running Springs, where State Route 330 from Redlands joins State Route 18, are two popular winter ski resorts. **Green Valley** caters to novice skiers, while **Snow Valley** – with a top elevation of 7,841 feet (2,390 meters) and a vertical rise of 1,141 feet (348 meters) – has many chair lifts and terrain suitable for more adventurous skiers.

Big Bear Lake ⑳ (tel: 909/866-4608) was created by a single-arch dam in 1883, built by civil engineer Frank E. Brown to irrigate the orange groves of Redlands.

Today, it is a summer and winter resort, featuring outdoor sports such as game-hunting and fishing, boating and horseback riding, camping and picnicking. There are sledding, skating, hiking and tobogganing activities in winter – plus skiing, of course. Snow Summit has 14 miles (23 km) of runs from a top elevation of 8,200 feet (2,500 meters). Farther east, the Goldmine ski area drops 1,500 feet (460 meters) from a top-level elevation of 8,600 feet (2,600 meters).

Near Big Bear Lake is the wooded Holcomb Valley, the scene of frenetic gold mining in the 1860s. The two bustling towns that once stood here are now only dim and distant memories.

Favorite Victorian home

East of San Bernardino is **Redlands** ㉑, founded in 1881 by two Connecticut-born orange planters and named for the color of its rich soil. In 1885, the Bear Valley Mutual Water Company – still in business today – began dispensing the water car-

BELOW: chateau-style Kimberly Crest was built in 1897.

Map on page 186

ried 25 miles (40 km) by gravity from Big Bear Lake all the way to Redlands. Water enabled Redlands to expand very fast, and by 1900 the colony was attracting wealthy Easterners in search of mild winters.

These well-heeled newcomers built lavish mansions with landscaped grounds and decorative gardens set among the citrus groves. Lovely **Kimberly Crest** (Thurs–Sun 1pm–4pm closed Aug, tel: 909/792-2111) was built in 1897. A chateau-style house, with around 5 acres (2 hectares) of Italian gardens, it is furnished with Tiffany lamps and antiques.

The 1890 **Morey House** describes itself as "America's favorite Victorian home." Its French mansard roof, onion dome, Queen Anne-style mill work and beautifully carved staircases have frequently caught the attention of moviemakers and advertising agencies.

In Smiley Park at the center of town is the **Lincoln Memorial Shrine,** the only library, museum and monument west of the Mississippi River honoring former President Abraham Lincoln. Built in 1932 by philanthropist Robert Watchorn, the shrine houses a collection of manuscripts, art, photos and other memorabilia from the Civil War period. The park is the site of the **Redlands Bowl**, where, since 1924, concerts and operas have been staged, especially during the summer musical series which features classical performers from around the world.

Model colony

About 12 miles (19 km) west of Riverside is **Ontario ㉒**, the San Bernardino Valley's third-largest city with a population of about 145,000. It was founded in 1882 by two Canadian brothers named George and William Chaffee, who arrived, established a "model colony" orange grove, and named it after their home province. Today, Ontario is the home of the Los Angeles area's second international airport.

Another high-speed location is the **Ontario Motor Speedway**, like its similar cousin in Riverside – the **Riverside Inter-**

BELOW: camping it up in the San Bernardino Mountains.

national **Raceway** – an important stop on the national motor-racing circuit. You can also attend olive-tastings at the attractive, century-old **Graber Olive House** (open daily 9am–5:30pm, Sun till 6pm, tel: 800/996-5483).

Gunfights and balloons

Geographically, the biggest chunk of the Inland Empire is southeast of Riverside near **Perris**, a major center for ballooning and other sky sports. Several outfits organize "champagne flights" in hot-air balloons offering superlative panoramic vistas. Perris is also the site of the **Orange Empire Railway Museum** (daily 9am–5pm, tel: 909/657-2605), with its 140 or so ancient trolleys, some of which you can ride.

Once known as Laguna Grande (Big Lake), **Lake Elsinore** ㉓ is 11 miles (18 km) west of Perris. Three investors launched the Elsinore Colony in 1883, naming it for the "pleasant sounding" Danish city in Shakespeare's Hamlet. Elsinore

is now a popular resort area except that heavy rains in recent years have raised the lake to such unprecedented levels that some lakeshore homes have found their property surrounded by water.

The gigantic Eastside Reservoir Project near the town of **Hemet** has created one of the largest freshwater lakes in the state, whose 25-mile (40-km) shoreline has become a major recreational area. Hundreds of mastodon fossils uncovered during construction are housed in a special museum at the site.

Just outside Hemet is the **Ramona Bowl** where the annual "Ramona Pageant" has been staged since 1923. Based on Helen Hunt Jackson's popular 1880s novel *Ramona*, it tells the sad love story of two Mission Indians in Mexican California. A local cast of hundreds, plus horses, stages the musical in late April and early May.

Nearby **Maze Stone County Park** contains a 15,000-year-old Indian petroglyph, in the form of a maze, on a large boulder. Just north of Hemet is **San Jacinto**, a charming old town in the San Jacinto foothills which is a popular base for hiking and rock-climbing in the Mount San Jacinto Wilderness.

Farther south and just above the San Diego County line, is the interesting little town of **Temecula**. The name comes from the Luiseno Indian world which translated means "where the sun breaks through the mist." The Luiseno tribe inhabited Temecula in the 1700s, after which it was discovered by Spanish *padres*.

The **Temecula Valley Museum** (Wed–Sun 11am–4pm, tel: 909/676-0021) exhibits articles from the Old West plus dioramas of a gunfight, stagecoach, a saloon peopled with wax figures. **Old Town Temecula** has one-of-a-kind shops, antique dealers and a **farmers market** every Saturday morning; Western days and classic car shows are held most years. There is an **information center** in the building called the Stage Stop. Visits can be paid to many vineyards close to town, an industry that is booming due to the geography, microclimate, well-drained soil and the efforts of the Temecula Valley Winegrowers Association. ❑

Map on page 186

LEFT: off-road vehicles are much favored. **RIGHT:** hiking Mount San Jacinto.

Map
on page
212

PALM SPRINGS AND THE DESERT

Because of springs discovered by the Agua Caliente tribe, eco-tours and upscale resorts thrive near Joshua Tree National Park

Although Palm Springs is the main city in the desert area, the name itself has come to refer also to several nearby communities, many of which have springs of their own. The springs were first judged to be therapeutic by the local Agua Caliente ("hot water") Native Americans, who still own vast sections of downtown Palm Springs. Ever-escalating real estate prices have made the Agua Caliente an immensely wealthy tribe.

All of these communities have stylish shopping malls and upscale housing, but what the area is best known for are literally hundreds of golf courses, tennis courts and swimming pools. A recent survey by the Palm Springs' convention bureau established that two-thirds of visitors named swimming and tanning as their main motive for coming to the area – a figure exceeded only by those who listed shopping in first place. The town of Palm Springs veers between excessive permissiveness and strict crackdowns on the hordes of young people who sometimes uninhibitedly fill the main streets, a tradition that began with the annual collegiate spring breaks centered here.

The San Bernardino Freeway, then Interstate Highway 10, will bring you to Palm Springs from Los Angeles in just under three hours, but you might like to take an alternative route, the Pomona Freeway (continuation of the Santa Monica Freeway), to pass through Riverside with its famous Mission Inn *(see page 201)*, about whom architect Charles Moore observed that if you could only see one building in Southern California, this ought to be it.

State Route 60 joins US Highway 10 a few miles east of Riverside. Just beyond that your attention will be caught while passing the truck stop at **Cabazon ❶**.

Many travelers stop off at the Wheel Inn to get a closer look at the giant model dinosaurs towering 30 feet (9 meters) above the highway. From this point there are spectacular views of hillsides covered with row after row of steel wind turbines generating power *(see page 219)*.

Palm Springs

Turn right onto State Route 111 to drive into the town of **Palm Springs ❷**, past the soaring-roof gas station designed by architect Albert Frey in 1965 and recently refurbished, and then down **Palm Canyon Drive**, one of the two parallel main streets around which the town is structured. The

PRECEDING PAGES: spooky Joshua Tree National Park. **LEFT:** Anza-Borrego's Palm Canyon. **RIGHT:** Palm Springs.

well-maintained **Desert Fashion Plaza** 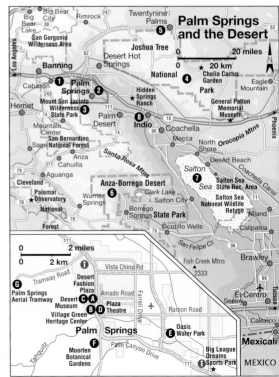 on this palm-lined thoroughfare is as upscale as it sounds.

A block or two farther down you'll come to what passes for an "old town", the **Village Green Heritage Center** , which consists of a restored adobe, several fairly old buildings and a recreated general store from the 1930s with genuine canned and packaged goods bearing their old labels.

In this ultra-chic, ultra-modern town, there are not a great many more attractions to see, but one that is definitely worthwhile is the **Desert Museum** (Tues–Sat 10am–5pm, Sun noon–5pm, tel: 760/325-0189), behind the Fashion Plaza, with its dioramas of the desert, old Indian artifacts and rotating exhibitions.

On Thursday nights a regular street fair includes stalls offering arts and crafts, antiques, plants, produce and jewelry. Each week is centered around a different musical theme: jazz, pop, country and western, classical or rock and roll. A tribute to the many world-class musicians who have chosen this region in which to live is the **National Big Band & Jazz Hall of Fame Museum** (tel: 760/329-3128). Specific information on all these things is available at the **Visitor Information Center** (tel: 800/967-3767) on North Palm Canyon Drive, where you can also reserve accommodation.

Tennis with the stars

Movie stars of the caliber of Clark Gable, Greta Garbo and Douglas Fairbanks came to play tennis when the famous Racquet Club first opened in 1933, and Palm Springs has been popular with Hollywood types ever since with streets named after Bob Hope, Frank Sinatra and Jack Benny, among others.

A reminder of those earlier star-studded days is the **Ballantines Movie Colony** (open daily, tel: 760/320-1178), where the ambiance (and the music) recreates the 1950s and the room furnishings are from the same era. If you're a fan of the music of the 1930s, 1940s and 1950s you'll also

BELOW: tribal baskets from the Desert Museum.

Map on page 212

enjoy an evening performance by the Palm Springs Follies at the **Plaza Theatre ⓓ** on S. Palm Canyon Drive.

Clark Gable and Walt Disney were among the big names who helped to launch the theater, whose opening – the 1937 world premiere of *Camille* – was attended by Greta Garbo. For years the CBS *Jack Benny Show* used to be telecast from the theater's stage. Also for music lovers are the free concerts on summer evenings in **Sunrise Park**. or the Sunday afternoon jazz concerts at the **Ingleside Inn**.

354 sunny days a year

Palm Springs' weather is usually superb – 354 sunny days each year – but in summertime when the temperature can go as high as 100°F (38°C) you'll welcome being able to sit at an outdoor café screened by its own artificial cloud of cooling mist. The younger crowd flock and frolic in the **Oasis Water Park ⓔ** (daily 11am–5pm, 11–6pm in winter, tel: 760/327-0499), located east of town,

which contains a health club, enormous swimming pool, volley ball courts and seven breathtaking, sky-high water slides.

At the lower end of the main street is the **Moorten Botanical Gardens ⓕ** (9am–4:30pm Mon–Sat, Sun 10am–4pm, tel: 760/327-6555), an attractive "living museum" with giant cacti, flowers and trees lining shaded nature trails. It is open daily until late afternoon; there is a small entry fee

One block east is **Indian Avenue**, Palm Springs' other main street, which heads north, towards Desert Hot Springs. If you don't have time to explore the wilderness be sure to visit **The Living Desert** (daily 9am–4:30pm, tel: 760/346-5694), an extensive nature park 15 miles (24 km) southeast of town, filled with eagles, zebras and gazelles (you'll probably love the playful meerkats), and hundreds of desert shrubs, flowers and cacti. Just north of town is the **Aerial Tramway ⓖ** (tel: 888/515 TRAM), with roomy tramcars that rotate as they climb.

BELOW: Palm Canyon Drive, Palm Springs.

During an awesome ride lasting about 15 minutes, the tram climbs to an 8,516-foot (2,596-meter) peak of the San Jacinto Mountains, which is part of **Mount San Jacinto Wilderness State Park ❸**.

From the restaurant, the panorama takes in a radius of 50 miles (80 km) with understandably magnificent views of Palm Springs, and (to the southeast), the Salton Sea and the Coachella Valley. Take a jacket because it's invariably very cool up there.

In **Desert Hot Springs** the adobe home built by the area's first settler, Cabot Xerxa, has been restored as **Cabot's Old Indian Pueblo Museum** (open weekends 9am–4pm, tel: 760/329-7610) and displays the variegated souvenirs of Cabot who traveled widely throughout the world before his death in 1965.

Just to the east of Desert Hot Springs is **Joshua Tree National Park ❹**, a vast parkland filled with strange rocks, fascinating flora and fauna and the tall, fibrous plants after which it is named. It's unlikely you'll see any of the mostly nocturnal ani-

mals – kangaroo rats, coyotes, rattlesnakes – other than the occasional lizard unless you stay overnight in one of the camp grounds. Sunday tours (information: 800/967-3767) from Palm Desert cover 100 miles (160 km) of the region.

Twentynine Palms ❺, at the northern edge of the park, is a pleasant place to stay, with a few reasonably priced accommodations. North of Desert Hot Springs is the renowned, pretty but fairly pricey resort of **Two Bunch Palms**, supposedly once used by Al Capone as a hideout, but subsequently a popular hideaway for movie stars (a role it filled in Robert Altman's 1992 movie, *The Player*).

Eco-minded

The easiest and most interesting way to visit the Joshua Tree region, the similarly unspoiled **Santa Rosa Mountains** and the **Indian Canyons** with their cool palm oases is via Desert Adventures (tel: 760/324-JEEP), an ecologically minded tour company with some very knowledge-

BELOW: aerial tramway into the San Jacinto Mountains.

Map on page 212

able guides. The Indian Canyons are surprisingly rich in flora and fauna. Hawks and bald eagles circle overhead; tiny kangaroo rats and fleet-footed bighorn sheep can occasionally be seen on the slopes. Palm and Andreas canyons have the largest stands of palm trees in the world.

"Leave nothing but footprints, take nothing but photographs," reads a sign in this highly protected area.

The Agua Caliente

The Agua Caliente tribe of the Cahuillas, which already operates the five-story Spa Hotel Resort and Mineral Springs at the intersection of Indian Canyon Drive and Tahquitz Canyon Way in downtown Palm Springs, plans to construct a $20 million hotel-casino in partnership with Nevada's Caesar's World on one of the large tracts of local property they own. This is but one of a score of similar plans projected for various Indian reservations which may eventually turn California into a major gambling state to rival Nevada itself. Vis-

itors are welcome at the attractive Agua Calientes' **Visitor Center** (tel: 760/325-5673) in Tahquitz Canyon. The much-admired wood and glass building follows the style of the region's most influential and prolific architect, Albert Frey, whose fire station building on N. Indian Canyon Drive is a local landmark. The **Agua Caliente Reservation**, a few miles south of town, has picnic areas and hiking trails.

There are picnic areas and inviting trails into the mountains and for those with exceptional stamina, even a trail to hike all the way back down to the 200-sq. mile (500-sq. km) valley which, incidentally, is huge enough to completely enclose 10 cities. It also includes a wildlife preserve renowned for a rarely seen lizard whose "fringe toes" allow it to swim through the sand as readily as a fish in water.

As might be imagined, the Palm Springs and desert area abounds in luxury resorts, many of whose guest registers are a litany of famous names. The **La Quinta Hotel Golf and Tennis**

BELOW: the desert, with its hot springs, is known for its therapeutic qualities.

Resort (tel: 800/598 3828), for example, is where Frank Capra checked in to polish the movie script of *Lost Horizon* (1937) and Irving Berlin composed *White Christmas*. Ahead of its time, the hotel refused to sell cigarettes, forcing Greta Garbo to wander off the grounds to patronize a nearby grocery store. Recent renovations uncovered some sketches by Diego Rivera on the high ceilings of the lobby.

Other resorts have also moved into the area to take advantage of the hot springs (and well-heeled tourists). Even the high-class French emporium Givenchy have gotten into the act, with the Merv Griffin owned **Resort Hotel and Givenchy Spa**, tel: 800/745-8883.

Frank Sinatra lived a few miles down State Route 111 in **Rancho Mirage**, a bedroom community of country clubs, golf courses and tennis courts. The former US president Gerald Ford and Leonard Firestone, an industrialist and former ambassador to Belgium, also resided here, side by side on a fairway at Thunderbird Country Club. The Annenberg estate is a few blocks away at the corner of Frank Sinatra and Bob Hope drives. (Having a street named after a person has become the desert's ultimate status symbol.)

Heading South

A couple of miles from the Salton Sea, whose salt waters provide a habitat for game fish and a recreation area with campsites, is the **Anza-Borrego Desert State Park** ➏, centered around the town of **Borrego Springs** through which the Butterfield Overland Stage ran in 1858. Visitors to the 600,000-acre (240,000-hectare) park, the largest state park in the continental United States, should first stop at the **Visitor Center** (daily 9am–5pm in winter, weekends rest of the year, tel: 769/767-5311).

At the Visitor Center, videotapes of the park are shown and valuable advice is handed out, such as the times of sunrise and sunset and the fact that cell phones

BELOW: serious tennis is played at La Quinta.

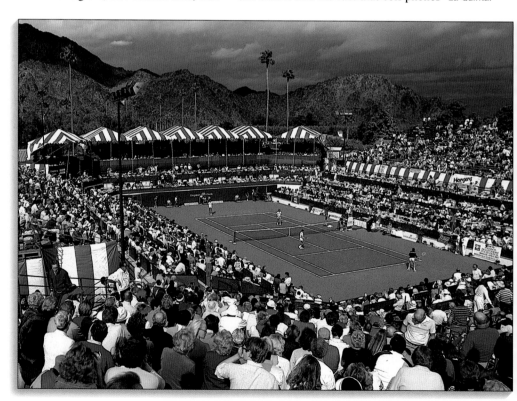

Map
on page
212

may not work in remote canyons. Be aware also that midsummer temperatures habitually reach 105° F (40° C). Its numerous canyons and gullies are easily accessible by car, but State Route 86 between the lake and the park is known by locals as "the killer highway" because of its high number of traffic deaths. Camping is permitted in the park, which is populated by jackrabbits, coyotes, chuckwalla lizards, kangaroo rats and snakes.

Near the Visitor Center is attractive **Palm Canyon**, with a pleasant campground where Park Rangers offer advice and organize nature walks. Wildflowers are especially attractive in the spring and a call to the Wildflower Hotline (760/767-4684) provides information on when blooms are at their peak.

More than 150 species of birds have been sighted in Anzo-Borrego park and the vegetation is equally varied, ranging from junipers and pines at the 5,000-foot (1,500-meter) level to palm trees at sea level. A short hike from Campfire Center to Palm Grove reveals a variety of plants used by the Cahuilla Indians for medicines, dyes and food *(see page 225)*.

The **Salton Sea** ➐ itself, which is only a couple of miles from the northeastern tip of the park, was all a big mistake. When engineers attempted in 1905 to divert Colorado River water to the Imperial Valley, the river changed course and reflooded the ancient Salton Basin, 235 feet (72 meters) below sea level. This formed a sea 35 miles long, 15 miles wide and 16 feet deep – or 56km by 24km by 5 meters – with royal blue water filling the area where the Coachella and Imperial valleys merge.

Salty sea

The sea's saltiness – it is 30 percent saltier than the ocean – creates a buoyancy popular with water skiers and swimmers. It also provides a habitat for saltwater game-fish. Adjoining marshlands are a refuge for migrating birds and

BELOW:
the Badlands,
Anza-Borrego
State Park.

a wonderful haven for birdwatchers. The **Salton Sea State Recreation Area** is an 18,000-acre (7,300-hectare) park with both developed and primitive campsites. There is a Bird Watch and Nature Trail (tel: 760-394 0062) and, 26 miles (42 km) away on SR86, a large boat basin at **Varner Harbor**, while geology buffs have a field day with ancient shorelines and layers of marine fossils which are visible along the base of the Santa Rosa Mountains.

May I have this date?

There is gambling in a 24-hour casino at Indio 8, which calls itself "the date capital of the world," and here the Coachella Valley Museum (closed Mon, Tues, tel: 760/342-6651) displays dioramas to explain the process of date-growing as well as housing tribal artifacts and old farm equipment. During World War II, thousands of soldiers trained for desert warfare in a handful of camps which are denoted on a relief map in the General Patton Memorial Museum (open daily 9:30am–4:30pm, tel: 760/227-3483), which itself sits on the site of an actual training camp off Interstate 10.

Indio is the site of the country's largest polo complex, the Pacific Coast Polo Center, where spectators are welcome on winter weekends. In February, the town celebrates its National Date Festival with camel races, cookouts and tasting of the semi-soft, amber-colored Deglet Noor, which accounts for 90 percent of the harvest and has come to be regarded as the "California date." Any time of the year, check out Shields Date Gardens where you can sample a Black Date ice cream cone and watch a continuous show called "The Romance and Sex Life of the Date."

Between Indio and the Salton Sea is a freshwater lake stocked with rainbow trout, striped bass and catfish. For non-anglers, there are hiking and equestrian trails, shady picnic spots, campsites and a children's play area on the sandy beach – away from fishermen. ❑

Map on page 212

BELOW: hairy palm; Indio, date capital of the world.

Power Plays

California, as well-known for its climate as for its automobile culture, is at the forefront in researching alternate forms of energy. Three of the state's utilities – Southern California Edison, the Los Angeles Department of Water & Power and the Sacramento Municipal Utility District – joined forces with financial help from the US Energy Department to construct a $39 million plant in the Mojave Desert that they hope will provide a feasible alternative to fossil fuels.

The initial 10–megawatt plant will produce a meager 10 percent or less of the current output of fuel-driven plants, but if it is successful, facilities will be built that are 10 or 20 times the size of the proposed plant.

At a plant known as Solar Two, hundreds of giant mirrors concentrate the sun's rays on a 300-feet (90-meter) tower, heating to a temperature of 1,050 degrees molten nitrate salt stored in an insulated tank. When needed the molten salt – a yellowish syrup which retains heat bettter than water or oil – will convert water into the steam required to power a turbine generator.

Earlier experimentation with solar energy has proved economically impractical partly because of the need for a lot of land and a consistently warm and sunny climate. The largest existing plant is one of nine owned by Luz International, which use the sun's rays to heat water rather than salt.

Although these generate enough light for 350,000 households in Southern California, Luz filed for bankruptcy due, the company claims, to confused Federal policies and "hidden subsidies" to utilities which use regular fossil fuels.

Similar problems have been faced by the pioneers of windpower. The country was originally the world's biggest producer of windpower – producing about 75 percent of the world's supply – but it has substantially down-sized. Now it aims at supplying 20 percent of California's energy by 2010, an enormous step down. Which is a major shame: nine-tenths of the US's windpower potential is located in the dozen Western states, where ranching and grain production are major industries and where ranchers have warmly welcomed the royalties that are paid for use of their land for such projects.

US Windpower Co. of Livermore, California, the nation's largest builder and operator of these machines, reports that its 3,700 turbines in the northern part of the state have accumulated 40 million operating hours in winds averaging 16 miles (26 km) an hour, driving the blades at almost ten times that speed.

Unfortunately, the development of new turbines, 75 feet (23 meters) high with 54-feet (16-meter) blades, could not sustain the industry's growth.

Government investment could make a huge difference, resulting in energy cheap enough to compete successfully with "dirty" (and diminishing) fossil fuels, so that windpower would become more significant than nuclear power within the next 25 years.

According to one expert in the field, it could provide up to 20 percent of the country's electricity needs, compared with what it presently supplies. ❑

RIGHT: windpower in the desert near Palm Springs.

Map on page 114

TRIBAL RESERVATIONS

*Despite widespread devastation in previous centuries,
there are still 300,000 Native Americans in California. If invited
to visit a reservation, it's important to remember that you are a guest*

Twice a year, at the old San Juan Bautista Mission near San Jose, California, an Indian market attracts native artists from as far away as Oklahoma, Washington, New Mexico, even Guatemala and Peru, and, of course, all parts of California. This gathering of native people is not unusual; California has a larger and more diverse Native American population than any other state.

Stone tools unearthed at the **Calico Early Man Site** in the Mojave Desert *(see page 238)*, date Indian occupation to about 15,000 years ago. Athabascans migrated into California about 3000 BC, pushing aside the earliest Hokan inhabitants. Penutians and Shoshoneans moved into the region some time later, settling on either side of the Sierra Nevada.

Although contact with Europeans occured late, the displacement of Indians was swift and devastating *(see pages 25–36)*. Today, the total area of Indian-occupied land is about 600,000 acres (243,000 hectares) for a population of some 300,000 Native Americans.

Fortunately, the old ways of most tribes were not entirely forgotten. The elders remembered, taught the young ones, and the cycle was renewed. Human and political rights were slowly, painfully, regained. Health and education improved. Families began to grow. Today, native California is undergoing a cultural renewal. The old spirits are being reawakened; dances and ceremonies are being performed, not for entertainment, but because they must be.

Where to find them

Starting in the desert country of California's southeasternmost corner, the **Fort Yuma Reservation** straddles the Colorado River. The first visible structure on this Quechan Indians' reservation is St Thomas Catholic Church (1922), which stands on the site of the original Mission Purísima Concepción, founded by Father Junípero Serra, but totally destroyed by the Quechans after only one year. Part of the old US Army fort still stands on the same prominent hill and contains an excellent period museum. The tribe maintains at least two RV parks, and plenty of bingo and high-stakes card play. Fishing is good here (with a tribal license), and powwows are held in March and September.

About 80 miles (130 km) north of Fort Yuma is the immense **Colorado River Indian Reservation.** The reservation is the ancestral home of the Chemehuevi Indians, although Mohave, Navajo and Hopi Indians also reside here. A visit to the Colorado River Reservation Museum at Parker is recommended. The Chemehuevi also live on

LEFT: Maidu dancer.
RIGHT: tools found near Calico date the time of Indian occupation.

the fairly barren **Chemehuevi Reservation**, a few miles north at Lake Havasu. To the east of the Colorado River Reservation, about 13 miles (21 km) north of Blythe on Highway 95, is one of the best works of rock art in California – the **Desert Intaglios** – giant figures of animals and hunters scooped out of the desert floor.

Rock maze

Farther north on Highway 95 is the tri-state **Fort Mojave Reservation**, home of the Hamákhava (Mohave) people. Most of the Indian land is in Arizona, and occurs in one-mile checkerboard squares (one of the peculiarities of some Southern California reservations). Ask someone at the tribal office in Needles to point you to the ancient **Rock Maze**, which is still used in ceremonies to prevent evil spirits from following spirits of the dead down the river. The reservation borders the **Havasu National Wildlife Preserve**, a year-round retreat.

Traveling across the state, near the Mexican border, there are a number of small, sparsely-settled Kamia reservations nestled in the rolling plateau of the Southern Coast Range west of San Diego. These include the Campo, La Posta and Manzanita reservations, unavailable to visitors but worth a glance from the highway just to see what a magnificent ecological preserve unspoiled Indian land can be. North, the Viejas and Barona reservations occupy the high, chapparal-green valleys of the Coast Range.

In San Diego itself is the oldest Indian mission in California, **San Diego de Alcalá** (1769); it never looked as good as it does today. In the excellent **Museum of Man** in Balboa Park, you can find a good presentation of early Kamia Indian (also called Kumeyaay, Ipai-Tipai or Diegueño) life, as well as other Indian artifacts.

North of San Diego, starting near the **Santa Ysabel Mission Asistencia** (a branch of the San Diego mission) is another cluster of small reservations, including Santa Ysabel, Mesa Grande, Los Coyotes, Rincon, La Jolla, Pauma and Pala. Several, **Mesa Grande** and **Los Coyotes** in partic-

BELOW: Shake Head Dance, California coast.

Map on page 114

ular, offer remarkable high-country scenery in what is practically a natural preserve, overlooked distant, sacred Mount Palomar. **La Jolla Reservation** is notable not only for its water park (slides, swimming, etc.) and full-service campground, but for its tiny mountain village with picturesque chapel and cactus-lined adobes.

But perhaps the **Pala Reservation** leaves the most lasting impression. The very moving **Pala Asistencia** chapel (1816) is probably the most emotional of the Indian missions – with unusual grave markers in the cemetery and strange Indian-painted faces on the walls. The people of three Indian cultures reside here – Luiseño, Cupa and Ipai. Although culturally similar, they still keep some degree of distinctiveness. Cupa Days are held in May, and a general fiesta is held in September. Corpus Christi, Easter, and Christmas services are also memorable. Staying at the full-service tribal campground is a good way to experience this quiet meeting of native cultures.

Want something completely different? A huge tract of the City of Palm Springs *is* the **Agua Caliente Reservation** of the Cahuilla people. The federal government checkerboarded this land when handing out reservations in 1896. Every other square mile is Indian land, and much of it is leased to developers, making the Agua Caliente band the wealthiest Indian people, per capita, in the US. The tribe carefully protects the area's extraordinary palm canyons.

For directions to the canyons, see either the tribal offices or the **Desert Museum**. The Agua Caliente **Indian Market** is usually held in late March.

Small but unusual

Just to the west of Palm Springs lies the **Morongo Reservation** and its small but interesting **Malki Museum**. Unusual here is the 1890 Moravian Church, a relic of days when the government used Christian organizations to supervise many reservations. Rare music is performed here on Memorial Day – their big time for fiesta and powwow.

BELOW: basket weaving, one of the skills still retained.

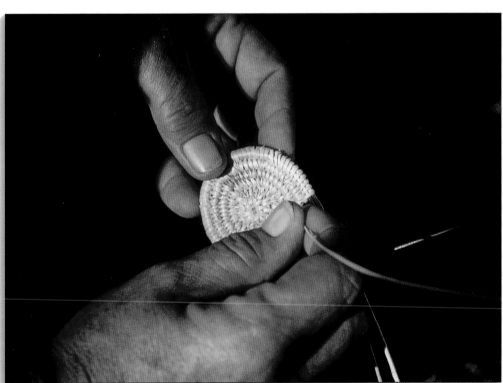

Heading west into Los Angeles County, the **San Manuel Reservation** in San Bernardino operates one of the most magnificent bingo palaces in the state, almost worthy of Las Vegas.

Elsewhere in the Los Angeles area, there is only one real spot of Indian-dedicated land – **Satwiwa**, site of an ancient village, located in the extensive **Santa Monica Mountains National Recreation Area.** This wild mountain spot is used by the Gabrielino (Tóngva) peoples of the Los Angeles basin and by the Chumash people to the west for ceremonies and for weekly Sunday storytelling and historical presentations open to the general public.

Excellent museums

Tens of thousands of Native Americans live in the Los Angeles area – people from all over the continent. It is no surprise, then, that powwows are scheduled most Saturdays somewhere in the area. Check the local American Indian Center for a listing. There are also three excellent museums: the

Los Angeles Museum of Natural History, the **Bowers Museum** in Santa Ana, and the stunning **Southwest Museum** towards Pasadena, which is dedicated exclusively to the Southwestern tribes.

San Fernando and **San Gabriel missions** also possess a number of Indian artifacts from the colonial period.

Painted cave

The mission trail continues north of Los Angeles at **Mission Santa Barbara**, an imposing structure built by the Chumash Indians. Nearby, the **Santa Barbara Museum of Natural History** features an excellent collection of Chumash artifacts. Ask the museum staff for directions to the **Chumash Painted Cave**, *the* most extraordinary ancient Indian painting in California. **Mission Purísima Concepción** is located in Lompoc about 50 miles (80 km) farther up the coast, and **Mission San Miguel**, once home of hundreds of Salinan Indians, is about another 80 miles (130 km) north on Highway 101. A few remnants of this small tribe are still members of the congregation at **Mission San Antonio de Padua**, about 20 miles (30 km) northwest.

Crossing the state into the Central Valley, the **Tule River Reservation**, occupied principally by Yokuts, offers quiet vistas of the Sierra Nevada and a fine rural atmosphere. An astounding rock painting is located beside the Tule River. To see this **Painted Rock**, you must hire a guide at the tribal office. Farther east, the tenacious band of Timbi-Sha Shoshone Indians have held onto their heritage in a most unlikely place, the aptly named Furnace Creek of **Death Valley National Park**. There is not much to see of their houses, but their homeland is fascinating.

The Owens Valley, deep between the Sierra Nevada and the Inyo and White mountains is home to other Shoshone and Paiute people. The largest of some five reservations is the **Bishop Reservation**, on an 875-acre (354-hectare) patch of land set dramatically alongside beautiful, plunging mountains. An architecturally fine museum displays dioramas, artifacts, crafts, and arts (some for sale). Horseback pack trips into the Sierra are also available. ❑

Map on page 114

LEFT: tribal rituals are still observed at powwows.

Medicine Men

The richest Native Americans in the country hit the headlines when they wanted to operate a full-scale gambling casino on their tribal land, several hundred acres of which are in the chic area around Palm Springs. It took the tireless efforts of dozens of legal friends before the Agua Caliente band of the Cahuilla Indians were able to break a legal deadlock allowing them to use their land at all. The canny exploitation of their terrain in the last three decades has put them on a par with – or maybe better than – many other American landowners.

Although the acquisition of a minor fortune is applauded, it has also resulted in the dilution of centuries-old wisdom and skills that enabled our earliest Native Americans to survive in what at first seems to be the totally inhospitable desert.

According to *Temalpakh* ("from the earth"), a seminal documentation about Indian knowledge and usage of plants, many of the Cahuilla themselves regret the loss of a more traditional way of life whose well-balanced diet produced longevity, mental alertness and good eyesight.

"They believe that adopted foods have brought about a general physical weakness, shortened lifespan, a tendency to obesity and proneness to such diseases as diabetes," write the authors, anthropologist Lowell John Bean and tribal authority Katherine Siva Sobel. "When Cahuilla speak of their grievances against the white man, they frequently mention the loss of traditional foods."

The Cahuilla survived in the hostile desert region not only because of their knowledge of desert plants and animals, but also because of the curing techniques of their shamans (witch doctors) who used natural substances that have enriched medicine ever since. Bean and Sobel say the shamans, because they employed both plant remedies and sacred power, occupied a more prominent place in the community than doctors.

"It is interesting to note that most of the prescribed drugs in use today trace their roots back to medicine plants known for centuries by indigenous cultures and their shamans," writes author Lynn V. Andrews. In her book *Jaguar Woman*, she says that the one rift between shamanism and modern medicine that she would like to see bridged "is the one caused by modern medicine's elitism and refusal to communicate."

Among the Cahuilla, as with other Native Americans, shamans – "technicians of the sacred" because they mediate between the world of mortals and the world of spirits, according to ethnologist Mircea Eliade – were believed to possess supernatural powers. They gave advice on political decisions, cured diseases and searched nature for signs from the spirit world. The origin and meaning of Cahuilla is unknown: "master" (in both mental and physical strength) has been suggested. Their territory ranges from valleys as high as 5,000 feet (1,525 meters) in the Santa Rosa Mountains to the desert area below sea level, around the Salton Sea (200 feet (60 meters) below sea level.

South of Palm Springs, the tribe still owns the five Indian Canyons in which their villages used to sit. There are still some traces of house foundations, ditches and dams. ❑

RIGHT: portrait by the pioneer and artist of the 1830s, George Catlin.

Map
on page
230

DEATH VALLEY AND THE MOJAVE DESERT

Travelers who visit the "fiery furnace" do so to escape the confines of urban life and to experience one of the most desolate and challenging landscapes in the Americas

The Mojave Desert (named after a southwestern native tribe and pronounced *"mo-hahv-ee"*) lies between US Highway 395 and Interstate 40, adjoining the Nevada state border. Its most visited and atmospheric section is famous **Death Valley National Park** ❶. The desert has come to mean different things to different people – a battleground of conflicting interests between backpackers, miners, ranchers, scientists, environmentalists and off-road vehicle groups.

Land of the Dead

Centuries ago, explorer Juan Bautista de Anza experienced the Mojave's fiery natural furnace and in his diary referred to the region as Tierra del Muertos, literally, "Land of the Dead." The first would-be settlers who had the misfortune to wander into Death Valley in 1849 on their way to the Gold Rush found this to be sadly true.

Mojave Desert ❷ travel these days, regardless of the season, is infinitely easier and safer, with well-supervised roads and accommodation which includes a few inns and even luxury hotels. The climate between November and April is ideal for outdoor travel, while May through October burn with heat not dissimilar to the North African Sahara.

The *WPA Guide* in 1939 reported that August travelers found "intense heat" even while over a thousand feet above the valley and said experienced travelers could estimate the temperature by putting their hand outside the car and checking how long it took the sunlight "to cause a sharp pain at the base of the nails."

From Los Angeles through the Mojave to Death Valley and back makes for a fascinating two- or three-day trip. Probably the best route is to set out from the San Fernando Valley on State Route 14

through Lancaster to Lone Pine, crossing the mountains into Death Valley via State Route 190.

At the junction of State Routes 14 and 58 is the small desert town of **Mojave** ❸. From borax to the B-1 bombers, the town has seen more history than places many times its size. Located near to **Edwards Air Force Base** (viewing by appointment, tel: 661/266-1110), Mojave was part of the Antelope Valley aerospace boom, serving as a bedroom community for the aerospace workers, as well as those employed in agriculture and railroads. The winter season is its busiest time, when weekend skiers, heading to and from Sierra slopes,

PRECEDING PAGES: Devil's Golf Course, Death Valley. **LEFT:** celebrating the land and the desert. **RIGHT:** the lonely road to Stovepipe Wells.

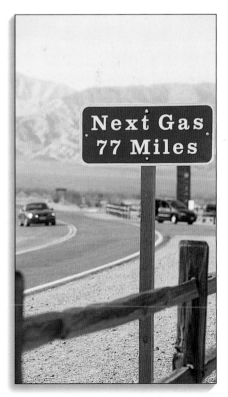

pack the area's motels and roadside cafés.

Approximately 25 miles (40 km) north of Mojave along State Route 14 is the **Red Rock Canyon State Recreation Area ❹**, an unusual camping and picnic spot that – despite its undeniable geological importanc – has remained relatively unexplored. Great, colored columns of sandstone rise off the desert floor on either side of the highway, sculpted towers in the foothills of the eastern Sierras that were once the home of a desert tribe now known only as "the old ones."

Gold nuggets

Much later, about the middle of the 19th century, traffic picked up considerably when desert prospectors began discovering gold nuggets on the surface of dry stream beds. A mini-boom followed, and subsequently about $16 million worth of ore was removed, including one 5-lb (2.3-kg) nugget.

On weekends, state rangers give guided nature walks. Picnic tables and about 50 primitive campsites are provided for tents and recreational vehicles. Visitors must bring their own food and water, however, as there are no concessions at the park.

Randsburg ❺, a 19th-century ghost town that is actually still a hilltop mining community, is about 20 miles (32 km) east of Red Rock Canyon on US Highway 395. Named after one of the highly lucrative gold towns of South Africa, Randsburg struck it mineral-rich three times between the years 1895 to 1947, first with gold, next with silver, and finally with tungsten. After its discovery late in the 19th century, its Yellow Aster mine yielded $20 million in gold before it was pretty quickly exhausted.

Randsburg in the early 1900s was as wild and woolly as any Western boomtown, with saloons and dance halls and the inevitable scoundrels and rogues.

Among the remains of the original wood-and-corrugated iron buildings on Randsburg's main street today is the **Desert Museum** (open some weekends),

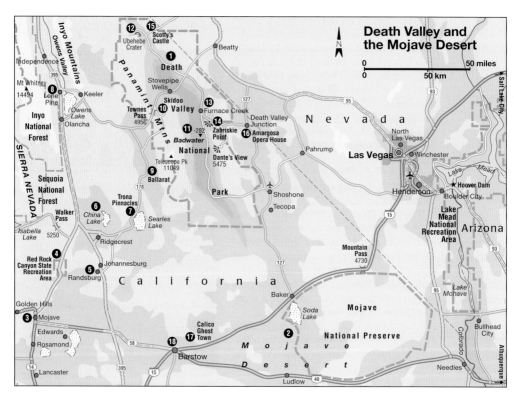

Map on page 230

with its collection of mining and geological artifacts. Also to be seen are the town's saloon, dance hall and barber shop, which have been quaintly converted to shops selling rocks, bottles and mining curios. At the **Randsburg General Store**, open daily, thirsty wayfarers can sip a chocolate soda at the same swivel-chaired soda fountain that was hauled into town by mules more than a century ago.

China Lake ❻ is a dry basin near Ridgecrest off US Highway 395. It is best known as the focus of the important China Lake Naval Weapons Center. Near the main gate of the naval station is the small **Maturango Museum**, open some weekend afternoons. The museum occasionally conducts public field trips to study aboriginal rock inscriptions that were found nearby, perhaps the best such collection in the state of California.

As a result of discoveries at China Lake, some scientists are tempted to say that humans migrated here from Asia at least 40,000 years ago, and perhaps as long as 100,000 years ago. Not far from China Lake are the **Trona Pinnacles ❼**. This great pincushion of ancient limestone columns in the middle of the Mojave Desert is both rare and bizarre. The spooky stone spires are "national natural landmarks," probably the most outstanding example of tufa formations in North America, and a challenging moonscape for hikers and rock climbers.

The Trona Pinnacles are situated on the west side of the bleakly awesome Searles Lake, access to which is via State Highway 178 north from **Johannesburg**. Camping is permitted at the Pinnacles.

Lone Pine

Ninety-four miles (151 km) north of Johannesburg on US Highway 395 is **Lone Pine ❽**, a picturesque village that has been a popular location for Hollywood westerns. From here, **Mount Whitney** *(see page 249)* is accessible although it's an almost three-day, 11-mile (18-km) challenge from the end of Whitney Portal

BELOW: over 900 plant species live in the Mojave.

Road to reach the summit. After rock climbing, take a look at **Keeler**, a ghost town about 10 miles (16 km) away from Lone Pine.

About 50 miles (80 km) to the east, beyond Towne's Pass, State Route 190 runs into the Panamint Mountains, some of whose rugged canyons were filled with life in 1873. The now-abandoned town of **Panamint** came into being when the robbers of a Wells Fargo express discovered silver while hiding out in Surprise Canyon.

Persuading two state senators to make a deal with the express company in return for part-ownership of the silverlode, they presided over an instant boom town with stores, saloons, boarding houses and banks – all along a main street that occupied the entire width of the narrow canyon. Within a year the boom was over but, perhaps with their own past careers in mind, the canny miners cast their silver in the form of 700-lb (320-kg) cannon balls to ship out, a burden too heavy for robbers to carry away.

Indian Ranch Road, an unpaved track off the Trona-Wildrose road and which forks off up Surprise Canyon, continues down to **Ballarat ❾**. Only crumbling adobe walls and ruined shacks remain here of what was a supply town for the miners, to which the stagecoach used to journey all the way from Johannesburg.

23 Skidoo

Another one-time mining town (now deserted) off Emigrant Canyon Road, was **Skidoo ❿**, its name derived from the phrase "23 Skidoo," the town having been 23 miles (37 km) from Telescope Peak. Skidoo is famous for its "million dollar slope" from which $1 million in gold ore was taken early in the century – "it could be scraped out in wheelbarrows," boasted its former owner.

But Skidoo has gone down in legend more as "the town that hanged its killer twice," after an incident in which a drunken saloon keeper killed a popular town banker.

BELOW: no gas here.

Map
on page
230

Skidoo's citizens were wary of what kind of justice might be administered from the nearest lawmen at Lone Pine, so they took it upon themselves to hang the killer. The next day – when an intrepid reporter from the *Los Angeles Herald* arrived – they dug up the body and hanged it again so the newsman could get a headline-grabbing picture.

Lowest spot on earth

State Route 190 is the main artery through **Death Valley National Park**, first established as a national monument in 1933. The name alone conjures visions of oppressive heat, blinding sunlight, bleached skeleons. A portion of the Mojave Desert, Death Valley is a 140-mile (225-km) long trough set between steep mountain walls of virtually naked rock.

The shallow Pleistocene lake that once filled the valley evaporated, leaving behind salt pans, cracked mud flats and undulating dunes. To the west, the deeply eroded walls of the Panamint Range tower to an elevation of 11,000 feet (3,400 meters), while to the east the Amargosa Range reaches 8,000 ft (2,500 meters).

Death Valley's fearsome reputation seems to attract as many as it intimidates. Winter or summer sightseers, hikers and amateur naturalists come to scramble up the sand dunes near Stovepipe Wells, marvel at the view from Zabriskie Point, study old mines and charcoal kilns, explore ghost towns and snap scores of pictures at humble **Badwater ⓫**, 282 feet (86 meters) below sea level, the lowest spot on earth.

The **Ubehebe Crater ⓬**, by the way, in the north end of Death Valley near Scotty's Castle, is a sort of reverse volcano in the shape of a 500-foot (152-meter) deep crater formed by a giant explosion of trapped steam somewhere around 4,000 years ago.

Death Valley's summer temperatures are exceeded only by those in the Libyan Sahara Desert. Autumn through spring, the climate is ideal for exploring, with day-

BELOW: the Amargosa Opera House.

time temperatures ranging between 60°–70°F (about 15–25°C), chillier at night. Skies are often eerily bright and free from rain. Despite the harshness of Death Valley's environment, about 900 types of plants grow in the national park, some throwing down roots 10 times the height of a man.

After the spring rains, the valley blooms with such species as desert star, poppies, verbena and evening primrose, which can be admired at lower elevations between mid-February and mid-April. From then until early May the most blooms – lupine, daisies – can be found between 2,000 and 4,000 feet (600 and 1,200 meters) in the Panamint Mountains. Above 4,000 feet, blooming time lasts into June

There is not much to admire in summertime. The average daily high in July for the past 50 years has been 116°F (47°C). It commonly soars past 120°F (49°C), and once hit a national high of 134°F (57°C). In short, May to October is one continuous heat wave.

This remarkable and justifiably famous valley is the result of a geological phenomenon. At least five million years ago the deep gap between the Panamint and Funeral mountains was formed by earthquakes and the folding of the earth's crust created technically, not a valley, but what geologists call a *graben*. Rock debris eroded from the mountains, filling a plateau which the Ice Age flattened and swathed in a vast cool sea.

Parched

This evaporated, leaving alternating layers of mud and salt. Cut off from cooling breezes by the surrounding mountains, this hemmed-in basin (4–16 miles/6–26 km wide) was left to parch, with an annual rainfall of under a couple of inches.

Death Valley's full-time human population seems indomitable, enduring terrific heat and isolation with the nearest big-city civilization in Las Vegas, Nevada, 140 miles (225 km) away, and television reception only mediocre. One compensation

BELOW: the 20-mule team carrying borax from the valley.

Map
on page
230

might be the glorious sunrises – look east towards the **Amargosa Range** – and sunsets (best seen, park rangers advise, from locations near to Dante's View, Zabriskie Point or Badwater).

Furnace Creek

Years ago, it was a tradition for all concessions to close down in the summer but the tourists kept on coming anyway. Nowadays, **Furnace Creek Inn** (tel: 760/786-2362) and the **Stovepipe Wells Motel** complex (tel: 760/786-2387) stay open throughout the year, and neither is ever very empty.

What may be surprising to learn is that virtually all the water supply for Furnace Creek and other desert regions areas comes from the underground aquifer that dates from the Ice Age. It is a non-renewable resource over which there will be inevitable battles in years to come, one contender clearly being expanding Las Vegas, which has insufficient water supplies of its own.

Furnace Creek ⑬ is a good focal point for a visit to the valley. Located not far from Badwater, its **Visitor Center** (tel: 760/786-2331) is open daily all year. The Furnace Creek Inn has an 18-hole golf course which, naturally, is the lowest on earth. Nobody would hire a caddy for the valley's other links, the so-called **Devil's Golf Course**, an otherworldly expanse of rugged and jagged salt crystals.

This area lies between the former sites of the Eagle Borax mill southwest of Badwater and the Harmony Borax Works just north of Furnace Creek, which was developed into a resort from what had been the workers' quarters. At the **Harmony Borax Works**, an old cleanser-processing plant has been restored to show visitors the 19th-century manufacturing method (tel: 760/786-2345).

Beginning in 1873, borax – a white, crystalline substance made into soap and used as a flux, cleansing agent and antiseptic – was a major product of the valley, transported by wagons hauled by

BELOW:
the Furnace
Creek Inn;
desert view.

20-mule teams 165 miles (266 km) from this site to the town of Mojave.

The company set up resting stations with water tanks and feedboxes every few miles. Eventually the price of borax was undercut by producers in Italy, and the valley companies suspended operations.

Overlooking Badwater to the east is **Dante's View** (5,475 feet/1,669 meters) and in the west, **Telescope Peak**, the highest point in the Panamint Mountains (11,049 feet/3,368 meters).

Among Death Valley's other natural beauty spots are **Zabriskie Point** ⓮, southeast of Furnace Creek in the Black Mountains and made famous in the 1960s by an arthouse movie of the same name; **Artists Drive** and the **Golden Canyon**, vivid displays of color among old outcroppings; and Ubehebe Crater.

Desert castle

Near Ubehebe Crater is **Scotty's Castle** ⓯ (open most days, tel: 760/786-2392), a 25-room Spanish palace that is Death Val-

ley's biggest visitor attraction. It is operated by the National Park Service which runs hourly tours although there is almost always a wait. Work on the castle began in 1926 at the foot of a natural spring-fed canyon at an elevation of 3,000 feet (about 900 meters). About 2,000 workmen assembled at the castle, completing it in 1931, all at the expense of a young Chicago millionaire and visionary named Albert Johnson.

Earlier, Johnson had been charmed into investing literally thousands of dollars in a fruitless search for gold by an affable roustabout named Walter Scott, popularly known as "Death Valley Scott." After years of waiting for Scott to strike gold, Johnson's patience ran out – but not before he had grown so fond of Death Valley that he decided to build a summer retreat here.

A replica of a Spanish-Mediterranean villa, Scotty's Castle contains beautiful continental furnishings and *objets d'art.* The Chicago financier and his wife lived on and off at the castle for many years

BELOW:
Scotty's Castle
has 25 rooms.

Map on page 230

until his death in 1948. "Death Valley Scotty," the good-natured rogue, also lived here, of course. He died in 1954, and his grave lies along a trail just behind the castle. To make the tour more authentic, rangers dress up in clothing of the 1930s.

If you have time to spend, consider exploring some of the park's backcountry trails and roads. From Ubehebe Crater. for example, it's a 25-mile (40-km) drive on a rough dirt road (four-wheel drive recommended) to the **Racetrack**, where rocks seem to move across the *playa* on their own power. (Geologists think the rocks are actually blown by high winds across a fine layer of ice or slippery clay.) Other popular backcountry drives include spectacular **Titus Canyon** (and the ghost town of **Leadville**); **Echo Canyon**, **Cottonwood Canyon** and **West Side Road**, which leads to several remote canyons popular among experienced hikers.

State Route 190 exits Death Valley National Park near the Nevada border, and joins State 127 at **Death Valley Junction**.

It is here that one of the more extraordinary sites of the desert is located – the **Amargosa Opera House** ⑯. Performances are held weekly from October through May, and tend to be sell-outs, so be sure to book ahead (tel: 760/852-4441).

Vision in the sand

In 1968, New York actress and performer Marta Becket was driving through the desert and saw the disused headquarters of a company that once produced borax. She leased the building, cleaned it up and took to the stage, with – and without – an audience. During her "resting" moments Becket painted vivid murals on the walls of the theater and also at the **Amargosa Hotel**. Whether the murals are worth traveling all the way across a desert for is a hard call to make, but the murals and the opera house *are* pretty extraordinary.

Becket is in her seventies and still performing. It is unclear what will happen once she stops treading the boards, but the building and murals have recently

BELOW:
Calico
Ghost Town.

been honored by the California Heritage Council, so it is likely they will survive.

It's a scenic 83-mile (134-km) drive south (via Tecopa Hot Springs) to Baker and Interstate 15. From Baker, another 50 road miles (80 km) and you eventually arrive at **Calico**. Some of the earliest traces of human habitation on the North American continent were discovered on this windblown desert.

Paleontologists are still carrying on the work of the late Dr Louis Leakey, leader of a team of scientists who believed they found a prehistoric "tool factory" estimated to be some 200,000 years old. The so-called **Calico Early Man Site** (closed Mon, Tues, tel: 679/256-5102) has guided tours available most days.

The town of Calico was established by silver miners in the 1880s whose boomtown has been restored as the **Calico Ghost Town** ⑰ (open daily, tel: 760/254-2122). Half history and half Hollywood, Calico is an amusement park where visitors can explore mining tunnels, ride the ore train,

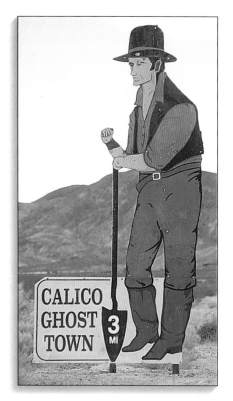

and browse through the dry-goods shops.

Just west of Calico is **Barstow** ⑱, a busy desert town which is largely the suburb of a military community. Situated at the junction of Interstates 15 and 40, it has miles of motels, gas stations and grocery stores that make it a good base for desert adventures.

Other hiking, trekking and backpacking trails include the 5-mile (8-km) round-trip from Golden Canyon to Zabriskie Point; the easy 2-mile (3-km) round trip to the **Keane Wonder Mine** (off Beatty Cut-Off Road, 16 miles/26 km northeast of the Visitor Center); and the 14½-mile (23-km) round-trip through **Mosaic Canyon** (off State Route 190, just to the west of Stovepipe Wells).

About 15 miles (24 km) southwest of Death Valley, on State Route 127, is the little town of **Shoshone**, which calls itself "the oasis where Death Valley began." During the 1920s, tourists arrived here on the Tonopah and Tidewater Railroad but today they drive in from Las Vegas, 84 miles (135 km) to the east, or Los Angeles, or fly into the nearby airport.

Just 10 minutes' drive away is another town named after local tribes, **Tecopa**, where several hundred camping sites adjoin a mineral hot springs. Nearby opal beds, cliffside amethysts and petrified wood have been attracting an increasing number of gemologists and rockhounds.

Survival techniques

The Mojave Desert covers an enormous amount of land – roughly that of the states of Massachusetts, Connecticut and Rhode Island combined. It's easy to get lost and, with conventional vehicles, to get stranded when off the main roads. Water can usually be found if one is equipped to dig deep enough – as the native Shoshone knew – but few visitors know anything about survival techniques.

The basics are simple: travel with a full tank of gas, and preferably with a reserve can in the trunk. Carry lots of water, and drink frequently. Use sunscreen, and wear a hat. And be alert: it is quite literally life-threatening to be under the desert sun too long, so carry a good map and tell people where you're going. ❑

Map on page 230

LEFT: ride the ore train here. **RIGHT:** Stovepipe Wells.

SAN JOAQUIN VALLEY

*The highest mountain peak on the mainland US, giant
sequoia trees, whitewater rapids, and food to feed the nation
greet visitors to the San Joaquin Valley*

Map
on page
244

When driving north out of Los Angeles County, it's only a matter of time before the urban landscape disappears and another California begins. This starts with a stretch of Interstate 5 called the **Grapevine**, one that loses almost a mile of elevation within five minutes of driving. Many think this 12-mile (19-km) section of freeway owes its name to its numerous curves, but in fact, two centuries ago a dusty track wound through Grapevine Canyon, so-called because of the abundance of wild grapes in the area.

In 1859 this trail, first used by tribal communities, was widened to accommodate freight wagons and stagecoaches, later to be replaced by a precipitous route along the ridge of the mountains. This has now been restored and is as sinuously dangerous (and as gloriously scenic) as ever. The original town of Grapevine is now only a truck stop consisting of gas stations and diners.

The road is frequently closed off after heavy winter storms. but sees an influx of visitors in the spring, when a colorful display of California poppies blanket the fields beside the highway. In 1991, the internationally known artist Christo lined the route with 1,760 giant yellow umbrellas, unfurling them at the same time at his similar installation in Japan.

Entering the valley

Crossing the **Tejon Pass** at 4,239 feet (1,292 meters), with the **Los Padres National Forest ❶** to the west, the view ahead is a seemingly endless checkerboard of fields divided occasionally by freeways, service roads and cement canals. At night, the string of highway lights is visible for 30 miles (50 km) – all the way to Bakersfield. Across the **Tehachapi Mountains** to the east, and visible from State Route 58, is a magnificent sight: thousands of totating wind-powered turbines, generat-

ing enough electricity for almost half a million people. Every May, people flock to the Tehachapi Wind Fair at Mountain Valley Airport to admire wind and solar technology, electric cars, take helicopter and glider rides, as well as do a 5-mile (8-km) trek around all the local wind farms.

The southern San Joaquin Valley between the two highways is an area of hardworking people with conservative values. There are no world-renowned tourist attractions like Disneyland or San Simeon, not even any tour buses, but there is a pleasant side of California that exemplifies the state's diversity.

The hub of the southern San Joaquin valley is Bakersfield, the largest city between Los Angeles and Fresno. The area

PRECEDING PAGES: artist Christo's 1991 project in the Tejon Pass, when 1,760 umbrellas were unfurled. **LEFT AND RIGHT:** the business in the San Joaquin is farming.

also includes small agricultural towns, a national forest and some of the country's most challenging whitewater rapids.

The small towns, most located near the two major highways (I-5 and State Highway 99) that bisect the valley north of Bakersfield, dot the flatland that produces everything the agriculturally rich state of California could think to cultivate. In fact, it's not the Southern states but the San Joaquin Valley that grows most of the cotton in the United States.

Enter the Oakies

This area originally appealed to the Yokut Indians, a peaceful tribe who inhabited the southern valley until the European settlers arrived. The Yokuts were largely an agricultural tribe, the first to recognize the potential of the land's bounty. The Yokuts believed that after death their spirits moved into the giant oak trees that lined the valley.

Gold mines in the hills and fights over water rights bred conflicts among the early immigrants, who included Anglos, Armenians, Asians, Mexicans and Basques. The Basques were first drawn to the valley in the late 1800s when the area emerged as the key sheep-raising part of the state. Skilled as shepherds, they took the sheep into the mountains for "summering," returning to the plains in the cooler weather. The winds of political change blew through the valley in the early 20th century. The Great Depression led to the "Dust Bowl" invasion of the 1930s, as farmers from Oklahoma and the prairie states packed their families and belongings into their jalopies and headed for what they hoped would be a better life, a tale told memorably by John Steinbeck in his 1939 novel *The Grapes of Wrath*.

As many as 500,000 "Okies" migrated here. One-eighth of the current California population claim Okie ancestry, and much of that gritty family-based community is still here in the heart of the San Joaquin. Stop by any valley town and, as one Dust Bowl survivor said, "You might as well be

BELOW LEFT: the Kern River is good for high-octane whitewater rafting.

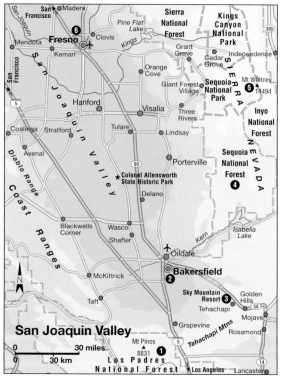

Map on page 244

in Tulsa or Little Rock or Amarillo… Same music, same values, same churches, same politics."

River route

Though its name is often mistakenly applied to California's entire Central Valley, the San Joaquin comprises just the southern two-thirds of that 450-mile (720-km) long, 50-mile (80-km) wide basin. It follows the course of the San Joaquin River, flowing south to north, to the Sacramento–San Joaquin Delta, where both rivers empty into San Francisco Bay.

The area is experienced by most travelers as something to be passed through quickly on the way to somewhere else. Interstate 5, running the length of the valley, is the main link between Los Angeles and the Bay Area, and the east–west routes to Lake Tahoe and the Sierras all cross the valley. So the region can only sell itself by virtue of being the crossroads to all these. Fresno, for instance, boasts of being the only community in the United States within an hour and a half of three national parks (Yosemite, Sequoia and Kings Canyon). The business of the valley is farming, and it succeeds at that like few other spots on earth. The nearby Gold Country mining claims were abandoned long ago, but the San Joaquin Valley is still enjoying general prosperity.

Agriculture, after all, is a major industry in California, worth many billions of dollars. Half of that is produced in the San Joaquin Valley, with Fresno County accounting for so much produce and farm goods it might well be the Number One farming community in America. The valley's alluvial soil, covering more than a million irrigated acres (400,000 hectares), is the reason for this agricultural richness. Major crops include cotton, grapes, tomatoes, corn, fruit and nuts.

Beneath the soil are deposits of oil and natural gas. In addition to its pastoral plenitude, the valley has always had oil to fall back on. Only three American states have more oil reserves than Kern County and

BELOW:
citrus groves
east of the
town of
Bakersfield.

the pumps, bobbing day and night in a slow but constant motion, are everywhere, blending into the environment whether their neighbors are ranches or restaurants. Some have even been decorated with cartoon characters.

The oil derricks, often topped by 50-foot (15-meter) flames burning off natural gas, provide the valley with some of its most stunning night scenes. Refineries and wells cast enough light to give the illusion of daylight.

The relentless sun

The area's other natural asset is the sun, unshaded by clouds for most of the year. But putting the sun and soil to work required water, lots of it. Since rainfall is typically less than 7 inches (178 mm) a year, nature wasn't much help. The early history of the valley was scarred with fights over the water rights to the Kern River, although these lacked the high drama and shenanigans of the LA disputes. Eventually two irrigation systems – the

Central Valley Project (1951) and the State Water Project (1973) – were constructed to help farmers.

Aside from the Sacramento River Delta and the mammoth irrigation projects it supports, several of California's great rivers flow through the area – the **San Joaquin**, the **Stanislaus**, the **Tuolumne**, the **Merced**, the **Kings**, and farther south, the Kern River. Most are renowned for outstanding, and occasionally terrifying, stretches of whitewater, perfect for high-octane rafting.

The arid-looking land is misleading: the water table below the fertile soil actually rises most years. But some of this water is harmful to crops due to accumulated mineral salts. Some agriculture pessimists fear that the brackish water will eventually destroy the ability to farm in the valley, in the same way that agriculture was eradicated in some parts of ancient Egypt.

Currently though, at least 200 agricultural commodities are produced in the San Joaquin Valley, a progress report that would have astonished the Spanish priest who reported in 1816 that "there is no fit land for sowing crops here because everywhere is sand."

Bakersfield is considered so typically American in attitudes and composition that it is a place often used for marketing studies of new products. Like many other towns in the valley, it appears unglamorous to the outsider and, as the butt of jokes for years, it has created in the locals a somewhat defensive attitude common to residents of frequently ridiculed cities. ("And second prize" the old joke goes, "is *two* weeks in Bakersfield.")

Another favorite local topic is the weather, the extreme climate being the single biggest factor in discouraging visitors. There is rarely a shower or even a cloud to be seen. In what is sometimes called "the San Joaquin blast furnace," August temperatures routinely top 100°F (38°C). It is a dry heat, with humidity usually under 20 percent. To visitors, however, the outdoors can seem like a moistureless sauna. The winter weather offers another extreme – a dense Tule fog, the like of which is rarely seen elsewhere. Unlike the low cloudiness

LEFT: California poppies are supplied to the nation.

Map
on page
244

found on the California coast, this winter blanket doesn't always burn off as the day goes on. It sometimes lingers for several weeks in winter months.

Bakersfield ❷ was largely swampland until Colonel Thomas Baker, an engineer in the state militia, received an 87,000-acre (35,200-hectare) grant in 1863. Baker began growing alfalfa on some of the drier land, and travelers began stopping at "Colonel Baker's field."

The city is the site of the enormous **Kern County Museum** (weekdays 8am–5pm, Sat noon–5pm, Sun 1–5pm, tel: 805/861-2132) on Chester Avenue, whose 40 buildings cover 14 acres (6 hectares) and depict local life during the last couple of centuries. A self-guided tour down the streets of the village includes a visit to a furnished Victorian mansion, a schoolhouse, a saloon and a railroad station. The **California Living Museum** (closed Mon, tel: 805/872-2256) on Old Alfred Harrell Highway is a combined zoo and botanical garden, including a petting zoo and endangered species such as mountain lions and bald eagles.

Country music

Bakersfield's most familiar contribution to culture has been in the field of country music. The city, known as "Nashville West," was the training ground for *Hee Haw* star Buck Owens (who still lives there) and singer Merle Haggard. Both honed their skills in the many small, rough-and-tumble country bars (some with sawdust on the floor) that thrived in the 1950s and later. Today, although they tend to come and go frequently, a few country clubs still operate.

The influence of the early settlers can be tasted in Bakersfield's famous Basque restaurants, where high-protein and carbohydrate feasts are served at low prices. It's all a family-style affair, with guests seated at long banquet tables and large platters of steaks and other foods passed around. There is only one seating time for lunch or dinner, so be sure to find out when that is.

Forty miles (65 kms) southeast of Bakersfield near the town of **Tehachapi**, the

Sky Mountain Resort ❸ was designed as a conference center but has since become popular with families because of its facilities like a health club, equestrian center (miles of attractive trails through the hills), swimming pool, golf course and restaurant.

Winding through Bakersfield from northeast of the city is the **Kern River**, which provides some of the most challenging whitewater rapids in the western states over three stretches: the Forks of the Kern (May to July), the upper Kern (May to early July) and the lower Kern (June to September). The rapids are rated class IV and V; the most dangerous rating is VI, but these are so treacherous that experts position rescue teams at strategic stations downstream, just in case.

Fortunately for neophytes, there are guided tours available, offering everything from a "get-your-paddle-wet" 90-minute jaunt to three-day trips that provide spectacular campfire meals at the end of a long day. Anyone feeling particularly adven-

RIGHT:
fruit, one of the Valley's main sources of income.

turous should head for the Forks. The sole access is a 3-mile (5-km) trail – mules are used to carry the rafts – and it's screened off from the highway, offering an isolated wilderness feeling. At the other extreme, anyone feeling particularly sybaritic should head for **Miracle Hot Springs**, where visitors can watch rafters float by while soaking in spring-fed hot pools right on the bank of the Kern.

Fishermen may want to stop in the **Lake Isabella-Kernville** area, between the upper and lower Kern, where a huge flood-control dam built in the early 1950s created the largest freshwater lake in Southern California. Kernville was once located where the lake itself is now, before it was moved by the government. In late fall, if the water is low, it is possible to wander among the old foundations and find remnants of the former village.

North of Bakersfield are a number of small agricultural villages with names such as **Pixley** and **Goshen**. Scattered among these villages are a few sights worth see-ing. **Colonel Allensworth State Historic Park** (open daily, tel: 805/849-3433) provides a unique look at one man's vision for his people. The agricultural colony of Allensworth was founded in 1908 by an ex-slave who wanted blacks to have polit-ical and economic independence.

After the colonel's death, Allensworth fell on hard times. The only American town to be founded and governed by blacks, it was scheduled to be bulldozed in the early 1960s before the state stepped in and began restoring the buildings. To get there by car, take State 99 to Tulare County Road J22 and turn left, then pro-ceed south on State 43.

Giant sequoias

Near the town of **Porterville** is the stun-ning **Sequoia National Forest ❹** featur-ing a redwood grove, the Kern Plateau, the Golden Trout Wilderness and numerous giant sequoias (naturally) over a 1.2-mil-lion-acre (490,000-hectare) area. The fall colors are as stupendous as can be seen

BELOW: autumn in Sequoia National Park.

Map on page 244

anywhere west of the Mississippi River, and winter sports such as skiing and snowmobiling are available because of the extremely high altitude.

Highest peak

At the park's eastern side is awesome, impressive **Mount Whitney ❺**, at 14,494 feet (4,418 meters) the highest peak in the continental United States. It's a steep 11-mile (18-km) climb from Whitney Portal Road to the summit, and a permit is required. (A less strenuous hike is simply to trek through the alpine meadows of Sequoia National Park, which are particularly stunning in springtime.) Mount Whitney was named for the first man to ascend to the top, geologist Josiah Whitney, who achieved this feat in 1873.

State Highway 99 connects Bakersfield with **Fresno ❻**, the sleeping giant of central California. From a train station by the edge of a wheat field, it has become a city with 11 freeway exits, rows of high-rise apartments and office buildings and a metropolitan population of over 400,000.

Fresno is the financial and cultural as well as the service and commercial center of the San Joaquin Valley. It is also as ethnically diverse as any city in the state, with large Mexican, Asian, Armenian and Basque communities. Cultural institutions include the **Metropolitan Museum of Art, Science and History** (closed Mon, tel: 559/441-1444) and **Storyland**, a children's fantasy park, and a zoo and water playground. Various wineries offer tours to the public. **Woodward Park**, in central Fresno, has a pretty Japanese Garden and a bird sanctuary.

The most bizarre attraction in town is **Forestiere Underground Gardens**, 5021 W. Shaw Avenue. These subterranean gardens once belonged to the sculptor-horticulturist Baldasare Forestiere, who over 40 years single-handedly – and using only hand tools – carved out a maze of rooms, passageways and courtyards, then filled them with rare trees. Telephone 559/271-0734 for tour information. ❑

BELOW: sunrise on Lake Isabella.

THE CENTRAL COAST

*Pretty towns, scenic wineries, perfect beaches
and chic hideaways are the main attractions of this region,
along with Santa Barbara and San Simeon*

Map
on page
254

It's a pleasant drive north from Los Angeles up the Pacific Coast Highway (PCH) along California's coast, with Santa Barbara roughly three hours away. However, you might want to consider a side trip off the PCH along State Route 150 to Ojai, hidden away on the edge of the Los Padres National Forest.

Ojai  is one of those pretty artists-and-writers' colonies that's remained determinedly unspoiled. Frank Capra's 1937 movie *Lost Horizon* was filmed at the eastern end of the valley (now filled with horse ranches and orange groves), and Shangri La is the way some residents think of it. The town itself is centered around a main street and a lovely tower with carillon, which offsets a row of unpretentious shops that includes a surprisingly elegant department store behind a covered arcade.

Pink moment

The predominantly Mediterranean-style architecture owes its origins to a glass tycoon, Edward Drummond Libby, who in 1917 built the elegant hotel opposite the library. Legendary to locals is the co-called "pink moment," when the sun sets over the surrounding mountain peaks, the highest of which is towering 6,000-foot (1,800-meter) Topa Topa. Artifacts in the **Ojai Valley Museum**, (closed Mon, Tues; open 1pm–4pm Wed–Fri, 10am–4pm weekends, tel: 805/640-1390) include those from Chumash Indian times through the ranching period.

The Oaks, a 46-room spa hotel, is owned by Sheila Cluff, a fitness buff who writes a syndicated column, and personally conducts her guests on brisk, pre-breakfast walks. Nearby is what may be the most unusual bookstore in California, **Bart's Corner**, with 100,000 used volumes on shelves that are open to the sky and a giant, 200-year-old oak tree growing through the roof.

Heading north to Santa Barbara, SR 150 winds along some 60 miles (100 km) of the shoreline of **Lake Casitas**, offering all kinds of water diversions from boat rides to swimming to water-side camping.

East of the 10-mile (16-km) Ojai Valley, the sleepy town of **Santa Paula** with its almost unchanged century-old main street lined with antique stores makes for a non-glitzy stop. A writer for the AAA magazine said it "wears the moniker 'old fashioned' with pride." One of Santa Paula's old buildings houses the **Union Oil Museum** (Thurs–Sat 10am–4pm, tel: 805/933-0076), which attractively illustrates the story of "black gold." Santa Paula is the halfway point for a trip on the fun **Fillmore and Western**

PRECEDING PAGES: Morro Bay, north of San Luis Obispo.
LEFT AND RIGHT: Mission Santa Barbara is the most beautiful of the missions.

Railway (tel: 805/524-2546), which on weekends offers two-hour excursions in vintage parlor cars past the citrus groves that lie between the towns of Fillmore and Ventura. There are also weekly Murder Mystery dinner trains.

Back on the coast

US101 bisects both **Oxnard** – scene of an annual **strawberry festival** (tel: 818/958-6634) and home to the **Carnegie Art Museum** (closed Mon–Wed, tel: 805/385-8157) – and the larger adjoining city of **Ventura ➋**, which is dominated by an ostentatious city hall on the hillside. This is outshone in style, however, by the **Mission San Buenaventura** (daily 10am–5pm, till 4pm on Sun, tel: 805/648-4496), the last of the California missions to be founded by the redoubtable Father Junípero Serra. The mission has a very pretty garden, cooling in the summer heat.

Across the street is the **Ventura County Museum of History and Art** (daily 10am–5pm, closed Mon, tel: 805/656-0323). Family photographs from the 1850s can be admired in the **Olivas Adobe** (weekend tours 10am–4pm, tel: 805/644-4346), which has a lovely garden open every day.

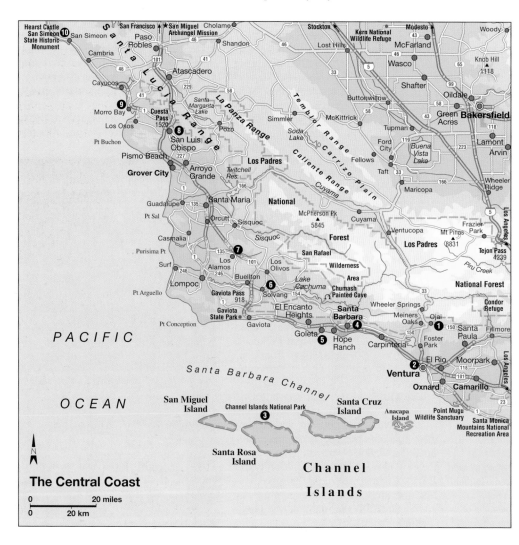

The Central Coast

0   20 miles

0   20 km

Map on page 254

West of town where the Ventura River flows into the ocean, the worthwhile **Seaside Wilderness Park** protects such exotic wildlife as pelicans and snowy plovers. The adjoining 121-year-old **Ventura Pier** was restored in 1993.

Channel Islands

From both Ventura and Santa Barbara, Island Packers (reservations: tel: 805/642-1393) runs boats 14 miles (23 km) across the ocean to **Channel Islands National Park ❸**, a group of five uninhabited islands whose headquarters are in Ventura Harbor (tel: 805/658-5730). Camping is permitted on **Anacapa** all year and on **Santa Barbara** and **San Miguel** islands in summer. Between Christmas and late March, there are sightseeing excursions to locate whales, thousands of which migrate from the Bering Sea through this area to the warmer waters off the Mexican Coast where they breed and spend the winter. The trip across to East Anacapa takes a couple of hours in seas that can be pretty rough,

but visitors are rewarded with an island that has remained pretty much as nature intended. A park ranger conducts a brief tour along paths which in springtime and early summer adjoin the nesting areas of thousands of aggressively protective seagulls and their fluffy chicks. Take along whatever you need to eat, because the island has no such facilities. **Santa Cruz** island is home to animals and plants found nowhere else in the world, many of which are endangered species. **Santa Rosa** is the fifth Channel Island;

Farther up the coast from Ventura is **Carpinteria**, a pedestrian-friendly town where few buildings are higher than two stories. Just north is **Summerland**, a tiny hillside community which took its name from a popular Spiritualist tract of 1887 and was planned as a colony devoted to believers in the occult. But when the following year a resident dug for water and struck oil, $25 lots quickly became worth 100 times that, and derricks went up everywhere, especially on the beach which

BELOW: wall mural, Ventura.

today is a secluded strand much favored for watching sunsets.

On the outskirts of Santa Barbara, the charming **Montecito Inn** has been popular with refugees from Hollywood since the 1920s, when one of its original owners was Charlie Chaplin. Guests included Fatty Arbuckle, Fred Astaire and Will Rogers. While the oil was flowing to the south, more than 1,000 two-reel movies were being shot in Santa Barbara, most of them between 1913 and 1918. Movies and television shows continue to be shot in the region today.

Another local hotel with a long and interesting history, the **Miramar**, has been renovated in his distinctive fashion by New York hotelier Ian Schrager. Among the residents of this affluent suburb are Michael Jackson and Michael Douglas, so it is no surprise there are so many upscale resorts in the area.

The legendary **San Ysidro Ranch** (1893), in a canyon lined with sycamore and eucalyptus trees, was where John F. Kennedy honeymooned with his wife Jackie, where Lauren Bacall says she fell in love with Humphrey Bogart and the site of a midnight wedding in 1940 between Laurence Olivier and Vivien Leigh.

Santa Barbara

Santa Barbara ❹, which got its start as a health resort after glowing articles by New York journalist Charles Nordhoff touted its mineral springs, is an attractive city whose architecture is almost entirely in idealized Spanish Colonial Revival style.

After a disastrous earthquake in 1925, the city's leaders imposed a building code that prohibited anything unharmonious, processing designs for 2,000 new structures in a remarkably short period of time. Before the earthquake, one author observed, it was "a wasteland of western junk that had spread over the original Spanish architecture like a smothering fungus."

But, its architecture notwithstanding and more because of its possession of the most

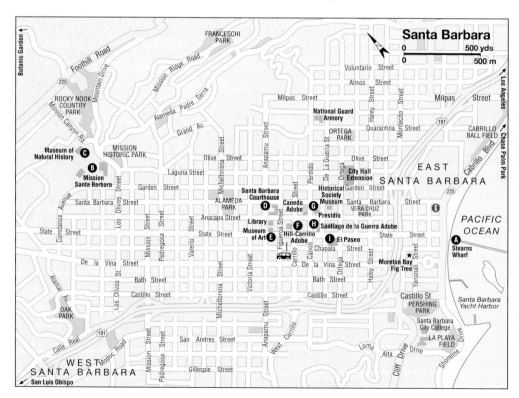

Maps,
page 254
& 256

handsome of all the missions, the city has long been admired. Over a century ago Baedeker referred to "the beauty of its surroundings, the luxuriance of its roses and other flowers, the excellence of its bathing beach and its pleasant society."

Most of Santa Barbara's modern attractions can be found along its main, busy thoroughfare, **State Street**, which, unfortunately, is changing its flavor as old mom-and-pop businesses have ceded space to the more solid, stress-proof structures demanded by new earthquake regulations.

Oldest pier

A shuttle operates down State Street all the way to century-old **Stearns Wharf** Ⓐ (tel: 805/564-5518), the oldest pier on the West Coast, which offers everything – fishing, seafood stands, restaurants, wine tasting, a marine museum and aquarium. It's also the starting point for whale-watching trips.

The **Santa Barbara Trolley** operates along the shore past the **Zoo** (daily 10am–5pm, till 6pm in summer, tel:

805/962-5339) and the **Andree Clark Bird Refuge** all the way to the Montecito Inn and back up through town to the Old Mission. Beaches line the shore on both sides of the pier, with the more expensive hotels at the eastern end. A path for bicycles follows this route, and rental bikes are available. The attractive 21-foot (6-meter) high **Chromatic Gate** on the waterfront was the work of Herbert Byer, last living master of the seminal Bauhaus school who spent his final years here.

After enjoying the pier, head north up State Street and turn right for three or four blocks to **Mission Santa Barbara** Ⓑ (daily 9am–5pm, Sunday 1pm–5pm, tel: 805/682-4149) which with its twin bell towers is generally regarded as the most beautiful of the remaining missions. Founded in 1786, it was damaged in both of the area's major earthquakes (1812 and 1925), but lovingly restored and still in use as a parish church. The museum displays relics from the days when the Chumash lived at the mission while being "trained"

BELOW: the harmonious roofscape of Santa Barbara.

to undertake useful tasks by their Spanish overlords. In May, an Italian street-painting festival takes place with entrants creating their chalked masterpieces on squares in the mission's plaza. More about Indian life can be studied two blocks to the north in the **Museum of Natural History** ● (daily 9am–5pm, tel: 805/682-4711), with its 80-foot (24-meter) blue whale skeleton and an interesting array of inanimate animals, birds, reptiles and fish.

There's one other attraction in this area, although it's more than a mile (2 km) to the north up Mission Canyon Road: the **Botanic Garden** (daily 9am–5pm, Sat, Sun till 6pm, tel: 805/682-4726). The garden has fragrant walking trails through 60 acres (24 hectares) of native flowers, shrubs and cacti.

Two blocks from the bus station in the center of Santa Barbara is the handsome, Spanish-Moorish-style **Santa Barbara Courthouse** ● built in the 1920s after the earthquake. Its attractive lobby is lined with mosaics and murals and there's a lovely view from the top of gently sloping red roofs and the lawn below. The courthouse is a favored place for weddings.

A short tour

Walk past the **Santa Barbara Library** to State Street, passing (or inspecting) the **Museum of Art** ● (closed Mon, Wed, tel: 805/963-4364). Turn left along Carrillo to visit the **Hill-Carrillo Adobe** ●, built by Daniel Hill in 1826 for his Spanish bride for whom he constructed the city's first home with a wooden floor.

Continue down Anacapa Street to Canon Perdido Street. The block to the left, bordered by the **Canedo Adobe** (*circa* 1782) is where Santa Barbara began, centered around the **Presidio** ● with its chapel and parade grounds, more restored adobes and the **Historical Society Museum** (Wed, Sat, Sun afternoons, tel: 805/966-1601). The city's **Conference & Visitor Bureau** (tel: 800/927-4688) offers a free map for a self-guided tour comprising most of these sites. Two of the city's oldest houses are the 1854

BELOW: tower atop the Santa Barbara Courthouse.

Maps,
page 254
& 256

Trussell-Winchester Adobe and the **Fernald House** (Sun 2–4pm, tel: 805/966-1601 for both). Head back one block towards State Street for the **Santiago de la Guerra Adobe** ⓗ (1827), the original home of the Presidio's commander. The plaza here is where the city council first met in 1850, an event still celebrated every August with a fiesta.

Here also is the enticing, cobbled area **El Paseo** ❶ (or "the street in Spain" as tourist officials call it). It is by far the most attractive place in town to shop and sip a cup of coffee at one of the outdoor cafés around the fountain. Half a century ago the El Paseo theater used to feature on its stage a group of Spanish dancers which included Rita Cansino (Rita Hayworth).

As befits its upscale nature, Santa Barbara has an active night-time cultural life centering around numerous theaters, including those on the UCSB campus. For show schedules, telephone the Santa Barbara Theatre Alliance.

Back down at the shore, kids love to play on the antique carousel in **Chase Palm Park**, a shady haven in the stretch of palm-fringed beaches; the park also features a riverbed maze and spouting whales.

Valley of the Flowers

For a contrast to upscale Santa Barbara, head up the coast a little farther north to **Lompoc,** whose Valley of the Flowers earned its name from the worldwide export of seeds and where an annual flower festival is still staged in late June. There's a relaxed, small-town feel to Lompoc, and its history is conveyed in countless murals and in the **Lompoc Museum** (open afternoons, closed Mon, tel: 805/796-3888).

Before Lompoc, though, the highway passes through **Goleta** ❺, home of a branch of the University of California and the 1873 **Stow House** (open Sat, Sun afternoons, tel: 805/964-4407), and skirts the shore past some gorgeous beaches before offering another side trip

BELOW: Santa Barbara's El Paseo and Stearns Wharf.

THE HARBOR
RESTAURANT

at **Solvang** ❻ (tel: 800/486 6765) a replica of a Scandinavian town whose horse-drawn streetcars and Danish bakeries attract around 5,000 visitors a day in season – double the population.

The largest freshwater reservoir in Southern California, **Lake Cachuma Recreation Area** (tel: 805/668-3018) is nearby, where in winter there are guided cruises to view a rare flock of migrating bald eagles. On the coast boating, sailing and surfing are available at the sandy beaches of **Gaviota State Park**.

Santa Ynez Valley

Solvang is a good base for visiting the wineries of the **Santa Ynez Valley**, most of which welcome visitors and offer free tastings. The Santa Barbara County Wineries Association (tel: 805/688-0881) offers a free touring map and guide to its many members in the area. The vineyards of the Santa Barbara missions were producing wine centuries ago, and wine grapes have now surpassed lettuce as the region's number one cash crop.

The Santa Ynez mountains and the San Rafael mountains which border the Santa Ynez Valley are gently rolling hills, sprinkled with oak trees and eucalyptus. Three charming little towns – **Santa Ynez**, **Los Olivos** and **Ballard** – in the northeastern portion of the valley are often overlooked, but all are worth visiting for their museums, galleries and quaintness.

Make a point of leaving US Highway 101 at the **Los Alamos** ❼ turnoff to view this town with its antique stores, frontier-style buildings and, especially, the handsome **Victorian Mansion** and adjoining **Union Hotel**. The latter has a wonderful saloon and poolroom as well as bedrooms and a restaurant furnished in 19th-century style. Operating as an upscale bed and breakfast inn, the hotel has a jacuzzi and swimming pool and offers visitors quick jaunts in its 1918 automobile.

The Victorian Mansion has to be seen to be believed: a three-story wooden edifice with half a dozen theme rooms in the style

BELOW: Victoria Mansion, Los Alamos.

Map on page 254

of gypsies, pirates, ancient Rome, provincial France, Egypt and a 1950s drive-in complete with bed-equipped Cadillac and movie screen.

Wedding bells

The first thought that comes to mind is how much honeymoon couples must love the mansion, and indeed the area seems to be romantically attuned to that notion with similarly exotic, but nicely tacky, theme rooms offered by the famous **Madonna Inn** (which can be admired from US Highway 101 just before San Luis Obispo), and old-fashioned wedding ceremonies performed at the nearby town of Nipono in its pretty 19th-century **Victorian Wedding Bells Chapel** or the **Kaleidoscope Inn**'s garden gazebo.

To the west of the little agricultural center of **Santa Maria**, which stages a Wednesday farmers' market, are a batch of wineries along State Route 174. Most of them have free tastings daily.

Southeast of San Luis Obispo is the historic village of **Arroyo Grande** (whose own farmers' market is on Saturdays) and **Lopez Lake**, with camping sites and facilities – boating, swimming, horseback riding, fishing and hilltop hikes. Just to the south is **Pismo Beach**, the only shore community actually on US Highway 101 between Santa Barbara and San Francisco. There's a wide range of places to stay and the usual attractions of a seaside community, including a pier and one of the few remaining beaches onto which you can still drive your car.

The famous Pismo clam, which grows nearly to the size of a dinner plate and can weigh as much as 1½ lb (nearly 700 grams), has almost disappeared and even with a license clammers are restricted to 10 per day, each clam at least 4½ inches (11 cms) across, if they can find them at all, that is. Undersized clams are supposed to be reburied in the sand but wardens say many people don't do the task properly.

A clam festival is held every year in October, but almost as many come to visit

BELOW:
Solvang is a replica of a Scandinavian town.

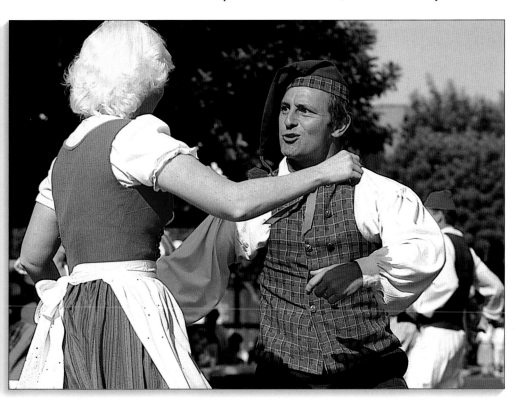

in January to see the hordes of colorful Monarch butterflies which spend the winter months in a grove of eucalyptus and Monterey pines.

Halfway to San Francisco

San Luis Obispo ❽, roughly halfway between Los Angeles and San Francisco, owes its beginnings to the 1772 mission, now a parish church, but its development to the arrival of the Southern Pacific Railroad in 1894. It's a pleasant town which offers historic strolls through its attractive streets from the restored adobe on Monterey Street in which Judge Walter Murray founded the local paper in 1850.

The Victorian homes in the Old Town neighborhood around Buchon and Broad streets are worth exploring, and there's a regular Thursday night farmers' market downtown that turns into a street festival with entertainment. The attractive **San Luis Obispo Mission** (daily 9am–5pm, till 4pm in winter, closed Jan, tel: 805/543-6850) remains in use as a parish church.

Morro Bay ❾ is a seaside resort dominated by a 576-foot (176-meter) rock just offshore, **Morro Rock**. Numerous seafood restaurants line the waterfront from which "clam taxis" ferry hopeful diggers to sand dunes across the bay.

There's a 60-mile (100-km) stretch of almost-deserted coastline between here and Monterey Bay, and most travelers who take the lovely longer route, rather than US 101 inland, are probably headed for the state's second-most popular attraction (after Disneyland), **Hearst Castle ❿** at **San Simeon** (first tour 8.20am, then throughout the day; for tickets tel: 1-916/414-8400 x 4100; www.hearst-castle.org).

Designed by William Randolph Hearst's architect Julia Morgan, the amazing complex includes the twin-towered main house, sumptuous guest houses and a fabulous indoor swimming pool *(see page 110)*. There are several tours a day to different parts of the estate. Although popular, timed tickets mean visitors can go away and come back closer to the hour of entry. ❑

Map on page 254

BELOW: San Luis Obispo.

Hearst's Castle

W illiam Randolph Hearst is said to have acquired his taste for collecting at 10 years old while visiting European castles and museums with his mother. Certainly, by the time Hearst and architect Julia Morgan began to create San Simeon "castle," the publishing magnate had the means to satisfy his hobby and provide a grand home for his acquisitions. The task that Hearst and Ms Morgan embarked upon was hardly a conventional building project.

All supplies had to be brought up the coast by steamer, then hauled 5 miles (8 km) up the hill. Tons of topsoil were brought up to create flower beds for the 127 acres (51 hectares) of gardens. Five greenhouses were erected to supply plants for year-round color. To hide a water tank on the adjoining hill, 6,000 Monterey pines were planted, plus an additional 4,000 trees each year.

White marble statues flanked the 104-foot (32-meter) outdoor Neptune Pool. A pair of tennis courts was sited near the indoor Roman pool. The 85-foot (26-meter) long assembly hall in the main house was constructed around a 400-year-old carved wooden ceiling from Italy.

By the time W.R. was advised by his doctors to move to Beverly Hills in 1947, the "ranch" had 165 rooms filled with mostly Spanish and Italian art and antiques spread over the Casa Grande and three guesthouses. Hearst moved into San Simeon when the last of his five sons went off to school. Instead of his wife Millicent – whom he had married when he was 39 and she 21 – he installed his longtime mistress, Marion Davies, who had been a teenaged chorus girl when he first wooed her with diamonds.

Almost every weekend San Simeon welcomed moviedom's elite. "The society people always wanted to meet the movie stars so I mixed them together," wrote Marion Davies. "Jean Harlow came up quite frequently. She was very nice and I liked her. She didn't have an awful lot to say... all the men used to flock around her. She was very attractive in an evening dress because she never wore anything under it." Clark Gable was another regular guest. "Women were always running after him but he'd just give them a look as if to say, 'How crazy these people are,' and he stayed pretty much to himself."

A special train with a jazz band and open bar from Glendale station in the San Fernando Valley brought the weekend party guests 210 miles (340 km) to San Luis Obispo, where limousines transported them through the estate's grounds filled with lions, bears, elephants, pumas and leopards.

On arrival at the floodlit mansion, each was allocated a personal maid or valet and was free to wander – except for a mandatory attendance at the late-night dinner over which W.R. would preside in the Great Hall, at the head of the 16th-century monastery table. Paper napkins, catsup from bottles and the absence of tablecloths preserved the illusion of "camping out." After dinner Hearst showed a movie, often one as yet unreleased; *Gone With the Wind*, for example, was screened six months before its premiere.

In 1957, six years after William Randolph Hearst's death, the Hearst Corporation deeded the San Simeon property to the state. ❑

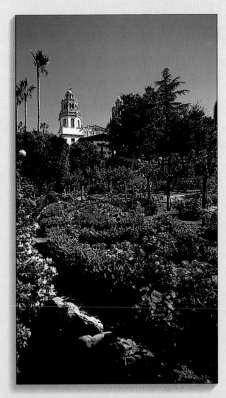

RIGHT: San Simeon's Hearst Castle is built from materials collected from around the world.

Map
on page
276

SANTA CATALINA

*With its steep and rugged canyons, miles of coastline
and lovely capital village, eco-friendly Catalina
charms even the most jaded traveler*

All the joys of living on an island (including Malibu-like floods in winter) are experienced by the few year-round residents of **Santa Catalina ❶**, located 26 miles (42 km) across the sea. Most of the year a trip to Catalina makes for a very pleasant one-day or weekend break via ferries which run frequently from the mainland.

With its steep and rugged canyons, 54 miles (87 km) of coastline and lovely capital of Avalon, Catalina charms even the most jaded traveler who has come to regard Southern California as the capital of auto-mania. Here there are no rental cars and the environmentally-oriented island authority has guaranteed that almost two-thirds of the island will always remain in its natural state. The first steamship service to the island began in 1888 at a time when pigeons were still being used to carry messages to and from the mainland.

Roses in Avalon

On arrival at **Avalon ❷**, it's a five-minute walk along the jetty into the tiny town, past a couple of places which rent bicycles or the ubiquitous golf carts. These are what most residents get around on until they have been here six years and are allowed to own a car. From the office of Island Tram Tours, you can take a 40-minute narrated trip around town.

Beside the pier is the helpful **Visitors' Information Center** (tel: 424/510-1520) where, if you're only here for the day, it's wise to book for an island tour before doing anything else. Among the other possible activities are fishing, boating or parasailing.

First stop on the basic tour, at the far side of the harbor, is **the Casino** which achieved national fame in the 1930s by broadcasting big bands such as Count Basie and Kay Kyser from the Art Deco ballroom filled with as many as 6,000 dancers at a time. Built in 1929 at a cost of around $2 mil-

lion, the casino's ground-floor theater with a full-size pipe organ was the first in America to be built especially for the new, all-talking motion pictures.

As you walk back into town past the Victorian hotels among the restaurants of **Solomon's Landing**, across from the Via Casino archway, there's a souvenir shop displaying products from the now defunct Catalina Pottery. Other memorabilia in the shop includes sheet music of songs about the island: *Catalina Is Calling Me, When Roses Bloom in Avalon, Catalina Aloha-Oe.*

Once the waters clear after the winter storms, there are regular 40-minute excursions from the **Pleasure Pier** in a glass-bottomed boat which traverses shallow waters filled with multi-colored fish (mostly dark

hues of olive or blue with the occasional orange garibaldi) darting in and out of a seaweed "garden." The fronds of kelp, swaying to the motion of the glass-bottomed boat, seem to be dancing to a hidden music with the little fish acting as random soloists. At night, says the local tour guide, nocturnal creatures take over including "wimpy" lobsters which lack the formidable (but oh-so-edible) claws of their Maine counterparts.

Arabian horses

To best appreciate Catalina, devote the afternoon to the four-hour **Inland Motor Tour** which heads up through the mountains to the island's airport and which makes a stop at **El Rancho Escondido**, the fascinating Wrigley-owned ranch where Arabian horses are reared. Immaculately trained horses are put through their paces to demonstratetheir skill and intelligence.

The tour then continues onwards along the old stage coach route across the island to various old tribal sites or secluded bays. The nicest parts of the island are these wilderness areas, popular with campers and hikers, some of whom find accommodation at the mountainous Blackjack Campsite.

Descendants of General Phineas Banning, who operated the earliest legendary stagecoach routes across the West, once owned most of Catalina island and began the process of turning it into the tourist resort it eventually became. William Wrigley, the chewing gum tycoon, continued this development when he acquired the island after the great fire of 1919.

He built the 1,000-bed luxury Hotel St Catherine at **Descanso Beach** west of town, a magnificent mansion on **Mount Ada** (now a bed & breakfast called the Inn of Mount Ada) and started the Catalina Pottery to provide tiles for other projects he was creating on the island. The Wrigley family still owns about 15 percent of Catalina, donating the remainder to the nonprofit Island Conservancy which takes its responsibilities seriously.

Catalina was "discovered" by the Portuguese navigator Juan Rodríguez Cabrillo

BELOW: the Wrigley Mansion on Mount Ada, built by the chewing-gun tycoon.

Map
on page
276

in 1542 and claimed for Spain as a safe anchorage for its Europe-bound treasure galleons 60 years later. Actually, of course, it had been inhabited by Native Americans for thousands of years. Two centuries after the Spaniards arrived, however, the Indians were pretty much eliminated by Russian hunters in their search for sea-otter pelts. In the 1860s there were almost 30,000 grazing animals on the island, among them 7,000 goats or sheep which de-vegetated most of the terrain.

Later visitors, mostly American, included traders, pirates, smugglers and even miners who mistakenly believed the island to be rich in gold and other minerals. All of them contributed to devastating the island by chopping down many of the trees.

Where the buffalo roam

Since the Conservancy took over, much of this damage has been repaired. Wild fauna such as the bald eagle, the fox, wild boar and buffalo have been protected and their numbers expanded. Passengers on the bus tour invariably spot a couple of buffalo – descendants of a herd brought here when Zane Grey's *The Vanishing American* was shot on the island in 1925. You can even buy a buffalo (for a few hundred dollars) when there's a surplus.

The house that Grey owned – he died in 1939 – has since become the **Zane Grey Pueblo Hotel** (tel: 310-510 0966) which, like the 40 or so other hotels on Catalina, tend to be booked up early in summer. Describing Catalina as the most delightful place he ever visited, Grey wrote about the way the sun shone after the morning fog had rolled away. "It is the kind of sunshine that salves the eye, elevates the spirit and warms the back. And out there rolls the vast blue Pacific – calm, slowly heaving, beautiful and mysterious."

At the airport, 1,620 feet (494 meters) above sea level, a small display includes historical pictures and a diorama featuring local animals. The local café sells buffalo burgers. Apart from flights to San Diego – offering spectacular views of the island –

BELOW:
buffalo were brought to the island to be a film backdrop; they still roam the hills.

there is no longer a scheduled service to the airport, which is used mostly by a freight company and a few private-plane owners.

An airport bus connects with Avalon several times each day; this is an alternative way to get into the mountains from the town. The island's highest point is **Mount Orizaba** (2,069 feet/631 meters).

Flying fish

For those lacking the stamina for a lengthy exploration other options include one-hour tours to see flying fish or sealions; two-hour inspections of the **Skyline Drive**; and evening tours, one of which includes dinner at **Two Harbors**, the island's other main community where so-called "buffalo milk" (a vodka drink) is served in the restaurant.

Even Downtown itself can be done in a tram tour, although Avalon is so small it's more fun to wander aimlessly, watching the boats in the harbor, admiring the Catalina Tile on the Serpentine Wall opposite the beach or on the fountain in Wrigley Plaza, shopping for crafts and eating well in a mul-

titude of little restaurants and stores. Leave some time for a stroll through the back streets, where most of the tiny houses are built on lots that originally housed tents. Drop by the bookshop on Metropole Street and look at old postcards.

If you go past the casino and climb the hill you'll pass the foundations, including swimming pool, of the old St Catherine Hotel which was pulled down in 1966. Perched on a hill at the other side of the bay is **Holly Hill House**. This Queen Anne-style mansion dates back to 1890 and is the third-oldest house in Avalon.

It's a stiff climb up Avalon Canyon, almost 2 miles (3 km), to the 37-acre (15-hectare) **Wrigley Memorial and Botanical Garden** (daily 8am–5pm, tel: 424/510-2288) where you can stroll among trees and plants many of which, like the flower St Catherine's lace, are endemic to this island. There are, of course, taxis available.

Island idyll

There are various packages available (round-trip transportation, two nights' accommodation, three tours) for reasonable fees. Hotels run the gamut from fairly moderate to expensive. There's a fully-equipped campground about a mile from town (with a shuttle bus), located close to the Botanical Garden and hiking trails. Reservations are required, especially in summer. Other campsites around the island are operated by Los Angeles County's Department of Parks and Recreation, as well as Catalina Island Camping.

The *Catalina Express* (beside the *Queen Mary* in Long Beach, tel: 800/668-5533) also operates daily boats from Dana Point. *Catalina Cruises* (tel: 800/ 228-2546) operates several daily trips from Long Beach and also services the other island port, Two Harbors. *Catalina Flyer* (tel: 714/673-5245) sails daily from Newport Beach. For those with more money than time, there's also Island Express Helicopters (tel: 310/510-252) which operate from both San Pedro and Long Beach. For information, contact the Catalina Island Visitors' Bureau and Chamber of Commerce, P.O. Box Avalon, CA 90704, tel: 310/510-1520 or visit www.catalina.com. ❑

Map on page 276

LEFT: peaceful anchorage on Catalina's windward side. **RIGHT:** beauty on the beach.

Map on page 276

ORANGE COUNTY TO SAN DIEGO

Heading south towards Mexico, features of the California coastline include sea breezes, surfing beaches, gondolas, telescopes and miniature cities made of toy brick

It takes a little longer to drive along the coast from Los Angeles to San Diego rather than whizzing down the freeway, but the route is much more interesting, passing through the various seaside resorts of the **South Bay**. All this area leading out from the City of Angels is still in Los Angeles County; the Orange County border begins after Long Beach.

If you have plenty of time after passing through the South Bay communities, you could make a short diversion around the **Palos Verdes** peninsula, admiring the magnificent seaside homes. Attractive **Abalone Cove**, the beach west of Narcissa Drive, is an ecological preserve located at the end of a steep path; it's perfect for divers and tidepoolers.

Whale watching

Just past the Golden Shores shopping center is a lighthouse beside which, at the **Point Vicente Interpretive Center ❸**, are telescopes to look for passing whales (December to spring); a small exhibit which includes an informative whale-watching video plus earphones to hear the mournful voices of these lovable monsters; and a relief map of the peninsula showing how mountainous is this surprising terrain. There are pleasant grassy grounds suitable for picnicking (bring your own food and drink) and leaflets identifying the various plants to be found on the **Botanic Trail**.

About a mile (2 km) farther on is the wood-and-glass **Wayfarers Chapel** (tel: 424/377-1650), designed by Frank Lloyd Wright's son Lloyd, whose inspiration is said to have been Northern California's majestic redwood trees. It was built in 1951 as a memorial to the 18th-century Swedish theologian Emmanuel Swedenborg. Walking around the peaceful gardens to the sound of songbirds, a fountain and the gurgling stream is a tranquilizing experience. There are services in the chapel most Sundays.

Head westwards along the coastal road to **San Pedro ❹**, headquarters of Southern California's fishing fleet which once distinguished this town as a fishing port. All the genuine old parts of what eons ago was a little fishing town are long gone, replaced by a pseudo-19th-century construction called **Ports O'Call Village** (tel: 424/831-0287), which, surprisingly, is imaginatively done: several blocks of New England saltbox-type, apparently weathered shops, plus more than a dozen restau-

PRECEDING PAGES: the *Queen Mary* and make-believe English village, Long Beach.
LEFT: SoCal pools inspired artist David Hockney.
RIGHT: canals in Naples.

rants – all in complementing and matching styles that are a pleasure to walk around. Harbor tours and fishing trips go from here, as well as helicopters to the isle of Catalina. There's oodles of free parking space beside which a heroic fisherman statue proclaims, *"Lo, the fisherman, for his harpoon, hook and net have long harvested the endless sea… etc., etc."*

Tied up opposite is the West Coast's largest commercial fishing fleet. A short walk away is **Pier 53** where you can look around – or even take a one-day cruise on – a preserved merchant ship from World War II, the *S.S. Lane Victory.*

Green and white trolleys run along San Pedro's waterfront area, making short stops at the **maritime museum, Ports O'Call Village** and the Frank Gehry-designed **Cabrillo Marine Aquarium** (afternoons Tues–Fri, 10am–5pm weekends, tel: 424/548-7652).

San Pedro's **Cabrillo Beach** has earned a reputation as one of the best places in the area to windsurf, and beginners espe-cially favor the sheltered waters inside the harbor breakwater. For lovers of the sea, the **Cabrillo Marine Museum** is on Stephen M. White Drive.

Long Beach

Palos Verdes Drive segues into 25th Street from which a left turn on Gaffey (State Route 110) and up to State Route 47 over the Vincent Thomas Bridge takes you straight ahead through **Long Beach ❺**, the world's largest man-made harbor, on Ocean Avenue. Out in the bay, take a close look at the palm-fringed island with the tall towers: it's actually one of four man-made islands created to conceal all the working oil derricks which for 30 years have been tapping one of the richest off-shore fields in the United States. The towers are lighted at night, creating an eerie and distinctive waterscape.

Long Beach is currently rethinking its image in order to attract tourists and new industry, and is prepared to spend money to make this happen. The city is in the

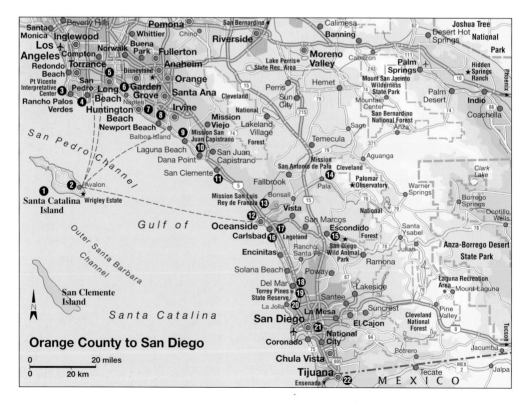

Orange County to San Diego

Map on page 276

process of developing hundreds of acres of pristine waterfront and spending $650 million on the Queensway Bay Project, whose centerpiece is **Rainbow Harbor**. At the **Irvine Spectrum**, an entertainment center where Interstate 405 merges with I-5, is one of Southern California's largest restaurants, the 700-person capacity **Yard House**. The world-class **Aquarium of the Pacific** (daily 10am–6pm, tel: 562/590-3100) is well worth a visit, and the respected **Museum of Art** (closed Mon, Tues, tel: 562/439-2119) has recently doubled its size. The *Catalina Express* runs from Long Beach to the island.

But Long Beach's main attraction – as well as being Los Angeles's harbor – is undoubtedly the *Queen Mary* ocean liner (daily guided tours, tel: 562/435-3511). The *Queen Mary* was built in 1936. One of the most stylish ships to sail the seas, royals and celebrities were regularly among her passengers.

During World War II, the ship was camouflaged with gray paint, and transported up to 800,000 soldiers in a series of daring cloak-and-dagger missions. Modern-day travelers can dine in the Art Deco restaurant, or even spend the night in one of the *Queen Mary*'s cabins, although the ship does not leave its berth.

At **Belmont**, a swing leftwards along Livingston Drive intersects with 2nd Street skirting the beach of **Alamitos Bay**. Here you can take a one-hour tour in a gondola along canals which pass the elegant homes of neighboring **Naples ⑥**. Operating from 11am to 11pm most days, the gondolas carry from two to six people, and are stocked with bread, cheese, salami, wine glasses and ice (bring your own drinks).

Surf City

Back, then, to the Pacific Coast Highway, which bypasses the sleepy town of **Seal Beach** and runs beside the ecological wetlands preserve just before Bolsa Chica state beach. At **Huntington Beach ⑦**, slow down to avoid the surfers carrying their boards across the road. Many of the

BELOW: rollerbladers by the beach.

communities around here are in dispute about which most deserves the title "Surf City," but Huntington Beach claims to have the best case, and in 1994 inaugurated a sidewalk **Surfers Walk of Fame**. The pier is among the most photogenic – and photographed – of the Southern California piers, and is particularly attractive at sunset. It is from Huntington that a vigorous campaign is being waged to preserve one of the state's favorite fish, the bright orange garibaldi, which flourishes all along this coast but has regrettably become too popular with collectors.

Yacht owners

At **Newport Beach ❽**, the Balboa peninsula with its 6 miles (10 km) of sandy shore encloses a harbor popular with yacht owners. On **Main Street** it's hard to miss the **Balboa Pavilion**, built in 1905 as a railroad terminal, with its distinctive but totally unnecessary steeple. Behind it you'll find fishing boats unloading their catch, if you get here early.

Almost as old is the ferry which makes the three-minute trip from the end of Palm Street to **Balboa Island** with its upscale homes and classy shops, restaurants and cafés. On your way back, somebody will surely point out the former homes of John Wayne and cowboy star Roy Rogers on nearby islands.

From **Balboa Pier**, you can admire the kite-flyers, frisbee-throwers, body-surfers and just plain sunbathers. Check out the restaurant at the end of the pier before finishing up at the **Balboa Fun Zone**, with its rides and rowdy video arcades. Almost a dozen luxury beachfront hotels have been built or are under construction along the coast between here and San Diego.

Near El Moro beach, an attractive cove before **Laguna Beach ❾**, an occasional pelican can be seen. Laguna's Pageant of the Masters (July and August) is a unique "living spectacle" with hundreds of participants, often volunteers, who do a remarkable job of creating replicas of art masterpieces using made-up performers

BELOW: Huntington Beach likes to think of itself as "Surf City."

Map on page 276

in full costume. The pageant has a different theme each year and is a remarkably ambitious enterprise; themes have included recreating the *Toll for Sunrise Mass* by J. Henry Sandham, and recreating the Serra Chapel Alter from nearby Mission San Juan Capistrano.

The Pageant of the Masters – which was first presented in 1933 and held at its Irvine Bowl Park location since the 1940s – is part of Laguna's Festival of Arts, which includes over 150 artists displaying and selling original work, plus music and dance performances.

In the past year, **Hermosa Beach** has become the local nightlife capital with a string of lively clubs dotted around the pier. Before turning inland, **Dana Point** harbor is worth a stop to browse through the cute shops and possibly stop for a drink in the attractive upstairs bar of the Jolly Roger.

Then it's off on Del Obispo Street to Camino Capistrano on which sits lovely **Mission San Juan Capistrano ⑩** (daily 9am–5pm, tel: 949/248-2048), seventh in the chain of 21 established by Franciscan *padres* late in the 18th century. Before leaving, be sure to stroll down narrow Los Rios Street, center of one of the country's oldest residential districts with its three historic adobes.

San Clemente

Just north of the controversial San Onofre Nuclear Power Plant is **San Clemente ⑪**, where former US president Richard Nixon was born on January 9, 1913 and where he set up his western White House until moving to New Jersey in 1980. The **Richard Nixon Library and Birthplace** (daily 10am–5pm, Sun 11am–5pm, tel: 714/993-5075) presents highlights of his life contained in 22 rooms.

San Clemente and Doheny beaches allow camping for a small fee, while Doheny, Dana Point, Laguna and Newport Beach have marine life preserves patrolled by state fish and game wardens, and are open to the public.

BELOW RIGHT: Mission San Juan Capistrano was seventh in the chain of 21 missions along the coast.

MISSION SAN JUAN CAPISTRANO

San Juan Capistrano is one of the most interesting of the 21 missions built along the coast of California. It is famous for the swallows' nests that can be found during the birds' scheduled arrival on St Joseph's Day, March 19 and their departure for Argentina on October 23. By some mysterious alchemy, the swallows until recent years have almost always been on time, their landing here marked by a week-long festival with *mariachi* bands and a parade.

Nowadays, perhaps as a result of climate change, tourists sometimes arrive to find only pigeons, but the mission is worth visiting nevertheless. Founded by Father Junípero Serra (his statue stands beside the ruined Great Stone Church to the right as you enter), the Serra chapel behind the church is the oldest still-in-use building in California.

At the mission's far-left corner, where the tanning vats, metal furnaces and tallow ovens can be inspected, is the archeological field office, which still uncovers old relics. The gardens were added in the 20th century, but the main courtyard itself was always the central focus of the mission, being the site of rodeos in older days with eager spectators watching from the surrounding roofs, including that of the west wing, which now houses the museum. A free map is available, which identifies and dates most of the artifacts.

A lagoon known as the **Buena Vista Audubon** (Tues–Sat 10am–4pm, Sun 1–4pm, tel: 760/439-BIRD) separates **Oceanside**  – whose major draw is the appropriate **California Surf Museum** (daily 10am–4pm, closed Tues in fall and winter, tel: 760/721-6876) – from the town of Carlsbad and Legoland *(see page 281)*. The water-obsessed museum displays the evolution of surfboards from 16-footers to fiber-glass creations known as potato- chip boards. There's an immense market among dudes for surfing memorabilia and thus much of the museum's collection is extremly valuable.

Four miles (6 km) inland from the beach on SR 14 is **Mission San Luis Rey de Francia** (daily 10am–4:30pm, tel: 760/757-3651), whose museum contains an 1865 document signed by Abraham Lincoln shortly before his assassination confirming the mission's right to its land. In its heyday, almost 3,000 Indians worked here at what was the 18th of the 21 California missions. There are pleasant strolls to be had among the acres of grounds; among the lush greenery is the first pepper tree brought to California from Peru in the mid-19th century.

From Oceanside, an interesting drive inland is along State Route 76 to the small village of **Pala**, site of the **Mission San Antonio de Pala**, an *asistancia* (extension mission) built in 1810. Located on the Pala Indian reservation, it is the only California mission still serving Native Americans and has celebrated Corpus Christi with an open-air mass, dances and games on the first Sunday in June since 1816.

Largest telescope

The road continues southeast to Rincon Springs, a community to the north of **Escondido** on County Highway S6, and the gateway to massive **Palomar Mountain**. Rising 6,100 feet (1,860 meters) above sea level and stretching some 20 miles (32 km) in length, Palomar is the home of the huge Hale Telescope inside the **Palomar Observatory** owned

BELOW: hats off to local visitors.

Map
on page
276

and operated by the California Institute of Technology. From 1948 until the 1970s, the 525-ton **Hale Telescope** with its huge reflector was the world's largest, and still enables astronomers to view galaxies million of miles away. Sitting under an Art-Deco-style dome around seven floors high, the telescope has a mirror made from a 14½-ton piece of Pyrex, the heaviest piece of glass in the world.

The observatory is credited with the discovery of quasars, which are defined by one dictionary as "celestial objects that resemble stars but whose large redshift and apparent brightness imply extreme distance and high energy output." A visitors' gallery contains an explanation of the workings of this and the observatory's other tools, and there are picnic areas nearby in the surrounding state park.

Between late February and April the **Flower Fields** (daily 10am–dusk, tel: 760/930-9123) at **Carlsbad ⑯** draw thousands of visitors who can walk among masses of red, yellow, orange and pink flowers which spread across acres of hillside in alternating bands. The Bird of Paradise, first commercially developed here, is the city's official flower. If you arrive out of season, either too late or too early for Carlsbad's big Street Faires (May and November), you might want to settle for some bird watching.

Legoland

Thirty million bricks are said to have gone into the recent construction of immense **Legoland California ⑰** (10am–6pm daily, 9am–9pm in summer, tel: 760/438-LEGO), the first of its chain in the US, which sprawls over 128 acres (52 hectares) of hills off Cannon Road, east of Interstate 5 near Carlsbad.

It's a kids' place through and through, and from shooting water into alligators' jaws and driving electric minicars, to taking a river ride under a bridge that rocks ominously as the boat passes, there's plenty to keep them occupied. The park's high spot is a series of meticulously repro-

BELOW:
Newport Beach
houses.

duced American cities–New York, Washington, New Orleans – with landmark buildings and moving vehicles which almost redeem the tackiness of the rest of the park.

Back on the coast, the little beachside community of **Del Mar** ⑱ is fine for a pleasant car-less vacation, having a railway station of its own on the Amtrak line. The town is the site of the Southern California Exposition and national horse show in June and July at the **Thoroughbred Club racetrack**. The track, whose season runs from July until mid-September, was rescued from collapse in the 1930s by actor Pat O'Brien and singer Bing Crosby, who pumped money into the facility, turning it into one of America's most popular racing circuit venues.

At the junction of I-5 and Via de la Valle, the **Del Mar Fairgrounds** (tel: 858/755-1161) is the scene of almost daily events all year – everything from monster truck racing to dog and bird shows. And on the main street, you can view, touch

and even buy million-year-old fossils at the **Dinosaur Gallery** (daily 11am–5pm, tel: 858/794-4855).

Turn off the Pacific Coast Highway towards the coast for the pretty **Torrey Pines State Reserve** ⑲. There's free parking in an unpaved lot atop the 300-foot (91-meter) cliffs. The **Torrey Pines Gliderport** offers introductory lessons in paragliding and hangliding, but spectators are welcome, too.

Worth a visit is the nearby and architecturally awesome **Salk Institute** (weekday tours by appointment, tel: 858/453-4100) on Torrey Pines Road. It was designed by the highly respected architect Louis I. Kahn and is named for its famous resident scientist, the late Jonas Salk, who devised the polio vaccine. At the northern end of the beach below the institute is Los Penasquitos Lagoon, a quiet venue for watching scores of birds.

Towards San Diego

A winding hill, La Jolla Shores Drive, leads through the affluent suburb of the same name where the trees which grow only here and on Santa Rosa island are environmentally protected. **La Jolla** ⑳ is the home of the San Diego campus of the **University of California**, whose well-designed La Jolla Playhouse draws locals to its first-rate productions. Its forerunner, an off-campus playhouse, was founded by actor Gregory Peck, a native of La Jolla.

Other popular attractions in La Jolla include the interesting clifftop **Stephen Birch Aquarium** (daily 9am–5pm, tel: 858/534-3474) on Expedition Way, which is located in the postmodern complex of the **Scripps Institution of Oceanography**. The institute offers whale-watching cruises in season. Among the 33 sea-filled tanks is a two-story one that replicates a kelp bed off the coast with all its familiar and unfamiliar creatures.

Superlative panoramic views of both coast and inland can be found atop 820-foot (250-meter) **Mount Soledad** in **Soledad Natural Park,** near the junction of Ardath and Torrey Pines roads. Not far away and just to the south lies California's second-biggest city, **San Diego** ㉑.

LEFT: preparing for Laguna's Pageant of the Masters, where real people pose as works of art. **RIGHT:** canalside living in Naples.

Map on page 276

SAN DIEGO

*California's second-largest city is also its oldest –
a good-looking town of missions and museums, Sea World,
and one of the finest zoos in the country*

Map
on page
288

On July 16, 1769 Father Junípero Serra conducted a solemn mass dedicating, first, the **Mission San Diego de Alcalá** ⓐ and then the military settlement which surrounded and protected it. The seeds for what was to become the state of California were sown.

The mission was moved from **Presidio Hill** to its present site in **Mission Valley** where it was twice destroyed by earthquakes and subsequently rebuilt. Today, flanked by Interstates 5 and 8 to the west and north, the hill and **Presidio Park** offer acres of tranquillity in a sea of traffic. Dominating the hillside is the elegant **Junípero Serra Museum** ⓑ (Tues–Sat 10am–4pm, Sun noon–4, tel: 619/297-3258), which looks like a mission but was actually built only in 1929.

Old Town

At the bottom of Presidio Hill is the area known as **Old Town** ⓒ. Old Town contains historic adobes and restored Victorian homes, plus shops, museums and charming patio restaurants, one of which, the Casa de Bandini, is located in an 1829 *hacienda*. It is also San Diego's most popular neighborhood for nightlife.

Free one-hour tours of Old Town at 11am and 2pm start from **Seeley Stables** which doubles as a **Visitor Center** (tel: 619/220-5422) and where *mariachis* and dancers roam the streets on weekends. Glassblowers, potters and diamond cutters pursue their trade in the **Bazaar del Mundo**, a collection of colorful shops and eating places at the north side of the plaza. On Wednesdays and Saturdays there are "living history" demonstrations of such old-time pastimes as making bricks or candles, baking bread in primitive ovens and producing salsa or tortillas. There is ample free parking in Old Town, which is on many bus-line routes.

Across the freeway is the 4,600-acre

(1,860-hectare) **Mission Bay Park** ⓓ area, comprising parkland, beaches and inner lagoons with almost every kind of outdoor leisure activity.

Located here at 500 Sea World Drive is **Sea World of California** ⓔ (opens 9am in summer, 10am in winter, closing hours vary, tel: 619/226-3901), a huge marine zoological park whose "killer" whales are as famous as some movie stars and whose appearances rarely fail to pack a 5,000-seat stadium. Seals, dolphins, otters and 400 penguins also draw admiring crowds. To the north on **Vacation Island** is Paradise Point Resort, offering soft, white beaches, a pool, sailboats, bicycles and a guided boat tour. There are panoramic views from an observation tower.

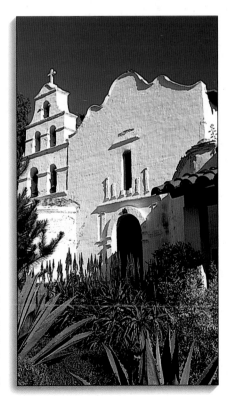

PRECEDING PAGES: Horton Plaza. **LEFT:** San Diego's Gaslamp Quarter has many Victorian buildings. **RIGHT:** Mission San Diego de Alcalá.

South of the channel leading into Mission Bay is **Ocean Beach** ❺. To the north of Mission Beach is **Pacific Beach** ❻, where activities tend to center around **Crystal Pier** and along busy **Mission Boulevard** and **Garnet Avenue**, where the locals shop and dine.

Miles of beaches

All three beaches are naturally a great draw for sun-seekers during most of the year (San Diego's climate is even more temperate than that of Los Angeles), but there are, in fact, wonderful beaches along most of this coast – 25 miles (40 km) of

them in an unbroken line between Del Mar and Oceanside, for example.

Buses run constantly along the coast road, and down the peninsula past the **Fort Rosecrans Military Reservation** to the **Cabrillo National Monument** ❽ (daily 9am–5pm, tel: 619/557-5450), which celebrates the day in September 1542 when Juan Rodríguez Cabrillo stepped ashore and claimed the territory for the Spanish Crown. There is a "birthday celebration" during the last week of September every year. The **Visitor Center** displays a Fresnel lens of the type used in the nearby lighthouse, and there are

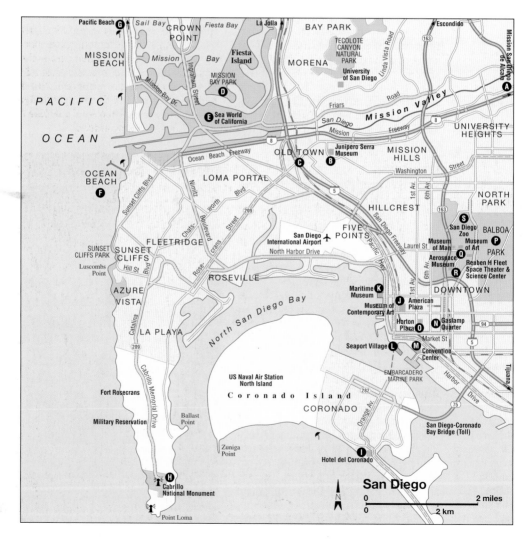

San Diego

0 _____ 2 miles
0 _____ 2 km

Map on page 288

regular daily screenings of movies and slide shows, plus an historical exhibit containing the kind of food found on ships in Cabrillo's day (olive oil, dried fish, beans, hardtack and wine). Outside are high-powered telescopes to enhance the views of Coronado and the bay area, as well as a statue of Cabrillo erected by the Portuguese navy.

Coronado peninsula

Farther up the hill is a charming two-story house high above the sea, from which the light tower arises like a chimney. Two tiny upstairs bedrooms above a kitchen, eating area and sitting room were shared by two families when the kerosene-fueled light was maintained from 1855 until 1891. Nearby is an observation point from which to view the gray whales that migrate south between December and March. And it's also a good spot for an overall view of the city, looking across the Coronado peninsula which loops up to fill most of the bay below.

This area west of Downtown is a peninsula-community of stately century-old homes best known for the superlative **Hotel del Coronado ❶**, a perfect example of elegant Victorian architecture with all its geegaws and eccentricities. A dozen presidents have stayed here since Thomas Edison personally installed the electric lighting; Great Britain's soon-to-be-king Edward met up with his future wife here, the notorious Mrs Simpson, who lived in a bungalow on the grounds (the bungalow is still there); Charles Lindbergh dropped by for dinner before and after making the first trans-Atlantic air flight; and author J Frank Baum is said to have used it as an inspiration for *The Wizard of Oz*.

Such milestones are memorialized in a history corridor lined with giant photographs. The hotel's extravagant architecture begs to be seen in the flesh. So eye-catching is the Coronado that it almost upstaged Tony Curtis and Marilyn Monroe in the 1959 movie *Some Like It Hot* – which is no mean feat.

BELOW: San Diego seen from the Coronado ferry.

San Diego's Downtown

San Diego (population: 1,111,000) is one of those places where the building never seems to stop, and Downtown has been undergoing extensive renovating for many years. There's some sensational architecture beside the bay, including the amazing Marriott Hotel, its two shiny wings resembling a ship in full sail, and the 40-story Hyatt Hotel, the tallest waterfront hotel in the country, which rises to twice the height of the arched Coronado Bridge. New structures are arising all around, revitalizing an area that was once filled with tuna factories.

Adjoining what was formerly the Santa Fe railroad station is a sleek satellite branch of the **Museum of Contemporary Art ❿** (Tues–Sat 10am–5pm, Sun noon–5pm, tel: 858/454-3541), a branch of the La Jolla museum, which is shoe-horned into a wedge of land originally planned to be retail space. Along the Embarcadero north of the train station is the much older **Maritime Museum ❿**

(daily 9am–8pm, tel: 619/234-9153), which encompasses three **historic ships**, the *Medea*, the *Berkel* and the *Star of India*, all built between 1863 and 1904 and containing nautical exhibits. The *USS Midway* is due to moor at Navy Pier in 2003 where it will serve as the **San Diego Aircraft Carrier Museum**. San Diego has always been a big naval town, and taking a **harbor cruise** will confirm that there is still plenty of activity on the water. In winter, **whale-watching tours** start from here.

South of the Museum of Contemporary Art is the attractive **Seaport Village ❿** (tel: 619/235-4014), a complex of restaurants (one is over the water) and shops of all kinds including one devoted to flags and others to music boxes and magic tricks. In addition, there's a video arcade, a century-old carousel and a Victorian clock tower from which chimes emanate. Next door is **Embarcadero Marina Park**, home to artists, clowns, kite flyers, and picnickers.

BELOW: La Casa de Machado y Stewart, Old Town.

Map
on page
288

Across the trolley route from the soaring **Convention Center**  is the interesting **Children's Museum** (Tues–Fri 10am–3pm, weekends 10am–4pm, tel: 619/233-KIDS), with a supervised play area where young visitors are encouraged to create artworks with paints or clay.

The **Historical Foundation** (tel: 619/233-4692) organizes Saturday morning walking tours starting from the yellow frame **William Heath Davis House** (Mon–Fri 10am–2pm, Sat 10am–1pm, tel: 619/233-5227), the 1850 home of the San Diego pioneer who made a premature attempt to build a new city here before abandoning the project.

Northeast of the Convention Center is the **Gaslamp Quarter** , the once-rowdy area to which every sailor headed as soon as his ship hit port. In the second half of the 19th century after the Civil War, when gas lamps illuminated the wooden sidewalks, ships chandlers here outfitted tall masted clippers on their last stop before rounding Cape Horn. Wyatt Earp, described by Yale University's John Mack Faragher as "a frontier *demimonde* – sometime lawman but full-time gambler, confidence man, associate of pimps and prostitutes," ran bawdy saloons on the nearby streets. Gambling halls and prostitution were rampant until 1912, when the police moved in to arrest the streetwalkers and close down the Red Light district. Today, horse-drawn carriages circulate through the old streets past Victorian buildings occupied by businesses, trendy restaurants, art galleries, and one-of-a-kind specialty stores.

Visionary mall

Almost next door to the Gaslamp Quarter is **Horton Plaza** , a curvilinear early project with Escher-like walkways by architect Jon Jerde who later designed Los Angeles' Universal City Walk. A visionary, Jerde believes architecture's prime task is to create a public space in which people can experience "a sense of common identity," and Horton Plaza has been

BELOW:
Museum of
Man in
Balboa Park.

much admired for its imaginative style and vibrant color scheme. There are five brightly colored floors of ramps, stairs, escalators, elevators, decorative pillars and levels that seem to colide with other levels. Anchored by big-name department stores, it contains a food court and is open until 9pm on weekdays, until 6 or 7pm on weekends. The multi-level mall was named after city founder Alonzo Horton, who in 1867 bought 960 acres (390 hectares) of waterfront land for $265, built a pier and sold residential lots. The rest, as they say, is history.

Trolley tours

An easy way to see all the local sights is to board one of the orange and green trackless trolleys which run every half-hour. Despite being called **Old Town Trolley Tours**, they actually cover a loop taking in Balboa Park and Coronado.

The (fairly expensive) ticket allows you to travel free on your next visit – as long as you bring a paying customer along with you. The bright red **San Diego Trolley** (cheap) runs every 15 minutes from Kettner and C streets along two routes: east to El Cajon and south to the Mexican border (a trip taking around 40 minutes).

At the northeast edge of town, the lush and handsome 1,400-acre (570-hectare) **Balboa Park ⓟ** contains most of the city's museums. The park has been in existence since 1868.

A pass to a group of museums is available at the park's **House of Hospitality**, which also offers maps and information. The beautiful white buildings with red tile roofs, towers and domes which form the park's impressive ceremonial entrance were built in Spanish-Moorish style by architect Bertram Grovesnor Goodhue for the 1915 Panama-California International Exposition which celebrated the completion of the Panama Canal.

Twenty years later, the buildings were refurbished for the California-Pacific Exposition and they have been an understandable object of local pride ever since.

BELOW: making a splash at Sea World.

Map on page 288

What's known as the California Quadrangle includes among its structure the impressive **California Tower**; its tile-crowned dome has become the city's logo, and the 100-bell carillon chimes every quarter hour. Behind the charming Lily Pond, the enormous **Botanical Building** with its hundreds of tropical plants may be the coolest place in the entire park.

Opening time for most of the dozen museums which flank the broad **Prado** is usually 10am, closing at 4 or 4:30 in the afternoon. Most are closed on Mondays. Outstanding is the **Museum of Art Q** (tel: 619/232-7931), whose ornate facade in 16th-century Spanish style is as attractive as anything inside.

The **Mingei International Museum** (tel: 619/239-0003) specializes in folk art; the **Model Railroad Museum** (tel: 800/446-8738) has trains for everyone; the **Historical Society Museum** (tel: 619/232-6203) houses files containing 2 million photographs; and the **Museum of Photographic Arts** (tel: 619/238-7559)

BELOW:
San Diego Zoo, one of the country's finest.

details the fascinating history of the photographic image.

Another fine museum, open daily, is the **Aerospace Museum R** (tel: 619/234-8291), with its 900-seat theater. This building is enormous, all the better to accommodate more than 60 full-size aircraft, some original and some reproductions. Among them are an early model of the primitive flying machine which the Wright Brothers first got off the ground at Kitty Hawk in North Carolina in 1903, and a replica of the *Spirit of St Louis* (another is at the San Diego International Airport; the original is in Washington, DC) in which in 1927 pilot Charles Lindbergh made the first solo crossing of the Atlantic Ocean.

Pandas and koalas

Occupying the western side of the park is the **San Diego Zoo S** (daily 9am–9pm, tel: 619/234 3153), whose more than 4,000 animals include rare giant pandas and the largest koala colony outside Australia. Most live in naturalistic habitats

behind moats in a lush, semi-tropical landscape. Posted on a board near the entrance are the day's highlights, which sometimes include notification of which animals have been given something new or different to play with. It's easy to get around the zoo, with pathways around the upper mesas and lower canyons. There are also kangaroo bus tours ("hop on and off at eight locations"), and the **Skyfari Aerial Tram** which is a pleasant overhead trip but offers no views of animals.

The 35-minute guided bus trip, on the other hand, takes you past polar bears, elephants and species you've never heard of such as takin, eland and quoll *. Escalators climb up from the most popular attraction, the pandas, on expensive rental from China (reputed to be $1 million a year). Shi Shi and Bai Yun mated and when the latter gave birth to Hua Mei in 1999, she was the first baby panda born in the Western hemisphere in a decade.

In the **Children's Zoo**, kids can pet fluffy creatures, race tortoises (the tortoises don't

know they're in a race) and watch baby animals being cared for by their substitute human mothers in the animal nursery.

The zoo also operates the fascinating **San Diego Wild Animal Park** (daily 9am–4pm, later in summer, tel: 760/747-8702), which is in San Diego County east of the town of Escondido, where only fences (and occasionally moats) keep different species in their own vast areas . To enjoy the park fully it's best to take the one-hour monorail ride past where more than 2,500 creatures including elephants, tigers and giraffes roam freely. There are daily shows in an area named Nairobi Village, and in summer the park operates an overnight camping stay which includes meals and informative lectures.

Gold-mining town

The Anza-Borrego Desert State Park *(see page 216)* is southeast of the animal park, accessible from San Diego through the one-time gold mining town of **Julian**, best known today for apple orchards, cattle ranches and springtime displays of lilacs and wildflowers. The main street, which hasn't changed much in a century *(see photo on page 16)*, contains a number of bakeries all claiming to sell the best apple pies in town. The white **Wilcox Building** on Main Street was built in 1872, while in the next block the attractive **Julian Hotel** has been operating continuously since 1897. Around the corner from the hotel on 4th Street, the **Julian Pioneer Museum** (Tues–Sun 10am–4pm in summer, weekends in winter, tel: 760/765-0227) is a typical small-town wonderland of Indian artifacts, stuffed birds and Victorian era curiosities.

As in any mining town, there was considerable rowdiness, and many a drunk ended up in the concrete, two-cell **Old Jail** situated at 4th and C streets. At the end of C Street, today's visitors can take one-hour tours in hillside tunnels of an old mine, the **Eagle Mining Company** (daily 10am–3pm, tel: 760/765-0036), which operated until 1942. Collectively, San Diego County's goldmines yielded more than $10 million worth of gold before the close of the 19th century. ❑

LEFT: San Diego has many trolley companies; some travel all the way to the border with Mexico. **RIGHT:** the historic Hotel del Coronado.

Map on page 288

Map on page 276

TIJUANA AND BAJA

Less than an hour away from the upscale charm of San Diego lies vibrant, throbbing Tijuana and, farther south, the best sandy beaches in northern Mexico

The **San Ysidro gateway** to and from Mexico south of San Diego claims to be the busiest border crossing in the world, and there is little reason to doubt it. Thousands of Mexicans pour into the United States each day, most working as laborers on a short-term basis, while many "Norteamericanos" head down south, drawn by the "exotic" ambiance of a foreign land or just simply to drink, eat or pick up a few souvenirs.

Tijuana ㉒ has always had a reputation as a free-wheeling town full of "genial *banditos*," a place for Americans seeking respite from minor misdemeanors: runaway lovers, small-time con artists, underage college kids drinking themselves into a stupor without supervision.

Their ranks have thinned out since the abduction and murder of an innocent American teenager, and the continuing publicity about drug-related violence and killings, whose victims have included government officials, a police chief, a presidential candidate and even a bishop of the Catholic church. Tijuana today is less genial than before and can cause nervousness even among those who know it well. So treat the town with caution, and don't linger too long after dark.

South of the border

Completely different in character and outlook is the arid but fascinating state of **Baja** itself, a relatively undeveloped sliver of land barely a few miles wide but stretching for almost 800 miles (1,290 km) alongside the Pacific Ocean, replete with rugged mountains, cactus-filled deserts and hundreds of pristine beaches. Daily buses operate from the north to Cabo San Lucas at the southern tip.

Mexican authorities permit US and Canadian citizens to head as far south as Ensenada, 76 miles (122 km) away, with no more than an ID, but beyond that (or for a stay longer than 72 hours) a tourist card, visa or passport is required. Non-US citizens should carry their relevant documents anyway, in case there are problems at the border crossing (unlikely, but possible). American car insurance that covers Mexico is strongly advised; vehicle ownership papers and a valid drivers' license are required.

San Diego's distinctive red trolley cars, in addition to providing transportation around town, also take passengers to the border. In daytime, the trolleys to Mexico run about every 15 minutes, with the ride itself taking about half an hour to 45 minutes. After being dropped off, there's a zig-zag walk into Mexico, where taxis and buses transport visitors

PRECEDING PAGES AND LEFT: things to see in Baja. **RIGHT:** border crossing.

to downtown Tijuana, about a 10-minute drive away. Of course, drivers can take their own cars to San Ysidro and walk or drive into Mexico themselves. But if Tijuana is your only destination, the trolley saves parking problems at the border and from waiting in the long line of automobiles coming back to the United States.

The **Tijuana Tourism and Convention Bureau** maintains an information booth in Tijuana, as you first enter through the San Ysidro border (open from 8am to 9pm Mon–Fri, till 10pm on Sat, and till 7pm on Sunday). There are also information booths at the **Otay border crossing** (daily 9am–4pm) and at **Third and Revolución streets** in downtown Tijuana (daily 9am–5pm).

Down Mexico Way

One of the first things visitors see as they drive or cross the footbridge into Tijuana (population 1,500,000) is the colorful outline of **Mexitlan** (daily 10am–6pm, closed Mon), a big building topped with a glass piñata. At Calle Benito Juarez (2nd Street) Number 8991, Mexitlan contains huge relief maps of all of Mexico, with 200 of its major landmarks and archaeological sites reproduced to scale on 20-foot (6-meter) square platforms. It is the work of one of the country's top architects, Pedro Ramirez Vásquez, who created Mexico City's well-known anthropology museum.

Next door is the arts and crafts market, **Mercado de Artesanías**. Walk two blocks west to the **Museo de Cera** (Wax Museum), where the 60 occupants include Madonna, Fidel Castro and the legendary Tia Juana (Aunt Jane), the owner of a lively cantina around which the city was reputedly founded.

Five blocks south on Avenida Revolución at Calle Galeana (7th Street), the **Jai Alai Fronton** has for years come to life on weekday nights when this dazzlingly fast game using a ball deftly tossed from a wicker basket enthralls exuberantly noisy crowds, most of whom are betting on their favorite player. (There is currently some

BELOW: Tijuana's Mexitlan, designed by Pedro Ramirez Vásquez.

Map on page 276

controversy over the playing of Jai Alai, however, so the stadium might be closed).

There's a winery down to the right on Calle Johnson at Hidalgo, but turn right on Calle Sarabia (10th Street) and head east. Avenida Revolución continues farther south, joining the Boulevard Agua Caliente and running past the city's old **bullring**, the **Sports Arena**, which is the venue for many big concerts, and the famous **Hipodromo Caliente racetrack** (grayhound races daily), among whose regulars used to be Charlie Chaplin, Jean Harlow and Laurel and Hardy.

Up broad Paseo de los Heroes at Calle Mina is the **Tijuana Cultural Center**, whose historical survey embraces Olmec stone heads; a meticulous model of the 16th-century capital, Tenochtitlan; plus skilfully embroidered tribal costumes. Adjoining the Cultural Center is the golf-ball-shaped concert hall and **Omnitheater**, on whose vast screen an English-language film about Mexico's culture is shown daily.

Walk one block over and along the river

for **Plaza Río Tijuana**, one of the largest shopping centers in northwestern Mexico. Across the way is the **Plaza del Zapato** (Plaza of Shoes), where many a good bargain can be found. Because Baja is a free port, most goods cost less than in San Diego, anyway. Shoppers should remember, however, that US Customs demands receipts for any daily purchases exceeding $400 per person. What the *Los Angeles Times* recently described as "a world class" dining area is developing in the **Zona Rio** with such fine restaurants as La Belle Claude and La Diferencia, whose chef Martin San Román aims to become Mexico's first celebrity chef.

Beginners' Baja

Stretching south of Tijuana, the narrow Baja peninsula originated about 4 million years ago, when the peninsula separated from the Mexican mainland. With most of its 54,000 sq. miles (140,000 sq. km) composed of mountains and desert, much of which receives less than 10 inches (25cm)

BELOW: Tijuana's best souvenirs include wool blankets and leather goods.

of rainfall a year, it can hardly have seemed the most attractive of regions to Hernando Cortés and the other Spaniards who came across from the Mexican mainland. Nevertheless, local legend has it that Cortés, stumbling upon a "peninsula" which stretched down between the sea and the gulf, thought he had found a long-lost fabled island, and dutifully named it "California." Baja becomes progressively more interesting the farther south you travel, ending up at the southern tip with two famous capes – Cabo San Lucas and San José del Cabo, but if you're heading this far, don't forget a passport or papers.

Yellowtail capital

The *cuota* (toll) road from Tijuana to the town of Ensenada includes some fine ocean scenery, and is recommended over the *libre* (free) road, which parallels the *cuota* as far as Rosarito, then dips inland.

About 17 miles (27 km) south of the California border, **Rosarito** is an over-commercialized beach town which gained

celebrity in 1927 when the newly opened **Rosarito Beach Hotel** began to attract the movie crowd as well as other celebrities and even heads of state. The hotel features glorious indoor murals by Matias Santoyo and a large swimming pool and bar area above the gray, sandy beach. Lobster is always a favorite meal in the town's numerous restaurants and there is a so-called "Lobster Village" – **Puerto Nuevo**, 6 miles (10 km) to the south, where the large New Port Baja Hotel promises an ocean view from each of its rooms.

At **El Sauzal**, just before Ensenada, Highway 3 heads across to the east coast, while its northbound section heads back towards the US via the beer-making town of **Tecate** near the border. The road passes through acres of vineyards on the boulder-strewn hills near the Guadalupe Valley, the center of Mexico's fast-growing wine business. The most interesting town on this route is **Francisco Zarco**, with both its cemetery and museum devoted to the history of the Russian immigrants who colonized the area at the turn of the last century.

Around 75 miles (120 km) south of Tijuana in a lovely setting between foothills and the sea, is **Ensenada** (population 193,000), a busy port, a stop for cruise ships and the farthest south that the vast majority of casual tourists penetrate. Popular with fishermen, it tags itself "the yellowtail capital of the world," with surf fishing along the rocky shoreline and organized trips from the sportfishing piers off **Boulevard Lazaro Cardenas**.

Daily winery tours are held at the Bodegas de Santo Tomás, and occasional summer bullfights.. At the El Mirador exit, there is a bluff-top view of **Bahia de Todos Santos**, home of Ensenada's deep-sea charter fleet, naval dry-dock and pleasure craft, which usually includes a couple of Los Angeles-based cruise liners.

Ensenada's tourist shopping zone is along **Avenida López Mateos** a few blocks inland from the bay, where there is also a **State Tourist Office**. Funkier and cheaper is the "non-tourist" part of town to the east, off Avenida Ruiz. Near the bus depot is **Hussongs**, a wooden-frame cantina which has been in business for over a century. ❑

LEFT AND RIGHT: Baja is the nearest place to the USA for Americans to feel they are in a foreign country.

Map on page 276

INSIGHT GUIDES
TRAVEL TIPS

INSIGHT GUIDES

The classic series that puts you in the picture

Alaska	Dominican Rep. & Haiti	London	Rio de Janeiro
Amazon Wildlife	Dublin	Los Angeles	Rome
American Southwest	East African Wildlife	Madeira	Russia
Amsterdam	Eastern Europe	Madrid	St Petersburg
Argentina	Ecuador	Malaysia	San Francisco
Arizona & Grand Canyon	Edinburgh	Mallorca & Ibiza	Sardinia
Asia, East	Egypt	Malta	Scandinavia
Asia, Southeast	England	Mauritius Réunion	Scotland
Australia	Finland	& Seychelles	Seattle
Austria	Florence	Melbourne	Sicily
Bahamas	Florida	Mexico	Singapore
Bali	France	Miami	South Africa
Baltic States	France, Southwest	Montreal	South America
Bangkok	French Riviera	Morocco	Spain
Barbados	Gambia & Senegal	Moscow	Spain, Northern
Barcelona	Germany	Namibia	Spain, Southern
Beijing	Glasgow	Nepal	Sri Lanka
Belgium	Gran Canaria	Netherlands	Sweden
Belize	Great Britain	New England	Switzerland
Berlin	Great Railway Journeys	New Orleans	Sydney
Bermuda	of Europe	New York City	Syria & Lebanon
Boston	Greece	New York State	Taiwan
Brazil	Greek Islands	New Zealand	Tenerife
Brittany	Guatemala, Belize	Nile	Texas
Brussels	& Yucatán	Normandy	Thailand
Buenos Aires	Hawaii	Norway	Tokyo
Burgundy	Hong Kong	Oman & The UAE	Trinidad & Tobago
Burma (Myanmar)	Hungary	Oxford	Tunisia
Cairo	Iceland	Pacific Northwest	Turkey
California	India	Pakistan	Tuscany
California, Southern	India, South	Paris	Umbria
Canada	Indonesia	Peru	USA: On The Road
Caribbean	Ireland	Philadelphia	USA: Western States
Caribbean Cruises	Israel	Philippines	US National Parks: West
Channel Islands	Istanbul	Poland	Venezuela
Chicago	Italy	Portugal	Venice
Chile	Italy, Northern	Prague	Vienna
China	Italy, Southern	Provence	Vietnam
Continental Europe	Jamaica	Puerto Rico	Wales
Corsica	Japan	Rajasthan	Walt Disney World/Orlando
Costa Rica	Jerusalem		
Crete	Jordan		
Cuba	Kenya		
Cyprus	Korea		
Czech & Slovak Republic	Laos & Cambodia		
Delhi, Jaipur & Agra	Las Vegas		
Denmark	Lisbon		

INSIGHT GUIDES

The world's largest collection of visual travel guides & maps

CONTENTS

Getting Acquainted

The Place

California is bordered by Mexico to the south, the state of Oregon to the north, and Nevada and Arizona to the east. Covering an area of 163,707 sq. miles (423,999 sq. km) – almost a quarter of which is water – it ranks third in size and first in population of all the US states. It contains the highest mountain range in the continental US, the Sierra Nevada, with deserts to the south and northeast; there is temperate rainforest in the northwest and a vast Central Valley (once the bed of an inland sea), which is one of the country's biggest agricultural regions.

Southern California's Mount Whitney (14,494 ft/4,418 meters) is its highest point and Death Valley (282 ft/86 meters below sea level) its lowest. Joshua Tree and the Mojave Desert are among its best-known natural beauty sites and the Channel Islands among its best-known national parks. State parks are visited by 77 million people each year.

The People

California's population is over 30 million, of which about two-thirds is white, one quarter Hispanic, roughly 10 percent Asian, 8 percent black and 6 percent Native American. The state has four of the country's largest cities (Los Angeles, San Francisco, San Jose and San Diego). The LA metropolitan area is home to over 13 million. San Diego has a population of about 3 million. More than 92 percent of the state's population is urban.

Language & Culture

The native language is English but as more than one-third of Southern California's population is Hispanic, Spanish is often spoken in many areas. The culture and customs of Southern California are influenced by its Mexican heritage. It is not uncommon to go to a downtown area at night and hear Mexican *mariachi* bands playing. Some of the best restaurants in Southern California are Mexican and many residents consider Mexican food to be the local cuisine.

Time Zones

California is situated entirely in the Pacific Time Zone, which is two hours behind Chicago, three hours behind New York and eight hours behind Greenwich Mean Time. On the first Sunday in April, the clock is moved ahead one hour for Daylight Savings Time. In late October, the clock is moved back one hour to return to Standard Time.

Climate

Southern California is one of the few places in the world where you can ski in the morning and surf in the afternoon. It is not uncommon for the temperature to vary 30–40°F (17–20°C) as you travel from mountains to deserts to the beach. The change of seasons is not as dramatic as it is elsewhere. The winters are mild, with a rainy season that lasts from January to March. In the summer months the humidity is usually low, so discomfort is rare. The famous LA smog is at its worst in August and September.

Electricity

The electricity California residents use in their homes is called standard, which is 110 volts. European appliances rated for 220–240 volts will require a voltage adaptor if used in the US. Some hotel bathrooms have electrical outlets suitable for use with European appliances, but an adaptor is always useful to have.

Economy

California's economy is the fifth largest in the world. Although America's top producer of fruits, nuts and vegetables (mostly from the 450-mile/724-km long Central Valley), agriculture ranks only tenth in the California's gross state product, with manufacturing as the leading industry.

California is also a leading state in fishery production and its mineral wealth includes oil, natural gas, iron ore, tungsten and the nation's only supply of boron. Aerospace, construction and electronics are its major manufacturing industries with Silicon Valley (south of San Francisco) regarded as the nation's center for electronic, computer and software development. And, of course, there is the concentration of movie production companies in the Los Angeles area.

Government

The state legislature comprises the Senate (40 members serving four-year terms) and the Assembly (80 members serving two-year terms) with powers, if necessary, to pass laws over the veto of the governor and the authority to conduct impeachment proceedings. The governor, to whom the California constitution gives supreme authority, serves a four-year term.

California is one of the few states whose citizens possess additional representation in the form of the ballot initiative. California citizens can initiate legislation by collecting the signatures of five percent of the people who voted in the previous elections for governor in support of a particular measure, which will then be put to popular vote.

Planning the Trip

What to Bring

Dress in Southern California is casual, and few restaurants require jackets and ties for men. Unless you are visiting the mountain areas, the moderate climate makes heavy clothing unnecessary. Sweaters or lightweight overcoats are sufficient for winter evenings, and a light jacket is adequate for summer evenings. Expect a few days of rain in winter and springtime.

Maps

Insight Map: California and also *Insight Map: Los Angeles* combine clear and detailed cartography with essential information about the state and the city, making them ideal maps to carry. The laminated finish makes the maps durable and easy to fold, and you can easily scribble directions on them with a non-permanent marker pen.

The **Automobile Association of Southern California**, with various branches in the area (consult a local phone book), has many street maps of the area as well as maps of California, Mexico and other states. It is worth joining if you are going to be driving, because the cost of being towed after one breakdown might be less than the annual membership fee. *Southern California Car Culture Landmarks* is a fun and informative AAA map listing quirky pieces of architecture – from gigantic doughnut-shaped buildings to the Wigwam Motel – that still survive in the region.

Another good source is the **California Map & Travel Center**, an LA bookstore at 3211 Pico Boulevard, tel: (310) 829-6277.

Entry Regulations

Most foreign travelers to the US must have a passport, a visa and, depending on where you are arriving from, a health record, In addition, you must make prior arrangements to leave the country. Those exempt from these rules at the moment are: Canadian citizens; certain European nationals; and certain government officials. Due to recent security alterations, non-US citizens may be required to produce photo ID when traveling within the US, so always have photocopies of your passport handy.

Any person who enters the US can visit Mexico or Canada for a period of less than 30 days and still be re-admitted to the US without a new visa. Visas can be obtained from any US embassy abroad.

If a visitor loses his or her visa while in the United States, a new one may be obtained from the embassy of the visitor's home country. Extensions are granted by the US Immigration and Naturalization Service, 425 I Street, Washington, DC 20536, tel: (202) 514-1000.

EXTENSION OF STAY

Most visitors are given a six-month visa. If after six months you wish to stay for a longer period, contact the immigration service *(address given above)*. Obtaining a six-month extension is often no problem.

QUARANTINE REGULATIONS

At the Mexico, Nevada and Oregon borders, the State Department of Food and Agriculture inspects all produce, plant materials and wild animals to see if they are admissable under current quarantine regulations. If you want to avoid a lengthy inspection, don't bring any agricultural products into California.

Customs

Everyone entering the country must go through US Customs, whether or not they have anything to declare. It can be a time-consuming process, but to speed things up, be prepared to open your luggage for inspection and keep the following restrictions in mind:

● There is no limit to the amount of money you can bring in from other countries. If the amount exceeds $10,000, however, you must fill out a report.

● Anything you have for your own personal use may be brought in duty- and tax-free. Adults are allowed to bring in 1 quart of alcohol for personal use.

● You can bring in gifts valued at less than $400 duty- and tax-free. Anything over $400 is subject to duty charges and taxes.

● Dogs, cats and other animals may be brought into the country with certain restrictions. For details, contact the US consulate nearest you or write to the US Department of Agriculture.

● Automobiles may be driven into the United States if they are for the personal use of the visitor, family and guests only.

US Customs: 1301 Constitution Avenue NW, Washington, DC Tel: (202) 354-1000.

Public Holidays

New Year's Day January 1
Martin Luther King Jr's Birthday Monday before or after January 15
Presidents' Day Third Monday in February
Easter Sunday, and often Good Friday
Memorial Day Last Monday in May
Independence Day July 4
Labor Day First Monday in September
Veterans' Day November 11
Thanksgiving Day Fourth Thursday in November
Christmas Day December 25

Reservations

Definitely make reservations at hotels and popular restaurants, especially during the tourist season, May–September. Resorts and inns near big cities like Los Angeles often get booked up at weekends year-round. Not all restaurants take reservations, but if you call ahead, the staff will usually let you know how long the wait will be. A no-smoking policy is usually enforced.

Health

If you should need medical assistance, consult the local Yellow Pages for the physician or pharmacist nearest you. In large cities, there is usually a physician referral service number listed. If you need immediate attention, go directly to a hospital emergency room. Most emergency rooms are open 24 hours a day.

There is nothing cheap about being sick in the United States. It is essential to be armed with adequate medical insurance and to carry an identification card or policy number at all times. If expense is a concern, turn first to county hospitals, which offer good service and do not tend to charge indigent patients.

In the case of an emergency, dial **911** from any telephone for the police, fire department or ambulance service.

Currency

Travelers checks are accepted in many places (when accompanied by identification) but, as with foreign currency, can be exchanged only at certain banks. Credit cards are widely accepted (again with ample identification). It is wise to acquire at least some dollars from one of the airport currency exchange booths on arrival.

Current exchange rates are listed on the inside back page of the *Los Angeles Times'* Sunday Travel section each week.

Practical Tips

Getting There

BY AIR

Los Angeles International

LAX is Southern California's largest airport, and it handles the major international, domestic and regional air traffic. Information booths just outside the terminal buildings direct you to a wide range of buses and limousine services. A free shuttle bus service runs to the parking lots, one of which is also a terminal for buses of the Metropolitan Transit Authority (NTA). Tel: (213) 626-4455 for bus schedules and information.

San Diego International

Travelers who want to start their tour in San Diego can fly there directly from most major American cities; currently there are no foreign carriers with service to San Diego. Public buses, taxis and limousines into the city and surrounding areas are readily available.

In addition to the international airports at Los Angeles and San Diego, there are regional airports in several locations throughout the southern part of the state, including Palm Springs, Ontario, Hollywood-Burbank, and Orange County. Shuttle flights are available at all of the larger air terminals.

A few airlines that fly into California airports are:
American Airlines, (800) 433-7300; www.americanairlines.com;
Delta Airlines, (800) 221-1212; www.delta.com;
Northwest, (800) 225-2525; www.nwa.com;

Southwest, (800) 435-9729; www.southwest.com;
United Airlines, (800) 241-6522; www.ual.com.

BY RAIL

Amtrak offers several major rail lines in Southern California. Although schedules are subject to change, these are the likely routes:

The *Sunset Limited* from New Orleans stops at Indio, Ontario and Pomona before reaching Los Angeles. The *Desert Wind*, from Chicago to Los Angeles, stops at Barstow, Victorville, San Bernardino and Fullerton. The *San Diegan* runs between Los Angeles and San Diego, with stops at Santa Ana, San Juan Capistrano, Oceanside and Delmar.

The state is linked together by the *Coast Starlight*, which travels north from Los Angeles all the way to Seattle, stopping at Glendale, Simi Valley, Oxnard, Santa Barbara, San Luis Obispo, San Jose, Oakland (from here there's a bus transfer to San Francisco before the route continues), Martinez, Davis, Sacramento, Marysville, Richmond, Chico, Reading and on across the Oregon border. Amtrak also offers regional rail passes for 15 or 30 days, and some local services. For information call: (800) 872-7245, (800) USA-RAIL, or visit their website: www.amtrak.com.

BY BUS

The national bus line, Greyhound/Trailways (tel: 800/231-2222; www.greyhound.com), as well as a number of smaller charter companies, provide an impressive network of ground travel throughout California, offering daily service to major towns and cities. Routes and schedules are subject to change; it is a good idea to check all arrangements with local stations – in advance. San Francisco, Oakland, Los Angeles, San Diego and other large towns also have municipal bus systems.

Bus service information numbers within major cities include:
Los Angeles Metropolitan Transit Authority. Tel: (213) 626-4455
San Diego Transit Company
Tel: (619) 233-3004

BY ROAD

California has a massive, intertwining freeway system that can be great if you understand maps and have ample patience.

The following list should help. For additional information, call the **Automobile Club of Southern California**, tel: (213) 741-4880.

The principal **north–south routes** in California are:

Interstate 5 (the Golden State and Santa Ana freeways), which covers the distance from Canada to Mexico via Seattle, Sacramento, Los Angeles and San Diego.

Interstate 15, which transits San Bernardino and San Diego after a long passage from Montana's Canadian border, via Salt Lake City and Las Vegas.

US Highway 101 (the Ventura and Hollywood freeways), which proceeds south down the Pacific coast from Washington state, crosses San Francisco's Golden Gate Bridge, and ends in downtown Los Angeles.

State Highway 1 (the Pacific Coast Highway), which hugs the coast from San Diego to San Francisco and further north.

The principal **east–west routes** in California are:

Interstate 8, which departs from I-10 at Casa Grande, Arizona and ends in San Diego.

Interstate 10 (the San Bernardino and Santa Monica freeways), which begins on the East Coast in Jacksonville, Florida and continues through New Orleans, Houston, El Paso, Tucson and Phoenix before cutting through Los Angeles and ending at the coast in Santa Monica.

Interstate 40, which connects Knoxville, Tennessee, with Barstow, California, via Memphis, Tennessee, Oklahoma City, Oklahoma and Albuquerque, New Mexico.

Local radio stations give road condition updates and traffic alerts. For **road condition information**, tel: (213) 628-7623.

Speed Limits

Keep in mind that the national speed limit on all interstate highways is now 65 miles (105 km) per hour, and 55 miles (89 km) per hour on most other local highways. California law requires that every passenger wears a seat belt, that small children and babies be secured in youth or infant seats, and that drivers carry a valid license. There is also a state law that requires all motorcycle riders to wear helmets.

Car Rental
National car rental companies are located at all airports and large towns. The best rates are usually available by booking in advance on the toll-free line. In most cases, you must be at least 21 years old to rent a car (often 25), and you must have a valid driver's license and at least one major credit card. Foreign travelers may need to produce an international driver's license or a license from their home country.

Always take out collision and liability insurance, which may not be included in the base price of the rental. It is also a good idea to inquire about an unlimited mileage package, especially on a long trip. If not, you may be charged 5–25¢ per mile in addition to your rental fee, and considering the vast area of California, your vacation miles add up quickly.

Alamo	(800) 327-9633
Avis	(800) 831-8000
Budget	(800) 527-0700
Dollar	(800) 800-4000
Enterprise	(800) 325-8007
Hertz	(800) 654-3131
National	(800) 227-7368
Thrifty	(800) 367-2277

Traveling with Kids

Because of the large number of world-famous playgrounds such as Disneyland and Knott's Berry Farm (see page 334), the state is a good place to take the kids. Hotels and motels are usually accommodating, allowing children to stay in their parents' rooms with only a nominal charge for extra beds.

Disabled Travelers

California has legislation requiring that all construction of buildings for public use should have access for the disabled. Handicapped travelers are offered some concessions: Greyhound buses, for example, allow a disabled person plus a companion to travel for one fare. The railroad system, Amtrak, offers a free booklet called Travel Planner, available from the National Railroad Corporation, 400 N. Capitol Street NW, Washington DC 20001.

Security & Crime

Like many metropolises all over the world, Californian cities have dangerous neighborhoods. Common sense is your most effective weapon:
● Don't walk alone at night.
● Keep an eye on your belongings.
● Never leave your car unlocked.
● Never leave small children by themselves.
● If you are driving, never pick up anyone you don't know, especially if you are alone. Be wary of who is around you. If you have trouble on the road, stay in the car and lock the doors, turn on your hazard lights and leave the hood up in order to increase your visibility and alert passing police cars.

Hotels usually warn that they do not guarantee the safety of belongings left in the rooms. If you have any valuables, you may want to lock them in the hotel safe.

The number to dial for all emergencies is **911**.

Medical Services

To locate a physician or a pharmacist consult the yellow pages of the phone book. If you need immediate attention, go directly to a hospital emergency room. Most hospitals have a 24-hour emergency service.
Here is a list of some of the larger Southern California hospitals:

Los Angeles
Cedars-Sinai Medical Center
8700 Beverly Boulevard
Tel: (310) 855-5000
Hollywood Presbyterian Medical Center
1300 N Vermont Avenue
Tel: (213) 413-3000
St John's
1328 22nd Street, Santa Monica
Tel: (310) 829-5511
UCLA
10833 Le Conte Avenue
Tel: (800) 825-2631

San Diego
Scripps Mercy Hospital
4077 Fifth Avenue
Hillcrest
Tel: (619) 294-8111
Sharp Memorial Hospital
7901 Frost Street
San Diego
Tel: (619) 543-6222

Business Hours

Standard business hours are 9am–5pm weekdays; some businesses operate weekend hours. Most department stores open at 10am and many stores, especially those in shopping malls, stay open until 9pm. Southern California has a number of 24-hour restaurants. A few local supermarkets and convenience stores are also open around the clock.
   Bank hours usually run from 9am–3pm, although some stay open later, especially on Friday. Although some branch offices keep Saturday morning hours, most banks are closed at weekends. However, most banks are equipped with 24-hour automated tellers on the outside of their building, and if

you have an account card you can use these machines for simple transactions at your convenience. Be careful at night.
   During holidays, post offices, banks, government offices and many private businesses are closed for the day.

Tipping

Just as in other parts of the country, service personnel in California rely on tips for a large part of their income. In most cases, 15–20 percent is the going rate for tipping waiters, taxi drivers, bartenders and barbers. In the larger cities, taxi drivers tend to expect 20 percent; for baggage handlers at airports or hotels, a tip of $1 per bag is usual.
   For overnight stays, it is not necessary to tip the chambermaid. For longer stays, the rule of thumb is to leave a minimum tip of one or two dollars per day. A doorman expects a small tip for helping unload your car or for other services. The final and the only tasteful rule in tipping is that the tip should be fair and commensurate with the service provided.

Weights & Measures

The US uses the Imperial system of weights and measures. Metric is rarely used. Below is a conversion chart.
1 inch = 2.54 centimeters
1 foot = 30.48 centimeters
1 yard = 0.9144 meters
1 mile = 1.609 kilometers
1 quart = 1.136 liters
1 gallon = 3.785 liters
1 ounce = 28.4 grams
1 pound = 0.453 kilograms

Rough temperature equivalents:
50°F = 10°C
60°F = 16°C
70°F = 21°C
80°F = 27°C
90°F = 32°C
100°F = 38°C

Media

TELEVISION & RADIO

Television and radio are invaluable sources of up-to-the-minute information about weather, road conditions and current events. It is now almost standard for decent hotels and motels to include televisions in the price of a room, although you may have to pay extra for cable service. Television and radio listings are published in local newspapers. Sunday papers usually have a detailed weekly guide.

PUBLICATIONS

The *Los Angeles Times*, the biggest daily and Sunday newspaper in the country, blankets the Southern California region with several editions with such smaller papers nipping at its heels as the *Daily News* (mostly in the San Fernando Valley), the *Evening Outlook* in Santa Monica, the *News Pilot* in San Pedro, the *Press Telegram* in Long Beach and the *Daily Breeze* in Torrance. There is also the *Long Beach Press Telegram*, *Santa Barbara News Press*, the *Orange County Register* and San Diego's *Union-Tribune* among many others.
   Many Southern Californian regions have individual glossy lifestyle magazines, as well as local listings magazines.

Postal Services

Post offices open 7–9am and usually close at 5pm, Monday–Friday. Many of them are also open for a few hours on Saturday morning. All post offices close Sunday. If you don't know where you will be staying in any particular town, you can receive mail by having it addressed to General Delivery at the main post office in that town. You have to pick up General Delivery mail in person and show proper identification. In LA, the Worldway Postal Center, 800 W Century Boulevard, tel: (310) 337-8845, is open 24 hours a day.

Telecommuications

TELEPHONE

To place a long-distance call from a public phone, dial 1 + area code + local number. Have plenty of change to deposit on the operator's prompting.

The quickest way to ask for assistance for a telephone-communications problem is to dial "0" for the operator from any phone. If the operator cannot be of assistance, he or she will most likely be able to connect you with the proper party. Another indispensable number is for information assistance, which can provide telephone listings if you do not have a phone book handy.

For **local information** dial 555-1212.

For **long-distance** dial 1-area code-555-1212.

For a **toll-free number** or directory dial (800) 555-1212.

TELEGRAMS, FAX & TELEX

Western Union, tel: (800) 325-6000 and International Telephone and Telegraph (ITT) will take messages as well as orders to wire money over the phone. Check the local directory, or call Information for local offices. Fax machines can be found in most hotels and stores.

Useful Addresses

TOURIST INFORMATION

Local organizations are often happy to give information and will also mail maps, lists of upcoming events or other literature in advance of your trip.

California State Office of Tourism
801 K Street
Suite 1600
Sacramento, CA 95812
Tel: (800) 862-2543
www.gocalif.ca.gov/index2.html

Local Dialing Codes

As computer modems, fax machines and mobile phones proliferate in gizmo-happy California, the state keeps adding codes at a dizzy rate: as we go to press these are correct, but if in doubt, call the operator

213 is Downtown Los Angeles
323 surrounds Downtown and includes Hollywood, West Hollywood, and Eagle Rock
310 is the western section, including Beverly Hills, West LA, and the coastal area stretching from Malibu south through Santa Monica, Venice, Manhattan Beach, Hermosa Beach, Redondo Beach, Torrance and Palos Verdes
562 is Long Beach, Downey, and Whittier
818 is the San Fernando Valley, including Glendale, Burbank, Sherman Oaks, Encino, and Calabasas

626 is the San Gabriel Valley including Pasadena
714 is North Orange County including Anaheim, Santa Ana, and Huntington Beach
909 includes the San Bernardino and Riverside areas
661 is the Santa Clarita and Valencia area
805 is Thousand Oaks north to Ventura and Santa Barbara
949 is South Orange County including Newport Beach, Irvine, Laguna Beach, San Juan Capistrano, and Dana Point
760 is North San Diego County including Carlsbad and stretching east and north including Palm Springs
858 is North Central San Diego County including Del Mar and La Jolla
619 is the San Diego city area

Visitors' Bureaux

Anaheim-Orange County Visitors' and Convention Bureau
800 W Katella Avenue
Anaheim, CA 92802
Anaheim, CA 92803
Tel: (714) 765-8888
www.anaheimoc.com

Beverly Hills Visitors' and Convention Bureau
239 South Beverly Drive
Beverly Hills, CA 90212
Tel: (310) 248-1015 or
(800) 345-2210
www.ci.beverly-hill.ca.us

Catalina Island Visitors' Bureau and Chamber of Commerce
PO Box Avalon 90704
Tel: (310) 510-1520
www.catalina.com

Hollywood Visitor Information Center
6541 Hollywood Boulevard
Tel: (213) 236-2331

Laguna Beach Visitors' Bureau
252 Broadway
Laguna Beach, CA 92651
Tel: (800) 877-1115 or
(969) 497-9229
www.lagunabeachinfo.org

Long Beach Area Convention and Visitors' Council
1 World Trade Center
Suite 300
Long Beach, CA 90831
Tel: (800) 234-3645 or
(562) 436-3645
www.golongbeach.org

Los Angeles Convention and Visitors' Bureau
685 South Figueroa Street
Los Angeles, CA 90071
Tel: (213) 689-8822 or
(800) 366-6116
www.lacvb.com

Ontario Convention and Visitors' Authority
Tel: (800) 455-5755
Fax: (909) 937-3080
www.ontariocva.org

Palm Springs Desert Resorts Convention and Visitors' Bureau
69–930 Highway 111
Suite 201
Rancho Mirage, CA 92270
Tel: (760) 770-9000 or
(800) 967-3767
www.palm-springs.org

Pasedena Convention and Visitors' Bureau
1715 Robles Avenue

Pasadena, CA 91101
Tel: (626) 795-9311
www.pasadenacal.com
San Bernardino Convention and Visitors' Center
(city information)
Tel: (909) 889-3980 or
(800) 867-8366
www.san-bernardino.org
San Bernardino County Tourism Development Council
(county information)
Tel: (909) 890-1090
San Diego Convention and Visitors' Bureau
401 B Street No. 1400
San Diego, CA. 92101
Tel: (619) 232-3101
Fax: (619) 696-9371
www.sandiego.org
Santa Barbara Conference & Visitors' Bureau
12 E. Carrillo Street
Santa Barbara, CA 93101
Tel: (805) 966-9222 or
(800) 927-4688
www.santabarbara.com
Santa Monica Convention and Visitors' Bureau
520 Broadway
Tel: (310) 319-6263 or
(800) 544-5319
www.santamonica.com
Ventura Visitors' and Convention Bureau
89c South California Street
Ventura, CA 93001
Tel: (805) 648-2075
www.ventura-usa.com

Chambers of Commerce
Big Bear Lake Valley Chamber of Commerce
630 Bartlett Road
Big Bear Lake, CA 92315
Mail: PO Box 2860
Big Bear Lake, CA 92315
Tel: (909) 866-4608
www.bigbear.chamber.com
Los Angeles Chamber of Commerce
404 South Bixel
Los Angeles, CA 90017
Mail: PO Box 3696
Los Angeles, CA 90051
Tel: (323) 629-0602
www.centurycitycc.com
Greater San Diego Chamber of Commerce
402 West Broadway

Suite 1000
San Diego, CA 92101
Tel: (619) 232-0124
www.sdchamber.org
Santa Barbara Chamber of Commerce
504 State Street
Santa Barbara, CA 93101
Mail: PO Box 299
Santa Barbara, CA 93102
Tel: (805) 965-3023
www.sbchamber.org

Consulates
Foreign visitors looking for home country representatives can find consulates in San Francisco and Los Angeles. Check in the Yellow Pages of local telephone books, available in libraries and post offices, or call "Information" (411 if calling within town; 1 + area code of city + 555-1212 if calling from out of town). Here are a few of the consulates in Los Angeles:
Australia: 2049 Century Park E, tel: (310) 229-4800
Britain: 11766 Wilshire Boulevard, tel: (310) 477-3322; fax: (310) 575-1450; www.britainusa.com
Canada: 550 S Hope Street, tel: (213) 346-2700; www.cdnconsulat-la.com
Netherlands: 11766 Wilshire Boulevard, tel: (323) 268-1598
New Zealand: 12400 Wilshire Boulevard, tel: (310) 207-1605
South Africa: 6300 Wilshire Bouevard, tel: (323) 651-0902; www.link2southafrica.com

Good Websites

In addition to the listed websites for Southern California tourist boards and chambers of commerce, try these for information on specific topics:
California Attractions & Events
www.gocalif.ca.gov/index
California State Parks
www.caohwy.com/c/caparks.htm
California Missions
www.ca-missions.org/contact.html
California Bed & Breakfast Inns
www.innaccess.com/home.html
Death Valley Ghost Towns
www.thesierraweb.com/sightseeing/death valley/dvghost.html

Getting Around

Public Transportation

Los Angeles
Public transportation into the city of LA is found on the lower level of Los Angeles airport, and this is where arriving passengers, after claiming baggage, will find shuttles, courtesy transport to various hotels and car rental offices, an information booth and a free bus to the MTA bus terminal about 1 mile (1.5 km) away. From here at Lot C, MTA buses run to different parts of LA and also a Big Blue Bus up into Santa Monica.

San Diego
San Diego has a comprehensive network of trolleys that connects the downtown area with neighboring districts and even to the Mexican border. The city has a good bus service, too, but this tends to serve local communities only.

Southern California
Southern California is currently implementing its most ambitious public transit plans for half a century which, when completed, will link areas as far apart as Los Angeles' port of Long Beach and Palmdale, 50 miles (81 km) north of the city. The 400-mile (644-km) system of light rail, subway and other transportation facilities will not be fully in place until 2010 although a few lines in central LA have opened already. The Red Line operates between North Hollywood and Downtown, one leg extending west to Wilshire and Western. The Blue Line operates between Downtown and Long Beach. The Green Line runs from Redondo Beach to Norwalk, crossing the Blue Line just north of Compton. Be careful if traveling after dark.

For information on getting around California by rail and bus, *see Getting There, page 308.*

Private Transportation

BY CAR

Drivers who yearn for a nostalgic drive through the California stretch of old US Route 66 can get a free map charting 29 points of interest along 62 miles (100 km) of the route. Pick it up from the LA Visitors' Center, 685 South Figueroa St, LA 90017, tel: (213) 689-8822. Or contact the Route 66 Territory Visitors' Bureau, tel: (800) 564-7866.

Driving is by far the most flexible and convenient means of travel in California, although newcomers are often confused by the many freeways. Roads are well-maintained throughout the state, and gasoline is relatively inexpensive. Before you set out, however, there are some important things to keep in mind *(see below).*

MOTORING ADVICE

A recent innovation in the Los Angeles area is the provision of 36 tow trucks patrolling the county's 200 miles (322 km) of freeway from 6–10am and 3–7pm in search of stalled automobiles. Called the **Freeway Service Patrol,** its operators provide emergency gasoline or offer help in changing tires or towing disabled cars to some public place with a telephone. Travelers should check local listings for the AAA office closest to them, or for reciprocal arrangements with international automobile organizations. Your greatest asset as a driver is a good road map. It is absolutely essential to make sense of the tangle of highways surrounding most large cities. It is also advisable to listen to local radio stations for updates on traffic and road conditions, and to check with highway officials for the latest information on weather and road conditions if you are planning a lengthy drive.

DESERT AND MOUNTAIN TRAVEL

The single most important precaution you can take is to tell someone your destination, route and expected time of arrival. Check tires carefully before long stretches of desert driving. Heat builds pressure, so have them at slightly below normal air pressure. The desert's arid climate makes carrying extra water – both for passengers and vehicles – one of the essentials. Carry at least one gallon per person. Keep an eye on the gas gauge. It's a good idea to have more than you think you need. Remember, if you should have car trouble or become lost, do not strike out on foot. A car, visible from the air and presumably on a road, is easier to spot than a person, and it affords shelter from the weather. Wait to be found rather than pursue your rescuers.

Mountain drivers are advised to be equally vigilant about weather conditions. Winter storms in the Sierras occasionally close major roads, and at times chains are required on tires. Phone ahead for road conditions before you depart: tel: (213) 628 7623.

TRAVELING TO TIJUANA AND BAJA

For entry into Mexico, non US citizens should bring their passports or green cards. US citizens don't need a passport unless they're visiting for more than 72 hours, or plan to go beyond the State Highway 1 checkpoint below Baja's Ensenada. If so, they must acquire a tourist visa in San Diego from any travel agent, the Mexican Consulate General, the Mexico Government Tourism Office or the Automobile Club of Southern California. Proof of nationality must accompany the visa.

US insurance is not valid in Mexico and short-term insurance is obtainable at innumerable sales offices just north or just south of the border.

Crossing into Mexico is easy, with immigration officers at both sides usually just waving you along. There are three major crossings: at **San Ysidro** 18 miles (29 km) south of downtown San Diego, which is the busy gateway to Tijuana; at **Tecate** off State 94, where there is rarely a wait, although the solitary customs officer tends to close the border in early evening; and at **Mexicali** (Baja's capital) a dreary industrial city opposite the California town of Calexico, which lies about 90 miles (144 km) to the east of the coast.

Because driving is not easy in Tijuana for those unfamiliar with the city (and the Spanish language), many drivers park in San Diego's San Ysidro, crossing into Tijuana via the elevated pedestrian walkway. Avoid leaving your car in the parking places of merchants unless you want to have it towed away by police.

There's an all-day secure lot off the "Last Exit US parking" ramp – turn right at the stop sign to the Tijuana side. Cheap taxis and buses are available.

CROSSING BACK

The return to California can be a bit more tense than the entry into Mexico, as US Border Patrol officers take far more interest in who's coming into the country. During busy American holiday periods, such as Independence Day (July 4) and Labor Day (early September), waiting up to two hours to cross is not uncommon.

HITCHHIKING

In California, as elsewhere in the US, hitchhiking is illegal, dangerous and unpredictable. In general, well-meaning people in California won't stop for hitchhikers as they might have 20 years ago because of fear – a fear the hitchhiker might do well to have of people who stop.

Where to Stay

Hotels and B&Bs

California offers the complete spectrum of accommodations – from elegant European-style hotels to inexpensive motels rented by the week. In cities, the most expensive hotels are usually situated either Downtown or by the beach, and have the best access to shopping and public transportation. These grand hotels are particularly well-suited to well-heeled international travelers, and many are attractive landmarks in their own right. The concierge at most finer hotels will arrange theater tickets, faxes, limousines with bilingual drivers and airline reservations. Rates average anywhere from $150–$500 per night, double occupancy. There are also a large number of smaller hotels and hotel chains. These establishments usually offer all of the essential comforts without the high prices or glamour of the grand hotels.

B&Bs: American Bed & Breakfasts tend to be both more elegant and more expensive than their European counterparts. Reservation services for B&Bs not listed here can be found on **US Bed & Breakfast**, tel: (800) 872-2632

Motels

If you're traveling by car, don't plan on spending a great deal of time in your room and want an inexpensive alternative, motels are the best solution. Whether set along busy Sunset Boulevard in Los Angeles or along the river bank in a remote town, most provide parking space – at a premium in most of California – within a few paces of your room.

Motel quality tends to vary considerably, but you can usually expect clean and simple accommodation. This is especially true for most of the national chains. A restaurant or coffee shop, swimming pool and sauna are often found on the premises. Room facilities generally include a telephone, television and radio, but don't hesitate to ask the motel manager if you may view a room before agreeing to take it.

Other than their accessibility by auto, the main attraction of motels is their extremely reasonable price: rates in California's cities range from $75–150 per night for double occupancy. They are less expensive in outlying areas.

Best Western	(800) 248-7234
Comfort Inn	(800) 228-5150
Embassy Suites	(800) 362-2779
Hilton	(800) 445-8667
Holiday Inn	(800) 465-4329
Hyatt	(800) 233-1234
Marriott	(800) 228-9290
Motel 6	(800) 466-8356
Quality Inn	(800) 228-5151
Ramada	(800) 272-6232

Campgrounds and Hostels

Public and private campgrounds are located in or near most of the state and national parks in California. Most public campgrounds offer primitive facilities – a place to park, rest rooms within walking distance and outdoor cooking. Fees are around $5 per site. Private campgrounds are usually a little more expensive and offer additional facilities such as RV hook-ups, coin laundries, swimming pools and restaurants. Most campgrounds are busy from mid-June to early September and are allotted on a first come-first served basis. If possible, make reservations.

For more information on camping grounds call or write:
California Department of Parks and Recreation, PO Box 1499, Sacramento, CA 95812-1499, tel: (800) 444-7275.

National Park Service, Department of the Interior, 1849 C Street NW Washington DC 20240, tel: (202) 208-4747; www.nps.gov.
USDA Forest Service, Mt Baldy Ranger District, 110 N Wabash, Glendora, CA 91740, tel: (626) 335-1251.
Santa Catalina: The Santa Catalina Island Company operates several fully equipped campgrounds including Hermit Gulch about a mile from town (shuttle bus), close to the Botanical Garden and hiking trails. Visiting www.scico.com/camping will secure a reservation request form.

Hostels are clean, comfortable and, on the opposite end of the spectrum from B&Bs, very inexpensive. Although suitable for people of all ages, they are definitely for the young at heart. Reservations are highly recommended.
Central California Council, PO Box 3755, Merced, CA 95344, tel: (209) 383-0686.
Los Angeles Council, 1434 Second Street, Santa Monica, CA 90404, tel: (310) 393-6263.
Also try:
www.hostels.com/us.ca.html for complete directory of hostels divided by region.

Los Angeles

LOS ANGELES (DOWNTOWN)

Best Western Hollywood Hills
6141 Franklin Avenue
CA 90028
Tel: (323) 464-5181
Fax: (323) 962-0536
Two blocks from Capitol Records and the Hollywood Metro Station. Pool, coffee shop. **$**
Best Western Mid-Wilshire Plaza Hotel
603 S New Hampshire Avenue
CA 90005
Tel: (213) 385-4444
Fax: (213) 380-5413
www.bestwesterncalifornia.com
Facilities include pool, sauna, Jacuzzi, exercise room, free parking. **$**

Regal Biltmore
506 S Grand Avenue
CA 90071
Tel: (213) 624-1011
Fax: (213) 612-1545
Restaurants, pool, Jacuzzi, impressively luxurious decor. **$$$**
Chancellor Hotel
3191 West 7th Street
CA 90005
Tel: (213) 383-1183
Fax: (213) 385-6658
Pool, laundromat, free parking, free breakfast. **$**
Comfort Inn
1710 West 7th Street
CA 90017
Tel: (213) 483-3470
Pool, waterbeds, free parking. **$**
Figueroa Hotel
939 S Figueroa Street
CA 90015
Tel: (213) 627-8971
or (800) 421-9092
Fax: (213) 689-0305
One block from Convention Center. Pool, Jacuzzi, restaurants, laundromat. **$**
Holiday Inn Downtown
750 Garland Avenue
CA 91423
Tel: (800) 628-5262
Fax: (213) 628-1201
Email: laxdt@aol.com
Pool, laundromat, free parking. **$**
LA Marriott Downtown
333 S Figueroa Street
CA 90071
Tel: (213) 617-1133
Fax: (213) 613-0291
Landscaped grounds with pool near Music Center. Luxurious. **$$$**
Metro Plaza Hotel
711 N Main Street
CA 90012
Tel: (213) 680-0200
or (800) 223-2223
Fax: (213) 620-0200
Downtown. Laundromat, sauna, whirlpool, restaurant. **$**
Miyako Inn
328 East 1st Street
CA 90012
Tel: (213) 617-2000
Fax: (213) 617-2700
Laundromat, whirlpool, sauna, restaurant. **$**
New Otani Hotel & Garden
120 S Los Angeles Street

CA 90012
Tel: (213) 629-1200
or (800) 273-2294
Fax: (213) 622-0980
www.newotani.com
Downtown beside Little Tokyo. Two shopping levels, pool, Japanese garden. **$$$**
The Standard
550 S Flower Street,
CA 90071
Tel: (213) 892-8080
Fax: (213) 892-8686
Hotelier Andre Balazs, who operates Hollywood's Chateau Marmont converted a 12-storey downtown office building into this hip hangout with a poolside bar on the roof. **$$$**

Price Guide

The price guide indicates rates for a standard double room:
$$$ = over $225
$$ = $150–225
$ = under $150
Always state whether you want a smoking or non-smoking room.

Westin Bonaventura
404 S Figueroa Street
CA 90071
Tel: (213) 624-1000
or (888) 625-6144
Fax: (213) 612-4800
Distinctive glass-towered building popular with film makers, pool, rooftop restaurant. **$$$**
Wilshire Grand
930 Wilshire Boulevard
CA 90017
Tel: (213) 688 7777
Fax: (213) 612-3989
Pool, exercise room, coffee shop. **$$$**

LOS ANGELES (WEST SIDE)

Bel Age Hotel
1020 N San Vicente Boulevard
West Hollywood
CA 90069
Tel: (310) 854-1111
Fax: (310) 854-0926
Deluxe, all suites, phones and TVs in bathrooms. **$$$**

Beverly Hilton Hotel
9876 Wilshire Boulevard
CA 90210
Tel: (310) 274-7777
Fax: (310) 285-1313
Near Rodeo Drive shopping. Pools, restaurants, coffee shops. **$$$**
Econolodge Hollywood
777 N. Vine St.
Hollywood, CA 90038
CA 90028
Tel: (323) 463-5671
or (800) 446-3916
Fax: (323) 463-5675
Near Universal studios. Laundromat, pool. **$**
Hollywood Celebrity Hotel
1775 Orchid Avenue
Hollywood, CA 90026
Tel: (323) 850-6464 or (800) 222-7017
Fax: (323) 850-7667
www.hotelcelebrity.com
Airport shuttle, free breakfast. **$**
Hollywood Roosevelt Hotel
7000 Hollywood Boulevard
CA 90028
Tel: (323) 466-7000
or (800) 537-3052
Fax: (323) 462-8056
www.hollywoodroosevelt.com
A legendary Hollywood landmark with Art Deco trimmings, palm-shaded pool, mezzanine museum. **$$$**
Hotel Bel Air
701 Stone Canyon Road
Bel Air
CA 90077
Tel: (310) 472-1211
Fax: (310) 476-5890
Deluxe hotel situated in landscaped grounds in secluded canyon, elegant suites. Prices to match the ambiance. **$$$**
Le Dufy Hotel
1000 Westmount Drive
West Hollywood
CA 90069
Tel: (310) 657-7400
Suites, kitchens, pool, sauna, laundromat. **$$$**
Ramada Hotel
6333 Bristol Parkway
Culver City
CA 90230
Tel: (310) 670-3200
Pool, whirlpool, and exercise room. **$**

Sheraton Universal
333 Universal Terrace Parkway.
Universal City, CA 91608
Tel: (818) 980-1212
or (800) 325-3535
Near Universal Studios. restaurant,
health club, pool. **$$–$$$**

Westwood Plaza Hotel
10740 Wilshire Boulevard
CA 90024
Tel: (310) 475-8711
Fax: (310) 475-5220
Pool, sauna, whirlpool, exercise
room. **$$**

LOS ANGELES (COASTAL)

Bayside Hotel
2001 Ocean Avenue
Santa Monica, CA 90405
Tel: (310) 396-6000
or (800) 525-4447
Fax: (310) 369-1000
Ocean views, kitchenettes,
multilingual staff. **$**

Cadillac Hotel
8 Dudley Avenue
Venice, CA 90291
Tel: (310) 399-8876
Fax: (310) 399-1930
Art Deco spot right on the
boardwalk with a roof sundeck.
$

Comfort Inn
2815 Santa Monica Boulevard
Santa Monica
CA 90404
Tel: (310) 828-5517
Fax: (310) 399-8876
www.comfortinn.com
A mile and a half (2 km) from
beach. Pool. **$$**

Georgian Hotel
1415 Ocean Ave.
Santa Monica, CA 90401
Tel: (310) 395-9945
or (800) 538-8147
Fax: (310) 656-0904
Historic Art Deco landmark. Easy
walk to pier and 3rd Street
Promenade. **$$$**

Hotel Santa Monica
3102 Pico Boulevard
Santa Monica, CA 90405
Tel: (310) 450-5766
Fax: (310) 450-8843
Kitchenettes, laundromat, rate
includes breakfast. **$**

Inn on Venice Beach
327 Washington Boulevard
Venice, CA 90291
Tel: (310) 821-2557
Fax: (310) 827-0289
Boutique-style hotel with 43 rooms.
Near Boardwalk. **$**

Loew's Santa Monica Beach Hotel
1700 Ocean Avenue
Santa Monica, CA 90401
Tel: (310) 458 -0200
Fax: (310) 458-2813
Pools, whirlpool, health club.
$$$

Malibu Beach Inn
22878 Pacific Coast Highway
Malibu, CA 90265
Tel: (310) 456-6444
or (800) 4-MALIBU
Fax: (310) 456-1499
www.malibubeachinn.com
Near the pier. Rooms with fireplaces,
fitness center, VCRs. **$$$**

Price Guide

The price guide indicates rates
for a standard double room:
$$$ = over $225
$$ = $150–225
$ = under $150

Marina Pacific Hotel
1697 Pacific Avenue
Venice, CA 90291
Tel: (310) 452-1111 or
(800) 421-8151
Fax: (310) 452-5479
Five miles (8 km) from airport.
Café. **$**

The Faimont Miramar
101 Wilshire Boulevard
Santa Monica
CA 90401
Tel: (310) 576-7777
or (800) 866-5377
Fax: (310) 319-3139
Landscaped grounds, pool, health
club, coffee shop. **$$$**

Pacific Shore Hotel
1819 Ocean Avenue
Santa Monica, CA 90401
Tel: (310) 451-8711
Fax: (310) 394-6657
Pool, sauna, laundromat. **$$**

Shangri La Hotel
1301 Ocean Avenue
Santa Monica, CA 90401

Tel: (310) 394-2791
or (800) 345-7829
Fax: (310) 451-3351
Art Deco landmark opposite
Palisades Park; kitchenettes,
laundromat. **$$$**

Shutters on the Beach
1 Pico Boulevard
Santa Monica
CA 90405
Tel: (310) 458-0030
Fax: (310) 458-4589
On the beach; pool, whirlpool,
restaurants. **$$$**

Venice Beach House
15 30th Avenue
CA 90291
Tel: (310) 823-1966
Fax: (310) 823-1842
A tranquil nine-room B&B with
garden that was once the
home of Venice founder Abbot
Kinney. **$$**

LOS ANGELES (UNIVERSAL CITY/ DISNEYLAND)

Angel Inn
1800 E Katella Avenue
Anaheim, CA 92805
Tel: (714) 634-9121
or (800) 358-4400
Fax: (714) 978-1608
Free transportation to Disneyland.
Multilingual staff. Pool. **$**

Convention Center Inn
2017 S Harbor Boulevard
CA 92802
Tel: (800) 521-5628
Fax: (714) 750-5676
Near Disneyland. Pool, spa,
restaurant, disabled-friendly. **$**

Days Inn Park South
2171 S Harbor Boulevard
CA 92802
Tel: (714) 703-1220
or (800) 654-7503
Fax: (714) 703-1401
Free shuttle to nearby Disneyland. **$**

Desert Palm Suites
631 W Katella Avenue
CA 92802
Tel: (714) 535-1133
or (800) 635-5423
Fax: (714) 491-7409
Near Disneyland. Pool, spa, games
room. **$**

Disneyland Hotel
1150 W. Magic Way
CA 92802
Tel: (714) 778-6600
or (800) 647-7900
Fax: (714) 956-6597
www.disneyland.com
Adjoins Disneyland. Pools, spa, 11
restaurants, tennis courts. **$$$**
Disney's Grand Californian Hotel
1600 South Disneyland Drive
Disneyland Resort
Anaheim, CA 92802
Tel: (714) 635-2300
or (800) 225-2024
Fax: (714) 300-7300
www.disneyland.com
Craftsman-style resort built as part
of Disney's California Adventure.
Pool, spa, restaurants. **$$$**
Jolly Roger Hotel
640 W Katella Avenue
CA 92802
Tel: (714) 772-7621
or (800) 446-1555
Fax: (714) 772-2308
Near Disneyland. Pool, restaurant,
spa. **$$**
Pan Pacific Hotel
1717 S West Street, CA 92802
Tel: (714) 999-0990
Fax: (714) 776-5763
Next to Disneyland monorail.
Restaurants, pool, shops, health
club. **$$$**
Penny Sleeper Inn
1441 S Manchester Avenue
CA 92802
Tel: (714) 991-8100
or (800) 854-6118
Free transport to nearby
Disneyland. Pool, games room. **$**
Sheraton Universal Hotel
333 Universal Terrace, Parkway
CA 91608
Tel: (818) 980-1212
or (800) 325-3536
Fax: (818) 509-0605
At Universal Studios. Pool,
whirlpool, exercise room. **$$$**
Tropicana Inn
1540 S Harbor Boulevard
CA 92802
Tel: (714) 635-4082
or (800) 828-4898
Fax: (714) 635-1535
Near Disneyland with free shuttle.
Pool, spa, restaurants nearby,
facilities for the disabled. **$$**

Universal City Hilton & Towers
555 Universal Terrace, Parkway
CA 91608
Tel: (818) 506-2500
or (800) HILTONS
Fax: (818) 509-2031
Near Universal Studios. Pool,
whirlpool, exercise room. **$$$**

BAJA CALIFORNIA

Ensenada
Bahia Resort Hotel
López Mateos & Alvarado
Tel: (011-52) 667-821-01
Midtown. Pool, ocean views,
outdoor dining plus La Tortuga
restaurant. **$$**
Days Inn
Lopez Matyeos 1050
Tel: (011-52) 617-838-34
or from the US dial (800) 432-9755
Motel comforts; pool and Jacuzzi. **$**
Hotel Paraiso Las Palmas
Boulevard Sangines 206
Tel: (011-52) 617-717-01,
Fax: 617-444-90
On the beach. Pool, Jacuzzi,
restaurant, ocean-view rooms. **$**

Mexicali
Holiday Inn Crowne Plaza
Av de los Heroes 201
Tel: (011-52) 655-736-00
or in the US (800) 465-4329
Five miles (8 km) below the border.
Pool, restaurants. **$$**

Rosarito
Baja Village Motel
Juarez & Via de las Olas 228
Tel: (011-52) 661-200-50
On main street, adjoining beach. **$**
Calafia
Km 35.5 Free Road Tijuana-
Ensenada
Tel: (011-52) 661-215-81
Vast, amusingly designed complex of
terrace restaurants, bars and bric-a-
brac. Pool, 24-hour coffee shop. **$$**
La Fonda
Km 59 Carretera Tijuana-Ensenada
Highway where Libre and Cuota
highways meet. Write for
reservations (no telephone) to
PO Box 430268
San Ysidro, CA 92143.
Charming oceanfront hacienda, bar

and restaurant on tropical patio;
4-person studios with kitchens. **$$**
Las Rocas Resort
On the highway 6 miles (10 km)
south of town
Tel & Fax: (011-52) 661-221-40
In attractive grounds with outdoor
restaurant. Tennis, pool, spa,
Jacuzzi. **$$$**
Rosarito Beach Hotel
PO Box 430145
San Diego, CA 92143
Tel: (011-52) 661-201-44
or in the U.S. (800) 343-8582
Legendary resort in midtown. Pools,
tennis, shopping arcade, all the
trimmings. **$$$**
San Felipe Marina Resort & Spa
Tel: (011-52) 657-711-55 or in the
US tel: (619) 558-0295
Restaurant, tennis, pools,
gymnasium, boat docks. **$$**

Tecate
Rancho Ojai RV/Campground
P.O. Box 2890, Tecate
Tel: (011-52) 665-447-72
Campsites and log cabins,
clubhouse **$**

Tijuana
Hotel Lucerna
Avenida Rodriguez & Paseo de los
Heroes, near the river
Tel: (011-52) 663-339-00
or in the US: (800) 582-3762
Restaurant, attractive coffee shop,
pool, tennis. **$$**

BUENA PARK

**Buena Park Radisson Resort at
Knott's Berry Farm**
7675 Crescent Avenue
CA 90620
Tel: (714) 995-1111
or (800) 333-3333
Fax: (714) 2205124
www.radisson.com/buenaparkca
Free shuttle to Disneyland.
Restaurant, pool, spa. **$**
Buena Park TraveLodge
7039 Orangethrope Avenue
CA 90620
Tel: (714) 521-9220
Free shuttle service to Knott's
Berry Farm and Disneyland. Pool,
spa, playground. **$**

Fairfield Inn by Marriott
7032 Orangethorpe Avenue
CA 90621
Tel: (714) 523-1488
or (800) 228-2800
Fax: (714) 523-1488
Near Knott's Berry Farm and the
Movieland Wax Museum. Pool,
facilities for the disabled. **$**

The Hanford Hotel
7828 Orangethorpe Avenue
CA 90620
Tel: (714) 670-7200
or (888) 560-1629
Eight miles (13 km) from
Disneyland with a free shuttle to the
Magic Kingdom and to Knott's Berry
Farm. Pool, spa. **$**

BURBANK

Burbank Airport Hilton
2500 Hollywood Way, CA 91505
Tel: (818) 843-6000
or (800) HILTONS
Fax: (818) 842-9720
At the airport. Pool, restaurant,
fitness center, sauna. **$$$**

DANA POINT

Best Western Marina Inn
24800 Dana Point Harbor Drive
CA 92629
Tel: (949) 496-1203
or (800) 255-6843,
Fax: 949 248-0360
Located beside the water. Pool,
restaurant. **$**

Blue Lantern Inn
34343 Street of Blue Lantern
CA 92929
Tel: (949) 661-1304
or (800) 753-9000
Fax: (949) 496-1483
www.foursisters.com
Overlooking Dana Point Harbor, many
rooms here have an ocean view. **$$**

DEATH VALLEY

Furnace Creek Inn
PO Box 1
CA 92328
Tel: (760) 786-2345
Fax: (760) 786-2514

www.furnacecreekresort.com
Restaurant, pool, golf, tennis,
horseback riding. **$$$**

Furnace Creek Ranch
Same address and phone as above.
Under the same management but
less expensive. **$$**

Stovepipe Wells Village
State Highway 190
CA 92328
Tel: (760) 786-2387
Restaurant, pool. **$**

HERMOSA BEACH

Quality Inn
901 Aviation Boulevard
CA 90254
Tel: (310) 374-2666
or (800) 553-1145
Fax: (310) 379-3797
A few hundred yards from beach.
Spas, kitchenettes. **$**

HUNTINGTON BEACH

Quality Inn
800 Pacific Coast Highway
CA 92648
Tel: (800) 228-5151
Near the beach. Spa, facilities for
the disabled. **$**

Waterfront Hilton Beach Resort
21100 Pacific Coast Highway
CA 92648
Tel: (800) 822-7873
Fax: (714) 845-8424
At the beach. Pool, spa, tennis,
restaurant, facilities for the
disabled. **$$**

INDIO

**Indian Palms Country Club
Resort**
48-630 Monroe Street
CA 92201
Tel: (760) 347-0688
Restaurant, pool, golf courses,
tennis. **$**

Indio Travelodge
80651 State Highway 111 west of
town
CA 92201
Tel: (760) 342-0882
Pool, tennis court. **$**

Royal Plaza Inn
82347 Highway 111 just east
of town
CA 92201
Tel: (760) 347-0911.
Fax: (760) 347-8644
Pool, laundromat, restaurant. **$**

LAGUNA BEACH

Aliso Creek Resort
31106 Coast Highway
CA 92677
Tel: (949) 499-2271
or (800) 223-3309
Fax: (949) 499-4601
Three miles (5 km) from
downtown, three minutes from
beach. Pool, spa, restaurant, golf
course. **$$**

Hotel Laguna
425 S Coast Highway
CA 92651
Tel: (949) 494-1151
or (800) 524-2927
Fax: (949) 497-2163
On beach. Near Pageant of
Masters. Restaurants, facilities for
the disabled. **$$**

LA JOLLA

La Jolla Beach & Tennis Club,
2000 Spindrift Drive
Tel: (858) 454-7126
or (800) 624-2582
Fax: (858) 456-3805
www.ljbtc.com
On the beach, and close to Sea
World. Restaurant, pool, golf,
tennis, some facilities for the
disabled. **$$–$$$**

La Valencia Hotel
1132 Prospect Street
Tel: (858) 454-0771
or (800) 451-0772
Greta Garbo stayed here, as did
Mary Pickford. Pool, spa,
restaurants. **$$$**

Sea Lodge Oceanfront Hotel
8110 Camino del Oro, CA 92037
Tel: (858) 459-8271
or (800) 237-5211
Fax: (858) 456-9346
www.sealodge.com
On the beach. Restaurant, pool, spa,
tennis and fitness facilities. **$$–$$$**

LAKE ARROWHEAD

Hilton Resort
PO Box 1699
27984 Highway 189
CA 92352
Tel: (909) 336-1511
Next to village. Pool, tennis, health club, restaurants **$$$**

LONG BEACH

Comfort Inn
3201 E Pacific Coast Highway
CA 90804
Tel: (562) 597-3374
or (800) 228-5150
Fax: (562) 985-3142
www.comfortinn.com
Pool, whirlpool, laundromat. **$**

Long Beach Airport Marriot
4700 Airport Plaza Drive
CA90815
Tel: (562) 425-5210
or (800) 944-9002
Fax: (562) 421-1075
www.gowestmarriott.com
Pools, sauna, whirlpool, exercise room. **$$$**

Guest House International
5325 E Pacific Coast Highway
CA 90804
Tel: (562) 597-1341
or (800) 21-GUEST
Fax: (562) 597-1664
www.guesthouseintl.com
Pool, deli-restaurant. **$$**

Queen Mary Hotel
1126 Queens Highway
Long Beach, CA 90802
Tel: (562) 499-1626
Fax: (562) 436-3685
www.queenmary.com
Restaurants, fitness center, nightly entertainment aboard one of the most historic ships in the world. **$$-$$$**

LOS ALAMOS

Victorian Mansion & Union Hotel
362 Bell Street, Box 616
CA 93440
Tel: (805) 344-2744
Unique theme rooms in two elegant Victorian structures. **$$$**

NEWPORT BEACH

Four Seasons Hotel
690 Newport Center Drive
CA 92660
Tel: (949) 759-0808
or (800) 332-3442
Fax: (949) 759-0568
One mile (1.5 km) from beach. Pool, restaurants, fitness club, tennis. **$$$**

Hyatt Newporter Resort
1107 Jamboree Road, CA 92660
Tel: (949) 729-1234
or (800) 233-1234
Fax: (949) 644-1552
www.hyatt.com
Near beach. Restaurants, pools, tennis, golf. **$$$**

Newport Classic Inn
2300 W Pacific Coast Highway
CA 92663
Tel: (949) 722-2999
or (800) 633-3199
Fax (949) 631-5659
On bay, short walk from beach. Restaurant, pool, sauna, facilities for the disabled . **$**

OJAI

Best Western Casa Ojai
1302 E Ojai Avenue
CA 93023
Tel: (805) 646-8175
Fax: (805) 640-8247
www.westerncalifornia.com
Pool, Jacuzzi, cable TV. **$$**

Ojai Valley Inn & Spa
Country Club Road
CA 93023
Tel: (805) 645-5511
or (800) 422-6524
Fax: (805) 646-7969
www.ojairesort.com
Enormous grounds include pools, tennis courts, saunas, restaurant. Kids stay free. **$$$**

PALM SPRINGS

Estrella
415 S Belardo Road
Palm Springs, CA 92260
Tel: (800) 237-3687
Poolside pavilions, terraced villas and nicely furnished studios, some with fireplaces. **$$**

Ingleside Inn
200 Ramon
CA 92264
Tel: (760) 325-0046
Fax: (760) 325-0710
Greta Garbo slept here. Garden, antiques, pool, restaurant. **$$$**

La Mancha
444 Avenida Caballeros
CA 92262
Tel: (760) 323-1773
or (800) 255-1773
Fax: (760) 323-5928
www.la-mancha.com
Attractively furnished villas, pools, sauna, putting green, lighted tennis courts, croquet. **$$$**

La Quinta Hotel & Resort
49-499 Eisenhower Drive
LA Quinta
CA 92253
Tel: (760) 564-4111
Fax: (760) 564-5758
Twenty miles (32 km) from Palm Springs. Numerous pools and spas, tennis and five restaurants. **$$$**

Marriott's Desert Springs Resort and Spa
74855 Country Club Drive
CA 92260
Tel: (760) 341-2211
Fax: (760) 341-1872
www.gowestmarriott.com
Features Venetian pond with gondolas, golf courses and tennis courts. **$$**

Orbit In
562 W Arena
Tel: (760) 323-3585
Fax: (760) 323-3599
Ten poolside rooms decorated and furnished in "mid-century" style, video library **$$**

Orchid Tree Inn
261 S Belardo Road
CA 92262

Tel: (760) 325-2791
or (800) 733-3435
Fax: (760) 325-3855
www.orchidtree.com
Landscaped grounds, pools, whirlpool, private villas with kitchens. **$$**

Quality Inn
1269 E Palm Canyon Drive
CA 92264
Tel: (760) 323-2775
or (800) 472-4339
Fax: 323-4234
www.qualityinn-palmsprings.com
Large grounds, pool, whirlpool, laundromat. **$**

Ramada Resort Inn
1800 E Palm Canyon Drive
CA 92264
Tel: (760) 323-1711
Fax: (760) 327-6941
www.psramada.com
Located close to airport, with pool, sauna, coffeeshop, laundromat. **$$**

Riviera Resort
1600 N Indian Canyon Road
CA 92262
Tel: (760) 327-8311
or (800) 727-8311
Fax: (760) 778-2560
Near Aerial Tramway. Floodlit tennis courts, pools, putting course, supervised children's camp. **$$$**

Royal Sun Inn
1700 S Palm Canyon Drive
CA 92264
Tel: (760) 327-1564
or (800) 619-4786
Fax: (760) 323-9092
Pools, sauna, adjoining restaurants, free breakfast. **$**

San Marino Hotel
225 W Baristo Rd
CA 92262
Tel: (800) 676-1214
Fax: (760) 325-6906
Central, pool and a special welcome to guests with dogs (dogsitting and grooming available). **$$**

Two Bunch Palms Resort & Spa
67–425 Two Bunch Palms Trail
Desert Hot Springs, CA 92240
Tel: (760) 329-8791
or (800) 472-4334
Fax: (760) 329-1317
Desert haven featured in the movie *The Player*. **$$–$$$**

Vagabond Inn
1699 S Palm Canyon Drive
CA 92264
Tel: (760) 325-7211
Fax: (760) 322-9269
www.vagabondinns.com
Pool, saunas, coffee shop. **$**

Villa Royale Inn
1620 Indian Trail
CA 92264
Tel: (760) 327-2314
Fax: (760) 322-3794
www.villaroyale.com
Suites decorated in styles of different countries, charming courtyards, pool. **$$–$$$**

Price Guide

The price guide indicates rates for a standard double room:
$$$ = over $225
$$ = $150–225
$ = under $150
Always state whether you want a smoking or non-smoking room.

PASADENA

Ritz Carlton Huntington Hotel
1401 Oak Knoll Avenue
CA 91109
Tel: (626) 568-3900
or (800) 241-3333
Fax: (626) 568-3700
Cottages, tennis courts, pool, free transportation to downtown LA. **$$$**

Vagabond Inn
1203 E Colorado Boulevard
CA 91106
Tel: (626) 449-3170
or (800) 522-1555
Fax: (626) 577-8873
Near Santa Anita racetrack. Pool.
$

REDONDO BEACH

Best Western Sunrise Hotel
400 N Harbor Drive
CA 90277
Tel: (310) 376-0746
or (800) 334-7384
Fax: (310) 376-7384
www.bestwestern-sunrise.com
At the marina. Pool, spa, restaurant. **$**

Portofino Hotel & Yacht Club
260 Portofino Way
CA 90277
Tel: (310) 798-5888
or (800) 468-4292
Fax: (310) 798-2766
Pool, restaurant, health club. **$$$**

RIVERSIDE

The Mission Inn
3649 Mission Inn Avenue
Riverside, CA 92505
Tel: (909) 784-0300
Fax: (909) 683-1342
Historic hostelry popular with presidents and movie stars. Unique Spanish Revival architecture. **$$**

SAN BERNARDINO

Sun Park Lodge
25300 E 3rd Street
CA 92410
Tel: (909) 884-2355
Three miles (5 km) from downtown. Kitchenettes, pool. **$**

Temecula Creek Inn
44501 Rainbow Canyon Road
CA 92390
Tel: (909) 694-1000
or (800) 96-CREEK
Pool, restaurant, golf, tennis.
$$$

SAN DIEGO

Balboa Park Inn
3402 Park Boulevard
CA 92103
Tel: (619) 298-0823
or (800) 938-8181
Fax: (619) 294-8070
www.balboaparkinn.com
Near the zoo. Bar, in-room Jacuzzi, free breakfast. **$–$$**

Clarion Hotel Bay View
660 K Street
CA 92101
Tel: (619) 696-0234
or (800) 766-0234
Fax: (619) 231-8199
www.clarionbayview.com
Sauna, whirlpool, exercise room, laundromat. **$$**

Comfort Inn and Suites
2485 Hotel Circle Place
CA 92108
Tel: (619) 881-6200
or (800) 824-0950
Fax: (619) 297-6179
www.comfortinn-sandiego.com
Just off I-8, close to Sea World
and San Diego Zoo. Pool,
whirlpool, laundromat, wheelchair
aaccess. **$**

Comfort Inn – Sea World Area
4610 DeSoto Street
CA 92109
Tel: (858) 483-9800
or (800) 824-0950
Fax: (858) 483-4010
Located just 5 minutes away from
Sea World. Ask for reduced-price
tickets, which are available from the
front desk. **$**

Crown City Inn
520 Orange Avenue
Coronado, CA 92118
Tel: (619) 435-3116
or (800) 422-1173
Fax: (619) 435-6750
www.crowncityinn.com
Near the beach and shops. Guests
have free use of bicycles. **$**

Westin Horton Plaza
910 Broadway Circle
CA 92101
Tel: (619) 239-2200
or (800) WESTIN
Fax: (619) 239-4806
www.westin.com
Pool, saunas, floodlit tennis courts,
health club. **$$**

Holiday Inn-Harbor View
1617 First Avenue
CA 92101
Tel: (619) 239-9600
or (800) 366-3164
Fax: (619) 233-6228
E-mail: ldmeglio@sanstonehotels.com
www.holiday-inn.com
Close to I-5. Pool, laundromat.
$$

**Holiday Inn Hotel & Suites Old
Town**
2435 Jefferson Street
CA 92110
Tel: (619) 260-8500
Fax: (619) 297-2078
E-mail: dosoldtownhi@sunstonehotels.com
www.sunstonehotelscom
Near historic attractions. Pool and
spa, free breakfast. **$$**

Hotel del Coronado
1500 Orange Avenue Coronado
CA 92118
Tel: (619) 522-8000
or (800) HOTELDEL
Fax: (619) 522-8262
www.hoteldel.com
One of the world's most stylish and
luxurious hotels, and a world-
famous Victorian-era landmark.
Tennis court, pool, restaurants,
prices to match. **$$$**

Hyatt Regency
One Market Place Harbor Drive and
Market Place
CA 92101
Tel: (619) 232-1234
or (800) 233-1234
Fax: (619) 233-6464
www.hyatt.com
Pool, sauna, tennis courts, exercise
room. **$$$**

The Inn at La Jolla
5440 La Jolla Boulevard
CA 92037
Tel: (858) 454-6121
Fax: (858) 459-1377
Close to beach. Pool, whirlpool,
putting green. **$$**

La Jolla Beach Travelodge
6750 La Jolla Boulevard
CA 92037
Tel: (858) 454-0716
Fax: (858) 454-1075
Pool, restaurant nearby. **$**

The Lodge at Torrey Pines
11480 N Torrey Pines Road
CA 92037
Tel: (800) 656-0087
Craftsman-type mansion on ocean
bluff. Meticulously furnished. Near
golf course. **$$$**

Mission Valley Hilton
901 Camino del Rio S
CA 92108
Tel: (619) 543-9000
or (800) 445-8667
Fax: (619) 296-9561
Pool, whirlpool, exercise room. **$$**

Quality Inn
2901 Nimitz Boulevard
CA 92106
Tel: (619) 696-0911
or (800) 404-6835
Fax: (619) 224-4025
Near airport, zoo and Seaworld.
Pool, coffee shop. **$**

Ramada Inn
830 Sixth Avenue, CA 92101

Tel: (619) 531-8877
or (800) 664-4400
Fax: (619) 231-8307
www.stjameshotel.com
Near Gaslamp Quarter. Harbor view,
rooftop, lobby bar and grill. **$**

San Diego Paradise Point Resort
1404 W Vacation Road
CA 92109
Tel: (858) 274-4630
or (800) 344-2626
Fax: (858) 581-5997
www.paradisepoint.com
Bungalows in spacious grounds
right on Mission Bay. Pools, lighted
tennis courts, boat rentals, jogging
facilities. **$$$**

**Town and Country Resort Hotel &
Convention Center**
500 Hotel Circle N
CA 92108
Tel: (619) 291-7131
or (800) 722-8527
Fax: (619) 291-3584
www.towncountry.com
Landscaped grounds, pools,
restaurants, coffee shops. Kids
stay free. **$$**

US Grant Hotel
326 Broadway
CA 92101
Tel: (619) 232-3121
or (800) 237-5029
Fax: (619) 232-3626
Historic downtown hotel near
shopping. Exercise room,
restaurant. **$$**

The Westgate Hotel
1055 2nd Avenue
CA 92101
Tel: (619) 238-1818
or (800) 221-3802
Fax: (619) 557-3737
Lovely interiors and furnishings,
exercise room, restaurant. **$$$**

Wyndham Garden Hotel
5975 Lusk Boulevard
CA 92121
Tel: (858) 558-1818
Fax: (858) 558-0421
North of town. Pool, whirlpool,
exercise room, restaurant. **$$**

SANTA BARBARA

Bath Street Inn
1720 Bath Street
CA 93101

Tel: (805) 682-9680
Fax: (805) 569-1281
Located in a quiet residential area, this Victorian house offers intimate and luxurious rooms. **$$**

Blue Quail Inn
1908 Bath Street
CA 93101
Tel: (805) 687-2300
Fax: (805) 687-4567
Main house and cottages in pleasantly landscaped grounds. **$$**

The Cheshire Cat
36 W Valerio Street
CA 93101
Tel: (805) 569-1610
Fax: (805) 682-1876
www.cheshirecat.com
Century-old house located in the suburbs. Rooms with fireplaces, whirlpool. **$$$**

Circle Bar B Guest Ranch
1800 Refugio Canyon Rd
CA 93117
Tel: (805) 968-1113
Just a few miles from the ocean, this quiet family ranch offers good accommodation in a most scenic canyon. **$$**

Fess Parker's Doubletree Resort
633 E Cabrillo Boulevard
CA 93103
Tel: (805) 564-4333
or (800) 879-2929
Fax: (805) 962-8198
www.fpdtr.com
Across from the beach in spacious grounds. Pool, sauna, putting green. **$$$**

Franciscan Inn
109 Bath Street, CA 93101
Tel: (805) 963-8845
Fax: (805) 564-3295
www.franciscaninn.com
At the beach. Health club, pool, tennis courts. **$**

Glenborough Inn
1327 Bath St
CA 93101
Tel: (805) 966-0589
Fax: (805) 564-8610
Built in the early 1900s, most rooms are graced with a fireplace. **$$–$$$**

Harbor View Inn
28 W Cabrillo Boulevard
CA 93101
Tel: (805) 963-0780
Fax: (805) 963-7967
www.santabarbara.com

Opposite Stearns Wharf with ocean views. Pool, whirlpool, adjacent restaurant. **$$**

Inn of the Spanish Garden
202 W Cabrillo Boulevard
CA 93101
Tel: (805) 564-4700
E-mail: info@spanishgardeninn.com
www.spanishgardeninn.com
Mediterranean-style complex in the Presidio District with pool and courtyard. 23 spacious, elegant rooms and underground parking. **$$**

Mary May Inn
324 W Mason Street
CA 93101
Tel: (805) 569-3398
Stylish rooms (some with fireplace) set in an 1886 Federal Style house with gabled roof and porches. **$$**

Olive House Inn

Price Guide

The price guide indicates rates for a standard double room:
$$$ = over $225
$$ = $150–225
$ = under $150
Always state whether you want a smoking or non-smoking room.

1604 Olive St
CA 93101
Tel: (805) 962-4902
Fax: (805) 962-9983
Historic bed and breakfast in a quiet residential area. **$$**

Polynesian Motel
433 W Montecito, CA 93101
Tel: (805) 963-7851
Near beach. Pool, kitchenettes, laundromat. **$**

Radisson Hotel Santa Barbara
1111 E Cabrillo Boulevard
CA 93101
Tel: (805) 963-0744
or (800) 643-1994
Fax: (805) 962-0985
www.radisson.com
Across from beach. Pool, whirlpool, health club. **$$$**

San Ysidro Ranch
900 San Ysidro Road
Montecito, CA 98108
Tel: (805) 969-5046
or (800) 368-6788
Fax: (805) 565-1995

www.sanysidroranch.com
Luxury resort with a celebrated history. **$$$**

Simpson House Inn
121 E Arrellaga Street
CA 93101
Tel: (805) 963-7067
Fax: (805) 564-4811
Beautifully decorated rooms in a historic bed and breakfast. Quiet, tree-shaded grounds. **$$–$$$**

Tiffany Country House
1323 De la Vina St
CA 93101
Tel: (805) 963-2283
Fax: (805) 962-0094
Historic bed and breakfast in the Colonial Revival Style. **$$**

The Upham,
1404 De La Vina
CA 93101
Tel: (805) 962-0058
Fax: (805) 963-2825
Last of the great, old SB hotels (founded 1872) with all the charm and style you'd expect. Beautifully furnished garden bungalows. **$$$**

Villa Rosa
15 Chapala Avenue
CA 93101
Tel: (805) 966-0851
Fax: (805) 962-7159
www.sbweb.com
Right on the beach, with swimming pool and spa. **$$**

SAN JUAN CAPISTRANO

Best Western Capistrano Inn,
27174 Ortega Highway
CA 92675
Tel: (949) 493-5661
or (800) 528-1234
Fax: (949) 661-8293
Three blocks from downtown. Restaurant, pool, spa. **$**

SAN LUIS OBISPO

The Garden Street Inn
1212 Garden Street
CA 93401
Tel: (805) 545-9802
Fax: (805) 545-9403
Historic B&B in Italianate Queen Anne-style house, some rooms with fireplace. **$–$$**

Madonna Inn
100 Madonna Road
CA 93405
Tel: (805) 543-5110
Fax: (805) 543-3406
A famous tourist site even for those just passing by. Outlandish rooms in Western, Hawaiian and Austrian styles. **$$**

Travel Lodge
345 Marsh Street
CA 93401
Tel: (805) 543-5110
Fax: (805) 543-3406
Near downtown. Usual facilities including pool, laundromat. **$**

SANTA CATALINA ISLAND

The Santa Catalina Island Company offers various packages and accommodations. Check www.scico.com for details.

Other island hotels include:
Best Western Catalina Canyon Hotel
PO Box 736
CA 90704
Tel: (310) 510-0325
or (800) 253-9361
Fax: (310) 510-0900
www.bestwesterncalifornia.com
In foothills overlooking Avalon Bay. Pool, sauna, golf, tennis, restaurant. **$$**

Cloud 7
137 Marilla Avenue
CA 90704
Tel: (310) 510-0454
or (800) 422-6836
Fax: (310) 510-0511
A B&B with some rooms having ocean views. Situated near beach. **$**

Hotel St Lauren
PO Box 497
CA 90704
Tel: (310) 510-2299
or (800) 645-2496
Fax: (310) 510-1369
Distinctive pseudo-Victorian structure with rooftop patio. **$$**

The Old Turner Inn
232 Catalina Avenue
CA 90704
Tel: (310) 510-2236
Stylish old wooden home turned into B&B. One block from pier. **$**

La Paloma Cottages
PO Box 1505
CA 90704
Tel: (310) 510-0737
or (800) 310-1505
Fax: (310) 510-2424
Self-contained properties within easy reach of the golf course. **$$**

Pavilion Lodge
513 Crescent Ave.
Avalon, CA 90704
Tel: (310) 510-2500
or (800) 428-2566
Fax: (310) 510-2073
In the center of the harbor with pleasant, sunny patio. **$**

Snug Harbor Inn,
108 Sumner
Tel: (310) 510-8400
Fax: (310 -510-8418.
Six luxurious bay view rooms in the century-old former Hotel Monterey. **$$$**

Villa Portofino
111 Crescent Avenue
PO Box 127
CA 90704
Tel: (310) 510-0555
or (888) 510-0555
Fax: (310) 510-1452
On the harbor. Restaurant with sundeck. **$$**

Vista del Mar
417 Crescent Avenue
PO Box 1979
CA 90704
Tel: (310) 510-1452
or (800) 601-3836
Luxury Mediterranean style on the beachfront. **$$$**

SOLVANG

Inns of California
1450 Mission Drive
CA 93463
Tel: (805) 688-3210
or (800) 457-5373
Fax: (805) 688-0026
On the edge of downtown, 25 minutes' drive from beach. Pool. **$**

Royal Scandinavian Inn
400 Alisal Road, Box 31
CA 93464
Tel: (805) 688-8000
or (800) 624-5572
Fax: (805) 688-0761

www.solvangasi.com
Pool, whirlpool, restaurant. **$$$**

Svendsgaards Danish Lodge
1711 Mission Drive
CA 93463
Tel: (805) 688-3277
Fax: (805) 686-5616
Pool, whirlpool, kitchenettes. **$**

TEHACHAPI

Best Western Mountain Inn
416 W Tehachapi Boulevard
CA 93561
Tel: (661) 822-5591
or (800) 528-1234
Fax: (661) 822-6197
www.bestwesterncalifornia.com
One mile (1.5 km) from airport. Restaurant, bowling center. **$**

Sky Mountain Resort
18100 Lucaya Way
CA 93561
Tel: (805) 822-5581
or (800) 244-0864
Cottages, bunkhouses, golf, tennis, volleyball, pools, restaurant. **$$**

TWENTYNINE PALMS

29 Palms Inn
73950 Inn Avenue
Twentynine Palms
CA 92277
Tel: (760) 367-3505
E-mail: 29palmsinn@eee.org
www.29palmsinn.com
Cabins in a quiet location overlooking the Mojave Desert. **$–$$**

VENTURA

Bella Maggiore Inn
67 S California Street
CA 93001
Tel: (805) 652-0277
Fax: (805) 648-5670
Architectural landmark from 1925. Downtown, near the beach. **$$**

Pierpont Inn
550 Sanjon Road
CA 93001
Tel: (805) 643-6144
Fax: (805) 641-1501
A mile (1.5 km) from town near beach. Pool, restaurant, tennis. **$**

Where to Eat

What to Eat

California is a food lover's paradise and has the statistics to prove it. It's been estimated that Southern Californians dine out an average of two or three times a week. The Golden State has also been the birthplace of several culinary trends over the years, including Szechuan, sushi, nouvelle, and of course, California cuisine.

Although the most prevalent ethnic food you'll encounter here is Mexican, there is an endless variety of other ethnic foods, as well as classic American cuisine. The following list is a mere sampling of some notable restaurants across the region.

Where to Eat

LOS ANGELES

ABC Seafood
205 Ord St, Chinatown
Tel: (213) 680-2887
Authentic dim sum at extremely low prices. You can't go wrong with any of the shrimp dishes, either. **$**

Angeli Caffe
7274 Melrose Avenue, Hollywood
Tel: (323) 936-9086
The original (and some will argue the best) of the burgeoning Angeli chain. Noisy, crowded and tiny, Angeli serves up some of the best rustic Italian cuisine in town. **$$**

Antica Pizzeria
8022 W Third Street, Near Fairfax
Tel: (323) 658-7607
One of Los Angeles' hippest magazines, *Buzz*, says it serves the best, most authentic Neapolitan pizza in town. **$$**

Aunt Kizzy's Back Porch
4325 Glencoe Ave, Marina del Rey
Tel: (310) 578-1005
Actors and athletes favor the ambiance (and fried chicken). **$**

Authentic Cafe
7605 Beverly Boulevard, Westwood
Tel: (323) 939-4626
A great neighborhood restaurant, serving an eclectic mix of Southwestern, Italian and American cuisines. Reservations are not taken here and there's always a wait. It's well worth it. **$$**

Balthazar
7119 Melrose Avenue
Tel: (323) 954-9931
French-Spanish cuisine with interesting tapas and great desserts **$$**

Barney's Beanery
8477 Santa Monica Boulevard
Tel: (323) 654-2287
Fax: (323) 654-5123
A newspaper-sized menu offering at least 200 international beers plus tables for a friendly game of pool. Casual, funky, and fun. **$**

Border Grill
7407 1–2 Melrose Avenue, Hollywood
Tel: (323) 658-7495
Susan Feniger and Mary Sue Milliken, who run City Restaurant on La Brea, offer perhaps the finest, modern Mexican cuisine eatery in the country. Tiny space, noise level shattering but the sweet, green corn tamales make up for it. **$**

Café Blanc
3706 Beverly Boulevard, Silverlake
Tel: (323) 380-2829
A small, unprepossessing hole-in-the-wall serving exquisite French-Japanese food. The presentations are gorgeous, the staff sweet and helpful, and the café offers one of the best lunch deals around. **$$**

Café Latte
6254 Wilshire Boulevard
Tel: (323) 936-5213
Coffee roasted on the premises. Simple food with great sausages. **$**

Cafe des Artistes
1534 N. McCadden Place
Tel: (323) 469-7300
"No dress code, no tablecloths" and music nightly **$$**

Café Pinot
700 W 5th Street, Downtown
Tel: (323) 960-1762
Delicious food in an unlikely elevated glass box adjoining the Central Library. **$$$**

California Pizza Kitchen
8600 S. Beverly Drive, Beverly Hills
Tel: (323) 278-9992
One of a chain and "the People's Spago" declares dining-out authority Merrill Shindler. **$**

Campanile
624 S La Brea
Tel: (323) 938-1447
Invariably dotted with celebrities and the ultimate in Gothic-California majesty. Inventive, delicious Mediterranean food and memorable bread. **$$$**

Canter's
419 Fairfax Avenue
Near Third Street
Tel: (323) 651-2030
Famous large and lively deli with classic 1950s interior. Open around the clock. **$**

Citrus
6703 Melrose Avenue
Tel: (323) 857-0034
Tagged by some as the best restaurant in town. A crisp white and glass restaurant is the setting for renowned pastry-chef Michel Richard's fabulous dishes. Allow room for dessert. **$$$**

Coles
118 East 6th Street, Downtown
Tel: (213) 622-4090
The city's oldest restaurant and a historic landmark. Inventor of the French Dip. **$**

Dar Maghreb
7651 Sunset Boulevard
Tel: (323) 876-7651
A popular tourist stop, this lushly decorated restaurant offers a solid Moroccan menu. **$$**

DC3
2800 Donald Douglas Loop
Near 28th Street
Tel: (310) 399-2323
Overlooking the tiny Santa Monica airport, a jazz group plays Wednesday–Saturday nights, free kids' care Tuesday–Thursday, and the food's good too. Try the salmon in Dijon cream sauce. **$$$**

Hollywood Athletic Club
6525 Hollywood Boulevard
Tel: (213) 468-9108
Small dinner menu (burgers, pasta) but diners are first in line for the popular pool tables. No time limit. **$**

House of Blues
8430 Sunset Boulevard
West Hollywood
Tel: (323) 848-5100
Owned, like its cousins in New Orleans and Boston, by Hard Rock Café founder Isaac Tigrett, it combines soul (and other) food with funky music. **$$$**

The Gumbo Pot
6333 W 3rd Street
Tel: (323) 933-0358
One of many great eating places in the Farmer's Market. Note: the market closes early evening. **$**

Literati Cafe
12081 Wilshire Boulevard
Tel: (310) 231-7484
Newspapers, mags, photos of old LA and famous authors, simple food, reasonable prices. **$**

Lowry's the Prime Rib
100 N La Cienega Boulevard
Tel: (323) 652-2827
Generations of Angelenos have come here for the flashy showmanship that accompanies the serving of great steaks. **$$$**

The Lunch to Latenight Kitchen
4348 Fountain Avenue
Tel: (323) 664-3663
Sandwiches, home-style cooking, delicious desserts and open till 1am (3am on weekends). **$**

Kate Mantilini
9101 Wilshire Boulevard
Tel: (310) 278-3699
In a distinctive-looking building, this popular late-night spot serves until at least 1.30am every night but Sunday. **$$**

Mandarin Deli
727 N Broadway
Tel: (213) 623-6054
It's worth going Downtown to sample these great Chinese dumplings. **$**

Moomba
665 N Robertson Boulevard
Tel: (310) 652-6364
Amish chicken with foie gras, ceviches and other delicious

delights. One critic called the desserts "a salute to sugar." **$$$**

Mizu 212
2000 Sawtelle Boulevard
Tel: (310) 478-8979
Japanese Shabu Shabu dishes of chicken, beef, fish and vegetables. **$$$**

Miceli's Italian Restaurant
3655 Cahuenga Boulevard
Universal City, CA 91608
Tel: (323) 851-3344
Operatically trained waiters serenade as you eat at this family-type spot. **$$**

Price Guide

The price guide refers to a meal for two without wine:
$$$ = $60 and above
$$ = $30–60
$ =   under $30

Morton's
8764 Melrose Avenue
West Hollywood
Tel: (310) 276-5205
One of LA's celeb watering holes, with food better than it has to be, and although you'll probably be seated in Siberia unless you're somebody special, you're really in the place for people-watching. **$$$**

Nate 'n Al
414 N Beverly Drive
Tel: (310) 274-0101
Sandwiches and other specialties are always superb at Beverly Hill's long-famous deli. **$**

Pangaea
Hotel Nikko
465 S La Cienega Boulevard
Tel: (310) 247-0400
Virtually part of the delightful Japanese garden that fills the hotel's ground floor. Asian cuisine, with the fish especially good. **$$$**

Pink's Famous Chili Dogs
709 N La Brea Avenue
Tel: (213) 931-4223
Heartburn city, but a quintessential LA experience. God only knows what this stuff does to your insides, but it's good for the soul. **$**

The Royal
7321 Santa Monica Boulevard
Tel: (323) 934-7777

A true American bistro with "old Hollywood" ambience and live jazz until 1.30am except Sundays. **$**

Ships
1016 La Cienega Boulevard
At Olympic
Tel: (310) 652-0401
One of the last of the old-time coffee shops with the familiar nursery food. Open all night. **$**

Sunset Room
1430 N. Caguenga
Tel: (323) 463-0004
Dressy-style ambiance and live music in a Havana-style nightclub. Try the lobster won ton. **$$**

Yamashiro
1999 North Sycamore Avenue
Hollywood
Tel: (323) 466-5125
www.yamashirola.com
Some claim it offers the nicest view in LA. Surrounded by Japanese gardens, this is a lovely place for dinner or drinks. **$$$**

ANAHEIM

Acapulco Mexican Restaurant
1410 S Harbor Boulevard
Tel: (714) 956-7380
Sample their award-winning Mexican food right across the street from Disneyland. **$$**

The Catch
1929 S. State College Boulevard
Tel: (714) 634-1829
Steak and seafood served in 1920s decor. **$$**

The Cellar Restaurant
305 North Harbor Boulevard
Fullerton
Tel: (714) 525-5682,
Superb French cuisine and expansive wine cellar 4 miles (6 km) from Disneyland. **$$$**

Five Crowns
3801 East Coast Highway
Corona del Mar
Tel: (949) 760-0331
Award-winning food served in a beautiful two-story building modeled after Ye Olde Bell, one of England's oldest inns. **$$$**

Hansa House Smorgasbord
1840 S Harbor Boulevard
Tel: (714) 750-2411

Scandinavian decor and cuisine served in buffet style. **$$**

Mini's Cafe
1240 N Euclid Avenue
Tel: (714) 535-1552
Frenchified café with family ambiance and American food. **$**

Plaza Garibaldi Dinner Theatre,
1490 S Anaheim Boulevard
Tel: (714) 758-9014
Mariachi singers, folklorico and tango dancers, accordians, Inca flutes and other entertainment accompanies the Mexican cuisine. **$$$**

The Stinking Rose
55 N La Cienega Boulevard
Tel: (310) 652-7673
California-Italian cuisine with lots of garlic. **$$**

LONG BEACH

Belmont Brewing Co.
25 39th Place
Tel: (562) 433-3891
Brew pub with good dishes and a view of the *Queen Mary*. **$**

Bobby Moore's Conglomeration
6501 E Pacific Coast Highway
Tel: (310) 594-8627
In the Market Place Shopping Center. Theme restaurant with waiters in costume; great for the kids. **$**

Fish Tale
5506 Britton Drive
Tel: (562) 594-8771
Seafood served in pleasant surroundings. **$**

Gazzella
525 E Broadway
Tel: (562) 495-7252
Italian cuisine. Live music Wednesday–Saturday evenings. **$$**

Yard House
401 Shoreline Drive
Tel: (562) 628-0455
Waterfront patio, huge menu and "the world's largest selection of draft beers." **$$**

NEWPORT BEACH

Bayside
900 Bayside Drive
Tel: (949) 721-1222

Minimalist interior with a wall-full of wine. Innovative cuisine. **$$$**

The Cannery Restaurant
3010 Lafayette Road
Tel: (714) 675-5777
Attractive surroundings in a former canning plant by the harbor. Seafood, steaks. Organizes weekend cruises. **$$**

Price Guide

The price guide refers to a meal for two without wine:
$$$ = $60 and above
$$ = $30–60
$ = under $30

Crab Cooker
2200 Newport Boulevard.
Tel: (949) 673-0100.
Grilled seafood on paper plates, reasonable prices but no reservations. **$$**

Daily Grill
957 Newport Center Drive
Tel: (714) 644-2223
Simple and unpretentious. **$**

21 Ocean Front
2100 W Ocean Front
Tel: (714) 673-2100
Not surprisingly, overlooking the sea, near the pier. Pasta, seafood, steaks. **$$$**

PALM SPRINGS

Banducci's Bit of Italy
1260 South Palm Canyon Drive
Tel: (760) 325-2537
Steak, lobster, and homemade canelloni cooked to perfection. **$$**

Elmer's Pancake and Steak House
1030 East Palm Canyon Drive
Tel: (760) 327-8419
The most crowded place in town on weekend mornings, with 25 varieties of pancakes and waffles for breakfast, and fine steaks and seafood for dinner. **$**

Kobe Japanese Steak House
Highway 111 at Frank Sinatra Drive
Tel: (760) 324-1717
Hibachi-style steak and chicken in a replica of a 300-year-old Japanese country inn. **$$$**

Las Casuelas Terraza
222 South Palm Canyon Drive
Tel: (760) 325-2794
Mexican-style cuisine served on a pleasant outdoor patio at reasonable prices. **$**

Siamese Gourmet Restaurant
4711 E Palm Canyon Drive
Tel: (760) 328-0057
In Rimrock Shopping Center. Thai food. **$**

Le St Germain
74-985 Highway 111
Indian Wells
Tel (760) 773-6511
Romantic stone-floored patio with blooming vines and candlelit tables. An attractive ambiance for Mediterranean cuisine. **$$$**

PASADENA

Clearwater Café
168 W Colorado Boulevard
Tel: (626) 356-0959
Seafood, healthy vegetable dishes, some Japanese touches. **$**

Nonya
61 N Raymond Avenue
Tel: (626) 883-8398
Spicy pumpkin soup and drunken shrimp are specialties of this fusion of Malay and Chinese cuisine. **$$**

Yujean Kang's
67 N Raymond Avenue
Tel: (626) 585-0855
Memorable Chinese food attractively presented. **$$$**

REDONDO BEACH

Aimee's
800 S Pacific Coast Highway
Tel: (310)-316-1081
Shrimp, salmon and tasty desserts, all prepared in a French manner. **$**

Marie Callender's
2979 Artesia Boulevard
Tel: (310) 371-5583
Wide choice of American dishes in the branch of this always reliable chain. Great pies. **$**

RIVERSIDE

Pitruzzelo's
287 W La Cadena Drive
Tel: (909) 683-9803
Italian cuisine. **$$**

SAN DIEGO

Anthony's Star of the Sea Room
1360 North Harbor Drive
Tel: (619) 232-7408
Fabulous seafood served with
dramatic flair. Located on the water.
Jackets, and reservations, required.
$$$
California Cafe Bar & Grill
502 Horton Plaza
Tel: (619) 238-5440
Pleasant patio in interesting
surroundings. Pizza and pasta. **$$**
Casa de Pico
2754 Calhoun Street
Tel: (619) 296-3267
Located in the Bazaar del Mundo in
Old Town. Fine Mexican food and
great margaritas. **$**
Charlie Brown's
880 East Harbor Island Drive
Tel: (619) 291-1870
Dine aboard the Reuben E Lee, a
genuine Mississippi steamboat with
a great view of the harbor. **$$$**
The Marine Room
2000 Spindrift Drive
La Jolla
Tel: (858) 459-7222
At high tide the waves crash just
outside the windows. **$$**
North China
5043 N Harbor Drive
Tel: (619) 224-3568
Bay views from outdoor patio.
Mandarin and Szechuan cuisine,
scores of seafood dishes,
Polynesian cocktails. **$$**
Old Spaghetti Factory
275 Fifth Avenue
Tel: (619) 233-4323
In the Gaslamp Quarter. Casual but
interesting decor including a real
trolley car. Popular with families.
Large portions, low prices. **$**
Old Trieste
2335 Morena Boulevard
Tel: (619) 276-1841
One of the best Italian restaurants
in town. **$$$**

Sky Room La Valencia Hotel
1132 Prospect Street
CA 92037
Tel: (858) 454-0771
Overlooks the sea. Delicious French
cuisine. **$$**

SAN FERNANDO VALLEY

Art's Deli
12224 Ventura Boulevard
Studio City
Tel: (818) 762-1221
Some say it's the best deli in
LA; it's certainly the best deli in
the Valley. Mile-high sandwiches,
great knishes and stuffed
cabbage. **$**
Bamboo Inn
14010 Ventura Boulevard
Tel: (818) 788-0202
Situated between Woodman and
Hazeltine avenues. A good
neighborhood place for Chinese
cuisine. **$$**
Dr Hogly Wogly's Tyler Texas BBQ
8136 N Sepulveda Boulevard
Van Nuys
Tel: (818) 780-6701
LA's top-rated ribs. **$**
La Parrilla
19601 Ventura Boulevard (Corbin
Ave.) Tarzana
Tel: (818) 708-7422
Authentic Mexican food in a fun
setting. **$$**
Moonlight Supper Club
13730 Ventura Boulevard
Sherman Oaks
Tel: (818) 788-2000
A late-night supper club with singing
waiters and a white-tuxedoed "big
band" combo that inspires conga
lines and other frivolity. **$**
Rubin's Red Hot
15322 Ventura Boulevard
Sherman Oaks
Tel: (818) 905-6515
A legendary hot dog dispensary in
unsurpassable Chicago style. **$**
Mistral
13422 Ventura Boulevard
Sherman Oaks
Tel: (818) 981-6650
Good food in the Valley's version of
a French bistro. **$$**
Sushi Nozawa
11288 Ventura Boulevard

Studio City
Tel: (818) 508-7017
Asian treats. **$$$**
Tempo
16610 Ventura Boulevard
Encino
Tel: (818) 905-5885
A Middle Eastern eatery in Little Tel
Aviv with a special sabbath dinner
every Friday night. **$$**
Ueru-Ka-Mu
19596 Ventura Boulevard
Tarzana
Tel: (818) 609-0993
A typical izakaya, or Japanese
drinking pub, specializing in the tiny
dishes that suit serious sake
drinkers. **$$**

Among the LA restaurants that have
branched out into the Valley, are:
Bistro Garden at Coldwater
12950 Ventura Boulevard
Studio City
Tel: (818) 501-0202
Beverly Hills' famed Bistro Garden
branches out with modern
continental cuisine from the
longtime LA favorite. **$$**
Posto
14928 Ventura Boulevard at Kester
Avenue
Sherman Oaks
Tel: (818) 784-4400
A casual cousin of Piero Selvaggio's
top-rated Valentino. **$$**
Salute
21300 Victory Boulevard
Woodland Hills
Tel: (818) 702-9638
The Valley extension of Silvio De
Mori's Tuttobene, offering refined
Italian cooking. **$$$**
Yang Chow
6443 Topanga Canyon Boulevard
Woodland Hills
Tel: (818) 347-2610
LA's long-time top-rated traditional
Chinese restaurant has one branch
in Chinatown and the other in the
Valley. **$$$**

SAN JOAQUIN VALLEY

Harland's
722 Shaw Avenue
Fresno
Tel: (209) 225-7100

Creative nouvelle cuisine: chicken in a raspberry vinaigrette or veal with morels in a lovely lemon sauce. Lunch, dinner, and Sunday brunch too. **$$$**

The Ripe Tomato
5064 North Palm, Fresno
Tel: (209) 225-1850
Quail and venison are standard menu items; typical specials include duck with apricot and garlic sauce and veal with oysters and mushrooms in vermouth sauce.**$$$**

Vintage Press
216 North Willis
Visalia
Tel: (209) 733-3355
Fresh food with a European flair. The fish, veal, vegetables, and desserts are personally prepared. Closed Sunday. **$$**

SAN LUIS OBISPO

Apple Farm Restaurant
2015 Monterey Street
Tel: (805) 544-6100
American food in delightfully rural atmosphere. **$**

Benvenuti Ristorante
450 Marsh Street
Tel: (805) 541-5393
Just south of downtown. Charming old building, tasty Italian food. **$**

Beau's Russia House Café and Tea Room
699 Higuera St
Tel: (805) 784-0172
This dressy Russian restaurant also offers traditional afternoon tea. **$**

SANTA BARBARA

Acapulco
1114 State Street
Tel: (805) 963-3469
Artfully prepared Mexican food for more than three decades. **$$**

Bay Cafe
131 Anacapa Street
Tel: (805) 963-2215
Excellent seafood. **$$**

Bucatini
436 State Sreet
Tel: (805) 957-4177
Named for the straw-shaped pasta. Tasty Northern Italian flavors. **$$**

Cafe Buenos Aires
1316 State St
Tel: (805) 963-0242
Spanish tapas, Argentine food, live music Wednesday–Sunday. **$$**

Citronelle
901 Cabrillo Boulevard
Tel: (805)-963-111.
French food from Michel Richard of LA's glorious Citrons. **$$$**

Michael's Waterside
50 Los Patos Way
Tel: (805)-969 0307
Gourmet cuisine in an elegant Victorian mansion. **$$$**

Price Guide

The price guide refers to a meal for two without wine:
$$$ = $60 and above
$$ = $30–60
$ = under $30

Crocodile Restaurant & Bar
2819 State St
Tel: (805) 687-6444
Opens 7am, closes late. Steaks, seafood, pasta, vegetarian. Open courtyard. **$**

Hibachi Restaurant
415 N Milpas
Tel: (805) 962-2687
Korean-style barbecue, fresh noodles, Mongolian beef. **$$**

Michael's Waterside
50 Los Patos Way
Tel: (805)-969 0307
Gourmet cuisine in an elegant Victorian mansion. **$$$**

Palace Grill
8 East Coia
Tel: (805) 963-5000
Blackened crawfish & other Cajun-Creole treats. **$$**

Paradise Cafe
702 Anacapa Street
Tel: (805) 962-4416
Go for the young chattering crowd as much as for the food. **$**

Playa Azul Cafe
914 Santa Barbara Street
Tel: (805) 966-2860
Mexican food near the Presidio. **$$**

Wine Cask Restaurant
813 Anacapa St
Tel: (805) 966-9463
Excellent California Cuisine offered

in an attractive outdoor courtyard and dining room. **$**

SANTA CATALINA ISLAND

The Channel House
205 Crescent Avenue
Tel: (310) 510-1617
Casual and attractive continental restaurant with excellent meat dishes. **$**

El Galleon
411 Crescent Avenue
Avalon
Tel: (310) 510-1188
Nicely decorated in seafaring style. Wide selection including seafood, pasta and Mexican. **$**

Ristorante Villa Portofino
101 Crescent Avenue, Avalon
Tel: (310) 510-0508
Italian cuisine featuring good seafood. **$$**

SOLVANG

Bit 'O Denmark Restaurant
490 First Street
Tel: (805) 688-5426
Casual Danish restaurant with afternoon smorgasbord and excellent entrees. **$**

Café Angelica
490 First Street
Tel: (805) 686-9970
Charming, casual Italian bistro also offering a good selection of California cuisine. **$$**

Massimi
1588 Mission Drive
Tel: (805) 688-0027
Italian cuisine, and outdoor dining in fine weather. **$$**

VENTURA

The Chart House
567 Sanjon Road
Tel: (805) 643-3725
Between the ocean and US 1. Seafood and steak. **$$**

Yolanda's Mexican Cafe
2753 E Main Street
Tel: (805) 643-2700
Interesting decor. Mexican food. **$**

Culture

Ticket Agencies

Front Center Ticket Services
1355 Westwood Boulevard
Tel: (310) 478-0848
Los Angeles 90024
Ticketmaster
591 Camino de la Reina
San Diego 92108
Tel: (619) 220-8497
www.ticketmaster.com
Tickets.com
An online ticketing website:
www.tickets.com

Nightlife

Evening diversions in California are as varied and all-encompassing as the state itself. Visitors can entertain themselves with events that range from world-class operas and musicals, theater and symphonies to first-rate comedy and funky live blues, jazz and rock'n'roll.

To track down nightlife, you would do best to refer to the local newspaper as a guide to what's on where. The "Calendar" section of Sunday's *Los Angeles Times* will fill you in on the action, not only in the City of Angels, but also in the surrounding communities. The *Union-Tribune* in San Diego should be able to do the same further south.

Many towns have their own listings magazines, like Los Angeles' *LA Weekly* and San Diego's the *Reader*, which give more detailed or off-beat venues and attractions.

If you arrive without any of the previously mentioned publications, the concierge at any larger hotels can usually help you in your quest for fun when the sun goes down in the Golden State.

Wildlife

Rural Refuges

Andree Clark Bird Refuge
1400 E Cabrillo Boulevard
Santa Barbara
Tel: (805) 564-5433.
Walking trails, bike path and lake in this haven for southbound migratory birds in winter.
Castaic Lake
Lake Hughes Road exit from Golden State freeway. For information tel: (661) 257-4050.
Open sunrise–sunset. Fishing, windsurfing, water skiing, and boating attract thousands of visitors, some of whom just want to relax, picnic and enjoy the playgrounds and sandy beaches.
Channel Islands
Information and reservations: Island Packers, 1867 Spinnaker Drive, Ventura, CA 93001
Tel: (805) 642-1393
Boats leave Ventura Harbor most mornings for the six to eight hour excursions to Anacapa, 12 miles (19 km) offshore, one of the half-dozen islands of the Channel Islands National Park. Wildlife, including sea lions, whales, and birds, are the main attractions.
Malibu Creek State Park
Las Virgenes exit off Ventura freeway, for information, tel: (818) 548-2000. Thirty miles (48 km) of rugged trails and a "hidden" lake. History and ecology explained on guided walks.
Mount Whitney
Towering an awesome 14,500 ft (4,420 meters) above sea level in the Sequoia National Park, about 200 miles (320 km) north of LA via Palmdale on State Highway 14 and US 395. The mountain can be seen from the highway, but the

best unobstructed views are from along Whitney Portal Road, westwards from Lone Pine. Beginning at Victorville, US-395 offers numerous landmarks and diversions along its route: Death Valley to the east; Edwards Air Force Base (landing site for the space shuttle); the once-fertile Owens Valley from which LA's water supply was stolen in 1913; the desolate camp at Manzanar where Japanese-Americans were held in World War II; and the Native American Museum at Independence.

National Parks

For information about accommodations, campgrounds, fishing, horseback riding, backpacking, and ranger programs, contact the National Park Service, Western Region Information Office, Fort Mason, San Francisco, CA 94123, tel: (415) 556-0560 or (800) 365-2267;
www.nps.gov/parks.html.

There are 20 National Park System areas in California. Although they come in a variety of guises (they are also known as National Monuments, National Recreation Areas, and National Seashores), they are all filled with helpful rangers and park personnel as well as more scenic vistas than you can point a camera at. About 30 million people visit California's national parks every year; you'll do best by visiting these areas during the week or in the off-season.

State Parks

The California State Park System's 285 parks, which include 250 miles (400 km) of coastline beaches, offer many opportunities for camping, some with full RV hookups. Campsites should be reserved, tel: (800) 444-7275. The Official Guide (available for a nominal fee) can be ordered from the Department of Parks and Recreation, PO Box 942896, Sacramento, CA 94296 and is also available at most parks.

Whale Watching

In the first three months of every year, several coastal communities organize whale-watching celebrations with parades, displays and street fairs. Among the biggest are Point Luma in San Diego tel: (619) 557-5450; Ventura (tel: (800) 333-2989; Oxnard tel: (800) 269-6273 and Dana Point tel: (800) 290-3262. The American Cetacean Society is among the many groups that organize trips to see some of the thousands of 40-ton California gray whales that start their 10,000-mile (17,700-km) migration from Alaska to South America in the fall, and back in the spring. Traveling 80–100 miles (130–160 km) per day, some of these mammals can be seen from high spots along the coast – particularly from the Palos Verdes Peninsula – and around the Channel Islands. Sightseeing boats operate out of Ventura Harbor and from Stearns Wharf in Santa Barbara. Seals and sea lions are also plentiful in the islands to which Island Packers (tel: 805-642 1393) run trips and about which the Channel Islands National Park (tel: 805- 658 5730) can provide a wealth of information. In addition, snowy plovers and cormorants are found on San Miguel; kestrels, larks and owls on Santa Barbara; and brown pelicans, who nest between May and August, on Anacapa, the closest island to the mainland. For information about Santa Cruz, the largest island of the group, call the Nature Conservancy (tel: 805-962 9111). Whale-watching trips further south in La Jolla near San Diego are organized by the Scripps Institution of Oceanography. Contact the Stephen Birch Aquarium in the Scripps building for details, tel: (858) 534 3474.

Parks & Gardens

Charmlee Nature Preserve
2577 Encinal Canyon off Pacific Coast Highway
Tel: (310) 457-7247
Lots of birds and a small nature musuem.

Descanso Gardens
1418 Descanso Drive
La Cañada, Flintridge
Tel: (818) 952-4401
Daily all year 9.30am–4.30pm. A camellia forest, Japanese garden and pretty walks are among the attractions of this tranquil place.

Earl Burns Miller Japanese Garden
California State University at Long Beach, 1250 Bellflower Boulevard, Long Beach
Tel: (562) 985-8885.
This garden has all the traditional Japanese garden components – teahouse, stone lanterns, azalea, iris, and pine – arranged with eminent and sympathetic grace.

Forest Lawn Memorial Park
Two LA locations flanking 4,000-acre (1,619-hectare) Griffith Park: Glendale, 1712 S Glendale Avenue, tel: (818) 241-4151 and Hollywood Hills, 6300 Forest Lawn Drive, Hollywood, tel: (213) 254-7251.

Franklin D. Murphy Sculpture Garden
Adjoins the Wright Art Gallery at the north end of the UCLA campus off LA's Sunset Boulevard, tel: (310) 825-3264. This much-loved and well-tended garden has more than fifty works of art representing such sculptors as Rodin, Henry Moore, and Calder.

Greystone Mansion
905 Loma Vista Drive
Hollywood
The 18-acre (7-hectare) garden is popular with visitors, but the house is usually closed.

Huntington Library, Art Collections and Botanical Gardens
1151 Oxford Road
San Marino
Tel: (626) 405-2141
www.huntington.org
Open Tuesday–Friday 1.30–4.30pm; weekends 10.30am–4.30pm.
Fifteen gorgeous gardens spread over 150 acres (61 hectares) with a library and world-renowned art collection.

The Japanese Garden
6100 Woodley Avenue
Van Nuys
Tel: (626) 989-8166
Tours at 9am, 9.45am, and 10.30am visit three gardens in distinctly different styles. In summer there are "sunset" tours on weekdays; reservations are essential. This 6-acre (2.5 hectare) botanical delight was created on the Donald C. Tillman Water Reclamation Plant.

Living Desert
47–900 Portola Avenue
Palm Desert
Tel: (760) 346-5694
Open daily September–June 9am–5pm. Admission charge. Fascinating wildlife and botanical park with rare cacti.

Los Angeles State and County Arboretum
301 N Baldwin Avenue
Arcadia
Tel: (626) 821-3222
This 127-acre (51-hectare) LA County-run arboretum was established to house the extensive collection of the world-traveling horticulturalist Dr Saumuel Ayres. There are some 30,000 permanent plants on the grounds admired by half a million visitors each year. There is a jungle garden, aquatic garden, tropical greenhouse, herb garden, bamboo grove, and lagoon; too much to cover on a single visit even with the aid of the tram. The peacocks are descendants of the original three pairs brought from India in the early 20th century.

Orcutt Ranch Horticulture Center
23600 Roscoe Boulevard
West Hills
Tel: (818) 883-6641
Open to the public on a weekend announced in June or July. Citrus groves bounded by majestic and stately oaks, statuary, and sundials.

Quail Botanical Gardens
230 Quail Gardens Drive
Encinitas
Tel: (760) 436-3036

Open daily 8am–5pm. Admission free with free tours Saturdays at 10am. Birds nest among rare and beautiful plants.

Rancho Los Alamitos
6400 Bixby Hill Road
Long Beach
Tel: (562) 431-3541
Some 7½ acres (3 hectares) are scant souvenir of the vast, semiarid spread of more than 28,000 acres (11,300 hectares) held by John Bixby and his partners in 1881, but the ranch house and other main buildings remain. There is not a plant sign in sight – visitors experience the garden directly, not as an institution or museum.

Rose Garden
900 Exposition Boulevard
Downtown LA
Tel: (213) 548-7671
Broad walkways firmly edged with white concrete bands define 200 rectangular rose beds. This 7½-acre (3-hectare) sunken garden, installed in 1926, is one of the oldest public gardens in Los Angeles. Flowering period late April–early November, but peak bloom occurs between June and September.

Santa Barbara Orchid Estate
1250 Orchid Drive
Santa Barbara
Tel: (805) 967-1284 or (800) 553-3387
Open daily 8am–5.30pm, Sunday 10am–4pm. Admission free. Thousands of flowers.

Sherman Library and Gardens
2647 E Pacific Coast Highway
Corona del Mar
Tel: (949) 673-2261
Established in 1958 in memory of industrialist M.H. Sherman by his beneficiary Arnold Haskell, a caring man who incorporated handicapped accessibility decades before its time. The horticultural objective at Sherman is to provide glorious color all year long – the Sun and Central gardens feature bedding plants rotated by season. The library specializes in the Pacific Southwest, including Sherman's papers.

South Coast Botanic Garden
26300 Crenshaw Boulevard

Palos Verdes Peninsula
Tel: (310) 544-6815
Open daily 9am–4.30pm. A former landfill now displaying fruit trees, roses, a desert garden with cacti and duck-filled lake.

UCLA Hannah Carter Japanese Garden
10619 Bellagio Road
Bel Air, Los Angeles
Tel: (310) 825-4574
(UCLA Visitors' Center)
An ingenious adaptation of Japanese themes to the vertical topography of Bel Air, the garden features asymmetry, naturalness and the subtlety of seasons with compromises made for the dry, bright and genial Southern California climate. Garden artifacts include Buddha carvings, stone water basins, pagoda, lanterns and more – all transported from Japan.

Virginia Robinson House and Gardens
1008 Eden Way
Beverly Hills
Tel: (310) 276-5367
Lushly landscaped gardens include a mini-forest of palm trees and flower-filled terraces. Only the gardens are open to the public.

Rancho de los Encinos

Originally the site of a Native American village, this historical park later became a ranch belonging to the de la Osa family, who planted vineyards and orchards and raised cattle. In among the 5 acres (2 hectares) of manicured lawns, duck ponds, and eucalyptus and citrus groves is the de la Osa Adobe, built in 1849 and restored with period furnishings. Other buildings in the park, which was hit badly in the 1994 earthquake, will be restored over the next few years.

Rancho de los Encinos Historical Park
16756 Moorpark Street, Encino, tel: (818) 784-4849.

Outdoor Activities

Horseback Riding

Horses to ride in LA's Griffith Park can be rented at several nearby stables among which are:

Bar S Stables
Glendale
Tel: (818) 242-8443.

Circle K
914 S. Mariposa St, Burbank
Tel: (818) 843-9890

Paddock Riding Club
3919 Rigali Ave, Los Feliz
Tel: (213) 662-7026

Other stables include:

Equestrian Education Center
Pepperdine University in Malibu
Tel: (310) 456-4367

Ranch Vista del Mar
33603 Pacific Coast Highway, Malibu
Tel: (310) 457-9203

Far West Farms
5155 N. Old Scandia Lane
Calabasas
Tel: (818) 591-2180

Foxfield Riding School
1250 E. Potrero Road
Westlake Village
Tel: (805) 495-5515

Mill Creek Equestrian Center
1881 Old Topanga Canyon Rd
Tel: (310) 445-1116

Will Rogers Equestrian Center
1501 Will Rogers State Park Road, Pacific Palisades
Tel: (310) 573-7270
J.P. Stables, tel: (818) 843-9890, and L.A. Equestrian Center, tel: (818) 840-8401, both in Burbank.

Sunset Stables
Hollywood
Tel: (213) 464-9612

Balloon Rides

These are popular attractions in scenic California towns. **California Dreamin'** launches hot-air balloons daily for flights that overlook the Temecula wine country or the Del Mar coastal valley, tel: (800) 748-5959; Call **DAE Flights**, tel: (909) 676-3902 or **Abobe All Balloon Charters**, tel: (909) 694-6287. **Skysurfer**, tel: (800) 660-6809, also covers Del Mar; **Dream Flights**, tel: (619) 321-5154, overlooks Palm Desert; **Gold Prospecting Expeditions** is in Jarrestown near Fresno, tel: (209) 984-4653. For trips over the Sierras contact **Sunshore Balloon Adventures**, tel: (800) 829-7238. Check local phone books for other listings.

Bicycle Tours

Pasadena operates an extensive cycling program and free bike maps are obtainable from City Hall, tel: (626) 405-4303.

For information about obtaining a free bike map for the Los Angeles County area, tel: (213) 244-6539. For information about cycling trips in the Santa Monica Mountains – one of the world's largest urban wilderness areas – telephone (800) 533-park.

Organized five-day bicycle adventures, which include accommodation, are operated in San Diego and other parts of the state by **Imagine Tours**, tel: (800) 924-2453. **Mammoth Mountain Bike Park**, tel: (800) 228-4947, offers 50 miles (80 km) of cycling trails and stunt tracks. Call **Backroads** (800) 245-3874 for details during the wildflower season in Death Valley (mid-March to early-April). They run four-day camping and bicycle trips departing from Furnace Creek to visit local landmarks.

Skiing

GREATER LOS ANGELES AREA

Bear Mountain Ski Resort
43101 Goldmine Drive
Big Bear Lake
Tel: (909) 585-2519

Mount Baldy
End of Mt. Baldy Road
Mount Baldy
Tel: (909) 981-3344
Mount Waterman
817 Lynn Haven Lane
La Canada Flintridge
Tel: (818) 790-2002
Snow Summit
880 Summit Boulevard State 18
east of Big Bear
Big Bear Lake
Tel: (909) 866-5766
Snow Valley
Highway. 18 (5 miles East of Running Springs)
Running Springs
Tel: (909) 867-2751

MAMMOTH AREA

June Mountain
State 158
June Lake
Tel: (619) 648-7733
Mammoth Mountain
North of Bishop off State 395
Mammoth Lakes
Tel: (760) 934-20745 or (800) MAMMOTH

Fishing

California's Department of Fish and Game oversees fishing areas at wildlife and ecological reserves in various parts of the state and offers a free copy of its magazine, *Outdoor California*, tel: (800) THE-WILD. One day in June and another in September each year are "Free Fishing Days" when a license is not needed to fish.

Hiking

The *Los Angeles Times*' popular columnist John McKinney details 150 favorite local walks in his *Day Hikers' Guide to Southern California* (Los Angeles Times, 2001).

Health Spas

Beverly Hot Springs
308 N Oxford Ave
Tel: (323) 734-7000
www.beverlyhotsprings.com

Spa Treatments

For those with the time (and money) to spare, a day or two at a health spa is sure to rejuvenate. Spas have naturally been a big hit with Southern Californians who, more than most people, are always ready for a little self-indulgence. Pedicures, rubdowns with vegetation from the Aegean Sea, lengthy sojourns in hot mud, and pricey body treatments are the kind of experiences offered by some of the upmarket places, but there are also simpler alternatives. Although prices vary, one dollar per minute is usually a working estimate – which mitigates against soaking for an hour in a mere hot tub, no matter how pleasurable.

Saunas, steam rooms and bathing areas in hot, alkaline mineral water, followed optionally with milk and cucumber body lotions.
Estee Lauder at Neiman Marcus
98700 Wilshire Boulevard
Tel: (310) 550-2056
A day at the spa package includes lunch and lavish use of perfumes.
Finland Baths
13257 Moorpark Street, Sherman Oaks
Tel: (818) 784-8966
A few movie stars favor the deep muscle massage and sauna that's been offered here for over half a century.
Skin Sense
8448 W 3rd Street
Tel: (323) 653-4701
Healing herbs, aromatic oils, body wraps, and rigorous massages are features at this salon.
The Spa at South Coast Plaza
695 Town Center Drive
Costa Mesa
Tel: (714) 850-0050
Elegant and opulent surroundings; have a pre-massage workout in the pool and gym.
Murad 365
2141 Rosecrans Avenue, El Segundo
Tel: (310) 726-0470

Alternatives include foot and leg treatment but you can also go for any of the many different massages.

Glen Ivy Hot Springs
25000 Glen Ivy Road, Corona
Tel: (909) 277-3529.
This internationally known outdoor spa in the Temescal Valley allows you the run of the estate with its pool and mud baths before you go indoors for the massages.

Givenchy Hotel and Spa
4200 E Palm Canyon Drive
Palm Springs
Tel: (800) 276-5000
Posh French-run resort in the desert, with gym, tennis courts, and four swimming pools.

Spa Hotel and Casino
100 N Indian Canyon Drive
Palm Springs
Tel: (800) 854-1279
A relaxing soak in bubbling, natural warm springs is a pleasant preliminary to Swedish massages, facials, body wraps, etc.

Four Seasons Biltmore Santa Barbara
1260 Channel Drive
Santa Barbara
Tel: (805) 969-2261 or (800) 332-3442.
www.fourseasons.com
Tennis, exercise facilities, a private beach, and the option of massages in your own room.

Sport

Participant Sports

GOLF COURSES

Greater Los Angeles Area
Brookside Golf Course
1133 N Rosemont Avenue
Pasadena
Tel: (626) 796-0177
Griffith Golf Courses
4730 Crystal Springs Drive
Los Angeles
Tel: (213) 664-2255
Industry Hills Golf Club
1 Industry Hills Parkway
City of Industry
Tel: (626) 810-4653
Rancho Park Golf Course
10460 W Pico Boulevard
Beverly Hills
Tel: (310) 839-4374

Orange County
Costa Mesa Golf Course
1701 Golf Course Drive
Costa Mesa
Tel: (714) 540-7500
Newport Beach Golf Course
3100 Irvine Avenue
Newport Beach
Tel: (714) 852-8681

San Diego Area
Balboa Park Municipal Golf Course
2600 Golf Course Drive
San Diego
Tel: (619) 570-1234.
La Costa Country Club
2100 Costa del Mar Road
Carlsbad
Tel: (760) 438-9111
www.lacosta.com
Mission Bay Golf Center
2702 N Mission Bay Drive
San Diego, CA 92109
Tel: (858) 490-3370.
Pala Mesa Resort
2001 State Highway 395

Fallbrook
Tel: (760) 728-5881
www.palamesa.com
Rancho Bernardo Inn & Country Club
17550 Bernardo Oaks Drive
San Diego
Tel: (858) 675-8470

Palm Springs Area
Indian Wells Golf Resort
Grand Champions Hotel
46000 Club Drive
Tel: (760) 360 0861.
La Quinta Hotel Golf & Tennis Resort
46–080 Jefferson Street
La Quinta (Dunes)
Tel: (760) 564-5729
La Quinta (Mountain)
50-503 Jefferson
Tel: (760) 564-7610
Mission Hills Resort Hotel & Golf Club
Rancho Mirage
Tel: (760) 321-8484
Palm Springs Municipal Golf Course
1885 Golf Club Drive
Tel: (760) 328-1005
PGA West
56150 PGA Boulevard
La Quinta
Tel: (760) 564-5729

Santa Barbara Area
Alisal Golf Course
1054 Alisal Road
Solvang
Tel: (805) 688-6411
www.alisal.com
La Purisima Golf Course
3455 E Highway 246
Lompoc
Tel: (805) 735-8395
Ojai Valley Inn & Country Club
905 Coun2try Club Road
Ojai
Tel: (805) 646-2420.
Sandpiper Golf Course
7925 Hollister Avenue
Santa Barbara
Tel: (805) 968-1541

TENNIS

Racquet Center of Universal City
10933 Ventura Boulevard

Studio City
Tel: (818) 760-2303
The Tennis Place
5880 W Third Street
Los Angeles
Tel (323) 931-1715**S**
Studio City Golf & Tennis
4141 Whitsett Avenue
Tel: (818) 769-5263

Public Courts
(Reservations advised):
Cheviot Hills Recreation Center
2551 Motor Avenue
Tel: (310) 838-8879
Pacific Palisades Recreation Center
851 Alma Road
Tel: (310) 454-1412
Poinsettia Recreation Center
7341 Willoughby Avenue
Tel: (213) 876-5014
Westwood Recreation Complex
1350 Sepulveda Boulevard
Westwood
Tel: (310) 575-8299

WATER ACTIVITIES

Whitewater rafting expeditions are organized further north in the Gold Country near Yosemite and Tahoe, and throughout the Sierras, by many companies including:
Earthtrek Whitewater Expeditions
Tel: (800) 229-8735
Whitewater Voyages
Tel: (800) 400-RAFT

Operating out of Lake Isabella, 3 hours north of Los Angeles, is:
Aqua Adventures Kayak School
Tel: (619) 523-9577 in San Diego
Kern River Tours
Tel: (760) 379-4616

Spectator Sports

BASEBALL

California possesses some of the finest sports teams. Baseball season runs from April–October. In Southern California, the Los Angeles Dodgers play at Dodger Stadium; the Anaheim Angels play at Anaheim Stadium; and the San Diego Padres play at Pac Bell Park.

BASKETBALL

The regular National Basketball Association (NBA) season runs from October through April, with championship playoffs continuing in June. The Los Angeles Lakers, who are almost always a league powerhouse, and the LA Clippers play home games at the downtown Staples Center

FOOTBALL

The National Football League (NFL) season begins in September and runs through December. The Los Angeles Raiders play at Anaheim Stadium. The Los Angeles Rams play at Los Angeles Memorial Coliseum, and the San Diego Chargers play at San Diego Jack Murphy Stadium.

The Rose Bowl in Pasedena is held every year on New Year's Day. Once every four years it hosts the national championship match. It is difficult to get tickets to either.

HOCKEY

California has two professional hockey teams, the Los Angeles Kings, who play at the downtown Staples Center and the younger San Jose Sharks, who play at the San Jose Arena. The hockey season runs from October through April.

HORSE RACING

For those who prefer the sport of kings, Southern California has three tracks to choose from:
Hollywood Park in Inglewood, tel: (310) 419-1500 hosts thoroughbred racing from April–July and harness racing in November and December; **Santa Anita Park**, tel: (626) 574-7223 in Arcadia hosts thoroughbred racing from October–mid-November and from December–late-April. The season at the **Del Mar Track** north of San Diego, tel: (858) 755-1141, runs from mid-July–September.

Sites

Visiting the Missions

From the beginning of California's history, the 21 missions set up along El Camino Real by Father Junípero Serra and his successors have played an important role. Today they are major tourist attractions. Seven of the missions are in Southern California, the quintet between Santa Barbara and San Diego being San Buenaventura, San Fernando, San Gabriel, San Juan Capistrano and San Luis Rey.

Originally developed by Spanish clerics with virtual slave labor from local native Americans, most of the missions were abandoned and fell into decay after the passing of the Secularization Act in 1834 and were forgotten for almost half a century. Helen Hunt Jackson's 1880 book about mistreatment of the Indians, *A Century of Dishonor*, revived interest in the buildings whose architecture thereafter became a much-emulated style.

San Gabriel is the nearest mission to Los Angeles, located in Baldwin Park, about 9 miles (14 km) east of Highway 10, tel: (818) 282-6191. It has unusual architecture, wonderful statues and paintings, and a September festival to celebrate its founding in 1771. Open daily 9.30am–4.30pm. Closed Easter, Thanksgiving and Christmas.
Mission San Fernando Rey de Espana
15151 San Fernando Mission Boulevard
Tel: (818) 361-0186
This was California's 17th mission, founded in 1797. Its long and tumultuous history has been marked by complete destruction in two major earthquakes

(1806 and 1971) and consequent reconstruction. The tour of the working, sleeping, and recreation areas, and an extensive collection of artifacts recreate a sense of early mission life.

San Juan Capistrano
Ortega Highway, CA 74
Near the South Bay town of Laguna Beach is Father Serra's original chapel and the ruins of an enormous church. A celebration on March 19 recognizes the famed return of the swallows. Open daily 8.30am–5pm. Closed between noon and 3pm on Good Friday and also closed on Thanksgiving and Christmas days.

San Diego de Alcala
Tel: (619) 281-8449
This was the first mission to be founded in California, originally 6 miles (10 km) south of its current site in the Old Town area, which it has occupied since 1769. Open daily 9am–5pm; check about hols.

San Buenaventura
Tel: (805) 643-4318
Located in the city of Ventura, it has ancient paintings, wooden bells, and original tiles and rafters. Open Monday–Saturday 10am–5pm, Sunday 10am–4pm. Closed most major holidays.

San Luis Rey
Just north of Oceanside off US 5
Tel: (619) 757-3651
Has a large collection of vestments and a fiesta each June to celebrate the founding of the mission. Open Monday–Saturday 10am–4.30pm, Sunday noon–4.30pm. Closed Thanksgiving and Christmas.

Santa Barbara
Tel: (619) 757-3651
This is the "Queen of the Missions" and has 60 Franciscan friars in residence. Open daily 9am–5pm; check about holidays.

Andres Pico Adobe
10940 Sepulveda Boulevard
Mission Hills
Tel: (818) 365-7810
Although not a mission, this adobe was built by Mission San Fernando Indians in 1834. It is the oldest home in San Fernando and the second oldest in the Greater Los Angeles area.

Children

Kids' Stuff

Bob Baker Marionette Theater
1345 W First Street
Downtown Los Angeles
Tel: (213) 250-9995.
Tuesday–Friday 10.30am, weekends 2.30pm. Admission.

Castle Park
3500 Polk Avenue, Riverside off the 91 Freeway
Tel: (909) 785-4141
Attractively landscaped family amusement park with videos, miniature golf courses, amusement rides, fountains, and waterfalls.

Griffith Park
A 4,100-acre (1,659-hectare) park , Griffith Park comprises many picnic areas and hiking trails, the famous "Hollywood" sign, and the 113-acre (46-hectare) Los Angeles Zoo. Rail buffs should visit Travel Town at the park's northwest corner with its collection of vintage trains (rides on first weekend of each month). The Griffith Park Observatory is closed to the public for major renovations until January 2005.

Legoland California
1 Lego Drive, Carlsbad
Tel: (760) 918-lEGO
www.lego.com
Hands-on models, rides, attractions, and shows. Open daily.

Monster Mansion
By appointment only. Call (213) MOON-FAN. The world's largest assemblage of such memorabilia, including life masks of Bela Lugosi, Boris Karloff and others.

Raging Waters
111 Raging Waters Drive
San Dimas
Tel: (909) 802-2200
www.ragingwaters.com
Open May–mid-September.

California's largest water park is located 20 minutes from Disneyland. The open water slides are breathtaking.

Ripley's Believe It or Not
Buena Park at 7850 Beach Boulevard
Tel: (714) 522-1152
Open daily. Admission charge. Oddities and scarcely believable artifacts.

San Diego Hall of Champions Sports Museum
2131 Pan American Plaza in Balboa Park
Tel: (619) 234-4542
Sports history museum featuring videos, photographs, uniforms, awards, and equipment from athletes in more than 40 sports.

San Diego Wild Animal Park
15500 San Pasqual Valley Road off Interstate 15 east of Escondido
Tel: (760) 747-8702
A 1,800-acre (728-hectare) preserve where wild animals roam freely. Open daily 9am–5pm. Admission and parking charge. Entrance fee includes animal shows and monorail tour.

San Diego Zoo-Balboa Park
2920 Zoo Drive
Tel: (619) 234-3153
www.sandiegozoo.org
In Balboa Park, the zoo houses almost 800 different species and is sometimes called the best zoo in the world. Open year-round 9am–5pm. Admission charge.

Santa Cruz Beach Boardwalk
400 Beach Street, Santa Cruz
Tel: (831) 426-7433
Winter hours: weekends only 11am–6pm, summer hours: (from May 28) daily 11am–10pm. No admission fee, but rides cost extra. California's first seashore amusement area (established 1868) offers rides, games, arcades, gift shops, entertainment and a mile-long beach. The magnificent casino, built 1907, now houses two restaurants. The antique merry-go-round dates back to 1911, and the Giant Dipper is among the best roller coaster rides in the world. Worth stopping off for if you're driving to San Francisco from Southern California.

Sea World of California
500 Sea World Drive, Mission Bay,
San Diego
Tel: (619) 226-3901
www.seaworld.com
Marine-life adventure park. This
park has wild marine animals, and
various attractions including a
rapids ride and live shows. Open
daily. Admission charge.

Shambala
Tel: (661) 268-0380
Actress Tippi Hedren's 130-acre
(53-hectare) game reserve at Acton,
40 miles (64 km) northwest of LA.
Tigers, lions, and leopards, mostly
abandoned by circuses and zoos
and rescued by Ms Hedren.

White Water Canyon
2052 Otay Valley Road, Chula Vista,
91911
Tel: (619) 661-7373
Rides, slides, and giant wavepool.

Wild Rivers Water Park
8770 Irvine Center Drive
Tel: (714) 768-WILD
Open mid-May–September.
Admission charge. Family playground
with 40 rides and attractions.

Theme Parks

Disneyland, Disneyland, PO Box
3232, Anaheim, CA 92803, tel:
(714) 999-4000, www.disneyland.com.
Write or call ahead for a map to
plan your strategy before you arrive.
Open daily year-round. Winter hours:
Mon–Fri 10am–6pm, weekends
9am–midnight. Summer hours: daily
8–1am. All-in-one daily admission
charge."The Happiest Place on
Earth" features dining, shopping,
entertainment, and more than 60
adventures and attractions in many
magical themed lands. "Disney's
California Adventure" is the newest.
Knott's Berry Farm, 8039 Beach
Boulevard, Buena Park, tel: (714)
220-5200; www.knotts.com. Winter
hours: Monday–Friday 10am–6pm;
Saturday 10am–10pm; Sunday
10am–7pm. Summer hours:
Sunday–Friday 9am–6pm; Saturday
10am–midnight. Admission charge.
A major Western-style park whose
six themed lands – Ghost Town,
Roaring 1920s, Camp Snoopy,
Indian Trails, Wildwater Wilderness,

and Fiesta Village – are funkier and
less automated than Disneyland, a
couple of miles to the south. There
are around 165 rides, shows and
adventures, 26 shops, and a
theater that books major stars.
Nearby are the **Movieland Wax
Museum**, open every day of the
year at 7711 Beach Boulevard, tel:
(714) 522-1154; and **Wild Bill's
Wild West Dinner Extravaganza**, at
7600 Beach Boulevard, tel: (714)
522-6414.

**Six Flags Magic Mountain/Six Flags
Hurricane Harbor**, 26101 Magic
Mountain Parkway, Valencia, CA
91355, tel: (661) 255 4100;
www.sixflags.com. Open daily Memorial
Day through Labor Day as well as
weekends, some holidays and
weekends year-round. A 260-acre
(105-hectare) theme park half an
hour north of Hollywood, with over
100 thrill-seeker rides and shows
and the world's largest dual-track
roller coaster, the Colossus. Gotham
City has a Batman ride described as
resembling "a ride on a high-speed
ski chairlift that spins upside down."

Children's Museums

*Most museums charge
admission and are closed on
Monday. Opening hours vary, so
call for details.*

Kidspace
390 South El Molino Avenue
Pasadena
Tel: (661) 449-9144
Participatory museum where
children are encouraged to touch
and explore the exhibits.

Children's Museum of San Diego
Front Street and Island Avenue
Tel: (669) 233-5437
This spacious, bright cornerfront
property, also called the **Museo
de Los Ninos**, encourages kids to
learn by doing things, like
working with paint and clay.

Children's Discovery Museum
300 Carlsbad Village Drive, #103
Carlsbad
Tel: (760) 720-0737
Located in the Village Faire
Shopping Centre, everybody
loves the solar-powered toy train.

Festivals

January

**Colorado River Country Music
Festival**, Blythe
Tel: (415) 974-4000
Desert Plein Air, Palm Springs
Tel: (760) 564-1244
Outdoor painting festival.
La Cienega Restaurant Row, Los
Angeles
Tel: (310) 271-8174
Ethnic food salute.
Native American Film Festival, Los
Angeles
Tel: (323) 221-2164
**Palm Springs International Film
Festival**
Tel: (619) 322-2930
Pasadena Folk Dance Festival
Tel: (310) 277-6699
San Diego Open Golf Tournament
Tel: (619) 281-4653
Southwest Arts Festival, Indio
Tel: (800) 44-INDIO
**Tournament of Roses Parade &
Rose Bowl Football Game**
Pasadena
Tel: (626) 449-4100

February

**Chinese New Year Food & Cultural
Faire**, Del Mar
Tel: (619) 234-4447
Tel: (805) 773-4811
National Date Festival, Indio
Arabian Nights pageant, camel and
ostrich races.
Saint Patrick's Day parades, Los
Angeles and San Diego
Sand Sculpture Contest, Dana Pont
Tel: (949) 496-6172
**Santa Barbara International Film
Festival**, Santa Barbara
Tel: (805) 963-0023
Southwest Arts Festival, Indio
Tel: (800) 44-INDIO

Whisky Flat Days, Kernville
Tel: (760) 376-2629.
Parade, rodeo, gunfighters, arts
and crafts, food.
Wildflower Walks, Penn Valley
Tel: (916) 273-3884
Guided tours along canyon trails.
Also in May.
Winter Barrel Tasting,Temecula
Tel: (800) 801-9463
Parade, rodeo, gunfighters, arts
and crafts, food.

March

Academy Awards, Beverly Hills
Tel: (800) 345-2210
Harvest & Wildflower Festival,
Palm Springs
Tel: (800) 34-SPRINGS
Street fair, arts and crafts, music,
car show.
International Orchid Show, Santa
Barbara
Tel: (805) 967-6331
Los Angeles Marathon
Tel: (310) 444-5544
Railfest, Filmore
Tel: (800) 773-8724
Ski Races, Big Bear Lake
Tel: (909) 585-2519
Taste of Solvang
Tel: (800) 468-6765
Danish cuisine, entertainment, golf.
Trout Fishing Derby, Lone Pine
Tel: (760) 876-4444

April

Desert Dixieland Jazz Festival,
Palm Springs
Tel: (760) 321-JASS
**Easter Sunrise Service in the
Hollywood Bowl**, Los Angeles
Tel: (213) 419-1500
**Easter Play in the Crystal
Cathedral**, Garden Grove
Tel: (714) 54-GLORY
The Freeway Series, Los Angeles
Tel: (714) 634-2000
A three-game series between the
Los Angeles Dodgers and the
California Angels.
**Joshua Tree National Park Arts
Festival**, Twentynine Palms
Tel: (760) 367-5522
Mexicayotl Azteca Dance Festival,
San Diego
Tel: (619) 691-1044

Orange Blossom Festival, Riverside
Tel: (909) 782-5676
Presidio Days, Santa Barbara
Tel: (805) 966-9719
Three-day celebration of the city's
birthday.
Renaissance Pleasure Faire, San
Bernardino
Tel: (800) 52-FAIRE
Music, theater, and country
dancing, on weekends late
April–late June.
Santa Fe Market, San Diego
Tel: (619) 296-3161
Indian crafts and culture.
Toyota Grand Prix, Long Beach
Tel: (562) 981-2600
Auto racing.

Festival Guide

For listings of festivals,
parades and other celebrations
in Southern California, check
the "Calendar" section of the
Los Angeles Times or a current
copy of the *LA Weekly* or *Los
Angeles Magazine*. Listings for
more specialized events will
appear in smaller local papers.
These are just some of the
most popular festivals and
events.

May

Applefest, Tehachapi
Tel: (661) 822-4180
Arts and crafts, entertainment,
apple dumplings. •
Bunka-Sai Festival, Torrance
Tel: (310) 827-4358
Japanese cultural event with
exhibits, entertainment.
California Festival of Beers,
San Luis Obispo
Tel: (805) 544-2266.
The largest regional beer-tasting
event in the country.
Cinco de Mayo, Los Angeles, San
Diego, Calexico, and Santa Barbara
Conejo Valley Days, Thousand Oaks
Tel: (805) 499-1993
Country & Western event with a
rodeo and carnival rides.
**Death Valley to Mount Whitney
Bicycle Race**, Lone Pine
Tel: (760) 876-4444

Desert Tortoise Days, California City
Tel: (760) 373-4926
Parade, arts and crafts,
entertainment.
Fiesta de las Artes, Hermosa
Beach
Tel: (310) 376-0951
Memorial Day Parade, Canoga Park
Tel: (818) 884-4222
Renaissance Pleasure Faire, San
Bernardino *(see April)*
Strawberry Festival, Garden Grove
Tel: (714) 638-0981
Street Painting Festival, Santa
Barbara Mission
Tel: (805) 966-9222
Tehachapi Wind Fair, Mountain
Valley Airport, Tehachapi
Tel: (661) 822-3222
**Urban American Indian Art
Exposition**, Los Angeles
Tel: (213) 221-2164.
Art, dances, demonstrations.

June

Auto Show,
Pacific Pallisades
Tel: (310) 459-7963
Back to Blue Treasure Hunt,
Malibu
Tel: (818) 789-7866
For divers and kids on the beach.
Concours d'Elegance, Escondido
Tel: (760) 749-1666
Classic cars, music, wine tasting.
Country Music Festival, Ojai
Tel: (805) 646-8126
Fabric Festival, San Diego
Tel: (619) 296-3161
Fashion shows, guest designers.
Festival de Caribe, Long Beach
Tel: (562) 677-2126
Music from Africa and the
Caribbean, food and dancing.
Indian Fair, San Diego
Tel: (619) 239-2749
Art and jewelry, traditional dancing,
ethnic foods.
Indian Pow Wow, Techahapi
Tel: (661) 822-1118
Crafts, ethnic foods, Indian dancing.
Open Sky Music Festival,
Big Bear Lake
Tel: (800) 4-BIG BEAR
Renaissance Pleasure Faire,
San Bernardino *(see April)*.
**Scottish Highland Games &
Festival**, Big Bear Lake

Southern California Exposition, San Diego
Tel: (619) 236-1212
A miniature world's fair.
Strawberry Festival, Susanville
Tel: (530) 257-4323
Arts and crafts, music, and food.
Threshing Bee & Tractor Show, Vista
Tel: (760) 941-1791
Weavers, blacksmiths, tractor parades and other rural pastimes.

July

Channel Islands Harbor Music Festival, Oxnard
Tel: (800) 994-4852
Three days of music at the water's edge.
Custom Car & Hot Rod Show, Lynwood
Tel: (310) 537-6484
Fourth of July, celebrations and fireworks state-wide.
French Festival, Santa Barbara
Tel: (805) 564-PARIS
Held in Oak Park, the largest French celebration in the western US.
Greek Festival, Santa Barbara
Tel: (805) 683-4492
International Surf Festival,
Hermosa, Manhattan, and Redondo beaches.
Exhibition surfing. Call beach city tourist bureaux for information.
Jazz in the Alley, Pasadena
Tel: (626) 568-1220
Lotus Festival, Los Angeles
Tel: (213) 485-8745
Highlights Asian culture.
Mozart Festival, San Luis Obispo
Tel: (805) 541-5425
Tel: (800) 487-3378
Sandcastle Days, Imperial Beach
Tel: (619) 424-6663
Three-day-long sandcastle building contest for serious contenders and curious onlookers.
Sawdust Festival, Laguna Beach
Tel: (714) 494-3030
Traditional arts and crafts festival.
Semana Nautica, Santa Barbara
Tel: (805) 564-2052
Multi-sports festival on land, water, and in the air.
Team Tennis, Newport Beach
Tel: (949) 644-5800
Professionals compete.

US Open Sand Castle competition, Imperial Beach
Tel: (619) 232-1707
Parade, fireworks, and castle-building for all ages.
West Coast Antique Fly-In, Merced
Tel: (209) 384-1144
Ancient aircraft fill the skies.

August

African Market Place & Cultural Fair, Los Angeles
Tel: (323) 734-1164
Catalina Ski Race, Long Beach
Tel: (562) 421-9431
Grueling race across the water.
Dune Run-Run, Grover City
Tel: (805) 489-9091
Footrace on the beach.
International Sea Festival, Long Beach
Tel: (562) 421-9431
International Surf Festival, Torrance
Tel: (310) 540-5511
Lifeguard championships, surfing, volleyball tournament on Redondo, Hermosa, and Manhattan beaches.
Latin American Festival, San Diego
Tel: (619) 296-43161
Long Beach Jazz Festival
Tel: (562) 436-7794
Mountain Festival, Tehachapi
Tel: (661) 822-4180
Nisei Week Japanese Festival
Los Angeles
Tel: (213) 687-6510
Old Spanish Days, Santa Barbara
Tel: (805) 962-8101
Pierfest, Huntington Beach
Tel: (714) 960-FEST

Festival Guide

For listings of festivals, parades and other celebrations in Southern California, check the "Calendar" section of the *Los Angeles Times* or a current copy of the *LA Weekly* or *Los Angeles Magazine*. Listings for more specialized events will appear in smaller local papers. These are just some of the most popular festivals and events.

Arts and crafts, music, spectator sports.
Professional Surfing Championship, Huntington Beach
Tel: (714) 731-3100
Summer Music Festival, Newport Beach
Tel: (949) 721-2022
Free Thursday night concerts.
Taste of San Pedro
Tel: (310) 832-7272
Food and entertainment.
Tehachapi Mountain Festival
Tel: (800) 822-4180
Rodeo, arts and crafts, food, entertainment.
Twilight Dance Series, Santa Monica Pier
Tel: (310) 458-8900
Weed & Craft Show, Julian
Tel: (760) 765-1857

September

Grecian Festival by the Sea, Long Beach
Tel: (562) 220-0730
Independence Day Celebration, Calexico
Tel: (760) 357-1166
KLON Blues Festival, Long Beach
Tel: (502) 985-1686
Los Angeles City Birthday Celebration
Tel: (213) 680-2821
Los Angeles County Fair, Pomona
Tel: (909) 623-3111
Mexican Cultural Festival, San Diego
Tel: (619) 482-0273
Mexican Fiesta, Ojai
Tel: (805) 646-4757
Mexican The People's Festival, Grover City
Tel: (805) 489-9091
Arts and crafts, ethnic food, music.
Oktoberfest, Big Bear Lake
Tel: (909) 866-5634; Torrance
Tel: (310) 327-4384; Huntington Beach Tel: (714) 898-8020
Route 66 Rendezvous, San Bernardino
Tel: (800) 669-8336
Hot rods, vintage cars, street dances, legal cruising, and golf tournament.
Sandcastle Contest, Newport Beach
Tel: (949) 729-4400

September Fiesta, Irwindale
Tel: (626) 962-3381
Annual celebration of city's
founding.
Street Scene, San Diego
Tel: (619) 557-8490
Watts Towers Day of The Drum,
Los Angeles
Tel: (213) 569-8181
Drummers, dancing, arts and
crafts.

October

**Antiques & Collectibles Show and
Sale**, Woodland Hills
Tel: (818) 985-3039
Outdoor show in country setting.
Banjo & Fiddle Contest, Julian
Tel: (760) 282-8380
California Avocado Festival,
Carpinteria
Tel: (805) 684-0038
California Countryfest, Solvang
Tel: (800) 468-6765
Western fine arts and crafts,
entertainment.
Clam Festival, Pismo Beach
Tel: (805) 773-3113
Cultural Heritage Festival,
Riverside
Tel: (909) 782-5407
Ethnic food, home-made crafts,
entertainment.
Dinner in the Canyons,
Palm Springs
Tel: (760) 778-1079
Festa Bella!, San Diego
Tel: (619) 483-9200.
Italian celebration.
Film Festival,
Lone Pine
Tel: (760) 876-9103
Great Glendora festival,
Tel: (626) 963-4128
Arts and crafts, classic cars,
entertainment.
Harvest Festival, Escondido
Tel: (760) 743-8207
Insite, San Diego
Tel: (619) 544-1482
Dozens of artists show at different
venues.
International Festival of Masks,
Los Angeles
Tel: (213) 937-5544
International Jazz Festival, Santa
Barbara
Tel: (805) 452-0309

Three days with famous musicians.
Johnny Appleseed Day, Paradise
Tel: (530) 877-9356
Arts and crafts, entertainment,
apple pie contest.
The Korean Festival, Garden
Grove
Tel: (714) 638-7950.
Pioneer Days Celebration, Twenty
Nine Palms
Tel: (760) 367-3445
Sierra Film Festival, Lone Pine
Tel: (760) 876-4725
Parade, films, arts and crafts.
Taste of Palm Springs
Tel: (800) 347-7746
Outdoor fair with food, wine, and
entertainment.

November

Christmas Parade, Hollywood
Tel: (213) 469-8311
Celebrities, bands, floats, classic
cars.
Death Valley 49ers Encampment,
Death Valley
Tel: (760) 852-4524
Fiddlers contest, valley trek.
Desert Holiday festival, Palm
Springs
Tel: (760) 327-4699
Parade, tree-lighting ceremonies,
carolers, carriage rides.
Dickens Celebration, Lake
Arrowhead Village
Tel: (909) 247-8237
Costumed carolers, horse and
carriage rides.
Doo Dah Parade, Pasadena
Tel: (626) 796-2591
Fall Flower Tour, Encinitas
Tel: (760) 7533-6270
Golf Cart Parade, Palm Desert
Tel: (760) 346-6111
Decorated golfcarts, marching
bands, etc.
Harvest Wine Celebration,
Temecula
Tel: (800) 801-9463
Holiday Lighting Ceremony, Beverly
Hills
Tel: (310) 271-8174
With carolers and real reindeer.
Intertribal Marketplace, Los
Angeles
Tel: (213) 221-2164
Native American pottery, jewelry,
arts and crafts.

National Amateur Horse Show,
Santa Barbara
Tel: (805) 687-0766
Training show for future Olympic
contestants.
Oktoberfest, Dana Point
Tel: (949) 496-6172
Very Merry Christmas Parade,
Anaheim
Tel: (714) 502-3938
Weed Sculpture Show,
Twentynine Palms
Tel: (760) 367-3445
Carriage rides, entertainment.

December

**Battle of San Pasquale
Re-enactment**, Escondido
Tel: (760) 238-3380
Volunteers in historic costume.
Candlelight Tours of Old Town,
San Diego
Tel: (619) 237-6766
**Channel Islands Harbor Parade of
Lights**, Oxnard
Tel: (805) 985-4852
Decorated boats float by.
Christmas Boat Parade, Newport
Beach
Tel: (949) 644-8211
Christmas on the Prado, San
Diego
Tel: (619) 239-0512
Candlelight processions, ethnic
food, arts and crafts.
Cruise of Lights, Huntington
Beach
Tel: (714) 840-7542
Elaborately decorated boats and
waterfront homes .
**Celebrations at Crystal Cathedral
Holiday Street Festival**, Ventura
Tel: (805) 654-7830
Hollywood Christmas Parade,
Tel: (323) 469-2337
Las Posadas, Los Angeles
Tel: (213) 628-7833
Candlelight procession.
Lighted Boat Parades, Marina del
Rey and San Diego
Call local tourist bureaux for
information.
New Year's Eve on Pine Square,
Long Beach
Tel: (562) 436-4259
Block party with entertainment,
dancing, food.

Shopping

Shopping Areas

For intrepid shoppers, Southern California is right up there with the big guns like Paris, New York and Hong Kong. No matter what your taste or budget, you are bound to find whatever you're looking for.

Of course, the glitziest shopping street is Los Angeles' renowned **Rodeo Drive**. While Rodeo has become quite a tourist trap, with more people window shopping than buying, there are some terrific, world-class shops along the drive; names like Chanel, Armani, Ungaro, Alaia, and Bottega Veneta are not to be ignored.

Rodeo Drive's luxurious amenities were increased by 40 percent with the ingenious addition of another street, **Two Rodeo** (or **Via Rodeo**), a curving, cobblestoned walkway lined with top-name stores like Tiffany, Christian Dior, and Cartier, whose classy emporiums feature granite colonnades and copper-toned roofs. Developer Douglas Stitzel and his Japanese partners compare Via Rodeo with its Rome counterpart, Via Condotti. An underground parking lot offering free valet parking feeds shoppers right into the middle of the street.

Although such trendy shopping streets as **La Brea Avenue** off Melrose and Santa Monica's **Third Street Promenade** and **Montana Avenue** have not lost their luster, there always seems to be a thriving newcomer. A recent one that has had people flocking is Venice's **Abbott Kinney Boulevard** (named after the visionary developer who created Venice early in the 20th century). Palm trees have been planted and now frame art

Clothing Sizes

This table gives a comparison of American, Continental and British clothing sizes. It is always best to try on articles before buying, however, as sizes may vary.

Women's

Dresses/Suits

American	Continental	British
6	38/34N	8/30
8	40/36N	10/32
10	42/38N	12/34
12	44/40N	14/36
14	46/42N	16/38
16	48/44N	18/40

Shoes

American	Continental	British
4½	36	3
5½	37	4
6½	38	5
7½	39	6
8½	40	7
9½	41	8
10½	42	9

Men's

Suits

American	Continental	British
34	44	34
–	46	36
38	48	38
–	50	40
42	52	42
–	54	44
46	56	46

Shirts

American	Continental	British
14	36	14
14½	37	14½
15	38	15
15½	39	15½
16	40	16
16½	41	16½
17	42	17

Shoes

American	Continental	British
6½	39	6
7½	40	7
8½	41	8
9½	42	9
10½	43	10
11½	44	11

galleries, vintage clothing and jewelry stores. Even more recently, the **Silver Lake** district – centered on Vermont Avenue and Sunset Boulevard – has become the not-to-be-missed area, full of fashion boutiques and street vendors.

And, of course, for mall-lovers Southern California is a shopper's Valhalla. One of the Southland's most famous landmarks, the outstanding former Uniroyal tire plant beside the Santa Ana Freeway in the City of Commerce, has re-emerged as the **Citadel Outlet Collection**, an enticing shopping plaza whose 42 stores spread around a tree-flanked courtyard. The mind reels at the number of mega-malls dotted throughout the region: **Century City, Beverly Center, Topanga Plaza, Del Amo Fashion Square, and Fashion Island** among them.

But you might want to concentrate your energies on the **South Coast Plaza** in Costa Mesa (just a stone's throw from Newport in Orange County), a shopping tour-de-force. South Coast Plaza is huge and all the shops are first-rate: J Crew (of mail-order fame), Armani, a Museum of Modern Art giftstore, Joan and David, Yves Saint-Laurent, and the West Coast's first Calvin Klein boutique, to name just a few, as well as a wide range of eateries.

Because of its upscale nature, the Palm Springs region is understandably one big shopping area, with the **Desert Fashion Plaza** on Palm Canyon Drive possibly outclassed only by Palm Desert's nearby **Town Center**, where dozens of shops and an outdoor ice-skating rink are flanked by several major department stores. Equally attractive is the charm and ambiance of Santa Barbara's **La Arcada** shopping paseo, a cheerful Spanish-style courtyard adorned with tiles, ornamental ironwork, and bright flags.

Yet another era is evoked by San Diego's **Gaslamp Quarter**, a 16-block, 38-acre (16-hectare) district recommended for arts and crafts browsers. In addition to that city's **Seaport Village** and the multilevel

A trip down LA's **Melrose Avenue** is a must. Some of Southern California's best people-watching goes on here, and there are plenty of little cafes to serve as rest stops. Those into avant-garde high fashion can go to Maxfield near Doheny and Melrose, an austere temple of haute style, where stars like Jack Nicholson, Robin Williams and a host of rock 'n' rollers find labels like Gaultier, Lagerfeld and Katherine Hamnett. For a change of pace you might want to browse among one of the country's largest collections of antique books at the Heritage Book Store in the 8500 block of Melrose, where an extensive autograph collection includes those of Dickens and Mark Twain.

Horton Plaza, it's location also allows a short excursion to the Mexican border town of Tijuana, where there are different souvenirs and lower prices.

In California there is a sales tax of 7.25 percent on most items (unprepared food, for example, is exempt), which is always assessed at the cash register, so prices never reflect the tax included price (unless indicated – gasoline prices always include the tax). To further complicate matters, various cities and counties levy an additional sales tax, usually approved by the voters to raise money to meet an urgent need. Residents of Los Angeles, for example, voted to increase the local sales tax to 8.25 percent in order to raise money to accelerate repairs after the 1994 earthquake.

Further Reading

General

A Guide to Architecture in LA by David Gebhardt & Robert Winter. Peregrine Smith Inc., 1977.
Behind the Mask of Innocence, by Kevin Brownlow. Alfred A. Knopf, 1990.
California: A Guide to the Golden State, by the Federal Writers Project. Hastings House, 1939.
California Coastal Access Guide, by the California Coastal Commission.
California Political Almanac, edited by Dan Walters. Pacific Data Resource.
LA Shortcuts, by Brian Roberts & Richard Schwadel. Red Car Press, 1989.
The City Observed: Los Angeles, by Charles Moore, Peter Becker & Regula Campbell. Vintage Books, 1984.
The Missions of California, by Melba Levick & Stanley Young. Chronicle Books, 1988.
Prismatic Metropolis: Inequality in Los Angeles. Russell Sage Foundation, 2001.
Los Angeles, A to Z by Leonard and Dale Pitt. University of California Press, 1997.
Iconic LA Stories of LA's Most Memorable Buildings, by Gloria Koenig. Chronicle books/Balcony Press, 2001.
Desert Lore of Southern California, by Choral Pepper. Sunbelt Publications, 1999.
Adventuring in the California Desert by Lynne Foster. Sierra Club, 1997.

History

The Age of Gold: The California Goldrush and the New American Dream by H.W. Brands. Doubleday, 2002.
California – The Great Exception by Carey McWilliams. University of California Press, 1999.

A Century of Dishonor, by Helen Hunt Jackson. Scholarly Press, 1880.
A Companion to California, by James Hart. Oxford University Press, 1978.
Hollywood: The First Hundred Years, by Bruce T. Torrence. New York Zoetrope, 1982.
Indians of Early Southern California, by Edna B. Ziebold. Sapsis, 1969.
Los Angeles, 1781–1981. California Historical Society.
The San Fernando Valley, Past & Present, by Lawrence C. Jorgensen. Pacific Rim Research, 1982.
Santa Monica Pier: A History from 1875–1990, by Jeffrey Stanton. Donahue Publications.
A Short History of the Movies, by Gerald Mast. University of Chicago Press, 1971.
The Times We Had: Life with William Randolph Hearst, by Marion Davis. Bobbs Merrill, 1975.
Two Years Before the Mast, by Richard Henry Dana. 1841.

Geography & Natural History

Amphibians and Reptiles of Baja California by L. Lee Grismer and Harry W. Greene. University of California Press, 2002.
California Patterns: A Geographical and Historical Atlas, by David Hornbeck. Mayfield, 1983.
California: The Geography of Diversity, by Crane Miller and Richard Hyslop. Mayfield, 1983.
Natural Los Angeles, by Bill Thomas. Harper & Row, 1989.
Where to see Wildlife in California, by Tom Taber. Oak Valley Press, 1983.

Literary

Grapes of Wrath, Wayward Bus and *To a God Unknown*, three books by John Steinbeck. Penguin USA, 1992.
The Big Sleep and *Farewell, My Lovely*, two books by Raymond Chandler. Vintage Books, 1992.
Oil, by Upton Sinclair. University of California Press, 1997.
The Valley of the Moon, Jack

London. University of California
Press, 1999.
The Loved One, by Evelyn Waugh.
Little Brown & Co., 1999.
The Last Tycoon, by F. Scott
Fitzgerald. Amereon Ltd, 1989.
*Writing Los Angeles: A Literary
Anthology* edited by David L. Ulin.
Library of America, 2002.
The Zoot Suit Murders, by
Thomas Sanchez. Vintage
Books, 1991.

People

*All the Stars in Heaven: Louis B.
Mayer's MGM*, by Gary Carey. E.P.
Dutton, 1981.
*California Characters – An Array of
Amazing People*, by Charles
Hillinger. Capra Press, 2001.
Contemporary Architects, St James
Press, 1987.
*The Great Movie Stars: The Golden
Years*, by David Shipman. Crown,
1970.
Hedda & Louella, by George Eells.
G.P. Putnams Sons, 1972.
Julia Morgan, by Sara Holmes
Boutelle. Abbeville Press, 1988.
*Life and Good Times of William
Randolph Hearst*, by John Tebbel.
E.P. Dutton, 1952.
The Life of Raymond Chandler, by
Frank McShane. E.P. Dutton, 1976.
This is Hollywood, by Ken
Schessler. Universal Books, 1989.
*Vamp: The Life & Times of Theda
Bara*, by Ron Genini. McFarland
Press, 1995.
*William Mulhollland and the
Inventing of Los Angeles*, by
Margaret Leslie Davis. Harper
Collins, 1994.

Places

Curbside LA, by Cecilia Rasmussen.
Los Angeles Times, 2001.
Death Valley & Its Country, by
George P. Putnam. 1946.
The Encyclopedia of Hollywood, by
Scott and Barbara Siegel. Facts on
File, 1990.
Hollywood, Land & Legend, by C.C.
& B. Crane. Arlington House, 1980.
Los Angeles: An Architectural Guide,
by David Gebhard and Ribert
Winter. Gibbs Smith, 1994.

*Santa Barbara Celebrities:
Conversations from the American
Riviera*, by Cork Millner. Santa
Barbara Press, 1989.
Santa Barbara Architecture, by Noel
Young and Herb Andree. Capra
Press, 1980.
*Southern California's Car Culture
Landmarks*. AAA, 2001.
Venice of America, by Jeffrey
Stanton. Donahue Publications,
1987.

Other Insight Guides

The 550-plus books and maps in
the Insight Guides range cover
every continent and include 75
titles to the United States, from
Alaska to Florida, from Seattle to
Boston.

Insight Guide: California is a
beautiful, comprehensive guide to
the entire state.
Insight Guide: San Francisco
explores this beautiful, diverse and
vibrant city.
Insight Guide: Los Angeles gets
under the skin of the glitz and the
glamour of America's movie
capital.
Insight Guide: Las Vegas is a full
run-down on the city, from the
Strip to Downtown and beyond.

Insight Pocket Guides to *San
Diego*, *San Francisco* and *Los
Angeles*. A volume to each city, with
personal recommendations from a
local host and large fold-out map.

Insight Compact Guides to *San
Francisco* and *Los Angeles* are
mini-encyclopedias to these cities,
keenly priced, extremely portable,
and perfect for on-the-spot
reference.

Insight Maps combine detailed
cartography with text and
photography of the destination's
top sights, plus useful
information. Their laminated
finish is durable and weather-
resistant. Titles include:
California, *San Francisco* and
Los Angeles.

Feedback

We do our best
to ensure the
information in
our books is as
accurate and
up-to-date as
possible. The
books are updated on a regular
basis, using local contacts, who
painstakingly add, amend and
correct as required. However,
some mistakes and omissions
are inevitable and we are
ultimately reliant on our readers
to put us in the picture.
    We would welcome your feed-
back on any details related to
your experiences using the book
"on the road". Maybe we
recommended a hotel that you
liked (or another that you didn't),
as well as interesting new
attractions, or facts and figures
you have found out about the
country itself. The more details
you can give us (particularly with
regard to addresses, e-mails and
telephone numbers), the better.
    We will acknowledge all contri-
butions, and we'll offer an Insight
Guide to the best letters received.

Please write to us at:
    Insight Guides
    PO Box 7910
    London SE1 1WE
    United Kingdom
Or send e-mail to:
insight@apaguide.demon.co.uk

ART & PHOTO CREDITS

INSIGHT GUIDE
SOUTHERN CALIFORNIA

Cartographic Editor **Zoë Goodwin**
Production **Linton Donaldson**
Design Consultant **Carlotta Junger**
Picture Research
Hilary Genin, Natasha Babaian

Map Production Laura Morris
© 2003 Apa Publications GmbH & Co.
Verlag KG (Singapore branch)

Index

Numbers in italics refer to photographs

A
B
b
D
E
F
G
H
I
J
a
b
c
d
e
f
g
h
i
j
I